ALSO BY THE EDITORS AT AMERICA'S TEST KITCHEN

The Science of Good Cooking
The Cook's Illustrated Cookbook
The America's Test Kitchen Menu Cookbook
The America's Test Kitchen Quick Family Cookbook
The America's Test Kitchen Healthy Family Cookbook
The America's Test Kitchen Family Baking Book
The America's Test Kitchen Family Cookbook

THE AMERICA'S TEST KITCHEN LIBRARY SERIES:
The America's Test Kitchen D.I.Y. Cookbook
Pasta Revolution
Simple Weeknight Favorites
Slow Cooker Revolution
The Best Simple Recipes

AMERICA'S TEST KITCHEN ANNUALS:
The Best of America's Test Kitchen (2007–2012 Editions)
Cooking for Two (2010–2012 Editions)
Light and Healthy (2010–2012 Editions)

THE TV COMPANION SERIES:
The Complete Cook's Country TV Show Cookbook
The Complete America's Test Kitchen TV Show Cookbook
America's Test Kitchen: The TV Companion Cookbook (2009, 2011, and 2012 Editions)
Behind the Scenes with America's Test Kitchen
Test Kitchen Favorites
Cooking at Home with America's Test Kitchen
America's Test Kitchen Live!
Inside America's Test Kitchen
Here in America's Test Kitchen

THE COOK'S COUNTRY SERIES:
From Our Grandmothers' Kitchens
Cook's Country Blue Ribbon Desserts
Cook's Country Best Potluck Recipes
Cook's Country Best Lost Suppers
Cook's Country Best Grilling Recipes
The Cook's Country Cookbook
America's Best Lost Recipes

THE BEST RECIPE SERIES:
The New Best Recipe
More Best Recipes
The Best One-Dish Suppers
Soups, Stews & Chilis
The Best Skillet Recipes
The Best Slow & Easy Recipes
The Best Chicken Recipes
The Best International Recipe
The Best Make-Ahead Recipe
The Best 30-Minute Recipe
The Best Light Recipe
The Cook's Illustrated Guide to Grilling & Barbecue
Best American Side Dishes
Cover & Bake
Steaks, Chops, Roasts & Ribs
Baking Illustrated
The Best Italian Classics
The Best American Classics
Perfect Vegetables

For a full listing of all our books or to order titles:
CooksIllustrated.com
AmericasTestKitchen.com
or call 800-611-0759

"Ideal as a reference for the bookshelf and as a book to curl up and get lost in, this volume will be turned to time and again for definitive instruction on just about any food-related matter."

PUBLISHERS WEEKLY ON
THE SCIENCE OF GOOD COOKING

"The perfect kitchen home companion. The practical side of things is very much on display . . . cook-friendly and kitchen-oriented, illuminating the process of preparing food instead of mystifying it."

THE WALL STREET JOURNAL ON
THE COOK'S ILLUSTRATED COOKBOOK

"If this were the only cookbook you owned, you would cook well, be everyone's favorite host, have a well-run kitchen, and eat happily every day."

THECITYCOOK.COM ON
THE AMERICA'S TEST KITCHEN MENU COOKBOOK

"This book upgrades slow cooking for discriminating, 21st-century palates—that is indeed revolutionary."

THE DALLAS MORNING NEWS ON
SLOW COOKER REVOLUTION

"Further proof that practice makes perfect, if not transcendent. . . . If an intermediate cook follows the directions exactly, the results will be better than takeout or Mom's."

NEW YORK TIMES ON *THE NEW BEST RECIPE*

"An instant classic."

CHICAGO SUN-TIMES ON *AMERICA'S BEST LOST RECIPES*

"Expert bakers and novices scared of baking's requisite exactitude can all learn something from this hefty, all-purpose home baking volume."

PUBLISHERS WEEKLY ON
THE AMERICA'S TEST KITCHEN FAMILY BAKING BOOK

"Scrupulously tested regional and heirloom recipes."

NEW YORK TIMES ON *THE COOK'S COUNTRY COOKBOOK*

"This tome definitely raises the bar for all-in-one, basic, must-have cookbooks. . . . Kimball and his company have scored another hit."

PORTLAND OREGONIAN ON
THE AMERICA'S TEST KITCHEN FAMILY COOKBOOK

"A foolproof, go-to resource for everyday cooking."

PUBLISHERS WEEKLY ON
THE AMERICA'S TEST KITCHEN FAMILY COOKBOOK

"The strength of the Best Recipe Series lies in the sheer thoughtfulness and details of the recipes."

PUBLISHERS WEEKLY ON *THE BEST RECIPE SERIES*

"These dishes taste as luxurious as their full-fat siblings. Even desserts are terrific."

PUBLISHERS WEEKLY ON *THE BEST LIGHT RECIPE*

"Like a mini–cooking school, the detailed instructions and illustrations ensure that even the most inexperienced cook can follow these recipes with success."

PUBLISHERS WEEKLY ON
BEST AMERICAN SIDE DISHES

"Makes one-dish dinners a reality for average cooks, with honest ingredients and detailed make-ahead instructions."

NEW YORK TIMES ON *COVER & BAKE*

"[*Steaks, Chops, Roasts & Ribs*] conquers every question one could have about all things meat."

SAN FRANCISCO CHRONICLE ON
STEAKS, CHOPS, ROASTS & RIBS

"The best instructional book on baking this reviewer has seen."

LIBRARY JOURNAL (STARRED REVIEW) ON
BAKING ILLUSTRATED

"A must-have for anyone into our nation's cooking traditions—and a good reference, too."

LOS ANGELES DAILY NEWS ON
THE BEST AMERICAN CLASSICS

America's TEST KITCHEN

THE TV COMPANION COOKBOOK

2013

America's TEST KITCHEN

THE TV COMPANION COOKBOOK

2013

BY THE EDITORS AT
AMERICA'S TEST KITCHEN

PHOTOGRAPHY BY
DANIEL J. VAN ACKERE
CARL TREMBLAY
STEVE KLISE

AMERICA'S TEST KITCHEN
BROOKLINE, MASSACHUSETTS

AMERICA'S TEST KITCHEN
17 Station Street, Brookline, MA 02445

AMERICA'S TEST KITCHEN: THE TV COMPANION COOKBOOK 2013
1st Edition

ISBN-13: 978-1-933615-95-0 ISBN-10: 1-933615-95-8
ISSN 2161-6671
Hardcover: $34.95 US

Manufactured in the United States of America

10 9 8 7 6 5 4 3 2 1

Distributed by America's Test Kitchen
17 Station Street, Brookline, MA 02445

EDITORIAL DIRECTOR: Jack Bishop
EDITORIAL DIRECTOR, BOOKS: Elizabeth Carduff
EXECUTIVE EDITOR: Lori Galvin
ASSOCIATE EDITOR: Kate Hartke
ASSISTANT EDITOR: Alyssa King
DESIGN DIRECTOR: Amy Klee
ART DIRECTOR: Greg Galvan
DESIGNERS: Taylor Argenzio and Sarah Horwitch Dailey
STAFF PHOTOGRAPHERS: Steve Klise and Daniel J. van Ackere
ILLUSTRATOR: Jay Layman
FOOD STYLISTS: Marie Piraino and Mary Jane Sawyer
PRODUCTION DIRECTOR: Guy Rochford
SENIOR PRODUCTION MANAGER: Jessica Lindheimer Quirk
SENIOR PROJECT MANAGER: Alice Carpenter
TRAFFIC AND PRODUCTION COORDINATOR: Brittany Allen
COLOR AND IMAGING SPECIALIST: Andrew Mannone
PRODUCTION AND IMAGING SPECIALISTS: Judy Blomquist and Lauren Pettapiece
COPYEDITOR: Cheryl Redmond
PROOFREADER: Debra Hudak
INDEXER: Elizabeth Parson

CONTENTS

PREFACE

THIRTEEN MAY BE AN UNLUCKY NUMBER FOR SOME but for all of us here at America's Test Kitchen, it represents the 13th season of our public television cooking show and the triumph of an idea that nobody thought would ever see the light of day.

Perhaps we ought to give credit to the quirky nature of public television for our longevity or, better yet, the enduring fascination that home cooks have with the whys and hows of cooking. This is a case where the audience was way ahead of the media. When our show began, home cooks were looking for useful, in-depth information while TV producers were providing more of the same culinary competitions and meals in minutes that still dominate the airwaves today. Nothing wrong with those shows, it's just that there was a large audience for something entirely different.

In this season of *America's Test Kitchen,* we have tackled and solved a host of new culinary challenges, from making a vegetarian chili that really tastes meaty to creating a turkey burger that is 500 percent better than the last one you ate to reinventing a lesser-known but spectacular dessert, French apple cake. We also bring you the results of a bevy of tests, in which we identify the best vegetable cleaver, the best pressure cooker, the best sauté pan, and more. And I had the privilege of taste-testing butter, cheddar cheese, chicken, spaghetti, tortillas, and a hot sauce that was so hot that it made me cry. (Literally.)

Many people do not feel that they have the skills to cook well. They often say, "I can't boil water." We have faith that everyone can cook if presented with well-tested recipes and enough information. Anyone can follow a well-constructed recipe as long as the author explains exactly why eggs have to be tempered, why meat must rest before being carved, or why a skillet should be preheated. With knowledge comes instant expertise—and some very, very good food.

Now it is true that, from time to time, folks get confused about cooking advice and end up making a mistake. That reminds me of the story of the two middle-aged ladies from New York who bought a place in northern Vermont back in the '60s. They were apprehensive about the coming winter and asked a nearby farmer what kind of winter it was likely to be. "Oh," the old-timer reassured them, "it's going to be a good winter." They didn't run into him again until March and it had been a severe winter with lots of snowfall. They were a bit out of sorts and commented, "We thought you said it was going to be a good winter." "I did," he replied, "What's been the matter with it?" One of the sisters replied hastily, "Why, my goodness, look at all this snow!" The old farmer looked them and smiled, "Lord," he said and paused for a moment, "I never told you it wasn't going to snow!"

I hope that all of us here at America's Test Kitchen are clear when we write a recipe and that you will come to trust our advice. We weren't born smart—we just cook everything so many times! When you try just about everything you can think of, well, you eventually end up on the right road. That's the benefit of our recipes. We have tried all the things you can think of (and maybe a few more besides).

Please enjoy this season of *America's Test Kitchen* and this companion book as well. For myself, I probably have forgotten half of what I know about cooking but that doesn't stop me from learning more. After all, I have to make room in my head for this year's new recipes!

Christopher Kimball
Founder and Editor, *Cook's Illustrated* and *Cook's Country*
Host, *America's Test Kitchen* and
Cook's Country from America's Test Kitchen

WELCOME TO AMERICA'S TEST KITCHEN

THIS BOOK HAS BEEN TESTED, WRITTEN, AND EDITED by the folks at America's Test Kitchen, a very real 2,500-square-foot kitchen located just outside of Boston. It is the home of *Cook's Illustrated* and *Cook's Country* magazines and is the Monday-through-Friday destination for more than three dozen test cooks, editors, food scientists, tasters, and cookware specialists. Our mission is to test recipes over and over again until we understand how and why they work and until we arrive at the "best" version.

Our television show highlights the best recipes developed in the test kitchen during the past year—those recipes that our test kitchen staff makes at home time and time again. These recipes are accompanied by our most exhaustive equipment tests and our most interesting food tastings.

Christopher Kimball, the founder and editor of *Cook's Illustrated* magazine, is host of the show and asks the questions you might ask. It's the job of our chefs, Julia Collin Davison, Bridget Lancaster, Becky Hays, Bryan Roof, and Dan Souza to demonstrate our recipes. The chefs show Chris what works and what doesn't, and they explain why. In the process, they discuss (and show you) the best examples from our development process as well as the worst.

Adam Ried, our equipment expert, and Lisa McManus, our gadget guru, share the highlights from our detailed testing process in equipment corner segments. They bring with them our favorite (and least favorite) gadgets and tools. Jack Bishop is our ingredient expert. He has Chris taste our favorite (and least favorite) brands of common food products. Chris may not always enjoy these exercises (hot sauce isn't exactly as fun to taste as mozzarella), but he usually learns something as Jack explains what makes one brand superior to another.

Although just 10 cooks and editors appear on the television show, another 50 people worked to make the show a reality. Executive Producer Melissa Baldino conceived and developed each episode with help from Associate Producer Stephanie Stender and Production Assistant Kaitlin Hammond. Rachael M. Stark and Debby Paddock assisted with all the historical recipe and photo research. Guy Crosby, our science expert on the show, researched the science behind the recipes. Along with the on-air crew, executive chefs Erin McMurrer and Keith Dresser helped plan and organize the 26 television episodes shot in May 2012 and ran the "back kitchen," where all the food that appeared on camera originated. Taizeth Sierra, Hannah Crowley, and Amy Graves organized the tasting and equipment segments.

During filming, chefs Andrea Geary, Nick Iverson, Andrew Janjigian, Lan Lam, Rebeccah Marsters, Suzannah McFerran, Rebecca Morris, Christie Morrison, Chris O'Connor, Celeste Rogers, and Diane Unger and interns Amy DeMello and Alexxa Grattan cooked all the food needed on set. Cooks Sarah Gabriel, Carolynn Purpura MacKay, Sacha Madadian, Addy Parker, and Cristin Walsh and interns Kelsey Branch, Joyce Liao, Blaire Newhard, and Lainey Seyler worked on set developing recipes for our magazines and books. Assistant Test Kitchen Director

Gina Nistico, Test Kitchen Manager Leah Rovner, and Senior Kitchen Assistant Meryl MacCormack were charged with making sure all the ingredients and kitchen equipment we needed were on hand. Kitchen assistants Maria Elena Delgado, Ena Gudiel, and Andrew Straaberg Finfrock also worked long hours. Chefs Dan Cellucci, Danielle DeSiato-Hallman, Sara Mayer, Ashley Moore, Kate Williams, and Dan Zuccarello helped coordinate the efforts of the kitchen with the television set by readying props, equipment, and food. Shannon Hatch, Kate May, and Christine Gordon led all tours of the test kitchen during filming.

Special thanks to director and editor Herb Sevush and director of photography Jan Maliszewski.

We also appreciate the hard work of the video production team, including Stephen Hussar, Michael McEachern, Peter Dingle, Roger Macie, Gilles Morin, Brenda Coffey, Ken Fraser, Joe Christofori, James Hirsch, Bob Hirsch, Griff Nash, Jeremy Bond, Eric Joslin, Heloise Borden, Amy Neben, and Ken Bauer. Thanks also to Nick Dakoulas, the second unit videographer.

We also would like to thank Nancy Bocchino, Bara Levin, and Victoria Yuen at WGBH Station Relations, and the team at American Public Television that presents the show: Cynthia Fenneman, Chris Funkhouser, Judy Barlow, and Tom Davison. Thanks also for production support from Elena Battista Malcom and DGA Productions, Boston, and Zebra Productions, New York.

DCS by Fisher & Paykel, Kohler, Diamond Crystal Salt, FOXY, Cooking.com, and Wente Vineyards helped underwrite the show, and we thank them for their support. We also thank Anne Traficante, Ann Naya, and Kate May for handling underwriter relations and Deborah Broide for managing publicity.

Meat was provided by Ronnie Savenor at Savenor's Market of Boston, Massachusetts. Fish was supplied by Ian Davison of Constitution Seafoods of Boston, Massachusetts. Live plants and garden items for the show were furnished by Mahoney's Garden Center of Brighton, Massachusetts. Aprons for Christopher Kimball were made by Nicole Romano and staff aprons were made by Crooked Brook. Props were designed and developed by Jay Layman, Christine Vo, and Erica Lee.

AMERICA'S TEST KITCHEN

THE TV COMPANION COOKBOOK 2013

Big, Bold
CHICKEN BRAISES

Browning meaty chicken thighs before braising them gives Chicken Marbella complex flavor.

COMPANY'S COMING AND YOU'RE MAKING CHICKEN. BUT ADMIT IT, for entertaining, chicken can be a bit ho-hum. How are you going to dress it up? Roast it? Stuff it? Take it easy on yourself and go for a braise. Braising is a mostly hands-off method where food is gently cooked in a small amount of liquid until tender. It's ideal for tough cuts of meat, but also works well for chicken, which doesn't take as long to cook through as a hefty roast. In this chapter, we turn to chicken Marbella and Filipino chicken adobo, two exceptionally flavorful braises.

Sweet, salty, tangy, and exotic (at the time), chicken Marbella became *the* party dish of the day thanks to its inclusion in *The Silver Palate Cookbook,* published in 1982. We wanted to tone down the party some, however—the original recipe serves 16 to 24 and requires an overnight marinade—and come up with a version for today's home cooks.

Chicken adobo hails from the Philippines. It's tangy and rich and can be made with pantry staples like soy sauce and garlic, although ingredients can vary widely—as can results. We encountered harsh, unbalanced sauces and greasy chicken with flabby skin. We wanted to nail down a foolproof recipe that yielded tender meat, crisp skin, a smooth sauce, and great flavor. Join us in the test kitchen as we update and upgrade two chicken braises for company or any night of the week.

CHICKEN MARBELLA

✓ WHY THIS RECIPE WORKS: More than 25 years ago, this dinner-party mainstay put *The Silver Palate Cookbook* on the map. We wanted to retool the recipe for today's tastes. To save time and boost flavor, we ditched the original marinade and made a paste of the prunes, olives, capers, garlic, and oregano, which we spread on the chicken and caramelized into the sauce. Instead of using whole birds, which require butchering, we chose easy-prep chicken parts. To intensify the dish's meaty flavor and to create complexity, we added anchovies and pepper flakes and browned the chicken in a skillet before baking it through.

IN 1977, A GOURMET SHOP CALLED THE SILVER PALATE opened on Manhattan's Upper West Side and introduced New Yorkers to their first bite of chicken Marbella. Inspired by the Moroccan tagines and Spanish braises that owners Julee Rosso and Sheila Lukins had sampled while traveling abroad in the 1960s, the shop's signature dish offered Americans a taste of then-exotic flavors: briny capers and bold Spanish olives baked with chicken and tender prunes in a sweet and tangy sauce. The shop closed in 1993, but the dish lives on in kitchens throughout America.

The original recipe starts with four whole chickens that are quartered into split breasts and legs and marinated overnight in olive oil, red wine vinegar, garlic, olives, prunes, capers, oregano, bay leaves, and plenty of salt and pepper. Everything is then transferred to shallow baking dishes, moistened with white wine, topped with a cup of brown sugar, and baked (with frequent basting) in a 350-degree oven for about an hour.

When we made this modern classic in the test kitchen, it was easy to see why its unique balance of flavors has made it such an enduring hit. But there were also a number of problems. While the chicken was juicy, its flavor was very subtle despite the overnight soak. The skin remained pale and flabby, and the sauce, though well seasoned, was quite sweet, lacking the pungency that its ingredient list would suggest. In the enterprising spirit

of Rosso and Lukins, we set out to create an updated version of this classic dinner-party favorite.

To make the dish more feasible as a weeknight supper, we first scaled it down to four to six servings (the original recipe serves 16 to 24). We also saved ourselves the trouble of butchering by switching from whole chickens to split breasts and leg quarters.

Next to go: the overnight marinade. Years of testing have taught us that marinades aren't miracle cure-alls for bland, dry meat. We've found that regardless of how long a marinade remains in contact with meat, its flavor never penetrates more than a few millimeters into the meat. And forget about crisp skin: The lengthy soak waterlogs poultry skin, which in turn inhibits rendering and browning. There is one element of a marinade that does live up to the hype, however: salt. Salt in a marinade acts like a brine, penetrating the muscle fibers, seasoning the meat, and helping it hold on to its juices. When we ran a side-by-side test pitting chicken pieces treated with the original marinade against a batch that was simply salted (both sat overnight in the fridge), both samples emerged equally succulent. In fact, tasters preferred the salted chicken, noting that the vinegar had turned the marinated chicken mealy.

Unfortunately, though salting worked well, it took at least 6 hours to have an impact (with better results after 24 hours). Brining was faster but—just like marinating—left us with limp, waterlogged chicken skin that resisted browning and diluted the sauce during baking. Reluctantly, we scratched these pretreatments off of our list and turned our attention to the cooking method, hoping to find an alternative path to moist, flavorful meat.

We decided to sear the chicken to jump-start browning and build a sauce from the fond. We seasoned two split breasts and two leg quarters with salt and pepper and placed them skin side down in a smoking-hot 12-inch skillet. Once the skin turned golden, we flipped the parts over and transferred them to a shallow baking dish. Then we set about building the sauce. We stirred in the oil, vinegar, olives, capers, and other ingredients and cooked them for a minute. We deglazed the skillet with white wine, poured the sauce around the chicken, and transferred everything to a 400-degree oven (leaving the skin exposed to the direct heat of the oven). To allow the skin

CHICKEN MARBELLA

to continue rendering, we scrapped the brown sugar coating (relying on the prunes for sweetness) and skipped the basting, since moist skin doesn't render or brown much.

The good news was that the sauce was more flavorful, albeit still a little thin. But despite our efforts, the skin hadn't rendered or colored much more than it had after the initial browning—the straight sides of the baking dish were trapping moisture. We'd already dirtied a skillet; could we take advantage of its shallow walls and cook the chicken through in the same pan? We gave it a shot, returning the seared chicken to the skillet after building the sauce and then placing the skillet in the oven to finish cooking. Sure enough, the skillet allowed more steam to escape, resulting in well-browned skin and a more concentrated sauce. Finally, we were getting somewhere.

But there was still more work to do. Tasters complained that the dish didn't seem cohesive, and none of the sauce's flavor had transferred to the chicken. Perhaps a more concentrated sauce was the answer. We ramped up the amounts of olives, capers, prunes, and garlic, and to boost meatiness and complexity, we tried adding onions, anchovies, and red pepper flakes. Onions didn't impress tasters, but minced anchovies added a rich depth without tasting fishy and a pinch of pepper flakes earned raves. The sauce finally came together with the addition of ¾ cup of chicken broth. The chicken, however, was still bland.

Desperate for a fix, we went back to basting, but the technique proved both inconvenient and ineffective. While mulling over how we could get the flavor to "stick" to the chicken, we hit on the solution: We'd make a paste that would literally adhere to the skin.

We prepped another batch, pureeing some of the prunes, olives, and capers with garlic, anchovies, oregano, pepper flakes, and olive oil. After searing the chicken, we spread an even layer of paste on each piece before transferring the skillet to the oven. Things looked promising during the first half of cooking, as the paste started to develop a rich, dark patina. But it continued to darken, and by the time the meat was cooked through, the surface was charred. For the next test, we waited until the chicken was about half cooked and the skin well rendered and browned before adding the paste. After another 10 minutes in the oven, the paste had caramelized and the flavors had bloomed, making this the best-tasting chicken yet.

Wondering if we could use the paste to deepen the flavor of the sauce as well, we caramelized some of the paste in the skillet after browning the chicken. Just as we had hoped, the sauce was deeply flavorful and possessed a velvety texture thanks to the pureed prunes. A last-minute knob of butter, a teaspoon of red wine vinegar, and a sprinkle of fresh parsley pulled everything into balance.

With these changes, our colleagues agreed we'd made a good dish even better—and a version that might live on for another 25 years.

Chicken Marbella
SERVES 4 TO 6

Any combination of split breasts and leg quarters can be used in this recipe.

PASTE

- ⅓ cup pitted green olives, rinsed
- ⅓ cup pitted prunes
- 3 tablespoons extra-virgin olive oil
- 2 tablespoons capers, rinsed
- 4 garlic cloves, peeled
- 3 anchovy fillets, rinsed
- ½ teaspoon dried oregano
- ½ teaspoon pepper
- ¼ teaspoon kosher salt
- Pinch red pepper flakes

CHICKEN

- 2½–3 pounds bone-in split chicken breasts and/or leg quarters, trimmed
- Kosher salt and pepper
- 2 teaspoons olive oil
- ¾ cup low-sodium chicken broth
- ⅓ cup white wine
- ⅓ cup pitted green olives, rinsed and halved
- 1 tablespoon capers, rinsed
- 2 bay leaves
- ⅓ cup pitted prunes, chopped coarse
- 1 tablespoon unsalted butter
- 1 teaspoon red wine vinegar
- 2 tablespoons minced fresh parsley

1. **FOR THE PASTE:** Adjust oven rack to middle position and heat oven to 400 degrees. Pulse all ingredients together in food processor until finely chopped, about 10 pulses. Scrape down bowl and continue to process until mostly smooth, 1 to 2 minutes. Transfer to bowl. (Paste can be refrigerated for up to 24 hours.)

2. **FOR THE CHICKEN:** Pat chicken dry with paper towels. Sprinkle chicken pieces with 1½ teaspoons salt and season with pepper.

3. Heat oil in 12-inch skillet over medium-high heat until just smoking. Add chicken, skin side down, and cook without moving until well browned, 5 to 8 minutes. Transfer chicken to large plate. Drain off all but 1 teaspoon fat from skillet and return to medium-low heat.

4. Add ⅓ cup paste to skillet and cook, stirring constantly, until fragrant and fond forms on bottom of pan, 1 to 2 minutes. Stir in broth, wine, olives, capers, and bay leaves, scraping up any browned bits. Return chicken, skin side up, to pan (skin should be above surface of liquid) and transfer to oven. Cook, uncovered, for 15 minutes.

5. Remove skillet from oven and use back of spoon to spread remaining paste over chicken pieces; sprinkle prunes around chicken. Continue to roast until paste begins to brown, breasts register 160 degrees, and leg quarters register 175 degrees, 7 to 12 minutes longer.

6. Transfer chicken to serving platter and tent loosely with aluminum foil. Remove bay leaves from sauce and whisk in butter, vinegar, and 1 tablespoon parsley; season with salt and pepper to taste. Pour sauce around chicken, sprinkle with remaining 1 tablespoon parsley, and serve.

FILIPINO CHICKEN ADOBO

✔ **WHY THIS RECIPE WORKS:** Adobo is the national dish of the Philippines, and chicken adobo is among the most popular versions. The dish consists of chicken simmered in a mixture of vinegar, soy sauce, garlic, bay leaves, and black pepper. The problem with most recipes we found was that they were aggressively tart and salty. Our secret to taming both of these elements was coconut milk. The coconut milk's richness tempered the bracing acidity of the vinegar and masked the briny soy sauce, bringing the sauce into balance. But the fat from the coconut milk and the chicken skin made the sauce somewhat greasy. To combat this, we borrowed a technique used in French bistros. We placed the meat skin side down in a cold pan and then turned up the heat. As the pan gradually got hotter, the fat under the chicken's skin melted away as the exterior browned.

ADOBO MAY BE CONSIDERED THE NATIONAL DISH OF the Philippines, but thanks to the country's melting-pot ancestry, the formula for making it is remarkably varied. The core concept is meat marinated and braised in vinegar and soy sauce, with lots of garlic, bay leaves, and black pepper. Everything from that point on, however, is open to interpretation. Chicken is the usual choice, but pork is also used. In the Philippines, coconut-sap vinegar is preferred, but when that isn't available, rice vinegar is a popular substitute. Plenty of recipes also call for cider vinegar or plain old distilled vinegar. Some versions go heavy on the soy sauce, rendering the dish a distant relative of Japanese teriyaki, while others use the soy more sparingly, with rich coconut milk stirred in for a result that is more currylike.

What most Filipino recipes do have in common: This dish is simple and easy to prepare, the ingredients are few and mostly pantry staples, and the finished product—tender meat napped with a reduction of the tangy braising liquid—boasts bold, well-developed flavors.

We armed ourselves with Filipino cookbooks and tried a bunch of recipes based on chicken, our protein

FILIPINO CHICKEN ADOBO

of choice. The recipes all started with combining all the ingredients in a large bowl. Marinating times, however, were anywhere from 30 minutes to as long as 24 hours. The results were predictably varied, but unfortunately all were problematic, with aggressively tart and salty flavors and sauce that was too thin to cling to the meat. Most troubling of all was the meat, which more often than not sported a tough, mealy outer layer. With the goal of bringing more balance and body to the dish and producing meat that was juicy and tender, we started to work up our own take on adobo.

Using the best elements of our research recipes, we built a working formula using bone-in, skin-on chicken thighs. With more fat and collagen than breasts and more meat on the bone than drumsticks, thighs are rich, flavorful, and particularly well suited to braising. And the meat's skin would give the sauce something to cling to.

We tested marinating times from one end of the spectrum to the other, using cider vinegar for its round, fruity flavor. Each test resulted in the same tough, mealy texture. If anything, we expected that the chicken would be mushy, as we've always found that to be the effect of acidic marinades on meat. Puzzled, we relayed the result to our science editor, who offered an explanation: While soaking meat in moderately acidic marinades causes its surface to become mushy, strongly acidic mixtures like this one can cause surface proteins to bind and squeeze out moisture, drying out and toughening the meat's exterior. And it doesn't take long; tasters reported that even the 30-minute samples showed the effects.

We tried skipping the marinade altogether, but that knee-jerk reaction was too drastic. While we'd done away with the meat's tough chew, we'd also inadvertently wiped out its flavor, and tasters complained that the chicken and sauce now tasted like separate entities. We reviewed our previous research on marinades and came up with our next idea: marinating in only soy sauce. Salt is one of the few marinade ingredients that actually makes its way beyond the surface of the meat; in fact, it's the most important one, as it both seasons and tenderizes the meat. Sure enough, when we repeated the marinade test using only soy sauce, the flavor and tenderness of the meat improved radically after only 30 minutes. But we were far from finished. The tartness of the sauce was still way off base, and even after reducing, it lacked enough body to cling to the meat.

As we found ourselves at an impasse, a colleague suggested that we stop into Filipino chef Romy Dorotan's acclaimed Purple Yam restaurant in Brooklyn to try his adobo. His version was terrific, and when we inquired about the recipe, Dorotan revealed that he adds coconut milk to the braising liquid, which is customary in adobos native to southern Luzon, the largest of the Philippine islands. We'd shied away from the super-rich milk in our earlier tests, fearing that it would muddy the flavor of the braise. But his version convinced us otherwise, as it perfectly tempered the salt and acidity while still allowing for plenty of tanginess.

We returned to the test kitchen and whisked a can of coconut milk into the braising liquid of our next batch. Tasters praised the balanced flavors and declared this our best adobo yet, save for one objection: The double dose of fat from the chicken skin and the coconut milk had rendered the sauce a little greasy. We also had a related complaint of our own: This being a braise, we weren't banking on crackly crisp skin, but thus far it had been downright soggy. Discarding the skin altogether might have been one option, but we were counting on its craggy exterior to grip the sauce.

The problem was that our one-step cooking method wasn't exposing the chicken to any high, dry heat, so there was no opportunity to render any of the skin's gummy fat layer and crisp its surface. We figured we could just throw

NOTES FROM THE TEST KITCHEN

BALANCING ACT

The two core components of Filipino adobo—vinegar and soy sauce—add up to a predictably sharp, salty braising liquid. To even out the acidity and salt, we took a cue from a regional variation and added a can of coconut milk. The thick, rich milk mellows those harsher flavors while still allowing for plenty of tanginess. It also adds welcome body to the sauce.

We'd been at the stove for less than an hour when we removed the chicken from the pan and briefly reduced the cooking liquid. We poured the tangy, coconut milk–enriched sauce over the tender pieces of chicken, sprinkled on a handful of sliced scallion for color and freshness, and dug in, admiring how perfectly these bold flavors had melded together.

Filipino Chicken Adobo

SERVES 4

Light coconut milk can be substituted for regular coconut milk. Serve this dish over rice.

8	(5- to 7-ounce) bone-in chicken thighs, trimmed
⅓	cup soy sauce
1	(13½-ounce) can coconut milk
¾	cup cider vinegar
8	garlic cloves, peeled
4	bay leaves
2	teaspoons pepper
1	scallion, sliced thin

1. Toss chicken with soy sauce in large bowl. Refrigerate for at least 30 minutes or up to 1 hour.

2. Remove chicken from soy sauce, allowing excess to drip back into bowl. Transfer chicken, skin side down, to 12-inch nonstick skillet; set aside soy sauce.

3. Place skillet over medium-high heat and cook until chicken skin is browned, 7 to 10 minutes. While chicken is browning, whisk coconut milk, vinegar, garlic, bay leaves, and pepper into soy sauce.

4. Transfer chicken to plate and discard fat in skillet. Return chicken to skillet skin side down, add coconut milk mixture, and bring to boil. Reduce heat to medium-low and simmer, uncovered, for 20 minutes. Flip chicken skin side up and continue to cook, uncovered, until chicken registers 175 degrees, about 15 minutes. Transfer chicken to platter and tent loosely with aluminum foil.

5. Remove bay leaves and skim any fat off surface of sauce. Return skillet to medium-high heat and cook until sauce is thickened, 5 to 7 minutes. Pour sauce over chicken, sprinkle with scallion, and serve.

the thighs skin side down into a ripping-hot skillet for a few minutes before moving them into the braising liquid. Easy fix, right? Wrong. Sure, the skin looked crisp and nicely browned, but slicing below the surface revealed that the thick fat pad was still there. Leaving the thighs in the hot pan for several more minutes to render the fat wasn't any better; by the time the skin had shed most of its fat, it was also literally burnt to a crisp.

The problem reminded us of cooking duck breasts. In French bistros, chefs often rely on this method for melting down the dense white fat layer in duck: Place the meat skin side down in a "cold" (read: room-temperature) pan and then turn up the heat. As the pan gradually gets hotter, the fat under the skin has enough time to melt away before the exterior burns. Hoping the technique would translate to chicken, we placed the marinated thighs skin side down in a 12-inch nonstick skillet and then turned the heat to medium-high. Sure enough, after about 10 minutes the skin was not only sheer but also gorgeously browned. Even better, when we emptied the pan, we dumped out nearly ⅓ cup of fat. Greasiness problem solved. And although we knew that the skin wouldn't stay super-crisp, we did employ one last trick to keep as much of its crackly texture as possible. When we braised the chicken thighs, we started them skin side down and then flipped them halfway through so that they finished skin side up, allowing the skin to dry out a little before serving.

RATING WHOLE CHICKENS

Long gone are the days when you simply selected a broiler or fryer from the supermarket poultry case. Nowadays, picking up a whole chicken for supper has gotten more complicated, with labels advertising birds that are "all-natural," "air-chilled," "organic," and "free range," just to name a few. To find out if any of these claims made a difference, we sampled eight birds that had been roasted, rating both light and dark meat. Though some of these terms didn't seem to make a difference, one clearly did. Our top-rated birds were both air-chilled. While other manufacturers use a cold-water chilling system, which leads to the absorption of water that can affect and dilute the flavor, our top two brands air-chill their birds, and these chickens took top marks for flavor and texture, and were juicy rather than soggy. They also contained more fat, so they have an inherent flavor advantage. Note that sodium is per 4-ounce serving. Brands are listed in order of preference. See AmericasTestKitchen.com for updates to this testing.

HIGHLY RECOMMENDED

MARY'S Free Range Air Chilled Chicken
PRICE: $1.99 per lb **FAT:** 14.2% **SODIUM:** 85 mg
DISTRIBUTION: California, Oregon, Washington, Hawaii, Arizona, and Nevada
ANTIBIOTIC USE: "No antibiotics ever"
CHILLING METHOD: Air
COMMENTS: Air chilling plus a higher percentage of fat added up to a bird that tasters raved was "clean," "sweet," "buttery," "savory," "chicken-y," and "juicy."

BELL & EVANS Air Chilled Premium Fresh Chicken
PRICE: $3.29 per lb **FAT:** 15.6% **SODIUM:** 75 mg
DISTRIBUTION: East of the Rockies
ANTIBIOTIC USE: "Raised without antibiotics"
CHILLING METHOD: Air
COMMENTS: Thanks to almost three hours of air chilling, this bird's white meat was "perfectly moist," "rich and nutty," "concentrated and chicken-y," and its dark meat "silky-tender" yet "firm."

RECOMMENDED

SPRINGER MOUNTAIN FARMS Fresh Chicken
PRICE: $1.89 per lb **FAT:** 6.3% **SODIUM:** 80 mg
DISTRIBUTION: National, with concentration east of Mississippi
ANTIBIOTIC USE: "No antibiotics ever"
CHILLING METHOD: Water, "may contain up to 5% retained water"
COMMENTS: Compared with our air-chilled winners, this water-chilled bird's meat was "extremely mild tasting." It also contained the least amount of fat. Even so, tasters thought both the white and dark meat boasted "nice chew."

COLEMAN Organic Whole Chicken
(also sold as Rosie Organic Whole Chicken)
PRICE: $2.29 per lb **FAT:** 12% **SODIUM:** 80 mg
DISTRIBUTION: National
ANTIBIOTIC USE: "No antibiotics"
CHILLING METHOD: Water, "may contain up to 5% retained water"
COMMENTS: This organic chicken's "super moist meat" came across as "tender" but "not mushy" in both white and dark meat. However, tasters ranked its flavor as "middle-of-the-road," only "moderately chicken-y."

RECOMMENDED (cont.)

EMPIRE Kosher Broiler Chicken
PRICE: $3.89 per lb **FAT:** 9.2% **SODIUM:** 290 mg
DISTRIBUTION: National
ANTIBIOTIC USE: "Never ever administered antibiotics"
CHILLING METHOD: Water, koshered (salted, soaked, and rinsed)
COMMENTS: Reactions to this kosher chicken's high sodium level were mixed: Some tasters found its white meat "rich" and "brothy"; others, a bit too "salty."

RECOMMENDED WITH RESERVATIONS

PERDUE Fresh Whole Chicken
PRICE: $1.99 per lb **FAT:** 9.8% **SODIUM:** 80 mg
DISTRIBUTION: National
ANTIBIOTIC USE: "Perdue does not use antibiotics for growth promotion"
CHILLING METHOD: Water, "may contain up to 4% retained water"
COMMENTS: Your "basic," "bland" chicken that some found "super tender" but others deemed "dry" with meat that "sticks to your teeth."

GOLD KIST FARMS Young 'n Tender All Natural Chicken
(also sold as Pilgrim's)
PRICE: $1.99 per lb **FAT:** 14.42% **SODIUM:** 65 mg
DISTRIBUTION: Florida to Arizona, in the South (half of chickens produced are sold as store brands across the U.S.)
ANTIBIOTIC USE: Yes
CHILLING METHOD: Water, "may contain up to 5% retained water"
COMMENTS: This somewhat "bland" bird had "soft-textured meat that kind of melted in [the] mouth." Others called it "mushy" and "spongy." In sum: "Pretty average chicken, not great."

TYSON Young Chicken
PRICE: $1.69 per lb **FAT:** 9.4% **SODIUM:** 150 mg
DISTRIBUTION: National
INGREDIENTS: Contains up to 12 percent chicken broth, sea salt, natural flavorings
ANTIBIOTIC USE: Yes
CHILLING METHOD: Water
COMMENTS: You know something's fishy when your chicken has an ingredient list. Though most judged it "OK," some found this broth-injected bird "spongy," "wet," and "bland beyond description."

Rethinking
SEAFOOD CLASSICS

Does a pair of seafood scissors belong in your kitchen drawer? Lisa explains why you might want to consider this purchase.

THERE ARE SOME SEAFOOD DISHES THAT PEOPLE DON'T BOTHER making at home, either because the main ingredient isn't always available—freshly shucked lump crabmeat for crab cakes, for example—or because they're considered so complicated that they're best left in the hands of a professional—such as smoked salmon. We set out to show you why you really *can* make both these dishes at home—without making a special trip to a fish market or investing in a smoker.

Have you ever made crab cakes with commonly available pasteurized crabmeat? We typically avoid it because of its fishy odor. Our first challenge: Find a way to rid supermarket crabmeat of this off-putting characteristic. A second goal for truly great homemade crab cakes was in finding a decent binder. Too often, "binder" equals "filler" and that filler, whether it's bread crumbs, mayonnaise, or eggs, dulls the flavor of the crab. We wanted crab cakes with sweet shellfish flavor front and center. Period.

We've enjoyed our fair share of firm, silky cold-smoked salmon, sliced thin with bagels, and we're also fans of salmon fillets grilled over coals with wood chunks, which does a decent job of imparting smoky flavor. We wanted to unite the two methods, so we could enjoy smooth, smoky dinnertime fillets. We wouldn't rely on specialized equipment, nor would we allow this to be an all-consuming project. Coming up, two seafood favorites anyone can make at home.

BEST CRAB CAKES

✔ **WHY THIS RECIPE WORKS:** We wanted to come up with the best possible crab cakes—sweet, plump meat delicately seasoned and seamlessly held together with a binder that didn't mask seafood flavor. And we didn't want shopping to be an issue—our crab cakes should work with either fresh crabmeat or the pasteurized variety found at the supermarket. Instead of flavor-muting bread crumbs, gloppy mayo, and eggs, we bound our cakes with a delicate shrimp mousse, which also enhanced the crabmeat's natural sweetness. Classic components like Old Bay seasoning and lemon juice bolstered the crab's flavor and panko bread crumbs helped ensure a crisp crust.

IT'S A GIVEN THAT THE BEST CRAB CAKES ARE MADE with meat that's just been picked from the shell. But since fresh crabmeat is usually impossible to come by, we almost never make the cakes at home. That's a shame, because crab cakes are relatively quick and easy to throw together. Most recipes call for simply mixing the shucked meat with aromatics, herbs, spices, and a binder like mayo or beaten egg; forming cakes and dredging them in bread crumbs; and quickly pan-frying them until they're golden brown and crisp.

But is fresh-shucked meat really the only acceptable option? We did some tasting and discovered that a couple of brands of pasteurized crabmeat (available either canned or in the refrigerated section of most supermarkets) are surprisingly good alternatives to the fresh stuff. We decided to make it our goal to come up with the best possible crab cakes—sweet, plump meat delicately seasoned and seamlessly held together with a binder that didn't detract from the seafood flavor—regardless of whether we were starting with fresh crabmeat or not.

The obvious first step: figuring out what type of packaged crabmeat to use. Species aside, all crabmeat is graded both by size and by the part of the crab from which it's taken. Most crab cake recipes call for plump (pricey) jumbo lump or lump, while some suggest finer, flakier backfin crabmeat.

We were pretty sure colleagues would prefer the meatier texture of jumbo lump or lump, but we made crab cakes with all three grades to be on the safe side. We put together a bare-bones recipe, mixing 1 pound of meat with mayonnaise and eggs, forming the mixture into eight cakes, rolling them in panko (super-crisp Japanese bread crumbs), and pan-frying them. No contest: Tasters overwhelmingly preferred the cakes made with jumbo lump or lump crabmeat. Flavor was another matter. Not only were the binders dulling the sweet crabmeat flavor, but all three batches tasted and smelled inescapably fishy. When we mentioned the results to our science editor, he suggested soaking the meat in milk to rid it of its unpleasant fishiness. It was a great quick trick. When we submerged the crabmeat in 1 cup of milk, the fishiness washed away after just a 20-minute soak.

Figuring we'd solved the toughest problem, we moved on to consider more conventional crab cake decisions like flavors and binders. Celery and onion (both briefly sautéed before joining the crabmeat) plus Old Bay seasoning were classic additions that nicely rounded out the rich flavor of the crabmeat. But the flavor-muting binders were a trickier issue. Reducing or leaving out the mayonnaise or egg allowed the clean crabmeat flavor to come through. However, the unfortunate (if predictable) consequence was that the binder-free batches fell apart during cooking.

Putting aside the mayo and eggs for the moment, we tried the first two out-of-the-box ideas that came to mind: a béchamel and a panade. Unfortunately, both tests flopped. The former, a combination of milk, flour, and butter, rendered the crab mixture mushy. The latter, a thick paste made from milk and bread that's often used in meatballs, was sticky and difficult to incorporate without breaking apart the crabmeat. Even worse, the starches and dairy in both binders deadened the crab flavor just as much as the mayonnaise and eggs had.

We were feeling short on ideas when we thought of a product used by high-end restaurants. "Meat glue," as it's commonly called, is a powdered protein that some chefs use to help bind foods together. Buying this stuff was out of the question here, but what about coming up with our own version? We couldn't turn protein into powder, but we could puree it. More specifically, we could call

BEST CRAB CAKES

on another restaurant idea: a mousseline. This delicate, savory mousse is composed mainly of pureed meat or fish and just a little cream. To enhance the briny sweetness and plump bite of the crabmeat, we figured we'd use shrimp. We wouldn't need much of it, and since the shrimp would be pureed, we could use whatever size was cheapest.

To that end, we pureed 6 ounces of shrimp in the food processor with 6 tablespoons of cream, plus the Old Bay, a little Dijon mustard, hot sauce, and fresh lemon juice for punchy flavor. As we'd hoped, the resulting mousse was a great stand-in; in fact, our science editor noted that this was a true meat glue. Pureeing the shrimp released fragments of sticky muscle proteins that delicately held the clumpy pieces of crabmeat together through the breading and cooking process. When tasters raved about the clean crab flavor that we had achieved, we knew this idea was a keeper. Their only quibble: The inside texture of the cakes was a bit too springy and bouncy, and a few

stray clumps of crabmeat were falling off during cooking. Scaling back the mousse mixture by a third took care of the bounce, but pieces were still breaking off as we flipped the cakes.

We had one other, more subtle idea in mind to help make the crab cakes a bit sturdier: Briefly chilling them before cooking allowed them to firm up, resulting in less fragile cakes. We ran a side-by-side test, refrigerating one batch for a half-hour before pan-frying, while immediately cooking the other. The chill paid off; these cakes not only felt noticeably sturdier than the unrested batch but also held up considerably better during cooking.

Our tasters' one lingering request concerned the breading. The panko was definitely crispier than traditional bread crumbs, but the flakes soaked up moisture from the cakes, losing some of their crunch and falling off the sides. Color was also a problem, as the only surfaces that browned nicely were those that came in contact with the pan. Our two quick fixes: crushing half of the panko to make smaller pieces that would adhere better to the cakes, and toasting all of the crumbs before coating to deepen and even out their color and beef up their crunch.

With just a few easy tricks to clean up the crab's flavor and keep the meat neatly bound, we'd created a recipe for classic crab cakes that were delicious whether made with the freshest crab or with readily available pasteurized crabmeat.

Best Crab Cakes

SERVES 4

Either fresh or pasteurized crabmeat can be used in this recipe. With packaged crab, if the meat smells clean and fresh when you first open the package, skip steps 1 and 4 and simply blot away any excess liquid. Serve the crab cakes with lemon wedges.

1	pound lump crabmeat, picked over for shells
1	cup milk
1½	cups panko bread crumbs
	Salt and pepper
2	celery ribs, chopped
½	cup chopped onion
1	garlic clove, peeled and smashed
1	tablespoon unsalted butter
4	ounces shrimp, peeled, deveined, and tails removed
¼	cup heavy cream
2	teaspoons Dijon mustard
1	teaspoon lemon juice
½	teaspoon hot sauce
½	teaspoon Old Bay seasoning
¼	cup vegetable oil

1. Place crabmeat and milk in bowl, making sure crab is totally submerged. Cover and refrigerate for 20 minutes.

2. Meanwhile, place ¾ cup panko in small zipper-lock bag and finely crush with rolling pin. Transfer crushed panko to 10-inch nonstick skillet and add remaining ¾ cup panko. Toast over medium-high heat, stirring constantly, until golden brown, about 5 minutes. Transfer panko to shallow dish and stir in ¼ teaspoon salt and pepper to taste. Wipe out skillet.

3. Pulse celery, onion, and garlic together in food processor until finely chopped, 5 to 8 pulses, scraping down bowl as needed. Transfer vegetables to large bowl. Rinse processor bowl and blade. Melt butter in now-empty skillet over medium heat. Add chopped vegetables, ½ teaspoon salt, and ⅛ teaspoon pepper; cook, stirring frequently, until vegetables are softened and all moisture has evaporated, 4 to 6 minutes. Return vegetables to large bowl and let cool to room temperature. Rinse out pan and wipe clean.

NOTES FROM THE TEST KITCHEN

FIX FOR "FISHY" SEAFOOD

Unless the fish or seafood you've bought is literally the catch of the day, chances are it will smell and taste at least a little fishy, thanks to a compound found in nearly all seafood called trimethylamine oxide, or TMAO. This compound is odorless when fish and shellfish are alive, but once they're killed, TMAO slowly transforms into TMA (trimethylamine), which has a fishy odor. But that doesn't mean that the seafood has gone bad or is unusable. We've found an easy way to eliminate the smell: Soak the fish or the shellfish meat in milk for 20 minutes and then drain and pat dry. The casein in milk binds to the TMA, and when drained away, it takes the fishy odor with it. The result is seafood that's sweet-smelling and clean-flavored.

DEVEINING SHRIMP

1. After removing shell, use paring knife or seafood scissors to make shallow cut along back of shrimp so vein is exposed.

2. Use tip of knife to lift vein out of shrimp. Discard vein by wiping blade against paper towel.

4. Strain crabmeat through fine-mesh strainer, pressing firmly to remove milk but being careful not to break up lumps of crabmeat.

5. Pulse shrimp in now-empty food processor until finely ground, 12 to 15 pulses, scraping down bowl as needed. Add cream and pulse to combine, 2 to 4 pulses, scraping down bowl as needed. Transfer shrimp puree to bowl with cooled vegetables. Add mustard, lemon juice, hot sauce, and Old Bay; stir until well combined. Add crabmeat and fold gently with rubber spatula, being careful not to overmix and break up lumps of crabmeat. Divide mixture into 8 balls and firmly press into ½-inch-thick patties. Place cakes in rimmed baking sheet lined with parchment paper, cover tightly with plastic wrap, and refrigerate for 30 minutes.

6. Coat each cake with panko, firmly pressing to adhere crumbs to exterior. Heat 1 tablespoon oil in now-empty skillet over medium heat until shimmering. Place 4 cakes in skillet and cook without moving them until golden brown, 3 to 4 minutes. Using 2 spatulas, carefully flip cakes. Add 1 tablespoon oil, reduce heat to medium-low, and continue to cook until second side is golden brown, 4 to 6 minutes. Transfer cakes to platter. Wipe out skillet and repeat with remaining 4 cakes and remaining 2 tablespoons oil. Serve immediately.

RATING CRABMEAT

Like most seafood, fresh-off-the-boat crabmeat is best—sweet and tender with a touch of salinity. But most crabmeat eaten in this country isn't fresh—it's prepackaged crab from the South Pacific. Though this prepackaged meat is quite pricey, the perks are that it's convenient and readily available (both refrigerated and canned) in most supermarkets. To find a worthy substitute for freshly picked crabmeat, we sampled five nationally available brands of crabmeat—only the more desirable lump and jumbo lump meat—plain and in crab cakes. In both the straight tasting and our crab cakes, we strongly preferred the two refrigerated products—and for good reason. To be shelf-stable, most canned crabmeat is typically pressure-heated at high temperatures (220 to 250 degrees), but the trade-off is drier, chewier meat. Manufacturers of canned crabmeat also often add additives such as citric acid to prevent discoloration or offset moisture loss during heat processing, but these can also negatively affect texture. (We did, however, find one brand of canned crabmeat that we can recommend.) Refrigerated crabmeat, on the other hand, is typically processed at lower temperatures (182 to 190 degrees) and is considerably juicier and more tender—and also pricier. Brands are listed in order of preference. See AmericasTestKitchen.com for updates to this testing.

RECOMMENDED

PHILLIPS Premium Crab Jumbo
PRICE: $26.99 for 16 oz ($1.69 per oz)
STYLE: Refrigerated; jumbo lump
SHELF LIFE: 18 months
COMMENTS: Our top-rated refrigerated brand boasted "moist," "plump," "meaty chunks" that tasters likened to fresh crab.

BLUE STAR Blue Swimming Crabmeat Lump Meat
PRICE: $8.99 for 6 oz ($1.50 per oz)
STYLE: Refrigerated; lump   SHELF LIFE: 18 months
COMMENTS: This brand earned praise for a taste that was "convincingly fresh" with "definite crab flavor."

MILLER'S SELECT Lump Crab Meat
PRICE: $9 for 6.5 oz ($1.38 per oz)   `BEST BUY`
STYLE: Canned; lump   SHELF LIFE: 4 years
COMMENTS: Tasters praised this shelf-stable canned brand's "high-quality," "light and tasty" flavor and "tender," distinct chunks of meat.

NOT RECOMMENDED

BUMBLE BEE Fancy Lump Crabmeat
PRICE: $5.79 for 6 oz ($0.97 per oz)
STYLE: Canned; lump   SHELF LIFE: 2–3 years
COMMENTS: Tasters complained that this crabmeat tasted like anything but crab, with a "dull" flavor that they likened to "Elmer's Glue" and "frozen fish sticks."

CROWN PRINCE Natural Fancy White-Lump Crab Meat
PRICE: $5.41 for 6 oz ($0.90 per oz)
STYLE: Canned; lump   SHELF LIFE: 3 years
COMMENTS: Don't bother with this bottom-ranking canned crabmeat. Tasters compared its taste to "dried squid" and "old fish-tank water."

RATING SEAFOOD SCISSORS

Cutting through thick, hard seafood shells to extract the meat within can be challenging, but luckily there's a tool that promises to make this job easier: seafood scissors. We recently tested two pairs, plus our favorite all-purpose kitchen shears, by snipping through pounds of lobster, king crab, and shrimp. Our favorite kitchen shears were a disappointment; their thick, straight blades, which are perfect for butterflying chicken and snipping herbs, were difficult to fit into narrow claws and legs and tended to hack up delicate meat in the process. One of the other brands tested shared the same problem; though they were sharp, they were too thick and large to be effective. The remaining pair worked much better. Its curved blades were easily able to follow the arc of shells, and they were thin enough to neatly extract meat from tight spots. Plus, they were strong enough to cut through knobby crab legs and hard lobster claws. Brands are listed in order of preference. See AmericasTestKitchen.com for updates to this testing.

HIGHLY RECOMMENDED

PROGRESSIVE INTERNATIONAL Seafood Scissors
MODEL: GT-3156   ITEM: 98-7832918   PRICE: $9.95
COMFORT: ★★★   PERFORMANCE: ★★★   BLADE: ★★★
HANDLE: ★★★
COMMENTS: These slender seafood scissors were strong enough to slice through knobby king crab legs and hard lobster claws. The curved blades fit perfectly along the arch of a shrimp shell, removing it in three efficient snips. They were the only pair that we tested that were dexterous enough to extract meat from long, skinny lobster legs.

NOT RECOMMENDED

THE ORIGINAL Sea Scissors
MODEL: 430   ITEM: sea01   PRICE: $14.95
COMFORT: ★½   PERFORMANCE: ★½   BLADE: ★½   HANDLE: ★★
COMMENTS: These sharp seafood scissors easily cut through lobster and crab shells, but their thick blades were too bulky to extract meat from spindly lobster legs and too large for shelling shrimp. The top blade was fitted with a wide plastic splatter guard that blocked our view, making it difficult to cut, and the wide, stiff handles were uncomfortable.

SHUN CLASSIC Kitchen Shears
MODEL: 1120M   ITEM: SUH1062   PRICE: $49.95
COMFORT: ★   PERFORMANCE: ★   BLADE: ★   HANDLE: ★
COMMENTS: These sturdy shears are excellent for butterflying chicken and snipping herbs, but the blades were too thick for most of the seafood tasks. They were also too wide to push into the shell far enough to get any cutting leverage. Inserting the blades into the lobster claws and crabs legs mangled the meat inside, and they felt clumsy and oversized while deveining shrimp.

GRILL-SMOKED SALMON

✔ WHY THIS RECIPE WORKS: We wanted to capture the intense, smoky flavor of hot-smoked fish and the firm but silky texture of the cold-smoked type, but we also wanted to skip specialized equipment and make this dish less of a project recipe. To prepare the salmon for smoking, we quick-cured the fish with a mixture of salt and sugar to draw moisture from the flesh, which firmed it up, and we seasoned it inside and out. We then cooked the fish indirectly over a gentle fire with ample smoke to produce salmon that was sweet, smoky, and tender. We also cut our large fillet into individual serving-size portions. This small step delivered big: First, it ensured more thorough smoke exposure (without increasing the time) by creating more surface area. Second, the smaller pieces of delicate salmon were far easier to get off the grill intact than one large fillet.

THE PROCESS OF SMOKING FISH OVER HARDWOOD TO preserve its delicate flesh has a long tradition, and rich, fatty salmon is well suited to the technique. But smoked salmon's unique taste and texture don't come easy: The translucent, mildly smoky slices piled on bagels are produced by ever-so-slowly smoking (but not fully cooking) salt-cured fillets at roughly 60 to 90 degrees, a project that requires specialized equipment and loads of time (at least 24 hours and as long as five days). Then there is hot smoking, a procedure in which cured fillets are fully cooked at higher temperatures (100 to 250 degrees) for 1 to 8 hours. The higher heat results in a drier texture and a more potent smokiness, so the fish is often flaked and mixed into dips and spreads.

Both approaches deliver terrific results but are impractical (if not impossible) for a home cook to pull off. Sure, you can impart a touch of smokiness by tossing wood chips onto hot charcoal and quickly grilling fish, but we had also heard of a lesser-known, more intriguing option that captures both the intense, smoky flavor of hot-smoked fish and the firm but silky texture of the cold-smoked type. It's easy because the fish is cooked via indirect heat on a grill—a familiar and uncomplicated technique. And although the resulting fillets have a distinctive taste, they are not overpoweringly salty or smoky, so they're suitable as an entrée either warm from the grill or at room temperature.

To try out these smoky, succulent fillets, we scoured cookbooks for recipes. The typical first step in smoking fish is to cure the flesh with salt; some authors recommend brining, others directly salting the fillet. To keep the preparation time in check, we steered away from recommendations for curing the fish for longer than an hour or two.

The other criteria, smoking temperature and length of exposure—both crucial to the final result—were all over the map. One recipe called for smoking the fish at 350 degrees for a modest 20 minutes; another let it go twice as long at only 275 degrees.

With so many factors at play, we decided to try a simple brine first, soaking a center-cut, skin-on fillet (retaining the skin would make it easier to remove the fillet from the grill) in the test kitchen's usual 9 percent solution of salt and water for 2 hours. For the time being, we used a moderate amount of coals, dumping 4 quarts of lit charcoal on one side of the grill, along with a few soaked wood chunks to provide the smoke. We placed the fish on the cooking grate opposite the coals, popped the cover on the grill, and smoked the fish until it was still a little translucent at the center, about 25 minutes.

The result was illuminating, if not exactly spectacular. The brine had the unfortunate effect of making the salmon terribly bloated, plus it seemed to highlight the fish's natural oiliness in an unpleasant way—a far cry from the supple but firm texture we were after. When we thought about it, it made sense: Unlike lean, dry proteins such as turkey breast and pork tenderloin, salmon contains so much fat and moisture that a brine only makes it seem waterlogged.

For our next try, we covered the salmon in a generous blanket of kosher salt (its coarse texture makes it cling to food better than table salt) and refrigerated it uncovered on a wire rack on a baking sheet. After an hour, a considerable amount of liquid had been drawn to the surface of the flesh. We knew that if we waited any longer, the fluid would start to migrate back into the salmon through the process of osmosis, once again leading to a bloated texture, so we promptly removed it from the refrigerator, blotted the moisture with a paper towel, and took it out to the grill for smoking. This sample was considerably better than the brined fish: incredibly moist yet still firm—and not at all soggy. It wasn't perfect, though, since most tasters found it too salty to be enjoyed as a main dish. We tried dialing down the amount of salt as well as salting for a shorter amount of time, but alas, the fish didn't achieve the proper texture.

Going back to our research, we looked for a solution in the recipes that we'd collected and came across a few that called for adding sugar to the cure. We knew that, like salt, sugar is hygroscopic, meaning it attracts water. Could sugar pull moisture from the salmon as effectively as salt? Not quite: Because individual molecules of sucrose are much larger than sodium and chloride ions, sugar is, pound for pound, about 12 times less effective than salt at attracting moisture. Still, it was a workable option; we just had to do some tinkering. Eventually, we determined that a ratio of 2 parts sugar to 1 part salt produced well-balanced taste and texture in the finished salmon. Using these proportions, the fish firmed up nicely, plus it was far less salty and the sugar counterbalanced its richness.

With a reliable curing method in hand, we could finally fine-tune our smoking technique. Our current setup was far from ideal: By the time the fish was sufficiently smoky,

GRILL-SMOKED SALMON

oil spray.) Finally, we found that we could now use an even cooler fire (produced with a mere 2 quarts of charcoal): The smaller fillets still reached their ideal serving temperature in the same amount of time that the single, larger fillet had taken. Plus, the gentler fire rendered the fillets incomparably tender.

With a smoky, rich taste and a silky, supple texture, our quickie smoked salmon recipe was complete. To provide some contrasting flavors, we devised a home-made mayonnaise that incorporates three of the garnishes that are commonly served on a smoked salmon platter—hard-cooked egg, capers, and dill and an apple-mustard sauce. With these sauces and a reliable method, we had a recipe that was, to put it plainly, smoking hot.

Grill-Smoked Salmon
SERVES 6

Use center-cut salmon fillets of similar thickness so that they cook at the same rate. The best way to ensure uniformity is to buy a 2½- to 3-pound whole center-cut fillet and cut it into six pieces. Avoid mesquite wood chunks for this recipe. Serve the salmon with lemon wedges or with our "Smoked Salmon Platter" Sauce or Apple-Mustard Sauce (recipes follow).

2 tablespoons sugar
1 tablespoon kosher salt
6 (6- to 8-ounce) center-cut skin-on salmon fillets
2 wood chunks soaked in water for 30 minutes and
   drained (if using charcoal) or 2 cups wood chips, half
   of chips soaked in water for 15 minutes and drained (if
   using gas)

1. Combine sugar and salt in bowl. Set wire rack in rimmed baking sheet, set salmon on rack, and sprinkle flesh side evenly with sugar mixture. Refrigerate, uncovered, for 1 hour. With paper towels, brush any excess salt and sugar from salmon and blot dry. Return fish on wire rack to refrigerator, uncovered, while preparing grill.

2A. FOR A CHARCOAL GRILL: Open bottom vent halfway. Light large chimney starter one-third filled with charcoal briquettes (2 quarts). When top coals are partially covered with ash, pour into steeply banked pile against

it was dry and flaky. Conversely, when it was cooked perfectly—still silky and slightly pink in the interior, or about 125 degrees—the smoke flavor was faint. Adding more wood chunks only gave the fillet a sooty flavor. Instead, we tried to cool down the temperature of the grill by reducing the amount of charcoal from 4 quarts to 3. This helped somewhat, since the fish cooked more slowly (a full 30 to 40 minutes) and had more time to absorb smoke.

But the smoke flavor still wasn't as bold as we wanted. Rather than manipulating the cooking time any further, we turned to the salmon itself, cutting the large fillet into individual serving-size portions. This seemingly minor tweak resulted in big payoffs: First, it ensured more thorough smoke exposure (in the same amount of time) by increasing the surface area. Second, the delicate pieces were far easier to get off the grill in one piece than a single bulky fillet. (To that end, we also started placing the fillets on a piece of foil coated with vegetable side of grill. Place wood chunks on top of coals. Set cooking grate in place, cover, and open lid vent halfway. Heat grill until hot and wood chunks begin to smoke, about 5 minutes.

2B. FOR A GAS GRILL: Combine soaked and unsoaked chips. Use large piece of heavy-duty aluminum foil to wrap chips into foil packet and cut several vent holes in top. Place wood chip packet directly on primary burner. Turn primary burner to high (leave other burners off), cover, and heat grill until hot and wood chips begin to smoke, 15 to 25 minutes. Turn primary burner to medium. (Adjust primary burner as needed to maintain grill temperature of 275 to 300 degrees.)

3. Clean and oil cooking grate. Fold piece of heavy-duty foil into 18 by 6-inch rectangle. Place foil rectangle over cool side of grill and place salmon pieces on foil, spaced at least ½ inch apart. Cover grill (positioning lid vent over fish if using charcoal) and cook until center of thickest part of fillet registers 125 degrees and is still translucent when checked with tip of paring knife, 30 to 40 minutes. Transfer to platter and serve, or allow to cool to room temperature.

"Smoked Salmon Platter" Sauce

MAKES 1½ CUPS

This sauce incorporates the three garnishes that are commonly served on a smoked salmon platter—hard-cooked egg, capers, and dill.

- 1 large egg yolk, plus 1 large hard-cooked egg, chopped fine
- 2 teaspoons Dijon mustard
- 2 teaspoons sherry vinegar
- ½ cup vegetable oil
- 2 tablespoons capers, rinsed, plus 1 teaspoon caper brine
- 2 tablespoons minced shallot
- 2 tablespoons minced fresh dill

Whisk egg yolk, mustard, and vinegar together in medium bowl. Whisking constantly, slowly drizzle in oil until emulsified, about 1 minute. Gently fold in capers and brine, hard-cooked egg, shallot, and dill.

Apple-Mustard Sauce

MAKES 1½ CUPS

This sweet and tangy sauce is a perfect complement to our Grill-Smoked Salmon.

- 2 Honeycrisp or Granny Smith apples, peeled, cored, and cut into ¼-inch dice
- ¼ cup whole-grain mustard
- 2 tablespoons Dijon mustard
- 2 tablespoons minced fresh chervil or parsley
- 1 tablespoon cider vinegar
- 1 tablespoon honey
- ¼ teaspoon salt

Combine all ingredients in bowl.

NOTES FROM THE TEST KITCHEN

NOW WE'RE SMOKIN'

The two most common methods for smoking fish are cold and hot smoking. Both approaches require special equipment and a serious time investment and result in a product that is more of an ingredient than a main dish. Our unique hybrid recipe produces an entrée that captures the exquisitely smooth and lush texture of cold-smoked salmon and the forward smokiness of hot-smoked salmon. The best part? It cooks in only 30 to 40 minutes on a regular charcoal or gas grill.

COLD-SMOKED
Slick and silky; mild smoke

HOT-SMOKED
Dry and firm; potent smoke

HYBRID GRILL-SMOKED
Ultra-moist; rich, balanced smoke

Great *Italian*
PASTA SAUCES

*Dressed as a mushroom,
Chris pokes a bit of fun at
himself as he introduces a
segment on mushroom ragu.*

AMERICANS EAT BETWEEN 14 AND 20 POUNDS OF PASTA PER PERSON per year. That's a lot of noodles. Although we don't have the statistics on what kind of sauce makes it onto that pasta, we're willing to bet that it's a fairly simple tomato sauce, such as a marinara. Hey, we're all for the classics, but Italy boasts dozens of pasta sauces. Let's expand our horizons, shall we? In this chapter, we develop recipes for two classic, but little-known (in the United States) pasta sauces: *amatriciana* and mushroom ragu.

You've most likely encountered *pasta all'amatriciana* on Italian restaurant menus. It's a tomato sauce made ultrarich by the addition of salty *guanciale* (pork jowl) and Pecorino Romano cheese. Other than tomatoes, cheese, and the hard-to-find pork, traditional recipes diverge on what other ingredients they rely on to produce bright, sweet flavor (some insist on white wine, others wouldn't hear of it; ditto for onions and garlic). Our goals were clear: Find a substitute for guanciale that delivers the same meaty flavor and richness to the sauce and suss out just what supporting players are needed to make this sauce truly special.

We've all heard of pasta with meat ragu, but mushroom ragu? This isn't a dish dreamed up by vegetarians (the dish typically includes pancetta), but an actual Tuscan specialty known as *spaghetti alla boscaiola*. While meat ragus require an hours-long simmer to become flavorful, mushroom ragu takes just 30 minutes. What better sauce for a busy weeknight? To that end, we set out to determine just what mushrooms would yield maximum flavor and meaty texture. Pull out your pasta pot; we've got two terrific sauces to add to your repertoire.

PASTA ALL'AMATRICIANA

✔ WHY THIS RECIPE WORKS: To create an authentic-tasting version of pasta all'amatriciana we needed an alternative to hard-to-find guanciale, or cured pork jowl. Humble salt pork, though an unlikely solution, provided the rich, clean meatiness we were after. To ensure tender bites of pork throughout, we first simmered it in water to gently cook it and render fat, a step that allowed the meat to quickly turn golden once the water evaporated. Finally, to ensure the grated Pecorino Romano didn't clump in the hot sauce, we first mixed it with a little cooled rendered pork fat. Now the flavor of pork, tomato, chili flakes, and Pecorino shone through in each bite.

IF THERE'S ONE THING ITALIANS LOVE MORE THAN eating, it's arguing about cooking. Case in point: pasta all'amatriciana. Residents of Amatrice (a mountain town northeast of Rome) claim ownership of the dish's name and outline an official recipe that includes spaghetti, *guanciale* (salt-cured pork jowl), white wine, fresh or canned tomatoes, hot pepper flakes, and freshly grated Pecorino Romano—nothing more, nothing less. Romans, on the other hand, insist on bucatini (long, thin, hollow pasta) and incorporate onions and sometimes garlic, but never wine. On a recent excursion through the region, we sampled both versions and sided with the Amatricians, whose wine-brightened take elegantly balances the bold flavors of the dish, with no alliums to distract. Leaving the cacophony of disagreement in the Italian countryside, we headed home to reproduce the Amatrician recipe.

Guanciale, the shining star of the dish, can be difficult to procure in the United States. Made by salting and drying hog jowls, it boasts unmatched pure pork flavor. Our first idea for a substitute was pancetta, which is essentially spiced, unsmoked Italian bacon. We prepared two sauces; one with guanciale that we had splurged on for testing purposes and one with pancetta. For each sauce, we sautéed pork pieces, bloomed red pepper flakes in the rendered fat, stirred in and cooked down wine and tomatoes, tossed the sauce with spaghetti, and finished with grated Pecorino. Our colleagues' frowns said it all: Pancetta produced an oddly sour-tasting dish that lacked the heady porkiness of the guanciale version. In addition, the spices used to cure the pancetta detracted from the staccato notes of pork, tomato, cheese, and chilis.

American bacon was another option, but we knew its smoky taste would be out of place. But how about bacon's cousin, salt pork? At first glance, it seemed an unlikely candidate due to its humble American pedigree, but its preparation closely matches that of guanciale as it is also simply salt-cured. The difference is that for salt pork, the meat comes not from the jowl but from the belly of the pig. And sure enough, tasters found that the clean, meaty flavor of salt pork closely mimicked that of guanciale. Now we just needed to weed through conflicting advice to figure out how best to cook it.

Some recipes recommend lightly browning the guanciale before simmering it in the sauce and others warn against doing so. In a side-by-side test, sauces made with pork that was lightly colored boasted a richer flavor that was preferred hands-down. What's more, this method rendered more fat from the pork, which boosted the meaty flavor and led to a more voluptuous sauce. There was just one problem: The pork pieces had turned tough during simmering. We tried folding the crisped pork into the finished dish, but that only resulted in disparate, crunchy chunks dotting a lackluster sauce.

To solve the problem, we looked to a recent test kitchen discovery: We found that simmering bacon in water until the moisture evaporates and the strips sizzle holds the temperature low enough to keep the bacon meltingly tender. Once the water boils away, the bacon quickly browns, without turning tough or brittle. We gave it a shot with the salt pork and were beyond pleased. It remained supple and tender even after simmering.

When it came to white versus red wine, it made sense to depart from tradition: The heartier red wine provided a deeper, richer background flavor. And while the cultural affairs office of Amatrice allows for fresh or canned tomatoes, we decisively preferred diced canned tomatoes, which offered satisfying, sweet bites throughout. To help the sauce cling to the pasta, we also added a couple spoonfuls of tomato paste.

PASTA ALL'AMATRICIANA

We now turned our attention to the Pecorino Romano. Unlike mellow, nutty Parmigiano Reggiano (made from cow's milk), Pecorino is a sheep's-milk cheese with real funk and bite that pairs extremely well with the rich pork, tomato, and chili. But we kept running into the perennial problem when stirring grated aged cheese into a hot pot of pasta—it clumped into unattractive globs. With most pastas, we work around the problem by simply passing the cheese at the table. But all'amatriciana relies on the tang and saltiness of the Pecorino throughout the dish. Another traditional solution is to mix the grated cheese with cream and starch to provide stability while the cheese melts into the pasta. Unfortunately, this only resulted in muted flavors. What if, instead of cream, we mixed the cheese with some cooled pork fat? Bingo: We now had a clump-free dish and extra pork flavor to boot. The fat acted as a barrier to prevent the proteins in the cheese from bonding together as the cheese melted.

By arguing like Italians and questioning each ingredient, we had finally developed an authentic-tasting version of this classic dish. Let the dining—and the disagreement—begin.

Pasta all'Amatriciana

SERVES 4 TO 6

Look for salt pork that is roughly 70 percent fat and 30 percent lean meat; leaner salt pork may not render enough fat. If difficult to slice, the salt pork can be put in the freezer for 15 minutes to firm up. In this dish, it is essential to use high-quality imported Pecorino Romano—not the bland domestic cheese labeled "Romano."

- 8 **ounces salt pork, rind removed, rinsed thoroughly, and patted dry**
- ½ **cup water**
- ½ **teaspoon red pepper flakes**
- 2 **tablespoons tomato paste**
- ¼ **cup red wine**
- 1 **(28-ounce) can diced tomatoes**
- 2 **ounces Pecorino Romano, grated fine (1 cup)**
- 1 **pound spaghetti**
- 1 **tablespoon salt**

1. Slice salt pork into ¼-inch-thick strips, then cut each strip crosswise into ¼-inch pieces. Bring pork and water to simmer in 10-inch nonstick skillet over medium heat; cook until water evaporates and pork begins to sizzle, 5 to 8 minutes. Reduce heat to medium-low and continue to cook, stirring frequently, until fat renders and pork turns golden, 5 to 8 minutes longer. Using slotted spoon, transfer salt pork to bowl. Pour off all but 1 tablespoon fat from skillet. Reserve remaining fat.

2. Return skillet to medium heat and add tomato paste and pepper flakes; cook, stirring constantly, for 20 seconds. Stir in wine and cook for 30 seconds. Stir in tomatoes and their juice and rendered pork and bring to simmer. Cook, stirring frequently, until thickened, 12 to 16 minutes. While sauce simmers, stir 2 tablespoons reserved fat and ½ cup Pecorino together in bowl to form paste.

3. Meanwhile, bring 4 quarts water to boil in large Dutch oven. Add pasta and salt and cook, stirring often, until al dente. Reserve 1 cup cooking water, then drain pasta and return it to pot.

4. Add sauce, ⅓ cup cooking water, and Pecorino mixture to pasta and toss well to coat, adding remaining cooking water as needed to adjust consistency. Serve, passing remaining ½ cup Pecorino separately.

RATING GRATERS

A box grater has always been our go-to tool when we need to shred lots of cheese by hand. But given that most of us only ever use one side, leaving the other three grating surfaces unused, shouldn't there be a better option? To find out, we gathered nine graters, including everything from four-sided graters to flat paddles and two- or three-sided designs, and got to work grating. It was quickly evident that sharp teeth weren't as important as a generous-size grating plane and large holes, which let us effortlessly produce long, perfect strips of cheese. Also, we preferred graters with holes that were stamped, rather than etched; stamped holes offered thicker, more rigid grating surfaces that didn't budge when we pressed firmly against them. Brands are listed in order of preference. See AmericasTestKitchen.com for updates and further information on this testing.

HIGHLY RECOMMENDED

RÖSLE Coarse Grater
MODEL: 95022 **PRICE:** $35
STYLE: Stamped stainless steel
GRATING SURFACE AREA: 7 in by 3.2 in
DISHWASHER-SAFE: Yes
EASE OF USE: ★★★ **PERFORMANCE:** ★★★ **DURABILITY:** ★★★
COMMENTS: This easy-to-store flat grater made shredding a breeze, thanks to big, sharp holes; a large surface for better efficiency; and a solid, rigid frame that enabled continuous grating (rather than short bursts). It fit over medium and large bowls, and grippy rubber feet stuck securely to any work surface.

RECOMMENDED

MICROPLANE Specialty Series 4-Sided Box Grater
MODEL: 34006 **PRICE:** $34.95
STYLE: Chemically etched stainless steel
GRATING SURFACE AREA: 4 in by 3.2 in
DISHWASHER-SAFE: Yes
EASE OF USE: ★★★ **PERFORMANCE:** ★★
DURABILITY: ★★★
COMMENTS: From the originators of chemical etching technology, this model frames four super-sharp grating planes with tough plastic, making it easier to handle than other etched graters. It quickly and flawlessly grated mozzarella on its large holes and rendered perfect shreds of ginger and Parmesan on its fine holes. But hard carrots and potatoes bounced off its thin metal surface.

CUISIPRO 4-Sided Box Grater with Bonus Ginger Base
MODEL: 74-6850 **PRICE:** $29.95
STYLE: Chemically etched stainless steel
GRATING SURFACE AREA: 5.25 in by 3.25 in
DISHWASHER-SAFE: No
EASE OF USE: ★★ **PERFORMANCE:** ★★
DURABILITY: ★★★
COMMENTS: With ultrasharp etched teeth, a sturdy base, and a comfortable handle, this four-sided grater zipped through mozzarella, Parmesan, and ginger. But as with the etched Microplane grater, its thin surface bent under pressure, making it hard to create the thickest possible shreds of carrots and potatoes. Its razorlike teeth were tricky to clean—and it's not dishwasher-safe.

NOT RECOMMENDED

OXO Good Grips Box Grater
MODEL: 1057961 **PRICE:** $17.95
STYLE: Stamped stainless steel
GRATING SURFACE AREA: 6 in by 3.25 in
DISHWASHER-SAFE: Yes
EASE OF USE: ★ **PERFORMANCE:** ★★
DURABILITY: ★★★
COMMENTS: The holes on this grater, open in two directions to enable upward and downward grating, but it left mozzarella stuck to the surface and turned carrots and potatoes into mince. And forget about cleaning: The dual openings trapped food.

ONEIDA Large Oval Shaped Grater
MODEL: 50967 **PRICE:** $12.99
STYLE: Stamped stainless steel
GRATING SURFACE AREA: 6.25 in by 4 in (at widest end)
DISHWASHER-SAFE: Top rack
EASE OF USE: ★ **PERFORMANCE:** ★★ **DURABILITY:** ★★★
COMMENTS: Shaped like a flattened box grater, this oval model was narrow and tippy and made grating feel like a dangerous operation. One side sports strips of both fine and medium holes, cutting grating space in half.

JOSEPH JOSEPH Fold Flat Grater
MODEL: FFGG011HC **PRICE:** $20
STYLE: Stamped stainless steel
GRATING SURFACE AREA: 5.5 in by 2.5 in (at widest end)
DISHWASHER-SAFE: Yes
EASE OF USE: ★ **PERFORMANCE:** ★★
DURABILITY: ★★★
COMMENTS: This dual-sided grater uses sharp stamped metal teeth that render medium and coarse shreds and folds completely flat for storage. But its grating surface was smaller than most other boxes, and the grater itself refused to stay unfolded for stable, comfortable use.

MICROPLANE Twist N Grate Dual Sided Grater
MODEL: 34304 **PRICE:** $19.95
STYLE: Chemically etched stainless steel
GRATING SURFACE AREA: 4 in by 2.5 in (at widest end)
DISHWASHER-SAFE: Yes
EASE OF USE: ★ **PERFORMANCE:** ★★ **DURABILITY:** ★★★
COMMENTS: The narrow planes of this round, collapsible grater made semicircular carvings in foods and slowed testers down. Worse, these curves were dangerous, enabling the teeth to snag testers' hands.

QUICK MUSHROOM RAGU

✓ WHY THIS RECIPE WORKS: We wanted a mushroom ragu that combined the naturally hearty texture of fresh mushrooms with the concentrated flavor of dried ones—and that could be on the table in about 30 minutes. Using pancetta and its fat in our Quick Mushroom Ragu compensated for the lean nature of the mushrooms and made our mushroom ragu meatier. Portobello mushrooms gave our dish bulk, while smoky porcini gave it concentrated flavor. Adding tomato paste and hand-crushed whole canned tomatoes to our mushrooms after they'd browned sweetened our sauce but also let the mushrooms shine through. Finally, fresh rosemary finished our dish with brightness.

YOU'D NEVER FIND A RESPECTABLE TUSCAN TRATTORIA saucing a bowl of pasta with an overly sweet, dried herb–infused red sauce and calling it a "ragu"—but that's exactly the profile that most Americans recognize from the jarred versions that line supermarket shelves. In Italy, a true ragu combines tomatoes, meat, and hours of slow simmering to produce a rib-sticking, ultra-savory sauce that clings tightly to the pasta. A proper Italian ragu, in other words, is a labor of love.

But there are plenty of occasions when all that love and simmering is simply not possible. For those times, the jarred stuff is one option. Another, which embodies real depth of flavor and meaty richness and can be on the table in about 30 minutes, is mushroom ragu. Based on a Tuscan dish known as *spaghetti alla boscaiola,* or "woodsman's pasta," this ragu combines the naturally hearty texture of fresh mushrooms with the concentrated meaty flavor of dried ones.

Our working recipe started with a carryover: Pancetta is one ingredient of a traditional meat ragu that also finds its way into mushroom ragu, helping to make up for the lean nature of the mushrooms. Chopped bits of the salt-cured pork are first rendered, then the fat is used to sauté the remaining ingredients. Pancetta's meaty flavor, though subtle in the grand scheme of things, adds backbone to the sauce while still relinquishing the leading role to the mushrooms.

Since fresh mushrooms give the sauce bulk, we decided to go with one of the meatiest kinds: portobellos. We started with just one, removing the mushroom's gills—the dark, feathery grooves on the cap's underside—prior to cooking to keep the sauce from turning muddy. We then chopped the portobello into bite-size pieces that would blend into the sauce yet maintain a noticeable presence.

If fresh mushrooms offer meaty texture, then dried mushrooms offer ultra-concentrated flavor. Smoky porcini are among the most savory of the dehydrated varieties, and they seemed the natural choice in this Tuscan-inspired dish. We began by soaking half an ounce in boiling water for 10 minutes, then mincing the damp, shriveled pieces and adding them to the skillet along with the rendered pancetta, a little olive oil, the chopped portobello, and sliced garlic. After about 5 minutes, the fresh mushrooms had started to brown. In went chopped fresh tomatoes, and after about 20 minutes of simmering, the sauce had thickened nicely. When we tasted it, however, we were disappointed to find that it had nothing close to the earthy richness we wanted.

We tried adding another portobello cap and liked the bulk it provided, but it barely made an impact on the flavor. A far more potent solution was to increase the dried porcini to a full ounce. This so greatly deepened the flavor that we decided to keep going. We strained the soaking liquid left over from rehydrating the mushrooms, which we knew would have picked up a lot of porcini flavor, and added it to the sauce. Replacing the water in the recipe with chicken broth fortified the ragu even more. The mushroom flavor was finally in a good place; now we could return to the tomatoes.

Canned tomatoes are far more reliable than fresh most of the year, and we tried several types. Crushed tomatoes proved too thick and diced tomatoes stayed unpleasantly firm. Tasters preferred the softer yet hearty texture of whole tomatoes that we had crushed by hand. A tablespoon of tomato paste rounded out the sauce.

With the last-minute addition of fresh rosemary and red pepper flakes, the sauce took on brightness and heat. Even without an abundance of meat or hours of simmering, this was a ragu worthy of the name.

SPAGHETTI WITH QUICK MUSHROOM RAGU

Spaghetti with Quick Mushroom Ragu

SERVES 4

Use a spoon to scrape the dark brown gills from the portobellos.

- 1 cup low-sodium chicken broth
- 1 ounce dried porcini mushrooms, rinsed
- 4 ounces pancetta, cut into ½-inch pieces
- 8 ounces portobello mushroom caps, gills removed, caps cut into ½-inch pieces (about 1½ cups)
- 3 tablespoons extra-virgin olive oil
- 4 medium garlic cloves, peeled and sliced thin
- 1 tablespoon tomato paste
- 2 teaspoons minced fresh rosemary leaves
- 1 (14.5-ounce) can whole peeled tomatoes, roughly crushed by hand
  Salt and pepper
- 1 pound spaghetti
  Grated Pecorino Romano cheese

1. Microwave broth and porcini in covered bowl until steaming, about 1 minute. Let sit until softened, about 10 minutes. Drain mushrooms through fine-mesh strainer lined with coffee filter into medium bowl, reserve broth, and chop mushrooms fine.

2. Heat pancetta in 12-inch skillet over medium heat; cook, stirring occasionally, until rendered and crisp, 7 to 10 minutes. Add portobellos, chopped porcini, oil, garlic, tomato paste, and rosemary; cook, stirring occasionally, until all liquid has evaporated and tomato paste starts to brown, 5 to 7 minutes. Add reserved broth and crushed tomatoes and their juice; increase heat to high and bring to simmer. Reduce heat to medium-low and simmer until thickened, 15 to 20 minutes. Season with salt and pepper to taste.

3. While sauce simmers, bring 4 quarts water to boil in large Dutch oven. Add pasta and 1 tablespoon salt; cook, stirring often, until al dente. Reserve ½ cup cooking water, then drain pasta and return it to pot. Add sauce to pasta and toss to combine. Add reserved cooking water as needed to adjust consistency and season with salt and pepper to taste. Serve, passing Pecorino separately.

RATING WHOLE CANNED TOMATOES

If you believe the hype, San Marzano tomatoes, with the elite Denominazione d'Origine Protetta CR: Italics(DOP) label that indicates they have been grown in a designated region of southern Italy with seeds dating back to the original cultivar, have long been held to be the best tomatoes in the world. In recent years, these tomatoes have become easier to find—partly because not all brands labeled "San Marzano" are DOP-certified, with some even grown in the United States from San Marzano seeds. To find out if San Marzanos, no matter if they were grown in Italian or American soil, really are the ultimate canned whole tomatoes, we held a taste-off: San Marzanos versus everything else. We sampled 10 brands plain, in a quick-cooked tomato sauce, and in a slow-simmered sauce. Disappointingly, none of the San Marzanos delivered the bold, deep taste we were expecting. Tasters liked tomatoes that had higher levels of sugar (judged according to the Brix scale, which measures amounts of sugar in liquid; a higher number indicates a greater level of sweetness) balanced by enough acidity; the San Marzanos were either not sweet enough or too sweet but lacking ample acidity to counter the sweetness. When it came to texture, we liked tomatoes with a firm yet tender bite, even after a lengthy simmer. San Marzanos again scored poorly, as they are not treated with calcium chloride, which is added to the domestic brands to help maintain firmness. Brands are listed in order of preference. See AmericasTestKitchen.com for updates and further information on this testing.

RECOMMENDED

MUIR GLEN Organic Whole Peeled Tomatoes

PRICE: $2.99 for 28 oz   **ORIGIN:** USA
CALCIUM CHLORIDE: Yes **pH:** 3.91 **BRIX:** 6
COMMENTS: "Reminds me of a real summer tomato," said one taster about our favorite sample. No wonder: Its strong acidity and high level of sweetness made for flavor that was "vibrant" and "sweet in a natural way." The addition of calcium chloride gave the tomatoes a "nice firm texture" that held up even after hours of simmering.

HUNT'S Whole Plum Tomatoes

PRICE: $1.95 for 28 oz   **ORIGIN:** USA
CALCIUM CHLORIDE: Yes **pH:** 4.16 **BRIX:** 5.5
COMMENTS: Even after 2 hours of simmering, these calcium chloride–treated tomatoes were "meaty," with a "distinct shape." A relatively high Brix value and low pH—an ideal combination for tomatoes—explained their "fruity," "bright" flavors.

RECOMMENDED WITH RESERVATIONS

RED GOLD Whole Peeled Tomatoes

PRICE: $1.36 for 14.5 oz   **ORIGIN:** USA
CALCIUM CHLORIDE: Yes **pH:** 3.91 **BRIX:** 4.7
COMMENTS: These nicely "firm," globe-shaped tomatoes shared the same low pH (i.e., strong acidity) as our favorite brand, but they lacked its sweetness. As a result, several tasters found them "a bit sharp," even in long-cooked sauce. Others liked the big acid punch.

CENTO San Marzano Certified Peeled Tomatoes

PRICE: $3.79 for 28 oz   **ORIGIN:** Italy
CALCIUM CHLORIDE: No **pH:** 4.25 **BRIX:** 7
COMMENTS: Although these non–DOP-certified San Marzano tomatoes scored highest for sweetness, they lacked acidity, and tasters found their flavor merely "average"—even "untomatoey." That said, they fared the best of all the Italian brands, particularly because their texture "held up" in sauce.

RECOMMENDED WITH RESERVATIONS *(cont.)*

BIONATURAE Organic Whole Peeled Tomatoes

PRICE: $3.39 for 28.2 oz   **ORIGIN:** Italy
CALCIUM CHLORIDE: No **pH:** 4.28 **BRIX:** 5.6
COMMENTS: Without calcium chloride, these Italian tomatoes were so "mushy" that they "tasted like sauce" before we cooked them, but their "sweet" flavor was praised by some tasters.

SAN MARZANO Whole Peeled Tomatoes

PRICE: $3.99 for 28 oz   **ORIGIN:** USA
CALCIUM CHLORIDE: Yes **pH:** 4.26 **BRIX:** 6.4
COMMENTS: What's in a name? In this case, not much. These tomatoes were grown domestically with seeds from Italy's famous varietal. Some tasters picked up on their high level of sweetness, but without equally high acidity, the tomatoes' flavor was also "muted."

RIENZI Selected Italian Plum Tomatoes

PRICE: $1.95 for 28 oz   **ORIGIN:** Italy
CALCIUM CHLORIDE: No **pH:** 4.22 **BRIX:** 5.4
COMMENTS: Tasters noticed this sample's lack of calcium chloride in all three applications, describing the tomatoes as "mushy" and "borderline soupy." Thanks to low acid and moderate sweetness, their flavor was middle-of-the-road.

EDEN Organic Whole Roma Tomatoes

PRICE: $3.79 for 28 oz   **ORIGIN:** Canada
CALCIUM CHLORIDE: No **pH:** 4.31 **BRIX:** 4.2
COMMENTS: With the least amount of sweetness, not much acidity, and no added salt, these tomatoes didn't "pack much punch." Some tasters considered that effect pleasantly "clean" and "light," whereas others complained that they offered "no real tomato flavor at all," particularly in the long-simmered sauce.

CHICKEN CLASSICS, *Improved*

Our Skillet Chicken Fajitas are so flavorful that they require just a modicum of garnishes such as a squeeze of fresh lime juice.

ALL-AMERICAN CHICKEN SALAD, A STAPLE OF SUMMERTIME PICNICS, and the Tex-Mex classic chicken fajitas seem worlds apart, but both seem to have fallen on hard times. Today, chicken salad is just about indistinguishable from the classic version of our youth. Most recipes either ditch the mayo and doll it up with vinaigrette or use so much mayo you can hardly find a chunk of chicken. It's true that if you don't know what you're doing, chicken salad can indeed be bland and dull. We wanted to develop a recipe for an exceptional chicken salad packed with moist chunks of chicken in a creamy, well-seasoned dressing.

Over 30 years ago when fajitas made their U.S. restaurant debut in Texas, who knew they'd become so popular that they'd be a fixture on restaurant menus throughout the country? But somewhere along the way chicken fajitas began to suffer; the chicken often turned out dry and tasteless and the peppers and onions, a greasy afterthought. Instead, the accompaniments became the source of flavor—salsa, guacamole, sour cream, and loads of cheddar cheese. We wanted fajitas with juicy, boldly seasoned chicken and perfectly cooked peppers and onions. And equally important, the accompaniments, if any, would complement, not camouflage this Tex-Mex classic. Head into the test kitchen with us to put the sizzle back into chicken fajitas.

CLASSIC CHICKEN SALAD

✔ WHY THIS RECIPE WORKS: Recipes for chicken salad are only as good as the chicken itself. If the chicken is dry or flavorless, no amount of dressing or add-ins will camouflage it. To ensure silky, juicy, and flavorful chicken, we used a method based on *sous vide* cooking (submerging vacuum-sealed foods in a temperature-controlled water bath.) Our ideal formula was four chicken breasts and 6 cups of cold water heated to 170 degrees and then removed from the heat, covered, and left to stand for about 15 minutes. This yielded incomparably moist chicken that was perfect for chicken salad.

CHICKEN SALAD CAN MEAN JUST ABOUT ANYTHING these days, from shredded meat dressed in vinaigrette to grilled strips tossed with leafy greens. But we think that there's no beating the classic version: tender chicken cubes lightly bound with creamy mayonnaise and freshened up with minced celery and herbs. It's ideal sandwiched between bread slices, scooped into crisp lettuce cups, or simply eaten by the forkful—provided, of course, that the chicken has been properly cooked. Over the years we've eaten enough disappointing versions to know that no amount of dressing or add-ins will camouflage dry, stringy meat.

We made it our goal to come up with a method for silky, juicy, delicately flavored chicken first and worry about finessing the accoutrements later. We paged through dozens of recipes, most of which specified the same cut of meat: bone-in, skin-on chicken breasts. (The bone, a poor conductor of heat, helps prevent the meat from overcooking.) For the cooking method, the majority of recipes called for poaching.

As with any chicken recipe, our target temperature for the white meat was 160 to 165 degrees, when it's safely cooked through but still juicy and tender. We stuck with a conventional poaching method, bringing a pot of water to a subsimmer of 180 degrees and adding four breasts. Then things got fussy: Because the water temperature plunged as soon as we added the meat,

we had to continually adjust the heat to maintain the temperature. The results were succulent and tender, but having to constantly fiddle with the stove was a pain. Cranking the heat higher from the start wasn't the answer: The outside of the meat dried out before the inside was done. There had to be a simpler way to prevent the meat from overcooking.

That's when our thoughts turned to *sous vide,* a technique in which vacuum-sealed foods are submerged in a water bath that's been preset to the food's ideal cooked temperature. The beauty of this method is that it's impossible to overcook the food because the water temperature never exceeds the target doneness temperature. Temperature-controlled sous vide ovens cost a fortune, but if we could approximate this technique using ordinary kitchen equipment, we'd have a foolproof way to get perfectly cooked chicken.

Rather than heating the water before adding the chicken, we tried placing the breasts in a Dutch oven, covering them with cold water, and turning the burner to medium. When the water reached 165 degrees, we moved the pot off the heat and let it sit, covered, so that the chicken could continue climbing toward 165 degrees with no risk of overshooting the mark.

Unfortunately, this first sous vide attempt was too gentle; the water cooled before the chicken could fully cook through. We went through a dozen more tests, adjusting the cooking time, water temperature, and amount of water. It was a delicate balance: We needed enough water to fully submerge the chicken and hold the heat, but we didn't want to wait for several quarts of water to heat up. At last, we hit on the ideal formula: four chicken breasts and 6 cups of water heated to 170 degrees then removed from the heat, covered, and left to stand for about 15 minutes until the meat was 165 degrees throughout. In fact, the method was so foolproof that we could swap bone-in meat for fuss-free boneless, skinless breasts and still get the same tender, juicy results. One final cooking trick: Adding 2 tablespoons of salt to the water seasoned the meat nicely. We popped the cooked meat onto a baking sheet to chill in the refrigerator while we finished the salad.

We knew that mayonnaise would be the dressing base, but we wanted to use as little of it as possible to keep

CLASSIC CHICKEN SALAD

the salad light and fresh-tasting. After some experimentation, we found that just ½ cup was sufficient to bind the meat together, and we brightened its rich flavor with lemon juice and Dijon mustard. Minced celery, shallot, tarragon, and parsley added freshness and a cool, contrasting crunch.

With the basic salad perfected, we updated a few other classic versions so that we'd have several options for picnic lunches: a curried salad punched up with fresh ginger and crunchy cashews; a Waldorf version with crisp apple and walnuts; and an iteration boasting juicy red grapes and smoked almonds.

Classic Chicken Salad

SERVES 4 TO 6

To ensure that the chicken cooks through, don't use breasts that weigh more than 8 ounces or are thicker than 1 inch. Make sure to start with cold water in step 1. We like the combination of parsley and tarragon, but 2 tablespoons of one or the other is fine. This salad can be served in a sandwich or spooned over leafy greens.

       Salt and pepper
   4   (6- to 8-ounce) boneless, skinless chicken breasts,
       no more than 1 inch thick, trimmed
   ½   cup mayonnaise
   2   tablespoons lemon juice
   1   teaspoon Dijon mustard
   2   celery ribs, minced
   1   shallot, minced
   1   tablespoon minced fresh parsley
   1   tablespoon minced fresh tarragon

1. Dissolve 2 tablespoons salt in 6 cups cold water in Dutch oven. Submerge chicken in water. Heat pot over medium heat until water registers 170 degrees. Turn off heat, cover pot, and let stand until chicken registers 165 degrees, 15 to 17 minutes.

2. Transfer chicken to paper towel–lined baking sheet. Refrigerate until chicken is cool, about 30 minutes. While chicken cools, whisk mayonnaise, lemon juice, mustard, and ¼ teaspoon pepper together in large bowl.

3. Pat chicken dry with paper towels and cut into ½-inch pieces. Transfer chicken to bowl with mayonnaise mixture. Add celery, shallot, parsley, and tarragon; toss to combine. Season with salt and pepper to taste. Serve. (Salad can be refrigerated for up to 2 days.)

VARIATIONS

Curried Chicken Salad with Cashews

Microwave 1 teaspoon vegetable oil, 1 teaspoon curry powder, and ⅛ teaspoon cayenne pepper together, uncovered, until oil is hot, about 30 seconds. Add curry oil to mayonnaise and substitute lime juice for lemon juice and 1 teaspoon grated fresh ginger for mustard in step 2. Substitute 2 tablespoons minced fresh cilantro for parsley and tarragon, and add ½ cup coarsely chopped toasted cashews and ⅓ cup golden raisins to salad with celery.

Waldorf Chicken Salad

Add ½ teaspoon ground fennel seeds to mayonnaise mixture in step 2. Substitute 1 teaspoon minced fresh thyme for parsley, and add 1 peeled Granny Smith apple, cut into ¼-inch pieces, and ½ cup coarsely chopped toasted walnuts to salad with celery.

Chicken Salad with Red Grapes and Smoked Almonds

Add ¼ teaspoon grated lemon zest to mayonnaise mixture in step 2. Substitute 1 teaspoon minced fresh rosemary for tarragon, and add 1 cup quartered red grapes and ½ cup coarsely chopped smoked almonds to salad with celery.

RATING NO-FRILLS KITCHEN GADGETS

We love our fancy, high-end kitchen appliances and tools, but sometimes simpler is better. Case in point: this collection of humble, no-frills gadgets, which won us over with their exceptional performance. Though a few call for some elbow grease, they were so easy and fun to use, we didn't mind at all. See AmericasTestKitchen.com for updates to these testings.

CAST-IRON PIZZA PAN

We consider a pizza baking stone a must-have when making pizza, but could a cast-iron pizza pan give it a run for its money? We recently tested the Lodge Pro Logic Cast-Iron 14-Inch Pizza Pan ($28) to find out. Since cast iron absorbs and maintains heat so well, it would seem the ideal material for creating a great pizza crust, which requires searingly hot temperatures. After preheating the cast-iron pan to 500 degrees, we used it to bake multiple batches of pizza, looking for crisp, golden crusts on par with those made with our favorite baking stone. The first surprise: While the stone takes an hour to reach 500 degrees, this pan was ready after a mere 30 minutes. And though it weighs nearly 10 pounds (not far off from a baking stone), it was easy to move thanks to a pair of looped handles. Best of all, the pan produced perfect crust. Our verdict? Although the 14-inch round pan does limit the size and shape of your pizza when compared to a larger, rectangular baking stone, it offers identical results in less time—which means you can enjoy your pizza a lot sooner.

WINNER: LODGE PRO LOGIC CAST-IRON 14-INCH PIZZA PAN

CAST-IRON POT SCRUBBER

Since soapy water can strip the seasoning off of cast-iron cookware—and the seasoning is essential because it ensures the surface releases food easily—our standard cleaning method is to heat a little oil in the pan, add salt, and use this coarse paste to rub away cooked-on food. But not long ago, we came across a tool that promises to make cleaning cast-iron cookware (and all other cookware surfaces except nonstick) easier: the CM Scrubber by KnappMade ($19.98). We decided to give it a try, and passed this 4-inch square of stainless steel chain mail over a cast-iron pan encrusted with charred bits of sausage and another that we'd used for frying bacon. We were pleased to find that the linked steel rings effortlessly lifted away any stuck-on bits without damaging the pan's finish. Though the scrubber itself took some scrubbing to become completely grit- and oil-free for the next use, it dried quickly and didn't rust. We're even fonder of our cast-iron skillet now that we have a faster, tidier way to clean it up.

WINNER: KNAPPMADE CM SCRUBBER

MANUAL ESPRESSO MAKER

Espresso from a great coffeehouse delivers an incomparably rich, deep flavor. Short of buying a fancy $500 machine, could we get the same flavor from a more reasonably priced manual espresso maker at home? To find out, we tried the Presso Espresso Machine, which costs just $150. This 11-inch tool consists of two long, curved levers attached to a wishbone-shaped body, a clear hot-water chamber with markings for single and double shots, and a filter for grounds. Also included are a measuring scoop that doubles as a tamper, an adapter for making two single shots simultaneously, and a syringelike milk foamer (you simply stick it into milk and pump the plunger to froth). The instructions were clear and it was easy to use—but what about the flavor? The results were superb; the espresso was rich and full-bodied, and topped with a nice *crema*. The Presso makes a great espresso at home—no barista necessary.

WINNER: PRESSO ESPRESSO MACHINE

SKILLET CHICKEN FAJITAS

✓ **WHY THIS RECIPE WORKS:** To create indoor chicken fajitas that didn't require a slew of compensatory garnishes to be tasty, we took a fresh look at the key ingredients. For well-charred, juicy chicken we marinated boneless, skinless breasts in a potent mix of smoked paprika, garlic, cumin, cayenne, and sugar before searing them on one side and finishing them gently in a low oven. We revamped the usual bland mix of bell pepper and onion by charring poblano chiles and thinly sliced onion, and then cooking them down with cream and lime. Finally, we finish the dish with moderate amounts of complementary garnishes: pickled radish, queso fresco, and fresh cilantro.

FAJITAS ORIGINATED IN THE 1930S WHEN HUNGRY cattle ranchers in the Rio Grande Valley of Texas gorged on grilled leftover beef trimmings wrapped in charred flour tortillas. In 1973, Houston restaurateur Ninfa Rodriguez Laurenzo picked up on the idea and started offering the dish in her restaurant, Ninfa's, much to the delight of the locals. Fast-forward almost a decade to 1982, when enterprising chef George Weidmann of the Hyatt Regency's La Vista restaurant in Austin broke commercial ground by putting "sizzling fajitas" on his menu. To say that his signature dish was a hit is putting it mildly: Surging sales made La Vista the most profitable restaurant in the Hyatt chain, and chefs across the country were quick to jump on the fajita bandwagon.

Today, fajitas are made with everything from steak to shrimp to chicken. But truth be told, it almost doesn't matter what the protein is, since it's usually buried under flavor-dulling gobs of sour cream and shredded cheese. We wanted to reinvigorate fajitas, using convenient boneless, skinless chicken breasts and finding a good way to cook them indoors for year-round appeal. Our lighter, contemporary twist would abandon the stodgy Tex-Mex garnishes and put the spotlight where it belongs: on the chicken and obligatory peppers and onions.

Boneless, skinless chicken breasts may be convenient, but the downside is that they're also lean and somewhat bland. Our first inclination was to pump them up with a brinerade—a concentrated liquid with the salt content of a brine plus the acid and seasonings of a marinade. The salt seasons the meat and helps keep it moist during cooking while the herbs, spices, and acid penetrate the surface of the flesh with robust flavor.

We gave it a shot, mixing up a punchy concoction of salt, lime juice, garlic, cumin, and cayenne pepper—some of the key flavors of Mexican cuisine. We also added oil—important because the flavor compounds in garlic, cayenne, and cumin are largely fat soluble. We pounded the breasts to a ½-inch thickness so they would fit tidily into tortillas and then slipped them into the brinerade. After 30 minutes, we removed the chicken, wiped off the excess moisture, and seared it in a hot skillet. Unfortunately, by the time the meat was adequately charred, it was also dry as a bone.

We needed a way to get the chicken to brown faster, and even blacken slightly in spots. Would adding sugar to the brinerade do the trick? Since it caramelizes much more quickly (and at lower temperatures) than meat browns, we had high hopes. Sure enough, 1 teaspoon of sugar was just right, enabling rapid charring without contributing a noticeable sweetness. To further allude to the smoky heat of the grill, we stirred heady smoked paprika into the brinerade.

We now had some seriously flavorful chicken, but in spite of the brinerade it was difficult to keep it moist in the blazing-hot skillet. What if we compromised by searing just one side of the chicken over high heat and finishing the other side over low heat?

We gave it a shot, and lo and behold, the chicken that we'd charred on only one side was indeed juicier. We had to wonder, though: If the low heat of a stove was good, would the indirect heat of the oven be even better? To find out, we seared a batch on one side over high heat and then flipped the breasts and transferred the skillet to a 200-degree oven for 10 minutes. After letting it rest, we sliced up our moistest chicken yet and then tossed it back into the skillet to soak up the flavorful pan juices. Next up: veggies.

Fajitas' ubiquitous peppers and onions have a firm footing in Mexican cuisine, where they are known as *rajas*, or strips. While most rajas we eat stateside seem like an afterthought, they frequently take center stage in Mexico. In fact, *rajas con crema*—strips of roasted pepper and onion cooked down with tangy Mexican cultured cream—are often served alone in a tortilla. Providing a rich counterpoint to the lean chicken seemed an ideal way to breathe new life into our fajitas.

We threw a final batch of chicken into its brinerade and then followed a promising-looking rajas recipe using poblano chiles (they have a fruitier, more complex flavor than the usual bell peppers), which we broiled to blister the skins. After the broiled chiles steamed in a covered bowl for about 10 minutes, most of the skins slipped right off (though we did leave some charred bits behind for flavor). We sliced the chiles and sautéed them along with onion strips and then stirred in sour cream (our substitute for hard-to-find crema). That's where things started to fall apart—literally. First, the sour cream curdled as it made contact with the hot pan. Then, as we stubbornly persevered, the roasted poblanos overcooked into green mush.

Our first move was to swap heavy cream for the sour cream. The latter's high level of acidity and relatively low fat content make it a prime candidate for curdling, whereas fattier heavy cream is remarkably stable. To make up for the cream's lack of tang, we added a splash of lime juice toward the end of cooking. And to preserve our perfectly roasted poblanos, we added them at the last minute to rewarm with the onions and cream. Final touches of garlic, thyme, and oregano tied everything together. These revamped rajas were tender-crisp yet luscious.

After searing the chicken, finishing it in the oven, and charring some flour tortillas, we proudly laid out our modern fajita feast, offering crumbled *queso fresco,* chopped cilantro, lime wedges, and spicy pickled radishes for garnishing. These skillet fajitas provide all of the easy-to-love flavor of their grilled forebears—no shredded cheddar or salsa required.

NOTES FROM THE TEST KITCHEN

OVERCOMING THE PITFALLS OF LEAN WHITE MEAT
We like the convenience of boneless, skinless chicken breasts, but their lack of fat and flavor is a hazard. Here's how we achieve meat that is well charred, juicy, and meaty-tasting.

SEAR ON ONE SIDE
Cook marinated breasts over high heat without moving until thoroughly charred.

TRANSFER TO OVEN
Flip breasts and finish in gentle 200-degree oven, which ensures they won't overcook.

TOSS IN PAN JUICES
After resting chicken, slice and return to pan. Toss in flavorful juices before serving.

PEPPING UP FAJITAS WITH POBLANOS

We charbroil strips of fruity, complex-tasting poblano chiles and then simmer them with onions, cream, and lime juice. The tangy concoction, called *rajas con crema*, provides a rich counterpoint to the lean chicken.

Skillet Chicken Fajitas

SERVES 4

We like to serve these fajitas with crumbled queso fresco or feta in addition to the other garnishes listed.

CHICKEN

- ¼ cup vegetable oil
- 2 tablespoons lime juice
- 4 garlic cloves, peeled and smashed
- 1½ teaspoons smoked paprika
- 1 teaspoon sugar
- 1 teaspoon salt
- ½ teaspoon ground cumin
- ½ teaspoon pepper
- ¼ teaspoon cayenne pepper
- 1½ pounds boneless, skinless chicken breasts, trimmed and pounded to ½-inch thickness

RAJAS CON CREMA

- 1 pound (3 to 4) poblano chiles, stemmed, halved, and seeded
- 1 tablespoon vegetable oil
- 1 onion, halved and sliced ¼ inch thick
- 2 garlic cloves, minced
- ¼ teaspoon dried thyme
- ¼ teaspoon dried oregano
- ½ cup heavy cream
- 1 tablespoon lime juice
- ½ teaspoon salt
- ¼ teaspoon pepper

- 8–12 (6-inch) flour tortillas, warmed
- ¼ cup minced fresh cilantro
  Spicy Pickled Radishes (recipe follows)
  Lime wedges

1. FOR THE CHICKEN: Whisk 3 tablespoons oil, lime juice, garlic, paprika, sugar, salt, cumin, pepper, and cayenne together in bowl. Add chicken and toss to coat. Cover and let stand at room temperature for at least 30 minutes or up to 1 hour.

2. FOR THE RAJAS CON CREMA: Meanwhile, adjust oven rack to highest position and heat broiler. Line rimmed baking sheet with aluminum foil, then arrange

poblanos skin side up on baking sheet and press to flatten. Broil until skin is charred and puffed, 4 to 10 minutes, rotating baking sheet halfway through cooking. Transfer poblanos to bowl, cover, and let steam for 10 minutes. Rub most of skin from poblanos (leaving a little attached for flavor); slice into ¼-inch-thick strips. Adjust oven racks to middle and lowest positions and heat oven to 200 degrees.

3. Heat oil in 12-inch nonstick skillet over high heat until just smoking. Add onion and cook until charred and just softened, about 3 minutes. Add garlic, thyme, and oregano and cook until fragrant, about 15 seconds. Add cream and cook, stirring frequently, until reduced and cream lightly coats onion, 1 to 2 minutes. Add poblano strips, lime juice, salt, and pepper and toss to coat. Transfer vegetables to bowl, cover, and place on middle oven rack. Wipe out skillet with paper towels.

4. Remove chicken from marinade and wipe off excess. Heat remaining 1 tablespoon oil in now-empty skillet over high heat until just smoking. Add chicken and cook without moving it until bottom side is well charred, about 4 minutes. Flip chicken; transfer skillet to lower oven rack. Bake until chicken registers 160 degrees, 7 to 10 minutes. Transfer to cutting board and let rest for 5 minutes; do not wash out skillet.

5. Slice chicken crosswise into ¼-inch-thick strips. Return chicken strips to skillet and toss to coat with pan juices. To serve, spoon few pieces of chicken into center of warmed tortilla and top with spoonful of vegetable mixture, cilantro, and pickled radishes. Serve with lime wedges.

Spicy Pickled Radishes

MAKES ABOUT 1¾ CUPS

If you'd like a less spicy version of these pickled radishes, omit the seeds from the jalapeño.

10 **radishes, trimmed and sliced thin**
½ **cup lime juice (4 limes)**
½ **jalapeño chile, stemmed and sliced thin**
1 **teaspoon sugar**
¼ **teaspoon salt**

Combine all ingredients in bowl. Cover and let stand at room temperature for 30 minutes (or refrigerate for up to 24 hours).

RATING FLOUR TORTILLAS

Tortillas are big business in the United States, second only to white sandwich bread in bread sales. So it's not surprising to see a number of different brands on supermarket shelves. To find the best one, we tasted four brands of 6-inch flour tortillas plain and with our Skillet Chicken Fajitas. The biggest difference among the brands was thickness. Tasters preferred thinner tortillas, otherwise all they tasted in the fajitas was tortilla. Flaky texture, fat, and salt were also important. Our winner featured three distinct layers, not to mention almost three times as much fat as the lowest-ranking brand and nearly double the salt. It's clear why tasters would prefer tortillas with more fat, as fat adds flavor. But it also has another benefit: a higher percentage of fat helps produce a more tender yet flaky tortilla by reducing gluten development. Note that fat and sodium are per 32-gram serving. Brands are listed in order of preference. See AmericasTestKitchen.com for updates to this testing.

RECOMMENDED

OLD EL PASO 6-Inch Flour Tortillas
PRICE: $2.09 for 10 tortillas, 8.2 oz (21 cents per tortilla)
THICKNESS: 1.13 mm FAT: 2.9 g, 11.8 percent by weight
SODIUM: 285 mg
COMMENTS: The winning "soft and pliable" tortillas, the thinnest we tasted, wrapped fajita fixings securely but didn't steal the show and had a "flaky yet substantial texture." "Tender" and "rich" (with the most fat per serving), they had a "nice, mild, wheaty flavor."

MISSION Small/Fajita Flour Tortillas
PRICE: $2.39 for 8 tortillas, 9.2 oz (30 cents per tortilla)
THICKNESS: 1.93 mm FAT: 2.5 g, 7.4 percent by weight SODIUM: 290 mg
COMMENTS: At just 0.8 millimeter thicker than our top pick, these "pillowy" tortillas were still thin enough to suit our tasters, who liked that they were "flexible and just moist enough," to "hold securely," and were "not too thick or tough or gummy." They also detected an appealing "almost sweet," "baked bread" flavor.

RECOMMENDED WITH RESERVATIONS

MISSION Restaurant Style Small/Fajita Flour Tortillas
PRICE: $3.15 for 10 tortillas, 11.5 oz (32 cents per tortilla)
THICKNESS: 2.47 mm FAT: 2.5 g, 7.5 percent by weight
SODIUM: 230 mg
COMMENTS: These "restaurant-style" tortillas are thicker than the same manufacturer's traditional version, which we preferred. While some tasters liked these "chewy," "bready" tortillas with dark, "authentic-looking" char marks, most deemed them "too heavy and thick."

LA BANDERITA Fajitas
PRICE: $2.69 for 10 tortillas, 11.2 oz (27 cents per tortilla)
THICKNESS: 2.57 mm FAT: 1 g, 3 percent by weight SODIUM: 154 mg
COMMENTS: These losing tortillas were the thickest we tried, with the least amount of fat and salt per serving. They "held the food well," with "no sogginess or tearing," but many tasters found them "too doughy and pillowy," and more than one taster complained that the tortilla "stuck on the roof of my mouth."

IRISH
Comfort Classics

*To ensure that cooking on TV
runs smoothly, the test cooks
prep and measure ingredients
before the cameras roll.*

THE IRISH HAVE THE MARKET CORNERED WHEN IT COMES TO MEAT and potatoes. If you live in New England and are of Irish heritage, we'd bet that you eat one of these classics, corned beef and cabbage, or the more aptly named, "boiled dinner," every Saint Patrick's day. And therein lies the problem. We've found the traditional cooking method of combining the meat and vegetables in a pot and letting it cook away does a disservice to the dish—mostly to the vegetables, which are typically cooked to death. And the corned beef? Ever notice how salty it can be? We decided to skirt tradition and see how we could turn this dish around to yield subtly seasoned, tender beef and sweet, perfectly cooked (not mushy!) vegetables.

Another Irish classic is shepherd's pie. And it's easy to see why it's so appealing. A meal of tender meat, rich gravy, and a blanket of mashed potatoes baked together until bubbling and hot is hard to resist. But when we looked at the many steps involved in traditional recipes, we did a double take. Does shepherd's pie really require hours and hours of preparation, starting with long-cooking braised lamb (or beef), followed by a homemade stock and gravy? By the time we got to reading about the mashed potato steps, we cried foul. We wanted our shepherd's pie, but we wanted it without putting our lives on hold for the day. Our goal was clear: develop a recipe for shepherd's pie that could be prepared in a reasonable amount of time—maybe even quickly enough for a weeknight. Now wouldn't that be comforting?

CORNED BEEF AND CABBAGE

✔ **WHY THIS RECIPE WORKS:** Corned beef and cabbage is a hearty winter favorite, but too many recipes result in overly salty beef and washed-out, mushy vegetables. To control the salt level in our beef, we eschewed commercially corned beef and set out to make our own with an easy dry rub. We cooked our corned beef at a steady, slow simmer and then kept it warm while we cooked our vegetables. Cooking the vegetables (we chose cabbage, carrots, potatoes, and rutabaga) separately in the meat's broth allowed the vegetables to be enriched by the meat's juices, but still retain their own flavor.

THE VENERABLE ONE-POT MEAL, CORNED BEEF AND cabbage, also known as New England boiled dinner (a tradition on Saint Patrick's Day throughout the region), has always struck us less as a dish with big flavor and genuine dinner table appeal than as a symbol of the stalwart Yankee ethics of hard work and thrift. That misconception, however, was the first of several to be busted during our testing. In the course of tasting umpteen corned beef and cabbages, we came to realize that this dish needn't be mushy, overwhelmingly salty, and one-dimensional. Instead, it can be a full-flavored medley of meaty, tender, well-seasoned beef, subtle spice, and sweet, earthy vegetables, each distinct in flavor and texture.

We commenced our research and testing with the usual spate of recipes, most of which were based on a 4- to 6-pound piece of corned beef. The term "corned" refers to the curing of meat with salt, often used as a method of preservation before refrigeration became widespread. Legend has it that the salt grains were roughly the same size as corn kernels, hence the name "corned beef." The cut of beef most commonly corned is boneless brisket, which is a trimmed, 12- or 13-pound piece taken from the front part of the cow's breast. For retail sale, the whole brisket is usually split into two parts, called the first, or flat, cut and second, or point, cut.

We brought home an example of each type and took to the stove. Cooking directions on the packages and in our research recipes really did not vary much. Generally, instructions were to cover the meat by 1 to 3 inches of water and simmer until tender, anywhere from 2½ to 3½ hours, depending on the size of the brisket.

To our surprise, the commercial corned beef disappointed us across the board. Our tasters described the flavor as overtly salty and "sharp and somewhat chemical." In addition, the texture was deemed to be grainy and noticeably chalky.

Ruling out commercial corned beef, we figured we'd stick to making our own. Our research turned up two methods of corning your own beef; wet curing and dry curing. Both methods do require close to a week, but they are also mindlessly easy: All you need to do is prepare the meat and its cure. Beyond that, there is no work whatsoever. Of course, we tested each method, using 5-pound fresh flat-cut briskets (as the flat cut is more widely available than the point cut).

We tested the wet method first, tasting briskets cured in a brine of 2 cups of salt and 3 quarts of water for five, seven, 10, 12, and 14 days. Among all of them, we liked best the brisket soaked for five days, noting a pleasing saltiness alongside the distinctive flavor of beef. At this point, we also gave the dry-cure method a go. Adapting a recipe from Julia Child's *The Way to Cook*, we rubbed our brisket with ½ cup of salt and a few crushed herbs and spices, placed it in a huge, 2-gallon zipper-lock bag, weighted the meat with a brick, and let it sit for five days in the fridge. Lo and behold, the result was the best corned beef of them all, even better than the five-day wet-cured corned beef, with a concentrated beef flavor, assertive yet not overpowering salt, and a pleasant spiciness. Curing the brisket for two extra days, seven in total, brought out the flavor of the spices a little more, without affecting the saltiness. In addition, we tinkered with the salt quantity in the dry-cure mixture, trying ¼ cup less and more, but neither improved the flavor.

Julia Child's recipe suggested desalting the dry-cured meat by soaking it in several changes of water for at least 24 hours or up to three days, depending on the size of the brisket. To be honest, we initially overlooked this step; we simply rinsed the surface of the meat to remove shards of crumbled bay leaf and cracked peppercorns and went ahead with the cooking. When we finally did try the full

NEW ENGLAND–STYLE CORNED BEEF AND CABBAGE

desalting, we found that the meat tasted slightly richer because of the diminished salt presence, but not so much better that it justified a 24-hour soak versus a quick rinse.

Corned beef and cabbage is typically simmered (or boiled) on the stove, but we often cook braises and stews in the oven where the meat has the advantage of steady, gentle heat. We decided to follow suit here.

As for the vegetables, we tested a wide variety from the appropriate to the exotic and settled on the traditional green cabbage, with the added interest of carrots, potatoes, and rutabagas, all borrowed from New England boiled dinner, as our favorites. We tried cooking the vegetables along with the meat, but there were two distinct disadvantages to this approach. First, it made it too difficult to judge when the vegetables were properly done. Second, it would require a pot larger than any that we had in the test kitchen or in our own homes.

The best method turned out to be removing the meat from the broth when done, then cooking the vegetables in the broth. We started the firmer vegetables first—the carrots, potatoes, and rutabaga, and added the cabbage last. This not only benefited the vegetables, giving them a full, round flavor from the salt and rendered fat in the broth, but it also allowed us time to let the meat rest before cutting. Now that it was no longer dull, we'd enjoy this corned beef and cabbage more than once a year.

New England-Style Corned Beef and Cabbage

SERVES 8

Leave a bit of fat attached to the brisket for better texture and flavor. A similar size point-cut brisket can be used in this recipe. The meat is cooked fully when it is tender, the muscle fibers have loosened visibly, and a skewer slides in with minimal resistance. Serve this dish with horseradish, either plain or mixed with whipped cream or sour cream, or with grainy mustard.

CORNED BEEF

- ½ cup kosher salt
- 1 tablespoon cracked black peppercorns
- 1 tablespoon dried thyme
- 2¼ teaspoons ground allspice
- 1½ teaspoons paprika
- 2 bay leaves, crumbled
- 1 (4- to 5-pound) beef brisket, flat cut, trimmed

VEGETABLES

- 1½ pounds carrots, peeled and halved crosswise, thick end halved lengthwise
- 1½ pounds small red potatoes
- 1 small rutabaga (1 pound), peeled and halved crosswise; each half cut into 6 chunks
- 1 small head green cabbage (2 pounds), uncored, cut into 8 wedges

1. FOR THE CORNED BEEF: Combine salt, peppercorns, thyme, allspice, paprika, and bay leaves in bowl.

2. Using metal skewer, poke about 30 holes on each side of brisket. Rub each side evenly with salt mixture. Place brisket in 2-gallon zipper-lock bag, forcing out as much air as possible. Place in 13 by 9-inch baking dish, cover with second, similar-size pan, and weight with 2 bricks or heavy cans of similar weight. Refrigerate 5 to 7 days, turning once a day.

3. Rinse brisket and pat it dry. Place brisket in Dutch oven and cover brisket with water by 1 inch. Bring to boil over high heat, skimming any scum that rises to surface. Reduce heat to medium-low, cover, and simmer until skewer inserted in thickest part of brisket slides in and out with ease, 2 to 3 hours.

4. Adjust oven rack to middle position and heat oven to 200 degrees. Transfer meat to large platter, ladle 1 cup cooking liquid over meat, cover with aluminum foil and place in oven to keep warm.

5. FOR THE VEGETABLES: Add carrots, potatoes, and rutabaga to Dutch oven and bring to a boil over high heat. Reduce heat to medium-low, cover, and simmer until vegetables begin to soften, about 7 minutes.

6. Add cabbage, increase heat to high and return to boil. Reduce heat to medium-low, cover, and simmer until all vegetables are tender, 13 to 18 minutes.

7. Meanwhile, remove meat from oven, transfer to carving board, and slice against grain into ¼-inch slices. Return meat to platter. Transfer vegetables to meat platter, moisten with additional broth, and serve.

SHEPHERD'S PIE

✓ WHY THIS RECIPE WORKS: Shepherd's pie, a hearty mix of meat, gravy, and mashed potatoes can take the better part of a day to prepare. And while the dish is indeed satisfying, traditional versions are simply too rich. We wanted to scale back its preparation and lighten the dish to fit in better with modern sensibilities. Per other modern recipes, we chose ground beef as our filling over ground lamb. To prevent the beef from turning dry and crumbly, we tossed it with a little baking soda (diluted in water) before browning it. This unusual step raises the pH level of the beef, resulting in more tender meat. An onion and mushroom gravy, spiked with Worcestershire sauce, complemented the beef filling. For the mashed potatoes, we took our cue from an Irish dish called champ and cut way back on the dairy in favor of fresh scallions, which made for a lighter, more flavorful topping for the rich meat filling underneath.

WE'VE HAD REALLY GREAT SHEPHERD'S PIE. BUT IT comes with a price—a good day of labor. After boning, trimming, and cutting up lamb shoulder, you must sear the meat in batches (making a greasy mess of the stovetop in the process) and braise it with vegetables and homemade stock for a couple of hours. From there, you reduce the cooking liquid to make a sauce, chop the cooked meat, replace the spent vegetables with fresh, and transfer the filling to a baking dish. And then there's the mashed potatoes: boiling, mashing, mixing, and piping them over the filling. While the top crisps in the oven, it's time to clean the kitchen—no small feat because almost every piece of cooking equipment will have been used.

Another thing: Though it makes a very satisfying meal, this pie is heavy. Shepherd's pie may be a holdover from a time when physical laborers needed robust sustenance, but today we can't really justify eating like a preindustrial farmer. That said, the classic combination of meat, gravy, and potatoes is undeniably attractive on chilly winter nights. Maybe we could come up with a modernized shepherd's pie—a bit lighter, much less messy, and a lot quicker to prepare. Now that would be comforting indeed.

SHEPHERD'S PIE

We're not the first to think shepherd's pie needs an overhaul, and the most common shortcut is to use ground meat. Ground lamb seemed the obvious choice until we learned in *Traditional Irish Cooking* by Darina Allen, godmother of the cuisine, that modern-day shepherd's pie in Ireland is almost always made with beef. Since beef is more popular in this country, ground beef it would be.

But it only took us one test to realize that we couldn't simply swap chunks of meat for the ground kind; the two do not cook the same way. Searing chunks produces tender meat with a lovely brown crust. Ground beef, on the other hand, presents so much surface area to the pan that it gives up considerably more moisture as it cooks. The result: nubbly, dry crumbles that don't brown well.

So, meat left unbrowned, we nonetheless persevered. We added onions and carrots and let them soften a bit, then some flour to thicken the eventual sauce. We stirred in herbs along with some beef broth, and let the whole thing simmer and reduce while we cooked and mashed the potatoes. We transferred the filling to a baking dish, and—thinking we were simplifying things—ditched our piping bag and spread the potatoes on top with a rubber spatula, which turned out to be messy and difficult because of the soupy filling. Finally, we placed the pie in the oven to crisp the top.

The meat, even unbrowned, was chewy; the carrots were cooked to mush; and the "gravy" tasted pretty much like what it was: thickened canned beef broth.

Fortunately, we had a good lead on how to improve the meat's texture. We recently discovered that treating pork with baking soda tenderizes the meat by raising its pH. Hoping to achieve the same effect here, we dissolved ½ teaspoon into 2 tablespoons of water (to ensure that it would distribute evenly), then stirred it into the raw ground meat and let the mixture rest while we prepared the mashed potatoes. That did the trick, rendering the meat soft and silky, even after several minutes of simmering. On to beefing up the filling's lackluster flavor.

Since our gravy would not be based on browned meat flavors, we looked to other options. An approach to vegetarian gravy looked promising: Cook onions and mushrooms in a skillet with a little bit of fat over fairly high heat until they're deep brown and a fond starts to form in the pan, then stir in tomato paste and garlic and allow the

fond to get quite dark. We went ahead with this method, deglazing the pan with some fortified wine (ordinary red wine required us to use so much it left the sauce boozy) after a good layer of fond had developed. Then we added flour and, when the mixture was very deeply browned, fresh thyme and bay leaves, followed by beef broth and Worcestershire sauce to liberate that valuable crust from the bottom of the skillet. We were rewarded with a sauce that boasted rich color and savory depth.

Once the sauce was bubbling and thick, we added 1½ pounds of ground beef in 2-inch pieces and covered the skillet for roughly 10 minutes, lifting the lid once during cooking to break up the pieces of meat and to stir everything around. That's when we noticed the small pools of grease exuded by the meat. One downside of not browning the meat was that we had no opportunity to pour off its fat. We wondered if switching from 85 percent lean ground beef to 93 percent lean beef would help. Happily, the leaner beef stayed moist and tender, thanks to the baking soda treatment, and only a few tiny pools of fat remained. To get rid of these, we first tried adding more flour, but mixed in so late in the process, it tasted raw and starchy. Instead, we turned to the Asian trick of stirring in a slurry of cornstarch and water, which worked very nicely.

As for the spuds, the recipe we'd been using called for a full stick of butter and a cup of half-and-half—not exactly the lighter approach we were going for. We cut the amount of butter in half and subbed milk for the half-and-half. Because soft, moist mashed potatoes would merge with the gravy rather than form a crust, we also decreased the dairy by 50 percent and added an egg yolk for extra structure.

For the sake of convenience, we elected to leave the cooked filling in the skillet—except that we still had to resolve the issue of spreading the solid potatoes over the soupy mixture. We decided to give piping another go, but this time, we eschewed the fancy pastry bag and star tip for a disposable plastic bag with a corner cut off. Depositing the potatoes onto the filling from above was far easier than trying to spread them over a wet base. Once they were in place, we smoothed them with the back of a spoon and traced ridges in them with a fork; that way they'd get really crusty under the broiler.

One last problem remained: The browned crispy potato topping certainly looked appealing, but its flavor paled in comparison to the robust filling. Looking to add some pizzazz, we reviewed the British Isles' various regional potato dishes and a recipe for champ, Ireland's simple mixture of mashed potatoes and chopped scallions, caught our attention. Stirring a handful of chopped scallion greens into our own mash was just what it needed, freshening the whole dish without adding heft.

With its simmered lean ground beef, rich but not heavy gravy, and lighter, fresher mash, our updated shepherd's pie was not just faster to make than the traditional version, it was also less guilt-inducing—but still every bit as delicious. At last, comfort food that even the cook could enjoy.

Shepherd's Pie
SERVES 4 TO 6

This recipe was developed with 93 percent lean ground beef. Using ground beef with a higher percentage of fat will make the dish too greasy.

1½	pounds 93 percent lean ground beef
2	tablespoons plus 2 teaspoons water
	Salt and pepper
½	teaspoon baking soda
2½	pounds russet potatoes, peeled and cut into 1-inch chunks
4	tablespoons unsalted butter, melted
½	cup milk
1	large egg yolk
8	scallions, green parts only, sliced thin
2	teaspoons vegetable oil
1	onion, chopped
4	ounces white mushrooms, trimmed and chopped
1	tablespoon tomato paste
2	garlic cloves, minced
2	tablespoons Madeira or ruby port
2	tablespoons all-purpose flour
2	carrots, peeled and chopped
1¼	cups beef broth
2	teaspoons Worcestershire sauce
1	bay leaf
2	sprigs fresh thyme
2	teaspoons cornstarch

1. Toss beef with 2 tablespoons water, 1 teaspoon salt, ¼ teaspoon pepper, and baking soda in bowl until thoroughly combined. Let sit for 20 minutes.

2. Meanwhile, place potatoes in medium saucepan; add water to just cover and 1 tablespoon salt. Bring to boil over high heat. Reduce heat to medium-low and simmer until potatoes are soft and tip of paring knife inserted into potato meets no resistance, 8 to 10 minutes. Drain potatoes and return to saucepan. Return saucepan to low heat and cook, shaking pot occasionally, until any surface moisture on potatoes has evaporated, about 1 minute. Remove pan from heat and mash potatoes well with potato masher. Stir in butter. Whisk together milk and egg yolk in small bowl, then stir into potatoes. Stir in scallions and season with salt and pepper to taste. Cover and set aside.

3. Heat oil in broiler-safe 10-inch skillet over medium heat until shimmering. Add onion, mushrooms, ½ teaspoon salt, and ¼ teaspoon pepper; cook, stirring occasionally, until vegetables are just starting to soften and dark bits form on bottom of skillet, 4 to 6 minutes. Stir in tomato paste and garlic; cook until bottom of skillet is dark brown, about 2 minutes. Add Madeira and cook, scraping up any browned bits, until evaporated, about 1 minute. Stir in flour and cook 1 minute. Add carrots, broth, Worcestershire, bay leaf, and thyme sprigs; bring to boil, scraping up any browned bits. Reduce heat to medium-low, add beef in 2-inch pieces to broth and bring to gentle simmer. Cover and cook until beef is cooked through, 10 to 12 minutes, stirring and breaking up meat chunks with 2 forks halfway through. Stir cornstarch and remaining 2 teaspoons water together in bowl. Stir cornstarch mixture into filling and continue to simmer for 30 seconds. Remove bay leaf and thyme sprigs. Season with salt and pepper to taste.

4. Adjust oven rack 5 inches from broiler element and heat broiler. Place mashed potatoes in large zipper-lock bag and snip off 1 corner to create 1-inch opening. Pipe potatoes in even layer over filling, making sure to cover entire surface. Smooth potatoes with back of spoon, then use tines of fork to make ridges over surface. Place skillet on rimmed baking sheet and broil until potatoes are golden brown and crusty and filling is bubbly, 10 to 15 minutes. Let cool for 10 minutes before serving.

RATING INNOVATIVE KITCHEN GADGETS AND KITCHENWARE

We've come across a lot of kitchen gadgets that don't deliver what they promise and end up simply being a waste of money and kitchen space. Here are a few tools we found that were worth buying. They live up to their claims and make a variety of cooking tasks easier—and more than earned their spot in the test kitchen. See AmericasTestKitchen.com for updates to these testings.

MICROWAVE RICE COOKERS

Electric rice cookers promise to deliver perfectly tender rice without having to monitor the stovetop, but they can be quite pricey. Enter the microwave rice cooker, which claims to produce perfect rice with almost no effort. We tested five models, each made from BPA-free plastic (bisphenol A is a compound that has been linked to cancer in some studies). It took some experimentation before we hit on a method that worked for all of the rice cookers; since microwave oven wattage varies, the instructions included were presented as "guidelines" and didn't work consistently. But we finally found a reliable formula: 5 minutes on full power, 15 minutes on 50 percent power, and then a 5-minute rest. Our favorite brand was the Progressive International Microwave Rice Cooker Set ($8.99). This rice cooker is sturdy and compact, holds 6 cups of rice, and is a cinch to clean—plus, it's much cheaper than a traditional rice cooker.

WINNER: PROGRESSIVE INTERNATIONAL MICROWAVE RICE COOKER SET

RECIPE ROCK

Not all recipes come from magazines and cookbooks, and a sheet of paper—whether it's a printout from an online resource or a handwritten index card—can easily get lost in the countertop shuffle. The Recipe Rock from Architec ($9.99) offers a clever way to keep these in one place and hold them upright for easy reading. This small, weighty plastic holder sits solidly on a flat surface while its concave front cradles pages at a perfect angle for comfortable viewing. The pages are held in place by a metal ball and an embedded magnet so strong that it gripped 10 sheets of 8½ by 11-inch paper. And its compact 2-inch size takes up very little counter space, and it tucks away neatly in a drawer.

WINNER: ARCHITEC RECIPE ROCK

COLLAPSIBLE MINI COLANDER

When all you need to rinse is a handful of berries, the last thing you want to do is unearth (and later clean) a big colander. The Collapsible Mini Colander from Progressive International ($6.13) holds 3½ cups and folds down to a height of just 1 inch. Unfolded, this 8-inch-long silicone colander is sturdy, and its oval shape made it easy to tip rinsed food into a container with no spills. But the best part is its plastic base, which pops on to seal the colander's holes so you can soak the contents before draining or set it on a counter without drips.

WINNER: PROGRESSIVE INTERNATIONAL COLLAPSIBLE MINI COLANDER

MINI BUNDT PANS

Mini desserts are all the rage, and nowadays, manufacturers make a wide array of mini bakeware. Looking for the best miniature Bundt pan, we tested four models, two single-cup molds and two 6-cup trays, ranging in price from $3.75 to $40. Our favorite pan was the Nordic Ware Platinum Anniversary Bundtlette Pan ($40). This tray-style pan featured handles that made flipping out the cakes easier than flipping out from the singleton pans. Though all of the pans were nonstick and released the cakes effortlessly, some of the pans produced mini Bundts that were lumpy and frumpy. The cakes from our winner, however, had a perfect little shape with attractive, well-defined ridges. Next time we want to bake mini Bundt cakes, we'll be reaching for our favorite, which happens to be the mini version of our winning full-size Bundt pan.

WINNER: NORDIC WARE PLATINUM ANNIVERSARY BUNDTLETTE PAN

PANCAKE BATTER DISPENSER

How do restaurants get their pancakes so perfectly round? They use a pancake batter dispenser. Seeking the same results at home, we tested five batter dispensers priced from about $10 to $30, comparing each with our usual method of scooping up batter with a quarter-cup measure. Although dispensers eliminate the messy batter trail left by that method, not all of them made pancake prep easier. A few models had narrow mouths that made filling them a challenge, while others had small capacities, requiring us to fill them repeatedly, or they became clogged with batter. Our favorite was a simple model, the Tovolo Pancake Pen ($9.99). Just a squeeze of this tall plastic cylinder allowed us to draw letters and shapes in addition to creating perfect pancakes. Now we can enjoy picture-perfect pancakes without having to go out for them.

WINNER: TOVOLO PANCAKE PEN

SIMPLE AND SATISFYING
Vegetable Mains

*Adam explains why
sometimes you might want to
reach for a vegetable cleaver
instead of a chef's knife.*

LET'S FACE IT, YOU DON'T NEED A BIG STEAK OR PORK CHOP TO fill you up. Vegetables as the main event can satisfy just as well. The trick is to make your vegetable main dish interesting (we'll pass on a plate of steamed greens for dinner), yet still allow the vegetables themselves to shine (careful with the cheese and creamy sauces). Here, we set out to develop two vegetable dishes: a rustic but elegant French-style vegetable tart, called a galette, and a hearty vegetable soup.

Vegetables married with buttery pastry and enriched with cheese? Yes, please. And even better, you don't need to be a whiz with pastry or even own a tart pan to make this tart. The tart is assembled on a baking sheet and the edges of the dough are simply folded over the vegetable filling. The effect is rustic, yet sophisticated. But what about soggy pastry and unevenly cooked vegetables? And just what vegetables work in a vegetable tart? These are just a few of the questions we'd tackle in our quest for a really great-tasting vegetable tart.

Truly flavorful vegetable soup starts with a rich, long-cooked broth. Or does it? Is there a way to fortify store-bought broth to make it just as satisfying as homemade? Which vegetables pair together in soup and what could we add to the vegetables to make our soup as hearty as a meat-based soup? Join us as we investigate.

MUSHROOM AND LEEK GALETTE WITH GORGONZOLA

MUSHROOM AND LEEK GALETTE WITH GORGONZOLA

✔ WHY THIS RECIPE WORKS: Most vegetable tarts rely on the same pastry dough used for fruit tarts. But vegetable tarts are more prone to leaking liquid into the crust or falling apart when the tart is sliced. We needed a crust that was extra sturdy and boasted a complex flavor of its own. To increase the flavor of the crust and keep it tender, we swapped out part of the white flour for nutty whole wheat, and we used butter rather than shortening. To punch up its flaky texture and introduce more structure, we gave the crust a series of folds to create numerous interlocking layers. For a filling that was both flavorful and cohesive, we paired mushrooms and leeks with rich, potent binders like Gorgonzola cheese and crème fraîche.

COMPARED WITH MORE FORMAL TARTS BAKED IN fluted pans, a free-form tart's beauty lies in its rustic simplicity. You roll out the dough, add the filling, and then draw in the edges of the dough to form a pleated crust. This method requires far less effort than precisely fitting pastry into a molded pan, and it looks just as attractive.

But when it comes to savory applications, free-form tarts can have their flaws. Many recipes simply borrow a standard pastry dough intended for fruit and swap in vegetables. After trying a few such versions, we realized that for vegetables, this wouldn't work. Vegetables have far less of the pectin that holds on to moisture and binds a fruit filling together, so they are particularly prone to leaking liquid into the crust or falling apart when the tart is sliced. What's more, vegetables don't pack the concentrated, bright flavors of fruit. To make up for these deficiencies, we needed a crust that was extra-sturdy and boasted a complex flavor of its own. We also wanted a robust-tasting filling with enough sticking power to hold together when cut.

We started by putting together a basic all-butter pie dough, trading half of the white flour for whole wheat. The earthy flavor of whole-wheat flour, we hoped, would complement the savory filling, and its coarser consistency would turn out a pleasantly hearty crust. We pulsed the dry ingredients and butter in the food processor a few times, then dumped the mixture into a bowl, added a little water, and stirred it until thoroughly combined. To ensure that the butter stayed firm enough to leave air pockets as it melted in the oven, creating flakiness, we chilled the dough for about an hour before rolling it out.

The good news: The butter and all of that whole-wheat flour added up to a great-tasting crust. The bad news: It had none of the flaky yet sturdy texture that we'd been looking for. Instead, it was crumbly and dense. And we were pretty sure we knew why. All doughs, pastry or otherwise, get their structure from gluten, the network of proteins that form when flour is mixed with water. The challenge when working with whole-wheat flour is that it contains the bran (the fibrous outer layers of the wheat berry) and the germ as well as the starchy endosperm (which is the only part of the berry used in white flour). Since the bran and germ contain none of the gluten-forming proteins found in the endosperm, the more whole-wheat flour there is in a dough, the heavier and more prone to falling apart it will be.

To strengthen the dough, we'd need to cut back on the whole-wheat flour, but 25 percent was as low as we could go before we lost too much of the whole wheat's nice nutty taste. And there was another problem: As the proportion of white flour, and therefore gluten, increased, the dough became tough. We didn't think we were overworking the dough (a typical cause). Then it occurred to us that the problem might be water. Because the bran and germ need more water than the endosperm to become fully hydrated, we'd added a little extra to the dough. We realized that the extra liquid was being absorbed by the white flour's gluten-forming proteins, thus creating more gluten and making the dough more susceptible to overworking. To reduce toughness, then, we'd need to either cut back on the water or find an even gentler way to handle the dough.

We knew that acids can weaken the bonds that form between gluten strands, so we decided to try adding vinegar. We found that a teaspoon—the most we could add before the dough tasted too vinegary—did tenderize it a little, but not enough. What if we took a hands-off

approach to mixing and let the flour absorb the water on its own? We hoped that partially mixing the dough so that not all of the flour was mixed in and then letting it rest before rolling it out might allow the water to migrate to drier parts and produce pastry that was workable—but not overworked.

We gave it a shot, just barely mixing the dry and wet ingredients together and then chilling the dough briefly. When we pulled the dough out an hour or so later, it was clear that we were on to something: Without any effort on our part, most of the dry flour had disappeared; even better, the dough was remarkably supple but not floppy. We gently nudged it together and then rolled it out and baked it at 375 degrees. The result: a tender, moist, and decently flaky crust without the least bit of toughness.

But being perfectionists, we wouldn't settle for decently flaky. We wanted a crust with the long, striated layers of puff pastry, which would also make the crust more resistant to splitting when sliced. But the hundreds of layers in puff pastry are created through a painstaking process of rolling and folding the dough, chilling it in between. Curious to see what would happen if we mimicked this approach in a more modest way, we dumped the rested dough onto the counter, rolled it into a rectangle, and folded it into thirds, like a business letter. We repeated the process just twice more. The results were even better than we'd hoped: The increase in layers rendered the crust wonderfully flaky and less apt to shatter when cut.

Working with a sturdy crust, however, didn't mean that we could just throw in the vegetables raw. The shiitake mushrooms and leeks we'd chosen for a hearty yet fresh and springlike filling still leached far too much moisture, rendering the crust soggy. Fortunately, sautéing the leeks took only a few minutes and helped concentrate their flavor as well as reduce their liquid. For the mushrooms, we hastened the evaporation process by heating them in the microwave. To introduce rich, complex flavor and not too much moisture, we worked in a hefty dollop of crème fraîche and some Dijon mustard and layered a few handfuls of crumbled Gorgonzola between the vegetables just before baking.

With its hearty filling bound by a buttery crust, this rustic tart amounted to a perfect cold-weather meal—one so good we'd be tempted to make it year-round.

Mushroom and Leek Galette with Gorgonzola

SERVES 6

Cutting a few small holes in the dough prevents it from lifting off the pan as it bakes. A pizza stone helps to crisp the crust but is not essential. An overturned baking sheet can be used in place of the pizza stone.

DOUGH

- 1¼ cups (6¼ ounces) all-purpose flour
- ½ cup (2¾ ounces) whole-wheat flour
- 1 tablespoon sugar
- ¾ teaspoon salt
- 10 tablespoons unsalted butter, cut into ½-inch pieces and chilled
- 7 tablespoons ice water
- 1 teaspoon distilled white vinegar

FILLING

- 1¼ pounds shiitake mushrooms, stemmed and sliced thin
- 5 teaspoons olive oil
- 1 pound leeks, white and light green parts only, sliced ½ inch thick and washed thoroughly (3 cups)
- 1 teaspoon minced fresh thyme
- 2 tablespoons crème fraîche
- 1 tablespoon Dijon mustard
  Salt and pepper
- 3 ounces Gorgonzola cheese, crumbled (¾ cup)
- 1 large egg, lightly beaten
  Kosher salt
- 2 tablespoons minced fresh parsley

1. FOR THE DOUGH: Pulse all-purpose flour, whole-wheat flour, sugar, and salt together in food processor until combined, 2 to 3 pulses. Add butter and pulse until it forms pea-size pieces, about 10 pulses. Transfer mixture to medium bowl.

2. Sprinkle water and vinegar over mixture. With rubber spatula, use folding motion to mix until loose, shaggy mass forms with some dry flour remaining (do not overwork). Transfer mixture to center of large sheet of plastic wrap, press gently into rough 4-inch square, and wrap tightly. Refrigerate for at least 45 minutes.

3. Transfer dough to lightly floured counter. Roll into 11 by 8-inch rectangle with short side of rectangle parallel to edge of counter. Using bench scraper, bring bottom third of dough up, then fold upper third over it, folding like business letter into 8 by 4-inch rectangle. Turn dough 90 degrees counterclockwise. Roll out dough again into 11 by 8-inch rectangle and fold into thirds again. Turn dough 90 degrees counterclockwise and repeat rolling and folding into thirds. After last fold, fold dough in half to create 4-inch square. Press top of dough gently to seal. Wrap in plastic and refrigerate for at least 45 minutes or up to 2 days.

4. FOR THE FILLING: Microwave mushrooms in covered bowl until just tender, 3 to 5 minutes. Transfer to colander to drain; return to bowl. Meanwhile, heat 1 tablespoon oil in 12-inch skillet over medium heat until shimmering. Add leeks and thyme, cover, and cook, stirring occasionally, until leeks are tender and beginning to brown, 5 to 7 minutes. Transfer to bowl with mushrooms. Stir in crème fraîche and mustard. Season with salt and pepper to taste. Set aside.

5. Adjust oven rack to lower-middle position, place pizza stone on rack, and heat oven to 400 degrees. Line rimmed baking sheet with parchment paper. Remove dough from refrigerator and let stand at room temperature for 15 to 20 minutes. Roll out on generously floured counter (use up to ¼ cup flour) to 14-inch circle about ⅛ inch thick. (Trim edges as needed to form rough circle.) Transfer dough to prepared baking sheet. With tip of paring knife, cut five ¼-inch circles in dough (one at center and four evenly spaced halfway from center to edge of dough). Brush top of dough with 1 teaspoon oil.

6. Spread half of filling evenly over dough, leaving 2-inch border around edge. Sprinkle with half of Gorgonzola, cover with remaining filling, and top with remaining Gorgonzola. Drizzle remaining 1 teaspoon oil over filling. Gently grasp 1 edge of dough and fold up outer 2 inches over filling. Repeat around circumference of tart, overlapping dough every 2 to 3 inches; gently pinch pleated dough to secure but do not press dough into filling. Brush dough with egg and sprinkle evenly with kosher salt.

7. Lower oven temperature to 375 degrees. Bake until crust is deep golden brown and filling is beginning to brown, 35 to 45 minutes. Let tart cool on baking sheet on wire rack for 10 minutes. Using offset or wide metal spatula, loosen tart from parchment and carefully slide tart off parchment onto cutting board. Sprinkle with parsley, cut into wedges, and serve.

Potato and Shallot Galette with Goat Cheese

Substitute 1 pound Yukon Gold potatoes, sliced ¼ inch thick, for mushrooms and increase microwave cooking time to 4 to 8 minutes. Substitute 4 ounces thinly sliced shallots for leeks and rosemary for thyme. Increase amount of crème fraîche to ¼ cup and substitute ¼ cup chopped pitted kalamata olives and 1 teaspoon finely grated lemon zest for Dijon mustard. Substitute goat cheese for Gorgonzola.

Butternut Squash Galette with Gruyère

1. Microwave 6 ounces baby spinach and ¼ cup water in bowl until spinach is wilted and decreased in volume by half, 3 to 4 minutes. Using potholders, remove bowl from microwave and keep covered for 1 minute. Carefully remove plate and transfer spinach to colander. Gently press spinach with rubber spatula to release excess liquid. Transfer spinach to cutting board and chop coarse. Return spinach to colander and press again with rubber spatula; set aside.

2. Substitute 1¼ pounds butternut squash, peeled and cut into ½-inch cubes, for mushrooms and increase microwave cooking time to about 8 minutes. Substitute 1 thinly sliced red onion for leeks and ½ teaspoon minced fresh oregano for thyme. Substitute 1 teaspoon sherry vinegar for Dijon mustard and stir reserved spinach and 3 ounces shredded Gruyère cheese into filling along with crème fraîche and vinegar in step 4. Omit Gorgonzola.

NOTES FROM THE TEST KITCHEN

PLEATING A FREE-FORM TART

It's surprisingly simple to create pleated edges around free-form tarts.

Gently grasp 1 edge of dough and make 2-inch-wide fold over filling. Lift and fold another segment of dough over first fold to form pleat. Repeat every 2 to 3 inches.

FARMHOUSE VEGETABLE AND BARLEY SOUP

✓ **WHY THIS RECIPE WORKS:** Most recipes for hearty winter vegetable soups, it turns out, are neither quick nor easy. For a satisfying soup that doesn't take the better part of a day to make, we started with canned vegetable broth. To this we added soy sauce and ground dried porcini mushrooms. These ingredients added a savory, almost meaty flavor to the soup base. To make the soup more filling, we added barley to the hearty combination of carrots, potatoes, leeks, cabbage, and turnips.

WINTERTIME IS SOUP TIME, AND ALSO THE TIME OF YEAR when our crisper drawers are overflowing with cold-weather vegetables like carrots, potatoes, leeks, cabbage, and turnips. That abundance of hearty produce would seem to have all the makings of a satisfying vegetable soup, but our attempts often turn out lackluster. The problem is time: The best soups—vegetable or otherwise—start with a rich, full-bodied broth, and we usually need the weekend to make a good one. Some recipes call for adding a little meat to the broth to beef up flavor, but it's hardly a shortcut. Many of the most flavorful cuts are also some of the toughest, and they take hours to turn tender. Cured meats such as bacon and pancetta impart distinctive smoky tastes that we sometimes don't want in a vegetable soup.

Rather than sideline rustic vegetable soup as a Sunday afternoon project, we wanted to pack all the rich, earthy flavor and depth of a long-simmered stock into a recipe that took only about an hour's work. That narrowed our focus to a soup based on store-bought broth.

Curious to see how much mileage we could get out of simply doctoring commercial broth and tossing in vegetables, we threw together a test batch in which we sweated leeks, carrots, and celery in a few pats of butter; added staple aromatics like crushed garlic, a few sprigs of fresh thyme, and a bay leaf; and poured in 10 cups of vegetable broth. We simmered this base for 20 minutes, strained out the solids, then stirred in small chunks of potato and turnip and chopped green cabbage and let everything cook until the vegetables were just tender. Our tasters had no complaints about the vegetables themselves; their flavors worked well together, and the crinkly cabbage leaves offered a nice crisp-tender crunch. Nor could we gripe about the time or labor involved, both of which were minimal. But there was no denying that the soup felt thin, in terms of both flavor and body.

The good news was that we'd been here before. A few years back the test kitchen developed a recipe for quick beef and vegetable soup and learned that the most effective way to get big flavor in a hurry is to bolster the prefab broth with ingredients rich in *umami*, the fifth taste that describes savory, "meaty" flavor. Among the ingredients at the top of the list were soy sauce and mushrooms, so we started our testing there, "seasoning" one pot with a few dashes of soy sauce and another with two large pieces of dried porcini (great for adding intense, earthy depth). The improvement to each batch was obvious but still insufficient. While both flavor boosters provided subtle depth, the commercial-broth taste still prevailed. We hesitantly added a little more of each ingredient to the pot in subsequent batches. But just as we'd feared, the soy and mushrooms began to overwhelm the broth.

Clearly soy sauce and mushrooms were imperfect solutions on their own, but we had yet to try them together. We worked up another batch of soup, this time limiting ourselves to 2 teaspoons of soy sauce and just a few of the dried mushroom slabs. To our delight, this broth was far better than we had expected. The soup took on a savory depth and complexity that had previously been missing. The only problem was that we couldn't reliably repeat the results. Sometimes the soup turned out a little less flavorful; other times it tasted a bit too mushroomy.

It occurred to us that the issue was the dried mushroom pieces, which can vary a lot in size. We wondered if it would work better to grind the dried porcini to a powder and then measure out a set amount to add to the pot instead of rehydrating whole slices in the soup. This turned out to be a great solution: After experimenting with amounts, we found that 2 teaspoons of the porcini powder along with 2 teaspoons of soy sauce perfectly enhanced the broth's savory flavor.

The broth was now so good, we even found that we could substitute water for a good bit of the store-bought broth to eliminate any vestige of commercial flavor. The acidity of a little white wine (added along with the first batch of vegetables) further improved the soup, as did the last-minute addition of frozen peas, a splash of fresh lemon juice, and a fistful of chopped parsley.

FARMHOUSE VEGETABLE AND BARLEY SOUP

Flavorwise, we were in pretty good shape. The bigger hurdle was the soup's lack of body. The vegetables themselves were substantial, and roughly chopping (rather than dicing) them amped up their heartiness, but even the starchy potatoes didn't do much to thicken the broth. We thought about adding dairy but knew that the fat would dull the flavor of the broth that we'd just worked so hard to build. Recalling that a colleague had mentioned eating some stellar vegetable soups while in Ireland, we started flipping through some Irish cookbooks, and stumbled on an interesting idea: adding oatmeal to the soup. We found this frugal trick for bulking up the broth charming in theory, but it didn't play out as we'd hoped. Tasters complained that even though the dish took on a certain nuttiness, the chewy oats turned it into a vegetable-heavy gruel.

Nonetheless, we liked the idea of bulking up the soup with a grain and turned our attention to a more obvious choice: barley. We added half a cup of the pearl variety to the pot just as we poured in the liquids. The beads were partially plumped by the time we were ready to add the potatoes, turnip, and cabbage, and they were perfectly al dente about 20 minutes later, when the soup was ready to be served.

This was exactly the heft and substance that the soup needed—well, almost. A few of our tasters weren't keen on letting us wrap up testing before getting another dimension of flavor and richness into the pot. We had a holdout idea that we'd come across in one of the Irish cookbooks: finishing the soup with flavored butter. It would be an unusual addition for sure. Still, we held out hope that stirring in a dollop at the table would contribute not only a burst of fresh flavor (lemon and fresh thyme seemed like good soup-brightening additions) but also the plush body that only dairy can give without the cloying, flavor-dampening effect of milk or cream. When we caught our tasters sneaking an extra dollop into their bowls, we knew that we'd hit it right.

At last, we had a rustic, full-bodied vegetable soup thrown together in under an hour that didn't need even a speck of meat to taste hearty and satisfying.

Farmhouse Vegetable and Barley Soup
SERVES 6 TO 8

We prefer an acidic, unoaked white wine such as Sauvignon Blanc for this recipe. We love the richness added by the Lemon-Thyme Butter and the crunch of Herbed Croutons (recipes follow) but the soup can also be garnished with crisp bacon or crumbled cheddar cheese. You will need at least a 6-quart Dutch oven for this recipe.

- ⅛ ounce dried porcini mushrooms, rinsed
- 8 sprigs fresh parsley plus 3 tablespoons minced
- 4 sprigs fresh thyme
- 1 bay leaf
- 2 tablespoons unsalted butter
- 1½ pounds leeks, white and light green parts sliced ½ inch thick and washed thoroughly
- 2 carrots, peeled and cut into ½-inch pieces
- 2 celery ribs, cut into ¼-inch pieces
- ⅓ cup dry white wine
- 2 teaspoons soy sauce
  Salt and pepper
- 6 cups water
- 4 cups low-sodium chicken broth or vegetable broth
- ½ cup pearl barley
- 1 garlic clove, peeled and smashed
- 1½ pounds Yukon Gold potatoes, peeled and cut into ½-inch pieces
- 1 turnip, peeled and cut into ¾-inch pieces
- 1½ cups chopped green cabbage
- 1 cup frozen peas
- 1 teaspoon lemon juice

1. Grind porcini with spice grinder until they resemble fine meal, 10 to 30 seconds. Measure out 2 teaspoons porcini powder; reserve remainder for another use. Using kitchen twine, tie together parsley sprigs, thyme sprigs, and bay leaf.

2. Melt butter in large Dutch oven over medium heat. Add leeks, carrots, celery, wine, soy sauce, and 2 teaspoons salt. Cook, stirring occasionally, until liquid has evaporated and celery is softened, about 10 minutes.

3. Add water, chicken broth, barley, porcini powder, herb bundle, and garlic; increase heat to high and bring to boil. Reduce heat to medium-low and simmer, partially covered, for 25 minutes.

4. Add potatoes, turnip, and cabbage; return to simmer and cook until barley, potatoes, turnip, and cabbage are tender, 18 to 20 minutes.

5. Remove pot from heat and remove herb bundle. Stir in peas, lemon juice, and minced parsley; season with salt and pepper to taste. Serve, passing Lemon-Thyme Butter separately.

Lemon-Thyme Butter
MAKES 6 TABLESPOONS

6   **tablespoons unsalted butter, softened**
1   **tablespoon minced fresh thyme**
¾   **teaspoon finely grated lemon zest plus ¼ teaspoon juice**
    Pinch salt

Combine all ingredients in bowl.

Herbed Croutons
MAKES ABOUT 2½ CUPS

1   **tablespoon unsalted butter**
1   **teaspoon minced fresh parsley**
½   **teaspoon minced fresh thyme**
4   **slices hearty white sandwich bread, cut into ½-inch pieces**
    Salt and pepper

Melt butter in 10-inch skillet over medium heat. Add parsley and thyme; cook, stirring constantly, for 20 seconds. Add bread and cook, stirring frequently, until light golden brown, 5 to 10 minutes. Season with salt and pepper to taste.

NOTES FROM THE TEST KITCHEN

BUILDING SAVORY FLAVOR ON THE DOUBLE
To ramp up savory flavor in our Farmhouse Vegetable and Barley Soup, we tried adding umami boosters like soy sauce and porcini mushrooms and made an interesting discovery. We found that using small amounts of both ingredients—versus lots of just one or the other—had a powerful impact on flavor. Here's why: Soy sauce contains high levels of naturally occurring, flavor-enhancing compounds called glutamates, while mushrooms are rich in flavor-amplifying compounds known as nucleotides. Used together, the two compounds can boost savory, umami-like flavors exponentially. Their effect is even more pronounced when the ratio of glutamates to nucleotides is very high. (Studies suggest that an effective ratio is 95:5.) Of course, we couldn't measure exactly how much of each compound was making it into the pot, so we tinkered with the amounts of soy and porcini we were adding until we hit it just right.

GLUTAMATES + NUCLEOTIDES
= BIG SAVORY FLAVOR

Thanks to the synergistic effect of combining their different flavor-enhancing compounds, small amounts of both soy sauce and porcini mushrooms add up to a profound impact on flavor.

RATING VEGETABLE CLEAVERS

Unlike curving Western-style knives, rectangular vegetable cleavers, which are traditional in Asia, have a straighter edge that stays in contact with food as you cut and chop, streamlining vegetable prep. But while a meat cleaver is a must-have when hacking through piles of bones, we wanted to know if a vegetable cleaver was really necessary when prepping veggies. To find out, we tested seven knives, using them to dice onions, mince parsley, slice potatoes, and quarter butternut squash. We included three Chinese-style vegetable cleavers, also known as Chinese chef's knives, plus four Japanese-style vegetable cleavers, which are available either as double-bevel *nakiri* or single-bevel *usuba*. Blade width turned out to be the most important factor. Slimmer blades glided effortlessly through food; thicker blades with a V-shaped taper from spine to cutting edge worked like a wedge, tearing instead of slicing. After lots of chopping, we had our winner. While it doesn't necessarily replace an all-purpose Western chef's knife, it is a pleasure to use if you chop a lot of vegetables. Brands are listed in order of preference. See AmericasTestKitchen.com for updates to this testing.

HIGHLY RECOMMENDED

MAC JAPANESE SERIES 6½-Inch Japanese Vegetable Cleaver

MODEL: JU-65 **PRICE:** $95 **TYPE:** Nakiri **WEIGHT:** 4⅞ oz
SPINE THICKNESS: 1.9 mm **PERFORMANCE:** ★★★ **DESIGN:** ★★★
COMMENTS: This small, lightweight cleaver was razor sharp and easy to control. Just about every tester who handled this knife wanted to take it home. It sailed through all of our tests, slicing through even butternut squash more effortlessly than heftier Chinese cleavers did.

SHUN CLASSIC SERIES 6½-Inch Nakiri

MODEL: DMO728 **PRICE:** $134.95 **TYPE:** Nakiri **WEIGHT:** 7¾ oz
SPINE THICKNESS: 2.2 mm **PERFORMANCE:** ★★★ **DESIGN:** ★★★
COMMENTS: Heavier and more substantial than our winner, this cleaver was the favorite among testers accustomed to weightier knives. We found it easy to make precise cuts with its well-balanced, sharp blade.

RECOMMENDED

SHUN CLASSIC SERIES 7¾-Inch Vegetable Cleaver

MODEL: BMO712 **PRICE:** $189.95 **TYPE:** Chinese Vegetable Cleaver/Chef's Knife **WEIGHT:** 10⅞ oz
SPINE THICKNESS: 2.2 mm **PERFORMANCE:** ★★★ **DESIGN:** ★★
COMMENTS: The best of the Chinese-style cleavers, this weighty product (nearly 11 ounces) was too large and heavy for users unaccustomed to this style of knife. But with its keen edge and comparatively slim spine, that weight did most of the work, slicing through almost everything with little effort.

RECOMMENDED WITH RESERVATIONS

KASUMI DAMASCUS 7-Inch Vegetable Knife

MODEL: 84017 **PRICE:** $136.16 **TYPE:** Nakiri **WEIGHT:** 8 oz
SPINE THICKNESS: 2.1 mm **PERFORMANCE:** ★★ **DESIGN:** ★★
COMMENTS: A solid, well-balanced knife that neither dazzled nor disappointed. Its sharp blade had the most curve, which made it easy to rock when mincing parsley but kept it from slicing completely through potatoes.

RECOMMENDED WITH RESERVATIONS (cont.)

ZWILLING J.A. HENCKELS Japan, Miyabi 5000s Usuba

MODEL: 34506-171 **PRICE:** $149.99 **TYPE:** Usuba **WEIGHT:** 8¼ oz
SPINE THICKNESS: 2.3 mm **PERFORMANCE:** ★★ **DESIGN:** ★★
COMMENTS: The cutting edge of this knife, the only usuba in our lineup, is beveled on only one side. Sharp and substantial, it performed fairly well in most tests, but the single-beveled edge pulled the blade off course when cutting through hard squash.

NOT RECOMMENDED

VICTORINOX Curved Chinese Cleaver

MODEL: 41589 **PRICE:** $29.95 **TYPE:** Chinese Vegetable Cleaver/Chef's Knife **WEIGHT:** 9¼ oz
SPINE THICKNESS: 2.5 mm **PERFORMANCE:** ★★ **DESIGN:** ★
COMMENTS: This knife was a drag (literally). The edge was sharp, but no matter what we tried to cut through, the blade lagged instead of slicing smoothly. When we tried quartering butternut squash, there was more tearing than cutting.

WÜSTHOF Gourmet Chinese Chef's Knife

MODEL: 4688-2 **PRICE:** $79.75 **TYPE:** Chinese Vegetable Cleaver/Chef's Knife **WEIGHT:** 12¾ oz
SPINE THICKNESS: 3.1 mm **PERFORMANCE:** ★ **DESIGN:** ★
COMMENTS: The heftiest of all the knives we tested, it also had the thickest spine and the most drag. The size and heft made this knife cumbersome for many testers. The blade had almost no curve, causing its tip to dig into the cutting board when we tried to mince parsley and leaving us with a combination of bruised, crushed parsley and splinters from the gouged board.

Meat and Potatoes
À LA FRANÇAISE

Chris and Becky share a laugh as she prepares French-style potato casserole.

POT ROAST. YOU'RE THINKING OF THE AMERICAN STALWART, BEEF pot roast, right? Well, what about pork loin? The French popularized the method of slow-cooking pork loin in a covered pot, called *enchaud périgourdin* (which is simply a pork pot roast), and it turns out succulent, incredibly juicy meat. We've always gussied up the mostly mild flavor of pork loin with a glaze or spent time stuffing it, so we were intrigued by this relatively hands-off method that delivered deep flavor. But we knew that we'd need to make some adjustments, both because American pork is relatively lean and because a French addition to the pot—a pig's trotter (yes, that's pig's foot)—just wouldn't pass muster on most American tables.

The French don't just know their meat, they know their potatoes as well. The dish known as *pommes de terre boulangère,* or baker's potatoes, started out as a simple potato casserole that baked on a lower rack of the village baker's oven. (At the time, the baker's oven was often a communal affair—once the bread was baked, village families could use the still-hot oven to cook their own meals.) In this hearty side dish, the savory juices and fat from a roast on the upper rack would drip down into the casserole, bathing the potatoes with luxurious flavor. Modern versions of the dish rely on complex, hearty meat stock mixed into the potatoes. But we wanted deep flavor and silky texture without meat drippings or hours spent making stock. Join us as we take a few cues from the French and add a dash of American ingenuity.

FRENCH-STYLE POT-ROASTED PORK LOIN

✔ **WHY THIS RECIPE WORKS:** Enchaud périgourdin is a fancy name for what's actually a relatively simple French dish: slow-cooked pork loin. But given that American pork is so lean, this cooking method leads to bland, stringy pork. To improve the flavor and texture of our center-cut loin, we lowered the oven temperature (to 225 degrees) and removed the roast from the oven when it was medium-rare. Searing just three sides of the roast, rather than all four, prevented the bottom of the roast from overcooking from direct contact with the pot. Butterflying the pork allowed us to salt a maximum amount of surface area for a roast that was thoroughly seasoned throughout. And while we eliminated the hard-to-find trotter (or pig's foot), we added butter for richness and sprinkled in gelatin to lend body to the sauce.

FRENCH CUISINE IS WELL KNOWN FOR ITS MANY DISHES featuring a lackluster cut of meat turned sumptuous and flavorful by surprisingly simple methods, but the one that impresses us most is *enchaud périgourdin*. A specialty in the southwest Périgord region of France, it consists of a seared loin—one of the least promising cuts for slow-cooking—thrown into a covered casserole with garlic and a trotter (or pig's foot) to bake for several hours. You'd expect that a roast with so little fat or collagen to protect it would emerge from the pot dried out and tasteless. Instead, the finished meat is astonishingly moist and flavorful, with plenty of rich-tasting, viscous jus to drizzle on top.

Unfortunately, our attempts to make this dish at home have always turned out exactly as we had expected: bland and stringy meat sitting in a flavorless pool of juice. We're never sure what gets lost in translation, but the promise of a dish that eked out juicy, tender, savory results from this bland roast was motivation enough for us to find a successful approach of our own. We had just one stipulation:

The trotter had to go. Though it imparts body and flavor to the sauce, hunting one down would complicate this genuinely simple dish.

We gave a few recipes a try, and when not one of the roasts—cooked at both high heat and more moderate temperatures—turned out like the juicy, rich-tasting pot-roasted loins we've heard about from Périgord, we realized we had a very fundamental problem to deal with: the pork itself. While French pigs are bred to have plenty of fat, American pork contains far less marbling, with the center-cut roast that we were using being perhaps the leanest cut of all.

We wondered if we could improve the results by dropping the oven temperature (the lowest we'd tried so far was 325 degrees) and pulling out the roast when it hit the medium mark (140 degrees). Sure enough, this test proved that the lower the oven temperature, the more succulent the roast. Our tasters clearly favored the pork cooked in the 225-degree oven for about 70 minutes. In this very low oven, the outer layers of the loin absorbed less heat (and consequently squeezed out less moisture) during the time it took the center to climb to 140 degrees. And not only was it far juicier than any of our previous attempts, but a small pool of concentrated jus had accumulated at the bottom of the pot. There was just one texture-related setback: The bottom of the roast, which was in direct contact with the pot, cooked more quickly than the top. We solved this problem by searing just the top and sides of the roast while leaving the bottom raw.

But we still had work to do. Engineering juicier meat hadn't improved its bland flavor. Plus, without the trotter, the sauce lacked body. Salting and brining are our go-to methods when we want to draw seasoning into large cuts of pork and help the meat retain moisture during cooking. Brining wouldn't be helpful here, because soaking in a salt solution adds extra water to the meat, which would simply leach out and dilute the jus. Salting was the better option. The downside was that it took at least 6 hours (with superior results after 24 hours) for the salt to penetrate deep into the thick roast. We wondered if we could find a faster way.

It seemed that splitting the loin lengthwise into two smaller pieces and liberally sprinkling each one with salt might hasten the seasoning process, but when we gave it

FRENCH-STYLE POT-ROASTED PORK LOIN

a shot, tasters complained that the interior of each mini loin was still bland. Slicing a pocket into the top of the loin and sprinkling the interior with salt was strike two. Though the center of the roast was well seasoned, we were just as likely to get an unseasoned bite.

After some further experimentation we landed on an effective technique: "double-butterflying." By making two sweeping cuts—the first one-third of the way up the loin and the second into the thicker portion that we created with the first cut—we were able to open up the loin like a trifold book and expose a vast amount of surface area. Then we rubbed each side with 1½ teaspoons of kosher salt, folded the loin back up, and secured it with twine. While this method required a bit more knife work, it produced perfectly seasoned meat. Even better, this technique made it possible to add fat and flavor directly to the meat, bringing us closer to the French original.

For "fattening up" the roast, bacon fat, rendered salt pork fat, and butter all seemed like viable options. Though each produced richly flavorful, supremely juicy roasts, tasters particularly enjoyed the subtly sweet flavor imparted by butter. In fact, we pushed that sweetness one step further and added 1 teaspoon of sugar to the salt rub. To round out the roast's savory depth, we then sliced a few garlic cloves and caramelized them in the butter before using the mixture to coat the meat. Finally, we sprinkled the rolled roast with herbes de Provence, a heady combination that includes dried basil, fennel, lavender, marjoram, rosemary, sage, and thyme.

That left just the flavorful but thin jus to attend to. We knew one way to bulk up the jus would be to put bones in the pot. Not only do the bones themselves contain gelatin, but the connective tissue surrounding them also turns into gelatin over the course of long cooking. We wanted to see what would happen if we started with a bone-in loin, removed the bones, and then used them to make a quick stock to add to the pork as it roasted. This worked beautifully. When we opened the pot about an hour later, the jus was as glossy and thickened as the trotter-enhanced liquid. The only problem was that making the stock tacked 30 minutes onto an already lengthy cooking time. We wondered if adding powdered gelatin, which we've used in the past to mimic slow-cooked stocks, would do the trick here; we found that 1 tablespoon bloomed in ¼ cup of chicken broth lent just the right viscosity.

But bones also contribute flavor, and we still had to make up for that loss. Reducing ⅓ cup of white wine (after sautéing the onions) and whisking in 1 tablespoon of butter along with the gelatin rendered the sauce rich and balanced but not remarkable. It was only our final inspiration—a diced apple cooked along with the onions—that really brought the sauce together. Enchaud is traditionally served with pickles as a counterpoint to its rich flavors, and tasters raved that the softened bits of sweet-tart fruit worked in the same way. A variation with port and figs was equally satisfying.

The French method had inspired us, but it was kitchen testing that made slow-cooking this super-lean cut something truly great.

French-Style Pot-Roasted Pork Loin
SERVES 4 TO 6

We strongly prefer the flavor of natural pork in this recipe, but if enhanced pork (injected with a salt solution) is used, reduce the salt to 2 teaspoons (1 teaspoon per side) in step 2.

- 2 tablespoons unsalted butter, cut into 2 pieces
- 6 garlic cloves, sliced thin
- 1 (2½-pound) boneless center-cut pork loin roast, trimmed
  Kosher salt and pepper

1 teaspoon sugar

2 teaspoons herbes de Provence

2 tablespoons vegetable oil

1 Granny Smith apple, peeled, cored, and cut into ¼-inch pieces

1 onion, chopped fine

⅓ cup dry white wine

2 sprigs fresh thyme

1 bay leaf

1 tablespoon unflavored gelatin

¼–¾ cup low-sodium chicken broth

1 tablespoon minced fresh parsley

1. Adjust oven rack to lower-middle position and heat oven to 225 degrees. Melt 1 tablespoon butter in 8-inch skillet over medium-low heat. Add half of garlic and cook, stirring frequently, until golden, 5 to 7 minutes. Transfer mixture to bowl and refrigerate.

2. Position roast fat side up. Insert knife one-third of way up from bottom of roast along 1 long side and cut horizontally, stopping ½ inch before edge. Open up flap. Keeping knife parallel to cutting board, cut through thicker portion of roast about ½ inch from bottom of roast, keeping knife level with first cut and stopping about ½ inch before edge. Open up this flap. If uneven, cover with plastic wrap and use meat pounder to even out. Sprinkle 1 tablespoon salt over both sides of loin (½ tablespoon per side) and rub into pork until slightly tacky. Sprinkle sugar over inside of loin, then spread with cooled toasted garlic mixture. Starting from short side, fold roast back together like business letter (keeping fat on outside) and tie with twine at 1-inch intervals. Sprinkle tied roast evenly with herbes de Provence and season with pepper.

3. Heat 1 tablespoon oil in Dutch oven over medium heat until just smoking. Add roast, fat side down, and brown on fat side and sides (do not brown bottom of roast), 5 to 8 minutes. Transfer to large plate. Add remaining 1 tablespoon oil, apple, and onion to pot; cook, stirring frequently, until onion is softened and browned, 5 to 7 minutes. Stir in remaining garlic and cook until fragrant, about 30 seconds. Stir in wine, thyme, and bay leaf; cook for 30 seconds. Return roast, fat side up, to pot; place large sheet of aluminum foil over pot and cover tightly with lid. Transfer pot to oven and cook until pork registers 140 degrees, 50 minutes to 1½ hours (short, thick roasts will take longer than long, thin ones).

4. Transfer roast to carving board, tent loosely with foil, and let rest for 20 minutes. While pork rests, sprinkle gelatin over ¼ cup chicken broth and let sit until gelatin softens, about 5 minutes. Remove and discard thyme sprigs and bay leaf from jus. Pour jus into 2-cup measuring cup and, if necessary, add chicken broth to measure 1¼ cups. Return jus to pot and bring to simmer over medium heat. Whisk softened gelatin mixture, remaining 1 tablespoon butter, and parsley into jus and season with salt and pepper to taste; remove from heat and cover to keep warm. Slice pork into ½-inch-thick slices, adding any accumulated juices to sauce. Serve pork, passing sauce separately.

VARIATION

French-Style Pot-Roasted Pork Loin with Port and Figs

Substitute ¾ cup chopped dried figs for apple and port for white wine. Add 1 tablespoon balsamic vinegar to sauce with butter in step 4.

NOTES FROM THE TEST KITCHEN

"DOUBLE-BUTTERFLYING" A ROAST

1. Holding chef's knife parallel to cutting board, insert knife one-third of way up from bottom of roast and cut horizontally, stopping ½ inch before edge. Open up flap.

2. Make another horizontal cut into thicker portion of roast about ½ inch from bottom, stopping about ½ inch before edge. Open up this flap, smoothing out rectangle of meat.

RATING KNIFE BLOCK SETS

The biggest selling point when it comes to knife block sets seems to be the number of pieces the manufacturer can cram into one block, not the usefulness or quality of the blades. To find out if there was a knife block set on the market that would prove this assumption wrong, we tested eight sets containing six to nine pieces each and costing anywhere from $100 to nearly $700. After evaluating these sets against each other, comparing like components in a variety of tasks, we evaluated them against an à la carte selection of the test kitchen's favorite knives. In the end, our testing confirmed our suspicion that you are better off shopping for knives individually; that way, you get only what you really need—no weak links—and what you get is well constructed and of high quality. Brands are listed in order of preference. See AmericasTestKitchen.com for updates and further information on this testing.

HIGHLY RECOMMENDED   PERFORMANCE   TESTERS' COMMENTS

Test Kitchen's à la Carte Knife Set (7 pieces)
TOTAL PRICE: $334.65
- Wüsthof Classic 3½-Inch Paring Knife (model 4066), $39.95
- Victorinox Fibrox 8-Inch Chef's Knife (model 40520), $29.95
- Wüsthof Classic 10-Inch Bread Knife (model 4151), $109.95
- Victorinox Fibrox 12-Inch Granton Edge Slicing/ Carving Knife (model 47645), $49.95
- Victorinox Fibrox 6-inch Straight Boning Knife: Flexible (model 40513), $19.95
- Shun Classic Kitchen Shears (model 1120M), $39.95
- Bodum Bistro Universal Knife Block (model 11089), $45

PERFORMANCE: ★★★
EASE OF USE: ★★★
USEFULNESS: ★★★
WEAK LINKS: 0 OF 7

This "all-star" set of test kitchen favorites (all best-in-class winners in past tests) fits neatly into our favorite universal knife block by Bodum, designed to hold any variety of blades securely in its nest of plastic sticks. Best of all, at $334.65, this ideal collection costs less than many prepackaged knife block sets.

RECOMMENDED WITH RESERVATIONS

WÜSTHOF Classic 8-Piece Deluxe Knife Set
MODEL: 8420   **PRICE:** $379.99
INCLUDES: 3½-inch paring, 5-inch boning, 8-inch chef's, 8-inch bread, 8-inch carving, sharpening steel, shears, 17-slot wood block

PERFORMANCE: ★★½
EASE OF USE: ★★
USEFULNESS: ★★
WEAK LINKS: 3 OF 8

We were eager to try this set featuring our favorite paring knife and a shorter version of our favorite 10-inch bread knife. The results were mixed: The paring and boning blades fared admirably, but the 8-inch bread knife couldn't slice through a large loaf, and the shears were wimpy.

VICTORINOX 7-Piece Rosewood Knife Set
MODEL: 46054   **PRICE:** $189.95
INCLUDES: 3¼-inch paring, 6-inch boning, 8-inch chef's, 8-inch bread, 10-inch slicing, sharpening steel, 6-slot wood block

PERFORMANCE: ★★½
EASE OF USE: ★★
USEFULNESS: ★★
WEAK LINKS: 2 OF 7

While the knives in this set performed well and very few were filler, the slots chipped as we slid the knives in and out, making the set look worn right away. The bread and slicing knives were sharp but a bit short.

SHUN Classic 9-Piece Knife Set
MODEL: DMS0910   **PRICE:** $699.95
INCLUDES: 2½-inch bird's beak, 3½-inch paring, 6-inch utility, 8-inch chef's, 9-inch bread, 9-inch slicing, sharpening steel, shears, 11-slot bamboo block

PERFORMANCE: ★★½
EASE OF USE: ★★
USEFULNESS: ★★
WEAK LINKS: 5 OF 9

These solidly constructed, razor-edged knives performed well overall. But the 9-inch bread knife couldn't handle large loaves, and the parer was like a mini chef's knife, making it hard to peel an apple.

NOT RECOMMENDED

MESSERMEISTER Meridian Elite 9-Piece Knife Block Set
MODEL: E/3000-9S   **PRICE:** $351.94
INCLUDES: 3½-inch paring, 5-inch scalloped utility, 6-inch utility, 7-inch santoku, 8-inch chef's, 9-inch bread, sharpening steel, shears, 16-slot wood block

PERFORMANCE: ★★
EASE OF USE: ★
USEFULNESS: ★
WEAK LINKS: 5 OF 9

While some blades (particularly the nimble paring knife) shone in tests, this set's two utility knives and santoku were easily outperformed by the chef's blade on identical tasks. The bread knife was also too short.

FRENCH POTATO CASEROLE

✔ **WHY THIS RECIPE WORKS:** In the old days, this casserole of potatoes and onions was baked beneath a roast, which allowed the casserole to be seasoned by the savory fat and juices of the roast. To get the same luxurious results without the roast, we started by rendering a small amount of bacon, which lent the dish a meaty flavor with a hint of smokiness. We then browned the onions in the rendered bacon fat, which gave the dish remarkable complexity.

IN THE FRENCH DISH KNOWN AS *POMMES DE TERRE boulangère,* or "baker's potatoes," incredibly tender potatoes nestle in a rich, meaty sauce beneath a delicately browned crust. The name dates to a time when villagers used the residual heat of the baker's oven to cook dinner at the end of the day. Chicken, pork, or beef would roast on an upper oven shelf while this casserole of thinly sliced potatoes and onions bubbled away underneath, seasoned by the savory fat and juices dripping from above.

Today French chefs no longer cook pommes de terre boulangère beneath a blistering roast, but they impart the same unctuous flavor, deep brown color, and supreme tenderness using hearty meat stock and a well-calibrated oven. While we could spend hours making stock from scratch, it seemed like too much time and effort for a side dish. We wanted a potato casserole with deep flavor and a super-tender texture—after a reasonable amount of work.

Since we were seeking a creamy consistency, only one potato variety would do: the moderately starchy, buttery-tasting Yukon Gold. A mandoline was an ideal tool for slicing the peeled spuds since we wanted them to be wafer-thin (about ⅛ inch)—any thicker and the casserole would be too chunky, losing its refined nature. We added a thinly sliced onion to the Yukons, packed the mixture into a greased baking dish, poured in 3 cups of store-bought beef broth, and slid the casserole into a 350-degree oven. It was no surprise when this test batch revealed two big flaws. First, the sauce was bland

and tasted, well, canned. And second, its consistency was soupy, lacking the requisite creaminess.

We tackled the flavor issue first. To temper the beef broth's undesirable qualities, we diluted it with an equal amount of commercial chicken broth. This mellowed the flavor of both, for a blend that didn't taste processed. But that doesn't mean it tasted meaty. Since potatoes boulangère were sometimes roasted beneath poultry, we experimented with scattering chicken wings atop the potatoes before baking, hoping that the wings would infuse the slices with rich flavor. But this was effective only if we first browned the chicken on both sides—an extra step that we weren't willing to incorporate.

Next, we turned to flavor-packed pork options like ham hocks, pancetta, and bacon. We simmered a hock briefly in the broth, expecting it to impart smokiness, but the effect was negligible. (We could have cooked it longer but we wanted a quick fix.) For the pancetta and bacon, we simply rendered them until crisp and then tossed the pieces with the potatoes and onion. Both were much more effective at boosting meatiness than the ham hock was, but in the end, tasters preferred the smoky bacon.

Next up was the onion. We found inspiration from another French classic: onion soup, in which onions are deeply caramelized to concentrate their flavor. Cooking the sliced onion to a deep molasses-y brown made it too sweet for this dish, but sautéing it in some of the leftover bacon fat until golden brown was enough to bring out remarkable complexity.

With a scattering of fresh thyme, sprinkles of salt and pepper, and a few pats of butter, the flavor of our potatoes was in really good shape. But we still needed to improve the too-thin sauce and somehow make the overall texture silkier and more luscious.

Our first attempt to remedy the consistency of the sauce was twofold: we decreased the amount of broth to 2½ cups and increased the oven temperature to 425 degrees so that more liquid would evaporate during baking. When we started to see improvement, we took things one step further by bringing the broth to a simmer in the pot used to cook the onion, giving it a jump start on reducing in the oven. As a bonus, this deglazing step captured all of the flavorful fond left behind by the bacon and caramelized onion.

POTATO CASSEROLE WITH BACON AND CARAMELIZED ONION

The broth had now cooked down, but it was still neither thick nor creamy. Then it dawned on us. We had been submerging our sliced potatoes in water to keep them from discoloring while we prepped the remaining ingredients—a common practice, but one that also washes away most of the spuds' starch. Without that starch, the sauce couldn't thicken up. We tried again with unsoaked potatoes and witnessed a striking difference. The sauce now glazed the potatoes and onion in a velvety cloak. As a final measure, we made sure to allow the casserole to rest for a good 20 minutes before serving it. This went a long way toward developing a silky, creamy texture, since the starch granules in the potatoes continued to absorb moisture and swell as they cooled.

With a few modifications, we had been able to achieve a satisfying version of pommes de terre boulangère within a reasonable time frame, making this once-obscure dish now easy enough for weeknight cooking.

Potato Casserole with Bacon and Caramelized Onion

SERVES 6 TO 8

Do not rinse or soak the potatoes, as this will wash away their starch, which is essential to the dish. A mandoline makes slicing the potatoes much easier. For the proper texture, make sure to let the casserole stand for 20 minutes before serving.

3	slices thick-cut bacon, cut into ½-inch pieces
1	large onion, halved and sliced thin
1¼	teaspoons salt
2	teaspoons chopped fresh thyme
½	teaspoon pepper
1¼	cups low-sodium chicken broth
1¼	cups beef broth
3	pounds Yukon Gold potatoes, peeled
2	tablespoons unsalted butter, cut into 4 pieces

1. Adjust oven rack to lower-middle position and heat oven to 425 degrees. Grease 13 by 9-inch baking dish.

2. Cook bacon in medium saucepan over medium-low heat until crisp, 10 to 13 minutes. Using slotted spoon, transfer bacon to paper towel–lined plate. Remove and discard all but 1 tablespoon fat from pot. Return pot to medium heat and add onion and ¼ teaspoon salt; cook, stirring frequently, until onion is soft and golden brown, about 25 minutes, adjusting heat and adding water 1 tablespoon at a time if onion or bottom of pot becomes too dark. Transfer onion to large bowl; add bacon, thyme, remaining 1 teaspoon salt, and pepper. Add broths to now-empty saucepan and bring to simmer over medium-high heat, scraping bottom of pan to loosen any browned bits.

3. Slice potatoes ⅛ inch thick. Transfer to bowl with onion mixture and toss to combine. Transfer to prepared baking dish. Firmly press down on mixture to compress into even layer. Carefully pour hot broth over top of potatoes. Dot surface evenly with butter.

4. Bake, uncovered, until potatoes are tender and golden brown on edges and most of liquid has been absorbed, 45 to 55 minutes. Transfer to wire rack and let stand for 20 minutes to fully absorb broth before cutting and serving.

EQUIPMENT CORNER

MANDOLINES

When we need to slice spuds, or anything else, wafer-thin, we reach for a mandoline. A mandoline is faster and more accurate than a chef's knife when you've got a lot of slicing to do. Plus, it delivers pieces that are the same thickness, guaranteeing that they will cook through evenly. Our favorite model is the **OXO Good Grips V-Blade Mandoline Slicer** ($49.99), which has a razor-sharp blade, for faster, more precise cutting. Since mandoline blades can be very sharp, it's important that they have sufficient safety features. This model has a wide, sturdy gripper guard to keep fingers safe. Also, it has a measurement-marked dial, which makes it easy to set the slice thickness, plus it can produce matchsticks or waffle cuts by changing the blade. One more thing we like about it: extra blades can be conveniently stored beneath the frame. For a more affordable option, we also like the Kyocera Adjustable Ceramic Mandoline Slicer, which is just half the price, at $22. It also has a razor-sharp blade, and it adjusts easily and fits in a drawer, although it doesn't come with julienne or waffle blades. See AmericasTestKitchen.com for updates to this testing.

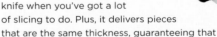

Company's COMING

Julia explains that meat should rest before it's sliced, but Chris is still eager for a taste of Best Prime Rib.

WHEN COMPANY'S COMING AND YOU'RE OUT TO IMPRESS, THERE ARE few main courses that mean business as much as prime rib. Prime-grade prime rib costs about $17 a pound. Given that this meal will be a splurge, you want a buttery, tender roast, guaranteed. One approach to cooking prime rib particularly intrigued us because we've heard the results are exceptional. It's from British restaurant chef Heston Blumenthal, who sears his rib roast with a blowtorch before cooking it for 18 hours in an ultraslow oven until the meat turns rosy. A blowtorch and 18 hours?! We set out to see if there was some method to his madness and if it could be modified for the home cook—without the kitchen theatrics and long stint in the oven.

What goes well with prime rib? Brussels sprouts. This cruciferous vegetable has been enjoying a resurgence in popularity since restaurant menus started roasting sprouts. Roasting mellows the vegetable's somewhat bitter bite, turning it sweet and nutty. Join us as we head into the test kitchen to uncover the best way to roast Brussels sprouts and produce a perfect roast prime rib.

BEST PRIME RIB

✔ **WHY THIS RECIPE WORKS:** The perfect prime rib should have a deep-colored, substantial crust encasing a tender, juicy rosy-pink center. To achieve this perfect roast, we started by salting the roast overnight. The salt enhanced the beefy flavor while dissolving some of the proteins, yielding a buttery-tender roast. To further enhance tenderness, we cooked the roast at a very low temperature, which allowed the meat's enzymes to act as natural tenderizers, breaking down its tough connective tissue. A brief stint under the broiler before serving ensured a crisp, flavorful crust.

A CHEF FRIEND RECENTLY SERVED US SLICES OF PRIME rib as close to beef perfection as anything we've ever tasted. The prime rib featured a crisp, salty crust encasing a large eye of juicy, rose-hued meat interspersed with soft pockets of richly flavored fat. The meat had the buttery texture of tenderloin but the beefiness of a chuck roast, and the usual gray band of overcooked meat under the surface of the crust was practically nonexistent. We found ourselves reassessing our expectations for this primo cut and asked for the recipe. While our friend wouldn't divulge all the details, he did direct us to the formula on which he based his own: famed British chef Heston Blumenthal's recipe for "steak" (translation: a two-rib roast from which he cuts steaks), published in his book *In Search of Perfection*.

To say that Blumenthal goes to extremes for his prime rib would be an understatement. The recipe breaks down as follows: Sear the exterior of the roast with a blowtorch, place the meat in a preheated 120-degree oven until the internal temperature hits 120 degrees—and then hold it there for 18 hours. (You read that right: 18 hours.) Finally, pull the meat out of the oven, let it rest, slice it into steaks, and pan-sear the slabs until crisp.

This exact approach was out of the question. For one thing, even if a cook were willing to keep the meat in the oven all night and most of a day, no home oven can reliably go below 200 degrees. But it did give us some ideas—and an ideal to strive for.

We had one major decision made before we even got started: the meat selection. In the test kitchen, our preferences for the exact grade and cut of beef are definitive: a Prime first-cut roast for its supreme marbling and large rib-eye muscle. As we would with any other roast, we patted the meat dry and seasoned it with a handful of coarse salt. Then came the first hurdle: how best to replicate the effects of a blowtorch. Blumenthal blast-sears meat with this instrument because its intense heat (over 3,000 degrees) immediately starts to render fat and brown the exterior while leaving the meat beneath the surface virtually untouched (hence the remarkably thin gray band). Our options were a hot oven or a skillet—and neither was ideal. Oven-searing at 500 degrees was easy but far too slow; by the time the roast got some decent color, a good half-inch of meat below the surface had turned ashen. Unacceptable. Meanwhile, a blazing-hot skillet seared the meat faster, but evenly browning a three-bone roast in a 12-inch pan was cumbersome to say the least.

We came up with a quick fix for the unwieldiness problem: we cut the bones off the roast before searing to make it easier to maneuver the meat in the skillet, then tied them back on before roasting so that they could still provide insulation, helping the roast cook more evenly. We even discovered two extra benefits to the method: The exposed meat on the bone side could now be thoroughly seasoned, and carving the finished roast required nothing more than snipping the twine before slicing. But getting a deep sear on the roast (even when we skipped browning the bone side) still took 10 minutes—not because the pan wasn't hot (it clocked 450 degrees), but because even after we had carefully blotted it dry, the meat straight out of the package was still damp. That meant that the surface directly underneath our roast couldn't rise above 212 degrees (the boiling point of water) until the moisture had evaporated. We didn't need a hotter pan. We needed drier meat.

Fortunately, this was familiar territory. We routinely air-dry poultry to allow its moisture to evaporate so that we can get the skin extra crisp. We took the same tack here, prepping and seasoning another roast before moving it into the fridge for a 24-hour rest. When we seared this roast, the exterior did indeed brown better (and faster) than it had in our previous attempts. But that wasn't the

BEST PRIME RIB

only perk. The meat below the surface was beefier and much more tender, and we had the combination of salt and time to thank for it. Given a chance to penetrate deep into the meat, salt enhanced the beefy flavor while dissolving some of the proteins, yielding a buttery-tender roast. In fact, we found that the longer we let the roast sit—up to four days—the beefier, juicier, and more tender the results. (If we let it sit any longer than four days, however, we risked desiccating the exterior.) We also scored the larger swaths of fat on the exterior, which gave the salt a head start on the meat and encouraged rendering.

Things were progressing nicely—but we still had a home oven to reckon with. There was good reason for Blumenthal's incredibly long cooking time and incredibly low temperature. By gently raising the temperature of the meat and then holding it at 120 degrees for all those hours, he was cleverly manipulating two active enzymes in the meat: calpains and cathepsins. When the meat is held around the 120-degree mark, these enzymes work at a rapid pace to break down connective tissues and tenderize the meat. (This tenderizing effect is equivalent to aging the beef for almost a month.) Since it was impossible to use the same method with our conventional home oven, we focused our efforts on finding another way to keep our beef close to 120 degrees for as long as we could.

The lowest our oven would go was 200 degrees, so we set the dial there and popped in another salted, seared roast. When the meat hit 125 degrees (medium-rare) almost 4 hours later, the crust was decent and the interior well seasoned and rosy from center to edge. But the texture wasn't ideal: more like run-of-the-mill strip steak than prime-grade rib eye. We weren't sure what to do next. Then it occurred to us that we actually did have a way to lower the temperature of our oven: We could turn it off. We ran a series of tests, shutting off the oven when the roasts hit various degrees of doneness. The magic number turned out to be 110 degrees, our trusty probe thermometer indicating exactly when the roast had hit the target temperature. This was a breakthrough technique. In the shut-off oven, the beef stayed in the enzyme sweet spot far longer, about an hour more to reach 120 for rare. We then took it out of the oven to let it

rest and to allow the exuded juices to be drawn back into the meat. Thanks to the roast's hefty size, the meat stayed at an ideal serving temperature for more than an hour, giving us plenty of time to cook or reheat side dishes.

Only one imperfection remained: The crust had lost some of its crispness as it rested under a tent of aluminum foil. A quick stint under the broiler before serving was all it took to restore it—well, almost all of it. To ensure that the fatty portion at the top of the ribs got enough exposure to the heat, we rolled up the piece of foil we'd used to tent the roast into a ball and sandwiched it under the ribs to elevate the fat.

All that was left was to snip the twine, lift the meat from the bones, and slice it into hefty ¾-inch-thick slabs. This prime rib was truly the king of all roasts—a deep-colored, substantial crust encasing a rosy-pink center. And making it took nothing more than a humble skillet and a regular oven.

Best Prime Rib

SERVES 6 TO 8

Look for a roast with an untrimmed fat cap (ideally ½ inch thick). We prefer the flavor and texture of Prime beef, but Choice grade will work as well. Monitoring the roast with a meat-probe thermometer is best. If you use an instant-read thermometer, open the oven door as little as possible and remove the roast from the oven while taking its temperature. If the roast has not reached the correct temperature in the time range specified in step 3, heat the oven to 200 degrees, wait for 5 minutes, then shut it off, and continue to cook the roast until it reaches the desired temperature.

1 (7-pound) first-cut beef standing rib roast (3 bones), meat removed from bones, bones reserved
  Kosher salt and pepper
2 teaspoons vegetable oil

1. Using sharp knife, cut slits in surface layer of fat, spaced 1 inch apart, in crosshatch pattern, being careful to cut down to, but not into, meat. Rub 2 tablespoons salt over entire roast and into slits. Place meat back on bones (to save space in refrigerator), transfer to large plate, and refrigerate, uncovered, for at least 24 hours or up to 4 days.

2. Adjust oven rack to middle position and heat oven to 200 degrees. Set wire rack in rimmed baking sheet. Heat oil in 12-inch skillet over high heat until just smoking. Sear sides and top of roast (reserving bones) until browned, 6 to 8 minutes total (do not sear side where roast was cut from bones). Place meat back on ribs so bones fit where they were cut and let cool for 10 minutes; tie meat to bones with 2 lengths of kitchen twine between ribs. Transfer roast, fat side up, to prepared wire rack and season with pepper. Roast until meat registers 110 degrees, 3 to 4 hours.

3. Turn off oven; leave roast in oven, opening door as little as possible, until meat registers about 120 degrees (for rare) or about 125 degrees (for medium-rare,) 30 minutes to 1¼ hours longer.

4. Remove roast from oven (leave roast on baking sheet), tent loosely with aluminum foil, and let rest for at least 30 minutes or up to 1¼ hours.

SCIENCE DESK

CARRYOVER COOKING

When you're cooking an expensive roast such as Best Prime Rib, getting it to the table cooked just the way you like it is critical. But judging precisely when meat is done is tricky, because what you're actually gauging is not whether the food is ready to eat right now but whether it will be ready to eat once it has rested. Meat will continue to cook even after it has been removed from the heat source, a phenomenon known as "carryover cooking." This happens for two reasons: First, the exterior of a large roast gets hot much more quickly than the interior. Second, because heat always moves from a hotter to a cooler area, as long as there is a difference in temperature between the two regions, heat will keep moving from the surface to the center even after you remove the meat from the heat source. This transfer will slow, and eventually stop, as internal and external temperatures approach each other and even out. But the process can result in a significant increase in temperature at the center of a large roast, bringing it from a perfect pink to a disappointing gray.

So when, exactly, should you remove meat from the heat source? Both the size of the roast and the heat level during cooking will affect the answer. A large roast will absorb more heat than a thin steak, which means there will be more heat in the meat and therefore a greater amount of carryover cooking. Similarly, meat cooked in a 400-degree oven absorbs more heat than meat cooked in a 200-degree oven, so carryover cooking is greater in a roast cooked in a hot oven.

Use our guidelines to determine exactly when to take meat off the heat so when you serve it, it's at the desired temperature. (Note: While carryover cooking can occur in poultry, for food safety reasons we usually don't recommend removing it from the heat until it's done.)

	FOR FINAL SERVING TEMPERATURE	STOP COOKING WHEN TEMPERATURE REACHES	
		LARGE ROASTS/ HIGH HEAT	THIN CUTS/ MODERATE HEAT
BEEF AND LAMB			
Rare	125°F	115°F	120°F
Medium-Rare	130°F	120°F	125°F
Medium	140°F	130°F	135°F
Well-Done	160°F	150°F	155°F
PORK			
Medium	150°F	140°F	145°F
Well-Done	160°F	150°F	155°F

5. Adjust oven rack to about 8 inches from broiler element and heat broiler. Remove foil from roast, form into 3-inch ball, and place under ribs to elevate fat cap. Broil until top of roast is well browned and crisp, 2 to 8 minutes.

6. Transfer roast to carving board; cut twine and remove ribs from roast. Slice meat into ¾-inch-thick slices. Season with salt to taste, and serve.

NOTES FROM THE TEST KITCHEN

PREPARING PRIME RIB

1. Removing ribs makes it easier to sear prime rib in skillet. Run sharp knife down length of bones, following contours as closely as possible to remove ribs.

2. Score fat cap in 1-inch crosshatch pattern to allow salt to contact meat directly and to improve fat rendering and crisping.

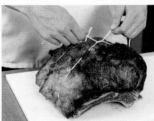

3. After searing meat, place meat back on ribs so bones fit where they were cut and let cool for 10 minutes; tie meat to bones with 2 lengths of twine between ribs. The bones provide insulation to the meat, so it cooks evenly.

ROASTED BRUSSELS SPROUTS

✔ **WHY THIS RECIPE WORKS:** Roasting is a simple and quick way to produce Brussels sprouts that are well caramelized on the outside and tender on the inside. To ensure we achieved this balance, we started out roasting the "tiny cabbages," covered, with a little bit of water. This created a steamy environment, which cooked the vegetable through. We then removed the foil and allowed the exterior to dry out and caramelize.

BRUSSELS SPROUTS ARE IN DIRE NEED OF A NEW publicist. The first order of business: to get the word out that this vegetable doesn't have to taste overly bitter or sulfurous. Like other members of the crucifer family (which also includes broccoli, cabbage, and mustard greens), Brussels sprouts are rich in flavor precursors that react with the vegetable's enzymes to produce pungent new compounds when the sprouts are cut, cooked, and even eaten. But when the sprouts are handled just right, this pungency takes on a nutty sweetness.

The problem is, achieving perfect results is usually a two-part process. To ensure that the interiors of this dense vegetable get sufficiently tender, the sprouts are first blanched or steamed, followed by roasting or pan searing. The latter process lightly crisps the outer leaves and creates the nice browning that mellows the sprouts' bitter kick. But when Brussels sprouts are part of a holiday feast, this two-step approach is a little too fussy. Could we get the results we wanted using just one step?

We decided to skip the pan searing, since one batch in a 12-inch skillet barely makes enough for four people, and we wanted our sprouts to feed a crowd. Roasting seemed like the best technique to play with.

We rounded up a little over 2 pounds of sprouts—enough for six to eight people—looking for same-size specimens about 1½ inches long. With parcooking ruled out, the obvious first step was to halve the sprouts, which would help ensure that they cooked through and would create a flat surface for browning. We then tossed them in a bowl with a bit of olive oil, salt, and pepper.

ROASTED BRUSSELS SPROUTS

To maximize browning and to jump-start cooking, we often preheat the baking sheet before roasting vegetables. We did precisely this, placing the sprouts cut side down on the hot sheet, which we then put back in a 500-degree oven. But when we pulled the vegetables out 20 minutes later, they were dry, chewy, and even burnt in spots on the outside, while practically crunchy on the inside. Starting with a cool baking sheet didn't help matters, and turning down the heat merely meant that it took a little longer for the sprouts to reach the same unsatisfactory state.

To prevent the outer leaves from drying out too much before the center achieved the ideal tender-firm texture, it seemed clear that we needed to introduce moisture to the equation. We wondered if just covering the sprouts with aluminum foil as they roasted would trap enough steam to do the trick. Once again, we arranged the sprouts cut side down on the baking sheet, but this time we covered the pan tightly with foil before placing it in the oven. After 10 minutes, we removed the foil so that the slightly softened sprouts could brown and get just a little crisp. After 10 minutes more, the Brussels sprouts were perfectly browned on the outside. And undercooked on the inside. And a bit dry and chewy all around.

We tried tossing the sprouts with a tablespoon of water along with the oil and seasonings before we put them in the oven. Covered in foil, each halved sprout acted like its own little steam chamber, holding on to a tiny bit of water to finish cooking its interior even as its outside began to brown. The results were perfect: tender, sweet insides and caramelized exteriors.

Now that we'd made perfectly cooked Brussels sprouts in one easy step, we devised some quick variations. They could show off their image makeover not just during the holidays, but all year long.

Roasted Brussels Sprouts
SERVES 6 TO 8

If you are buying loose Brussels sprouts, select those that are about 1½ inches long. Quarter Brussels sprouts longer than 2½ inches; don't cut sprouts shorter than 1 inch.

2¼ **pounds Brussels sprouts, trimmed and halved**
3 **tablespoons olive oil**
1 **tablespoon water**
  Salt and pepper

1. Adjust oven rack to upper-middle position and heat oven to 500 degrees. Toss Brussels sprouts, oil, water, ¾ teaspoon salt, and ¼ teaspoon pepper together in large bowl until sprouts are coated. Transfer sprouts to rimmed baking sheet and arrange cut sides down.

2. Cover baking sheet tightly with aluminum foil and roast for 10 minutes. Remove foil and continue to cook until Brussels sprouts are well browned and tender, 10 to 12 minutes longer. Transfer to serving platter, season with salt and pepper to taste, and serve.

VARIATIONS

Roasted Brussels Sprouts with Garlic, Red Pepper Flakes, and Parmesan
While Brussels sprouts roast, heat 3 tablespoons olive oil in 8-inch skillet over medium heat until shimmering. Add 2 minced garlic cloves and ½ teaspoon red pepper flakes; cook until garlic is golden and fragrant, about 1 minute. Remove from heat. Toss roasted Brussels sprouts with garlic oil and season with salt and pepper to taste. Transfer to platter and sprinkle with ¼ cup grated Parmesan cheese before serving.

Roasted Brussels Sprouts with Bacon and Pecans
While Brussels sprouts roast, cook 4 slices bacon in 10-inch skillet over medium heat until crisp, 7 to 10 minutes. Using slotted spoon, transfer bacon to paper towel–lined plate and reserve 1 tablespoon bacon fat. Finely chop bacon. Toss roasted Brussels sprouts with 2 tablespoons olive oil, reserved bacon fat, chopped bacon, and ½ cup finely chopped toasted pecans. Season with salt and pepper to taste; transfer to platter and serve.

RATING UNSALTED BUTTER

Not too long ago, cultured butter, also known as European butter, was hard to come by. Nowadays, there are as many brands of this rich, pricey ingredient in the dairy case as there are of the standard sweet-cream variety. We wanted to know if we really had to spend more money for the best butter, so we sampled 10 brands, seven cultured and three sweet-cream, spread on crackers and baked into French butter cookies. While sweet-cream butters are quickly and cheaply mass-produced by churning cream that has undergone little or no storage, cultured butters are made more slowly, with cream that's allowed to ripen for a few days to develop flavor and then inoculated with bacterial cultures before churning. The higher-ranking brands nailed their mix of cultures, nicely balancing sweet, fresh-cream flavor with complex tang. They also included enough butterfat to make them decadent and glossy but not so rich that baked goods were dense or greasy. Only one sweet-cream variety made it into the top tier, coming in second, most likely because of its packaging; sticks of this butter are protected from refrigerator odors by a specially patented wrapper. Brands are listed in order of preference. See AmericasTestKitchen.com for updates to this testing.

HIGHLY RECOMMENDED

PLUGRÁ European-Style Unsalted Butter
PRICE: $9.98 for 16 oz
STYLE: Cultured cream **BUTTERFAT:** 83%
COMMENTS: The cream of the crop, this "thick and luscious" cultured butter was "complex" and "just a bit tangy" and "grassy." Some deemed its flavor the most "robust" of all the samples.

RECOMMENDED

LAND O'LAKES Unsalted Sweet Butter
PRICE: $4.79 for 16 oz `BEST BUY`
STYLE: Sweet cream **BUTTERFAT:** 82%
COMMENTS: The most widely available supermarket butter—and the only sweet-cream sample to earn our recommendation—this product impressed tasters in spite of its plainer-tasting profile. We liked its "fresh-cream," "clean dairy flavor."

VERMONT CREAMERY European-Style Cultured Butter, Unsalted
PRICE: $11.98 for 16 oz
STYLE: Cultured cream **BUTTERFAT:** 86%
COMMENTS: This high-priced, high-fat cultured butter balanced "fresh-sweet dairy richness" with flavor that tasters described as "rich," "refreshing," and "barnyard-y" but also "mineral-y."

PRÉSIDENT Unsalted Butter
PRICE: $7.52 for 16 oz
STYLE: Cultured cream **BUTTERFAT:** 82%
COMMENTS: Though leaner than other cultured butters, this French import came across as "firm" and "silky," with "beautifully sweet and creamy" flavor that was also "buttermilk-y" and "slightly grassy."

ORGANIC VALLEY European-Style Cultured Butter, Unsalted
PRICE: $7.58 for 16 oz
STYLE: Cultured cream **BUTTERFAT:** 86%
COMMENTS: This sample was on the mellow side for a cultured butter, with some tasters deeming it "a bit timid." Others praised its "simple buttery flavor" and "floral undertones."

RECOMMENDED (cont.)

ORGANIC VALLEY Cultured Butter, Unsalted
PRICE: $5.99 for 16 oz
STYLE: Cultured cream **BUTTERFAT:** 83%
COMMENTS: Though some tasters picked up on nothing but this butter's "rich" flavor and "welcome tartness," several detected an apparent storage problem. Seeping through this sample's waxed parchment wrapper were flavors that tasted "like the inside of a fridge."

LURPAK Imported Butter, Unsalted
PRICE: $11.98 for 16 oz
STYLE: Cultured cream **BUTTERFAT:** 83%
COMMENTS: Though enough tasters praised this butter for its "richness" and "complexity," it barely skated into the "recommended" category, as others found it so "fake"-tasting that it drew comparisons to margarine.

RECOMMENDED WITH RESERVATIONS

CABOT Natural Creamery Unsalted Butter
PRICE: $5.29 for 16 oz
STYLE: Sweet cream **BUTTERFAT:** 81%
COMMENTS: At best, this butter was "mild"; but it was a little "boring," too. It was also another victim of poor wrapping: More than a few tasters detected "odd" flavors that reminded them of "the fridge."

KERRYGOLD Pure Irish Butter, Unsalted
PRICE: $5.98 for 16 oz
STYLE: Cultured cream **BUTTERFAT:** 83%
COMMENTS: It wasn't this Irish butter's texture that tasters objected to; in fact, several deemed it "luxurious" and "velvety." It was the "artificial," "movie-theater-popcorn flavor" that put many tasters off.

HORIZON Organic Unsalted Butter
PRICE: $5.49 for 16 oz
STYLE: Sweet cream **BUTTERFAT:** 81%
COMMENTS: Like the Cabot butter, this brand was "nothing special" and even struck some tasters as "watery" and "thin." Poor wrapping likely contributed to off-flavors that reminded one taster of "refrozen melted ice cream."

Chili and Stew
GO VEGETARIAN

Rather than using the traditional deep pot for our Italian Vegetable Stew, we rely on a skillet, whose wide surface area and dry heat help preserve the texture of the vegetables.

SOME PEOPLE MIGHT ARGUE THAT VEGETARIAN CHILI AND STEW ARE the ugly stepsisters of their meat counterparts. We beg to differ. To prove our point, we made it our goal to develop an outstanding recipe for each one.

Most vegetarian chilis rely on beans as their base ingredient and that's where we'd start in building our version. Since we were pulling out all the stops, we'd pick two bean varieties for maximum complexity—and we wouldn't be relying on canned beans—only dried would do in this chili. We also knew we'd need to replace the dusty commercial chili powder with a homemade mixture that delivered not just heat, but deep flavor. Finally, we wanted a thick, rich chili. Some recipes attempt to thicken chili with diced vegetables while others rely on nuts or a starch, such as rice. Whatever we landed on, we didn't want it to be distracting to the nature of the dish. We wanted real chili.

Ciambotta is a summery Italian vegetable stew that's much like France's ratatouille. Eggplant, potatoes, zucchini, onions, and bell peppers mingle together in a tomatoey broth infused with herbs. But this typically one-pot dish often results in mushy vegetables and muddy flavors. What is the secret to producing an Italian vegetable stew that retains the character of each vegetable, harmonizes their flavors, and yields a dish rich enough that no one misses the meat? Let's get to work in the test kitchen to find out.

BEST VEGETARIAN CHILI

BEST VEGETARIAN CHILI

✓ **WHY THIS RECIPE WORKS:** Vegetarian chilis are often little more than a mishmash of beans and vegetables. In order to create a robust, complex-flavored chili—not a bean and vegetable stew—we found replacements for the different ways in which meat adds depth and flavor to chili. Walnuts, soy sauce, dried shiitake mushrooms, and tomatoes add hearty savoriness. Bulgur fills out the chili, giving it a substantial texture. The added oil and nuts lend a richness to the chili, for full, lingering flavor.

WE LOVE CHILI. BUT MOST VEGETARIAN CHILIS disappoint. They rely on beans and chunky veggies for heartiness—but in truth that heartiness is just an illusion. Neither ingredient offers any real replacement for the flavor, texture, and unctuous richness that meat provides. It doesn't help matters that such chilis are typically made with canned beans and lackluster commercial chili powder.

But do vegetarian chilis really have to be this way? We set out to build a version as rich, savory, and deeply satisfying as any meat chili out there—one that even meat lovers would make on its own merits, not just to serve to vegetarian friends.

The first ingredient to tackle was the seasoning that gives the dish its name. Though we've found premade chili powders to recommend, even the best can't compete with a powder that you grind yourself from dried chiles. Plus, the commercial products tend to have a gritty, dusty texture that comes from grinding chiles whole—including the stems and seeds, which never fully break down. For our homemade blend, we opted for two widely available dried chiles: mild, sweet ancho and earthy New Mexican. We toasted them to bring out their flavor and then, after removing the stems and seeds, pulverized the peppers to a fine powder in a spice grinder with some dried oregano.

Next up: the beans. For greater complexity, we wanted to use a mix of beans with different characteristics, singling out sweet, nutty cannellinis and meaty, earthy pintos.

Canned beans are certainly convenient, but they also tend to be bland and mushy, so we opted for dried, calling on our quick-brining method. This entails bringing the beans to a boil in a pot of salted water and then letting them sit, covered, for an hour. The brine ensures soft, creamy beans (sodium ions from salt allow more water to penetrate the bean skins, for a softer texture) that are well seasoned and evenly cooked.

Meanwhile, the beans' hour-long rest gave us plenty of time to prep the remaining ingredients. We started out with the dried chile and oregano powder, some fresh jalapeños to kick up the heat, cumin for earthy depth, onions and garlic for sweetness and pungency, and a can of diced tomatoes for bright acidity. We sautéed the finely chopped onions just until they began to brown and then added the spices to bloom in the hot oil. In went our brined beans and water; then we covered the pot and placed it in a 300-degree oven. (If they were on the stovetop we'd have to stir the beans to prevent scorching, but in the more even, gentle heat of the oven they could simmer unattended.) We checked the beans periodically as they cooked. After 45 minutes, they were just tender. This was a great time to introduce the tomatoes, which we had processed with the garlic and the jalapeños. The tomatoes would keep the beans from falling apart during the remainder of cooking, since the basic building blocks of legumes—polysaccharides—do not readily dissolve in acidic conditions. Another 2 hours and the beans were perfectly cooked: creamy and tender but not blown out. But we still had just a pot of flavored beans. Now to turn it into a real chili...

Besides the beans, most vegetarian chilis replace the bulk that meat contributes with some combination of diced vegetables. But these recipes miss a major point: In addition to adding volume and flavor, meat gives chili its distinctive texture. A spoonful of chili should be a homogeneous mixture of ground or diced meat coated with a thick, spicy sauce. No matter how you slice or dice them, cut vegetables can't deliver that same sturdy texture. They also tend to water down the dish.

In our research we'd come across vegetarian chilis that called for nuts or grains and, with nothing to lose, we decided to try a few of these more unusual add-ins. Chopped pumpkin seeds were a failure: They didn't break down during cooking, leaving sharp, crunchy bits that tasters found distracting. Long-grain rice, meanwhile, turned to mush by the time the beans were cooked through, and large, round grains of pearl barley were too chewy and gummy. Finally, we hit the jackpot: We stirred in some nutty little granules of bulgur when we added the tomatoes to the pot. Even after the long simmer, these precooked wheat kernels (which normally plump up after a quick soak in water) retained their shape, giving the chili the textural dimension that it had been missing.

Our recipe was progressing nicely, but it still didn't have the rich depth of flavor that could help turn what was a good chili into something great. We knew that the canned tomatoes were introducing some savory flavor, but we needed a more potent source, so we added a few dollops of *umami*-packed tomato paste as well as a few tablespoons of soy sauce.

But the flavor was still too one-dimensional. While developing a vegetable soup recently, we'd learned that umami boosters fall into two categories—glutamates and nucleotides—and that they have a synergistic effect when used together. Dried mushrooms are rich in nucleotides and could amplify the effect of the glutamate-rich soy sauce and tomatoes. Since we were already grinding the chile peppers, we simply tossed in some chopped, dried shiitake mushrooms at the same time, in order to take advantage of their flavor-boosting qualities without adding distinct chunks of mushroom. Sure enough, this batch was the meatiest yet. But could we take things even further? We reviewed a list of umami-rich foods and were surprised to see that walnuts contain more than twice as many glutamates as do tomatoes. From the failed pumpkin seed test we knew that we didn't want to add crunch, so for our next batch we toasted and ground some walnuts in a food processor and then stirred them into the chili along with the tomatoes and bulgur. In terms of savory depth, tasters unanimously deemed this batch the winner to date, and there were added bonuses: The fat from the nuts offered some richness, and the tannins in the skins contributed a slightly bitter note that balanced the other flavors.

Now our chili had complexity, but it still didn't have the lingering depth of a meat chili. We took a step back and thought about what meat really brings to chili. Its fat not only contributes flavor but also boosts that of the other ingredients and affects how you taste them. The flavor compounds in spices (chile peppers and cumin, in particular) are far more soluble in fat than in water, so a watery sauce dulls their flavor, whereas oils and fats allow them to bloom. What's more, fat coats the surface of your mouth, giving flavors staying power on the palate. We began slowly increasing the amount of vegetable oil that we were using to sauté the aromatics and found that ¼ cup brought the flavors into focus and allowed them to linger pleasantly instead of disappearing after a few seconds.

Everything was perfect but for one issue: When we took the chili out of the oven, we found that some of the fat had separated out, leaving a slick on top. A quick stir helped, but at the suggestion of our science editor we tried a more vigorous stir followed by a 20-minute rest. This led to a thick, velvety chili that you could almost stand a spoon in. Here's why: Stirring released starches from the beans and bulgur, which thickened the water in the sauce, allowing it to stabilize around the fat droplets and prevent the sauce from separating out again—in a sense creating a kind of emulsion.

There was nothing left to do but stir some cilantro into the chili for a touch of freshness and then let our tasters loose on the topping bar. Whether garnished with a little of everything or just a dollop of sour cream, each bite of chili was hearty and full-flavored—and no one missed the meat.

SCIENCE DESK

THE FLAVOR-BOOSTING FUNCTION OF FAT

Everyone knows that fat is a source of richness, but it wasn't until we enriched our chili with a little more fat than usual—in the form of ground walnuts and a judicious amount of vegetable oil—that the flavors in this meatless version really came through. This is because fat makes food stick to the tongue, prolonging the sensation of taste and leading to a dish that's ultimately more satisfying to eat.

Best Vegetarian Chili

SERVES 6 TO 8

We prefer to make this chili with whole dried chiles, but it can be prepared with jarred chili powder. If using chili powder, grind the shiitakes and oregano and add them to the pot with ¼ cup of chili powder in step 4. Pinto, black, red kidney, small red, cannellini, or navy beans can be used in this recipe, either a single variety or a combination of beans. For a spicier chili use both jalapeños. Serve the chili with diced avocado, chopped red onion, lime wedges, sour cream, and shredded Monterey Jack or cheddar cheese. You will need at least a 6-quart Dutch oven for this recipe.

    Salt
  1 pound (2½ cups) dried beans, rinsed and picked over
  2 dried ancho chiles
  2 dried New Mexican chiles
  ½ ounce shiitake mushrooms, chopped coarse
  4 teaspoons dried oregano
  ½ cup walnuts, toasted
  1 (28-ounce) can diced tomatoes, drained with juice reserved
  3 tablespoons tomato paste
1-2 jalapeño chiles, stemmed and chopped coarse
  6 garlic cloves, minced
  3 tablespoons soy sauce
  ¼ cup vegetable oil
  2 pounds onions, chopped fine
  1 tablespoon ground cumin
  7 cups water
  ⅔ cup medium-grain bulgur
  ¼ cup chopped fresh cilantro

1. Bring 4 quarts water, 3 tablespoons salt, and beans to boil in Dutch oven over high heat. Remove pot from heat, cover, and let stand 1 hour. Drain beans and rinse well.

2. Adjust oven rack to middle position and heat oven to 300 degrees. Arrange anchos and New Mexican chiles on rimmed baking sheet and toast until fragrant and puffed, about 8 minutes. Transfer to plate and let cool, about 5 minutes. Stem and seed toasted chiles. Working in batches, grind toasted chiles, shiitakes, and oregano in spice grinder or with mortar with pestle until finely ground.

ITALIAN VEGETABLE STEW

✔ **WHY THIS RECIPE WORKS:** Italy's ciambotta is a ratatouille-like stew of summery vegetables seasoned with herbs and olive oil. We wanted to avoid the sad fate of most recipes, which end in mushy vegetables drowning in a weak broth. In order to optimize the texture of the zucchini and peppers, we employed the dry heat of a skillet. To address the broth, we embraced eggplant's natural tendency to fall apart and cooked it until it completely assimilated into a thickened tomato-enriched sauce. Finally, we found that a traditional *pestata* (similar to pesto) of garlic and herbs provided the biggest flavor punch when added near the end of cooking.

SOUTHERN ITALY'S CIAMBOTTA IS A RATATOUILLE-LIKE stew that peasant farmers have been feasting on for centuries, and it's easy to understand why. When mopped up with a piece of crusty bread, this chock-full-of-veggies stew makes a substantial, stick-to-your-ribs meal—with nary a trace of meat. The key components—chunks of potatoes, bell peppers, onions, zucchini, eggplant, and tomatoes—cook with plenty of fruity olive oil until the vegetables soften and thicken the tomatoey broth.

To bring ciambotta into the American kitchen, we combed through Italian cookbooks and earmarked a range of recipes. Each one called on a Dutch oven or other high-sided pot, and many instructed to simply throw in the vegetables all at once and let the mixture simmer until the flavors had melded. While we appreciated the ease of the walk-away method, when we gave these recipes a try, the universal result was a muddy-tasting, mushy stew that lacked depth. What we'd had in mind was tender-firm vegetables sunken into a thick, luxurious sauce. Most of all, we wanted both elements to boast rich, complex flavor.

The first task: Concentrate the flavor of each vegetable. Our instinct was to roast them, reasoning that the dry heat of the oven would drive off excess moisture and develop flavorful browning, so we oiled and lightly salted

3. Process walnuts in food processor until finely ground, about 30 seconds. Transfer to bowl. Process drained tomatoes, tomato paste, jalapeño(s), garlic, and soy sauce in food processor until tomatoes are finely chopped, about 45 seconds, scraping down bowl as needed.

4. Heat oil in Dutch oven over medium-high heat until shimmering. Add onions and 1¼ teaspoons salt; cook, stirring occasionally until onions begin to brown, 8 to 10 minutes. Lower heat to medium, add ground chile mixture and cumin, and cook, stirring constantly, until fragrant, about 1 minute. Add rinsed beans and water and bring to boil. Cover pot, transfer to oven, and cook 45 minutes.

5. Remove pot from oven. Stir in bulgur, ground walnuts, tomato mixture and reserved tomato juice. Return to oven and cook until beans are fully tender, about 2 hours.

6. Remove pot from oven, stir chili well, and let stand, uncovered, for 20 minutes. Stir in cilantro and serve. (Chili can be made up to 3 days in advance.)

ITALIAN VEGETABLE STEW

red bell pepper, eggplant, zucchini, and potato (Yukon Gold for now) pieces; placed them on separate baking sheets; and got the oven going. A long, slow roast yielded slightly dehydrated, wonderfully caramelized results, but since we could roast only two sheets at a time, the process was taking 50 minutes per batch—and that was before we'd even gotten to making the broth.

So we took a 180-degree turn, limiting ourselves to the stovetop and Dutch oven. We sautéed the veggies in individual batches over high heat before adding a can of whole tomatoes that we'd roughly chopped and a couple of cups of water that would form the base of the broth. But while cooking each vegetable separately helped them develop better color and flavor, the vessel's high sides still trapped steam and prevented them from burning off enough moisture—particularly the waterlogged eggplant, peppers, and zucchini. But this was only the beginning of our problems: The eggplant had soaked up a good bit of the cooking oil and tasted greasy, the potatoes were a tad underdone and weren't absorbing enough flavor from the stew, the zucchini and peppers were too mushy, and the broth was woefully thin.

We decided to tackle the eggplant first, calling on our favorite pretreatment to help curb its tendency to soak up oil: salting and microwaving the eggplant before sautéing it, which collapses its spongy flesh and limits its capacity to absorb oil. But while those steps kept the greasiness issue at bay, they also created another glitch: The parcooked eggplant started to disintegrate as it simmered in the stew, and the mushy result was unacceptable.

Or was it? It dawned on us that the eggplant's finicky texture might be a perfect solution to our too-thin broth. Deciding to embrace its mushiness, we made another batch in which we treated the eggplant, sautéed it, and allowed it to simmer in the broth until it had broken down completely. The results were a revelation: Our previously thin broth had transformed into a full-bodied, silky sauce. We also incorporated one more step to build up the stew's flavor: After batch-sautéing the vegetables and bringing them back together in the Dutch oven, we pushed them to the edges of the pan to form a clearing and browned a healthy spoonful of tomato paste. This left a valuable fond (flavorful browned bits) on the bottom of the pot, which we then deglazed with the canned tomatoes and water. Flavorful, full-bodied sauce? Check. Now we were getting somewhere.

However, we still had the mushy peppers and zucchini to deal with. If we wanted to preserve their crisp-tender bite, we'd have to limit how long they cooked. We also wanted to increase their flavor. The solution: Get them out of the high-sided Dutch oven and sauté them on their own in a skillet, whose shallow sides would allow the vegetables' exuded water to quickly evaporate. We gave it a try while the rest of the stew simmered, browning the peppers and zucchini together for about 10 minutes and then adding them to the Dutch oven, off the heat, once the eggplant had broken down completely. After letting the stew sit for 20 minutes to meld the flavors, we called our colleagues for a tasting. When they applauded the firm-tender bite of the skillet-sautéed vegetables, we knew that adding another pan to the recipe had been well worth it.

The last item on our to-do list was the potatoes. We'd assumed that the Yukon Golds' moderately waxy, moderately starchy flesh would resist breaking down in the stew, and it did—to a fault. In fact, the potatoes were not only too firm but also strangely bland. When we did a little research, we learned that acid from the tomato broth was actually retarding the breakdown of the potatoes' cell walls, preventing their flesh from softening and soaking up flavor from the broth. The obvious solution: Start with the least waxy (read: most delicate) potato available—the russet. Sure enough, the texture of the potatoes in the next batch was markedly better. Though these floury spuds typically crumble apart when cooked, the acid from the tomato broth ensured that they held their shape just enough but still absorbed some of the savory broth.

Though the flavor of our ciambotta was rich and round, we still felt that it could benefit from an additional burst of flavor and immediately thought of a *pestata*. While not a traditional player in ciambotta recipes, this pestolike garnish features a pulverized mixture of garlic, olive oil, hot pepper flakes, and fresh herbs, and is often incorporated into soups and stews to add brightness. For our version, we processed heady oregano and basil, six cloves of garlic, a couple of tablespoons of extra-virgin olive oil, and a touch of hot red pepper flakes in a food processor until the mixture was finely ground.

Cooking the pestata as a first step in the recipe (as is sometimes done in Italy) resulted in long exposure to heat that muted much of its punch. Instead, we preserved its potency by adding the paste to the zucchini and peppers during the final minutes of cooking. Presto. As a finishing touch, we stirred loads of shredded fresh basil into the stew just before serving. The herb's fragrance intensified when it was incorporated into the hot stew, adding a powerful blast of summery flavor. At last, we had a ciambotta that was satisfying, rich, and complex.

NOTES FROM THE TEST KITCHEN

WHAT'S A PESTATA?
A relative of pesto, pistou, picada, and gremolata, pestata is a potent garlic, herb, and olive oil puree. When stirred into the ciambotta toward the end of cooking, its grassy bite freshens the rich, earthy flavors of the stew.

Our pestata, made with olive oil, fresh oregano and basil, garlic, and red pepper flakes brightens the stew.

Italian Vegetable Stew (Ciambotta)
SERVES 6 TO 8

Serve this hearty vegetable stew with crusty bread.

PESTATA
- ⅓ cup chopped fresh basil
- ⅓ cup fresh oregano leaves
- 6 garlic cloves, minced
- 2 tablespoons extra-virgin olive oil
- ¼ teaspoon red pepper flakes

STEW
- 12 ounces eggplant, peeled and cut into ½-inch pieces
  Salt
- ¼ cup extra-virgin olive oil
- 1 large onion, chopped
- 1 pound russet potatoes, peeled and cut into ½-inch pieces
- 2 tablespoons tomato paste
- 2¼ cups water
- 1 (28-ounce) can whole peeled tomatoes, drained with juice reserved, chopped coarse
- 2 zucchini (8 ounces each), halved lengthwise, seeded, and cut into ½-inch pieces
- 2 red or yellow bell peppers, stemmed, seeded, and cut into ½-inch pieces
- 1 cup shredded fresh basil

1. FOR THE PESTATA: Process all ingredients in food processor until finely ground, about 1 minute, scraping down sides as needed. Set aside.

2. FOR THE STEW: Toss eggplant with 1½ teaspoons salt in bowl. Line surface of large plate with double layer of coffee filters and lightly spray with vegetable oil spray. Spread eggplant in even layer over coffee filters. Microwave eggplant, uncovered, until dry to touch and slightly shriveled, 8 to 12 minutes, tossing once halfway through to ensure that eggplant cooks evenly.

3. Heat 2 tablespoons oil in Dutch oven over high heat until shimmering. Add eggplant, onion, and potatoes; cook, stirring frequently, until eggplant browns and surface of potatoes becomes translucent, about 2 minutes. Push vegetables to sides of pot; add 1 tablespoon oil and tomato paste to clearing. Cook paste, stirring frequently, until brown fond develops on bottom of pot, about 2 minutes. Add 2 cups water and chopped tomatoes and juice, scraping up any browned bits, and bring to boil. Reduce heat to medium, cover, and gently simmer until eggplant is completely broken down and potatoes are tender, 20 to 25 minutes.

4. Meanwhile, heat remaining 1 tablespoon oil in 12-inch skillet over high heat until smoking. Add zucchini, bell peppers, and ½ teaspoon salt; cook, stirring occasionally, until vegetables are browned and tender, 10 to 12 minutes. Push vegetables to sides of skillet; add pestata and cook until fragrant, about 1 minute. Stir pestata into vegetables and transfer vegetables to bowl. Add remaining ¼ cup water to skillet off heat, scraping up browned bits.

5. Remove Dutch oven from heat and stir reserved vegetables and water from skillet into vegetables in Dutch oven. Cover pot and let stand for 20 minutes to allow flavors to meld. Stir in basil and season with salt to taste; serve.

NOTES FROM THE TEST KITCHEN

COAXING BIG FLAVOR OUT OF WATERY PRODUCE

BUILD STEW BASE
To deepen their flavors, cook the potatoes, onion, and eggplant (parcooked so it breaks down to thicken stew) in a Dutch oven.

ENHANCE FOND
Sautéing the tomato paste builds up a savory crust, which we deglaze with water and canned tomatoes to boost the stew's flavor.

SAUTÉ WATERY VEGGIES IN SKILLET
Browning the peppers and zucchini separately in a shallow pan cooks off the moisture and deepens their flavor.

ADD PESTATA
Clear the center of pan, add the pestata, and briefly sauté. The herb-garlic mixture will add a fresh burst of flavor.

COMBINE AND WAIT
After marrying the two batches of vegetables, let the stew stand for 20 minutes to allow the flavors to meld.

RATING VEGETABLE PEELERS

A good peeler should be fast and smooth, and should handle bumps and curves with ease and without clogging or losing its edge. And when the work is done, your hand shouldn't feel worse for the wear. We recently gathered 10 peelers and put them to work, looking to find a comfortable peeler that would make quick work of both lightweight peeling tasks like potatoes, carrots, and apples and more challenging terrain, such as celery root and ginger. We also ran precision tests by using the peelers on blocks of Parmesan and chocolate. For the most part, vegetable peelers fall into two main categories: "straight" peelers, whose blade extends directly out from the handle, and Y-shaped peelers, which look like wishbones, with a blade running perpendicular to the handle. Two models quickly rose to the top of the heap—one was a traditional peeler, while the other a Y-shaped model. In the end, the latter won out, though both are stellar choices. Brands are listed in order of preference. See AmericasTestKitchen.com for updates and further information on this testing.

HIGHLY RECOMMENDED

KUHN RIKON Original Swiss Peeler
MODEL: 2212   **PRICE:** $3.50   **BLADE:** Carbon steel   **WEIGHT:** ⅜ oz   **AVG. PEEL THICKNESS:** 0.90 mm   **PERFORMANCE** ★★★   **EASE OF USE** ★★★   **DESIGN** ★★★
COMMENTS: Don't be fooled by its featherweight design and cheap price tag. This Y-shaped peeler easily tackled every task, thanks to a razor-sharp blade and a ridged guide, which ensured a smooth ride with minimal surface drag.

MESSERMEISTER Pro-Touch Fine Edge Swivel Peeler
MODEL: 800–58   **PRICE:** $10   **BLADE:** Stainless steel   **WEIGHT:** 1½ oz   **AVG. PEEL THICKNESS:** 0.82 mm   **PERFORMANCE** ★★★   **EASE OF USE** ★★★   **DESIGN** ★★★
COMMENTS: A stellar choice for those who prefer a straight peeler. Lightweight, sharp, and comfortable, this model rivaled the winner, gliding over fruits and vegetables and producing almost transparent peels. Its high arch meant no clogging.

RECOMMENDED

WMF Profi Plus Horizontal Vegetable Peeler
MODEL: 1872616030   **PRICE:** $18   **BLADE:** Stainless steel   **WEIGHT:** 3¼ oz   **AVG. PEEL THICKNESS:** 1.08 mm   **PERFORMANCE** ★★½   **EASE OF USE** ★★★   **DESIGN** ★★★
COMMENTS: The other model with a ridged guide, this sturdy, sharp—and most expensive—peeler glided over everything from carrots to rough-textured celery root, though its peels were thicker than some.

MESSERMEISTER Culinary Instruments Swivel Peeler, Y Shape
MODEL: 900–189   **PRICE:** $7.50   **BLADE:** Stainless steel   **WEIGHT:** 1 oz   **AVG. PEEL THICKNESS:** 1.11 mm   **PERFORMANCE** ★★½   **EASE OF USE** ★★   **DESIGN** ★★
COMMENTS: Though it quickly removed wide swaths of peel and off-loaded waste easily, this Y peeler was outshone by its sibling when it skinned a little too deep. Its broad blade was a bit tricky to maneuver around smaller potatoes and curvy, bumpy celery root.

RECOMMENDED (cont.)

SWISSMAR Swiss Classic Peeler, Scalpel Blade
MODEL: 00447   **PRICE:** $10.17   **BLADE:** Stainless steel   **WEIGHT:** ⅝ oz   **AVG. PEEL THICKNESS:** 1.05 mm   **PERFORMANCE** ★★½   **EASE OF USE** ★★   **DESIGN** ★★
COMMENTS: Sharp and maneuverable, this lightweight peeler bit through the toughest peels with ease but also stripped away a good bit of flesh. A closer look revealed why: Its blade has a curved belly that bites deeply, creating more waste.

RECOMMENDED WITH RESERVATIONS

RACHAEL RAY TOOLS 3-in-1 Veg-a-Peel Vegetable Peeler/Brush
MODEL: 55250   **PRICE:** $9.06   **BLADE:** Stainless steel   **WEIGHT:** 1⅜ oz   **AVG. PEEL THICKNESS:** 1.05 mm   **PERFORMANCE** ★★½   **EASE OF USE** ★★   **DESIGN** ★½
COMMENTS: Peels were thin and waste was minimal; in fact, this model often required a few extra strokes. We might have liked this peeler's attached vegetable brush if it didn't mean that our thumb was prone to gripping the blade on the other side as we scrubbed—ouch.

OXO Good Grips Swivel Peeler
MODEL: 20081   **PRICE:** $7.99   **BLADE:** Stainless steel   **WEIGHT:** 2⅜ oz   **AVG. PEEL THICKNESS:** 0.71 mm   **PERFORMANCE** ★★   **EASE OF USE** ★½   **DESIGN** ★★
COMMENTS: This model produced the thinnest peels and the least amount of waste, but we often needed to go over patches again to finish the job. Many testers found the thick handle fatiguing and clunky. Its low bridge clogged frequently.

NOT RECOMMENDED

KYOCERA Ceramic Y Peeler
MODEL: CP-10N   **PRICE:** $8.12   **BLADE:** Ceramic   **WEIGHT:** 1 oz   **AVG. PEEL THICKNESS:** 1.05 mm   **PERFORMANCE** ★½   **EASE OF USE** ★   **DESIGN** ★★
COMMENTS: Potatoes and carrots were no problem, but the high bridge provided less leverage and control. This peeler struggled with celery root and utterly failed to skin butternut squash. Its ceramic blade was noticeably duller after testing.

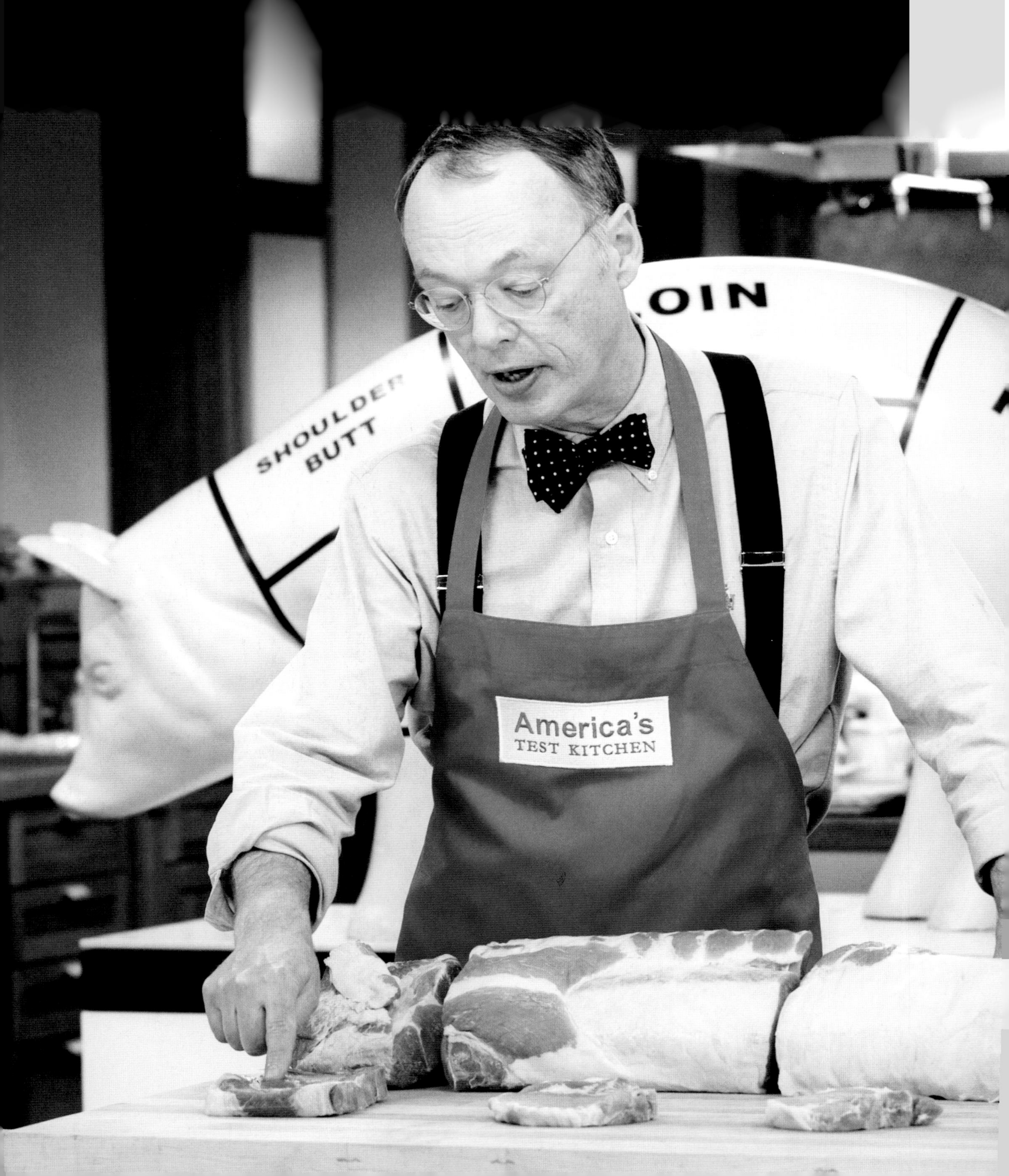
LOIN
SHOULDER
BUTT
America's
TEST KITCHEN

Pork Chops
AND LENTIL SALAD

CHAPTER 10

THE RECIPES

Braised pork chops can't be made with just any chop. Chris explains the differences among pork chops and why it matters in our recipe.

INEVITABLY WHEN WE THINK OF COOKING PORK CHOPS WE THINK OF two approaches: simple pan-seared chops for weeknight cooking and, for more special occasions, chops stuffed with a savory filling. But then we heard about braising pork chops, and the idea intrigued us. We envisioned tender meat in an unctuous sauce cooked down from the braising liquid and, unlike many other braises, no carving necessary—simply plop a chop onto a plate and you're done. But in our testing, it became apparent that not all chops take well to braising. Our first order of business: Find the variety of pork chop that would become tender and juicy when braised, not dry and stringy. Next, we'd need to sort out the braising liquid. We wanted a flavorful pan sauce as our end result, one that cut some of the richness of the pork and clung to the meat—weak, watery sauces need not apply.

Lentils make a terrific partner to pork chops. And lentil salads offer even more versatility, because they can be served on their own as a light meal. For our salads, we first wanted to determine the best cooking method for lentils, as they can easily become blown-out and mushy or remain undercooked and chewy. When cooked right, lentils boast a buttery, but still earthy, flavor. Once we had a cooking method down, we could concentrate on choosing how to dress our lentils and which vegetables and other supporting players, such as nuts and cheeses, would complement this underappreciated legume. Pork chops and lentils, here we come.

BRAISED PORK CHOPS

![checkmark] **WHY THIS RECIPE WORKS:** When braising pork chops, we found it's important to avoid lean loin chops that have a tendency to dry out when even slightly overcooked. For moist, tender chops, we began with blade chops, which, like other braising cuts, have a larger amount of fat and connective tissue. We trimmed the chops of excess fat and connective tissue to prevent buckling when cooked, and used those trimmings to build a rich and flavorful braising liquid. When the chops were done braising, we used the flavorful liquid as the foundation for a quick and tasty sauce.

WHEN WE THINK OF PORK CHOPS, WE THINK OF A simple, no-frills cut that we can just slap into a hot skillet and have on the table in minutes. But lately we've been hearing people talk about braised pork chops. The more we considered this option, the better it seemed. Not only did the slow, gentle approach of braising promise flavorful, tender chops, but it also meant that we'd end up with a rich, glossy sauce. This, we thought, would take pork chops to a whole new level. We were also attracted to the idea of braising smaller cuts like chops in place of the more typical roast—we wouldn't have to trim intramuscular fat or tough silverskin from the roast and retie it with twine before it went into the pan, nor would there be any carving to do after cooking. Sounded good to us.

But when we went into the test kitchen to try out a few recipes, none lived up to their promise. The meat was dry and bland, swimming in liquid that lacked both complexity and the silky body of a long, gently simmered sauce. Clearly we had some work to do.

Before we started fiddling with the cooking method, we had an important decision to make at the supermarket: exactly which chops to buy. Butchers cut four different chops: blade, rib, center cut, and sirloin. We knew that the muscle and fat makeup of the four chops varies considerably and that the only way to find the best cut for the job would be to test them all. We brined each set of chops (to season the chops and ensure juiciness),

patted them dry, and seared them in a Dutch oven just long enough to develop some flavorful browning on the meat and the fond on the bottom of the pot—a crucial step for creating a richly flavored sauce. Then we browned the aromatics and deglazed the pot with red wine, which we hoped would temper the meaty richness of the chops. Finally, we poured in some chicken broth, covered the pot, and pushed it into a low (275-degree) oven to simmer gently for about 90 minutes.

When we sliced the meat and called our tasters, the results were unanimous: All but one of the chops had cooked up stringy and bland, officially disqualifying the center-cut, rib, and sirloin contenders from the running. But the blade chops were promising; they contained a good bit of marbling and connective tissue, both of which broke down during cooking, lending the meat flavor and also helping to preserve its juiciness. The drawback was that the chops buckled considerably during searing and, as a result, didn't take on much browning or supply much fond to the bottom of the pot. Without that foundation of flavor, the sauce was lackluster and thin, and the wine's contribution one-dimensional and a bit harsh. Blade chops were also a little harder to find in the store, but we decided they were worth seeking out. All in all, this was a good start.

We seared another batch to get a closer look at the buckling problem and watched as the chops' dense rim of connective tissues immediately began to contract like a rubber band. The chops' contortions were keeping them from browning evenly, and the lack of fond on the bottom of the vessel also explained why the sauce tasted so anemic. For the sake of both aesthetics and flavor, we had to figure out a way to keep the chops flat. What would happen if we trimmed away the offending portion of connective tissue before searing?

We placed a new batch of trimmed chops in the hot Dutch oven, where they stayed flat and took on an even layer of color. Everything looked great until we took a peek at the bottom of the pot. Where we expected to find a thick, crusty layer of fond we found a few faint patches of browning—hardly the makings of a flavorful sauce. Where had all the fond gone? We realized that the real ingredient for fond was the pile of fatty scraps we were about to pitch into the trash.

RED WINE–BRAISED PORK CHOPS

TRIM YOUR CHOPS

The band of fatty connective tissue and shoulder meat along the outer edge of blade chops contributes body and flavor to the braise—but it also causes the chops to buckle. To cut out the structural issues without sacrificing flavor, we trim away the band, chop it up, and save the pieces for searing.

ON THE CHOPPING BLOCK
Trim off the swath of fatty meat and any cartilage running along the edge of the chop. Cut the scraps into 1-inch pieces.

That gave us an idea: Rather than toss the fatty trimmings, we chopped them into 1-inch pieces and seared them to generate fond. In less than 10 minutes, we had the most substantial layer of browning yet, thanks to the increased surface area of the smaller pieces. In fact, the fond was so impressive that we wondered if we needed to sear the chops themselves. One side-by-side test gave us the answer: The braise made with unseared chops was every bit as meaty as that made with the seared batch. To take full advantage of their flavor, we left the chunks in the pot during braising, knowing that their rich fat would only add to the porky flavor and unctuousness of the sauce.

As an added bonus, the chopped-up scraps served a structural function as well. When we nestled the chops on top of the fatty chunks, they rested well above the liquid line. When we pulled this batch out of the oven roughly 90 minutes later, not only was the sauce richer and more flavorful, but the chops were noticeably juicier than they had been when they'd cooked more thoroughly submerged in the liquid.

Our science editor had an explanation: The secret to braising is ensuring that the temperature of the meat hovers for as long as possible between 160 and 180 degrees. In that range, the meat's collagen converts into gelatin, which holds on to the meat's juices. Too little heat and the meat won't produce enough gelatin; too much and

its muscle fibers will wring out moisture before the gelatin can soak it up. In this case, the combination of air and liquid was holding the less-submerged chops at a temperature that allowed them to produce a good bit of gelatin and retain their moisture. And to ensure that they held on to every bit of their flavorful juices, we rested the braised chops for 30 minutes before slicing into them, which gave the juices ample time to redistribute throughout the meat.

Thanks to the trimmings and staple aromatics like garlic, thyme, and bay leaves, the braising liquid now had decent flavor, but a few tasters remarked that it lacked body, depth, and even some brightness. Fixing the first problem was easy; we simply strained and defatted the liquid and reduced it for about 5 minutes. A pat of butter whisked in off the heat added silkiness and a bit more viscosity.

As for the latter critiques, we tried finishing the pot with a splash of wine, but everyone agreed that only furthered the harshness we'd detected early on. To take the edge off, we went in search of something sweeter in the pantry and came across a bottle of ruby port. Replacing some of the red wine with the fortified stuff went a long way but also flattened the flavor a bit. We weren't crazy about upping the booziness, so instead we added a touch of red wine vinegar along with the wines, the bright acidity of which brought the sweet-tart balance into equilibrium. We also tossed in a knob of crushed fresh ginger and a dash of allspice, both of which lent this latest batch a rich, spicy aroma.

Just before serving, we added a final splash of vinegar and a handful of chopped parsley, spooned the liquid over the tender, juicy chops, and knew we had finally done right by this classic technique.

Red Wine–Braised Pork Chops
SERVES 4

Look for chops with a small eye and a large amount of marbling, as these are the best suited to braising. The pork scraps can be removed when straining the sauce in step 4 and served alongside the chops. (They taste great.)

    Salt and pepper
4 (10- to 12-ounce) bone-in pork blade chops, 1 inch thick
2 teaspoons vegetable oil
2 onions, halved and sliced thin
5 sprigs fresh thyme plus ¼ teaspoon minced
2 garlic cloves, peeled
2 bay leaves
1 (½-inch) piece ginger, peeled and crushed
⅛ teaspoon ground allspice
½ cup red wine
¼ cup ruby port
2 tablespoons plus ½ teaspoon red wine vinegar
1 cup low-sodium chicken broth
2 tablespoons unsalted butter
1 tablespoon minced fresh parsley

1. Dissolve 3 tablespoons salt in 1½ quarts cold water in large container. Submerge chops in brine, cover, and refrigerate for 30 minutes or up to 1 hour.

2. Adjust oven rack to lower-middle position and heat oven to 275 degrees. Remove chops from brine and pat dry with paper towels. Trim off meat cap and any fat and cartilage opposite rib bones. Cut trimmings into 1-inch pieces. Heat oil in Dutch oven over medium-high heat until shimmering. Add trimmings and brown on all sides, 6 to 9 minutes.

3. Reduce heat to medium and add onions, thyme sprigs, garlic, bay leaves, ginger, and allspice. Cook, stirring occasionally, until onions are golden brown, 5 to 10 minutes. Stir in wine, port, and 2 tablespoons vinegar and cook until reduced to thin syrup, 5 to 7 minutes. Add chicken broth, spread onions and pork scraps into even layer, and bring to simmer. Arrange pork chops on top of pork scraps and onions.

4. Cover, transfer to oven, and cook until meat is tender, 1¼ to 1½ hours. Remove from oven and let chops rest in pot, covered, for 30 minutes. Transfer chops to serving platter and tent with aluminum foil. Strain braising liquid through fine-mesh strainer; discard solids. Transfer braising liquid to fat separator and let stand for 5 minutes.

5. Wipe out now-empty pot with wad of paper towels. Return defatted braising liquid to pot and cook over medium-high heat until reduced to 1 cup, 3 to 7 minutes. Off heat, whisk in butter, minced thyme, and remaining ½ teaspoon vinegar. Season with salt and pepper to taste. Pour sauce over chops, sprinkle with parsley, and serve.

LENTIL SALAD

✔ **WHY THIS RECIPE WORKS:** The most important step in making a lentil salad is perfecting the cooking of the lentils so they maintain their shape and firm-tender bite. It turns out there are two key steps. The first is to brine the lentils in warm salt water. With brining, the lentils' skins soften, which leads to fewer blowouts. The second step is to cook the lentils in the oven, which heats them gently and uniformly. Once we had perfectly cooked lentils, all we had left to do was to pair the earthy beans with a tart vinaigrette and boldly flavored mix-ins.

LENTILS MAY NOT GET POINTS FOR GLAMOUR, BUT when properly cooked and dressed up in a salad with a bright vinaigrette and herbs, nuts, and cheeses, the legumes' earthy, almost meaty depth and firm-tender bite make a satisfying side dish for almost any meal.

The trouble is, perfectly cooked lentils are never a given. Too often, either their skins burst and their flesh disintegrates into unappealing starchy mush, or they don't cook through completely and retain chewy skins and hard, crunchy cores. Before we started adding accoutrements, we had to nail down a reliable way to produce tender, buttery lentils with soft, unbroken skins. And because the tiny, shape-retaining French green lentils we favor can be hard to come by, we were also determined to develop an approach that would yield perfect results with whatever lentil variety our supermarket had to offer.

Fortunately, the test kitchen's previous work with bean cookery gave us a good idea for how to keep the lentil skins intact. We've discovered that, odd as it may sound, brining beans overnight softens their outer shells and makes them less likely to burst. The explanation is twofold: As the beans soak, the sodium ions from the salt replace some of the calcium and magnesium ions in the skins. By replacing some of the mineral ions, the sodium ions weaken the pectin in the skins, allowing more water to penetrate and leading to a more pliable, forgiving texture. But with beans it takes an overnight soak for the brining to be most effective. Fortunately, due to the lentils' smaller, flatter shape, we found that

LENTIL SALAD WITH OLIVES, MINT, AND FETA

just a few hours of brining dramatically cuts down on blowouts. We also had one more idea for hastening the process: Since heat speeds up all chemical reactions, we managed to reduce the brining time to just an hour by using warm water in the salt solution.

To further reduce blowouts, we tried to cook the lentils as gently as possible. But we could see that even our stovetop's low setting still agitated the lentils too vigorously. We decided to try the oven, hoping that its indirect heat would get the job done more gently—and it did. And while the oven did increase the cooking time from less than 30 minutes to nearly an hour, the results were worth the wait: Virtually all of the lentil skins were tender yet intact.

Despite the lentils' soft, perfect skins, their insides tended to be mushy, not creamy. It occurred to us that we could try another simple trick with salt: adding it to the cooking water. Many bean recipes (including ours) shy away from adding salt during cooking because it produces firm, often gritty interiors. Here's why: While a brine's impact is mainly confined to the skin, heat (from cooking) affects the inside of the bean, causing sodium ions to move to the interior, where they slow the starches' ability to absorb water. But a firmed-up texture was exactly what our mushy lentils needed. Could a problem for beans prove to be the solution for lentils? Sure enough, when we added ½ teaspoon of salt to the cooking water, the lentils went from mushy to firm yet creamy.

We had just two remaining tasks to tackle: enriching the flavor of the lentils and creating a few salad variations.

Swapping some of the cooking water for chicken broth solved the first problem, and tossing the lentils with tart vinaigrette and bold mix-ins—feta, olives, and mint in one salad; spinach, walnuts, and Parmesan in another; hazelnuts and goat cheese in another; and carrots and cilantro in a final version—brightened and balanced their rich, earthy flavor.

Lentil Salad with Olives, Mint, and Feta
SERVES 4 TO 6

French green lentils, or *lentilles du Puy,* are our preferred choice for this recipe, but it works with any type of lentil except red or yellow. Brining helps keep the lentils intact, but if you don't have time, they'll still taste good without it. The salad can be served warm or at room temperature.

- 1 **cup lentils, picked over and rinsed**
  Salt and pepper
- 6 **cups water**
- 2 **cups low-sodium chicken broth**
- 5 **garlic cloves, lightly crushed and peeled**
- 1 **bay leaf**
- 5 **tablespoons extra-virgin olive oil**
- 3 **tablespoons white wine vinegar**
- ½ **cup pitted kalamata olives, chopped coarse**
- ½ **cup minced fresh mint**
- 1 **large shallot, minced**
- 1 **ounce feta cheese, crumbled (¼ cup)**

ALL ABOUT LENTILS

Lentils come in numerous varieties, each of which has a distinct appearance, flavor, and texture. We prepared different types using the slow-cooking method developed for our lentil salad recipes and asked our tasters to evaluate them.

TYPE	APPEARANCE	FLAVOR	TEXTURE	APPLICATION
French green	Small, dark green	Earthy, slightly starchy taste	Firm, resilient texture that won't fall apart even when long-cooked	Salads and side dishes
Black or "beluga"	Tiny, jet black	Robust, meaty taste	Firm, creamy texture that holds shape well	Salads and side dishes
Green, brown	Medium, pale green or brown	Vegetal, mineral taste	Relatively firm texture when cooked	Salads, soups, and side dishes
Red	Small, orange	Delicate taste with floral hints	Disintegrate completely when cooked	Soups, Indian dal
Yellow	Medium, pale golden	Bland, starchy taste	Disintegrate completely when cooked	Soups, Indian dal

1. Place lentils and 1 teaspoon salt in bowl. Cover with 4 cups warm water (about 110 degrees) and soak for 1 hour. Drain well. (Drained lentils can be refrigerated for up to 2 days before cooking.)

2. Adjust oven rack to middle position and heat oven to 325 degrees. Combine drained lentils, 2 cups water, broth, garlic, bay leaf, and ½ teaspoon salt in ovenproof medium saucepan. Cover and bake until lentils are tender but remain intact, 40 minutes to 1 hour. Meanwhile, whisk oil and vinegar together in large bowl.

3. Drain lentils well; remove and discard garlic and bay leaf. Add drained lentils, olives, mint, and shallot to dressing and toss to combine. Season with salt and pepper to taste. Transfer to serving dish, sprinkle with feta, and serve.

VARIATIONS

Lentil Salad with Spinach, Walnuts, and Parmesan Cheese

Substitute sherry vinegar for white wine vinegar. Place 4 ounces baby spinach and 2 tablespoons water in bowl. Cover and microwave until spinach is wilted and volume is halved, 3 to 4 minutes. Remove bowl from microwave and keep covered for 1 minute. Transfer spinach to colander; gently press to release liquid. Transfer spinach to cutting board and chop coarse. Return to colander and press again. Substitute chopped spinach for olives and mint and ¾ cup coarsely grated Parmesan cheese for feta. Sprinkle with ⅓ cup coarsely chopped toasted walnuts before serving.

Lentil Salad with Hazelnuts and Goat Cheese

Substitute red wine vinegar for white wine vinegar and add 2 teaspoons Dijon mustard to dressing in step 2. Omit olives and substitute ¼ cup chopped parsley for mint. Substitute ½ cup crumbled goat cheese for feta and sprinkle with ⅓ cup coarsely chopped toasted hazelnuts before serving.

Lentil Salad with Carrots and Cilantro

Substitute lemon juice for white wine vinegar. Toss 2 carrots, peeled and cut into 2-inch-long matchsticks, with 1 teaspoon ground cumin, ½ teaspoon ground cinnamon, and ⅛ teaspoon cayenne pepper in bowl. Cover and microwave until carrots are tender but still crisp, 2 to 4 minutes. Substitute carrots for olives and ¼ cup minced fresh cilantro for mint. Omit shallot and feta.

Two Ways WITH FISH

Read on to find out what an onion half has to do with olive oil–poached fish.

WE ADMIT THAT WHEN IT COMES TO COOKING FISH, WE OFTEN RESORT to simply pan-searing fillets or popping them in the oven with some buttery bread crumbs sprinkled on top. It's high time we expanded our horizons—with poached fish and salmon cakes.

Poaching fish is typically a method for cooking with less fat. But that's if you're poaching in the usual liquid—water, broth, or wine or some combination. What about olive oil? Yes, swanky restaurants have been oil-poaching fish, with great results. Rather than turning the fish greasy, the oil imparts a lush moistness to the fillets and the cooking oil can then be used to make a sauce. The downside? The fillets are submerged in the oil, which means you need to use an awful lot of it. Our goal—turn this restaurant technique home-friendly, beginning with scaling back that oil.

We have a fondness for old-fashioned fish cakes, which were originally designed as a way to use up leftover fish and potatoes. On the other end of the spectrum are more elegant, restaurant-style fish cakes, which are hardly made from recycled seconds, but from fresh fish. But honestly, chefs can go overboard with seasonings (and sauces), taking the focus off the fish. We imagined a fish cake that fell somewhere in between. Easy-to-make cakes made with moist, rich salmon; more fish than filler, modestly seasoned, and with a crisp bread-crumb coating. Let's head into the test kitchen to find out how to get there.

POACHED FISH FILLETS WITH CRISPY ARTICHOKES AND SHERRY-TOMATO VINAIGRETTE

POACHED FISH FILLETS WITH SHERRY-TOMATO VINAIGRETTE

✓ **WHY THIS RECIPE WORKS:** This restaurant-style dish requires a potful of pricey olive oil and promises super-moist, delicately cooked fish. Using a small skillet and flipping the fish halfway through cooking allowed us to cut back to ¾ cup of oil, which we then used to crisp flavorful garnishes. We then blended the flavorful oil into a creamy vinaigrette.

IF YOUR EXPERIENCE WITH POACHED FISH IS LIMITED to the lean, bland fillets you might be served at a wedding or a weight-loss spa, a poaching technique popular at high-end restaurants will permanently change your perception. Submerging fish in liquid and gently cooking it at below-simmering temperatures—anywhere from 130 to 180 degrees—renders the delicate flesh silky and supple. But some chefs give this technique a twist that elevates their poached fish above any other: Rather than the usual lean bath of water, wine, or broth, the poaching liquid is olive oil.

On paper, cooking delicate fish fillets in a pot of fat sounded like a recipe for greasy disaster, but after trying it at a restaurant we had to admit the results were stunning—lighter, moister, and more fragrant than any traditionally poached fish—and they explained why this technique has become so popular. Another plus: The flavor-infused poaching oil can be whirled into a rich, glossy emulsion and drizzled over the fish as a sauce. The dish would make elegant fare, provided we could get around one obvious challenge: the cost—and mess—of heating up a large amount of olive oil for just one meal. We would have to figure out how to scale the oil way back.

Since the oil would never get hot enough to crisp the skin, we went with skinless fillets. We settled on cod for its firm, meaty flesh and clean flavor. As for the amount of oil, we reasoned that the smaller the surface area of the cooking vessel, the deeper the liquid would pool, so we swapped our trusty 12-inch nonstick skillet for its 10-inch sibling. Unfortunately, this setup still demanded about 1½ cups of oil to cover the four 6-ounce fillets. Our only other idea was to displace some of the oil by placing half an onion in the skillet and arranging the fillets around it—a trick that helped but got us down only another ¼ cup. Clearly, we needed a more drastic solution.

That's when we started to wonder if completely immersing the fillets in oil was necessary. The alternative—pouring enough oil into the pan to come roughly halfway up the sides of the fish (about ¾ cup)—would mean flipping the fish partway through poaching to ensure that it cooked through. But that seemed a small price to pay for significantly reducing the amount of expensive oil. We gave it a shot, basting the exposed half of each fillet with a few spoonfuls of oil (to prevent evaporation), popping a lid on the pan, and placing the skillet over the lowest burner setting. The good news was that the method worked; the fillets were supremely moist and tender and not at all oily.

The bad news was that it was fussy. With relatively little oil in the pan, the temperature spiked quickly and required that we constantly fiddle with the burner knob to keep the oil in our target range (140 to 150 degrees), which would slowly bring our fish to an ideal internal temperature of 130 degrees with little risk of overcooking. What we needed was a steadier, less direct heat source—and for that we turned to the oven.

We figured that we could simply bring the oil to 140 degrees on the stovetop, add the fish, then transfer the skillet into a low oven. But the oil temperature immediately plummeted when we added the still-cold fillets, and the temperature recovery time in the oven was slow. We had an idea: We'd heat the oil on the stovetop to well above our target temperature then rely on the oven's even heat to keep it in the poaching sweet spot.

After a slew of tests, we hit upon a winning combination: Heat the oil to 180 degrees, nestle in the fillets (each sprinkled with kosher salt), and set the pan in a 250-degree oven. The oil temperature recovered within 15 minutes, by which point the lower half of the fish was cooked. We flipped the fillets, replaced the lid, and returned the pan to the oven. This batch emerged incredibly moist and velvety and, thanks to our oven method,

the process was now largely hands-off. What we had was good—but we wanted to make it even better.

We often salt meat and allow it to rest before cooking, both to enhance juiciness and to bring seasoning deep into the interior. Why not try this with fish? For our next round of testing, we salted the fillets about 20 minutes before cooking. This technique worked beautifully: Moisture beaded on the surface of the fish, where it dissolved the salt and created a concentrated brine that was eventually absorbed back into the flesh to bolster flavor.

We also wanted something that could serve as a textural contrast to the silky fish. Restaurants often garnish their oil-poached fillets with lightly fried vegetables and fresh herbs, and we reasoned that we could approximate that by crisping something in the oil before cooking the fish. Fried artichoke hearts would be a nice match here, so we defrosted a bag of artichokes, patted them dry, and halved them lengthwise before tossing them with cornstarch (for extra crunch) and dropping them into the shimmering oil with some minced garlic.

Tasters loved the crisp garnish, but after cranking up the heat to fry, we then had to wait more than 10 minutes for the oil to cool to our target of 180 degrees before the pan went into the oven. The solution proved easy: Rather than dump in all the oil at once, we'd fry the garnishes in ½ cup of oil, strain it, and add the remaining ¼ cup of room-temperature oil to the pan to speed the cooling. The tweak made all the difference; about 5 minutes after frying, the oil was cool enough for poaching.

Frying up a garnish had also left us with an added bonus: flavor-infused oil to use for a sauce. We poured ½ cup into the blender and whirled it with whole cherry tomatoes (for bright sweetness), half a shallot, sherry vinegar, and salt and pepper. After giving the mixture a quick spin on high speed and a pass through a fine-mesh strainer, we had a silky-smooth vinaigrette.

Dressed up with the sauce, crispy artichoke garnish, a few slices of fresh cherry tomato, and a fistful of minced parsley, our elegant plate was complete—not to mention simple enough to pull off at home.

Poached Fish Fillets with Crispy Artichokes and Sherry-Tomato Vinaigrette

SERVES 4

Fillets of meaty white fish like cod, halibut, sea bass, or snapper work best in this recipe. Just make sure the fillets are at least 1 inch thick. A neutral oil such as canola can be substituted for the pure olive oil. The onion half in step 3 is used to displace the oil; a 4-ounce porcelain ramekin may be used instead. Serve with couscous or steamed white rice.

FISH

- 4 (6-ounce) skinless white fish fillets, 1 inch thick
  Kosher salt
- 4 ounces frozen artichoke hearts, thawed, patted dry, and sliced in half lengthwise
- 1 tablespoon cornstarch
- ¾ cup olive oil
- 3 garlic cloves, minced
- ½ onion, peeled

VINAIGRETTE

- 4 ounces cherry tomatoes
- ½ small shallot, peeled
- 4 teaspoons sherry vinegar
  Kosher salt and pepper

- 2 ounces cherry tomatoes, cut into ⅛-inch-thick rounds
- 1 tablespoon minced fresh parsley

1. FOR THE FISH: Adjust oven racks to middle and lower-middle positions and heat oven to 250 degrees. Pat fish dry with paper towels and season each fillet with ¼ teaspoon salt. Let sit at room temperature for 20 minutes.

2. Meanwhile, toss artichokes with cornstarch in bowl to coat. Heat ½ cup oil in 10-inch nonstick ovenproof skillet over medium heat until shimmering. Shake excess cornstarch from artichokes and add to skillet; cook, stirring occasionally, until crisp and golden, 2 to 4 minutes. Add garlic and continue to cook until garlic is golden, 30 to 60 seconds. Strain oil through fine-mesh strainer into bowl. Transfer artichokes and garlic to ovenproof paper towel–lined plate and season with salt. Do not wash strainer.

POACHING FISH OUT OF WATER
Oil poaching is not only a foolproof technique for cooking delicate fish but also a seamless way to create a crispy garnish and elegant sauce from the same oil.

1. Fry artichoke hearts and garlic in oil for crisp garnish that provides nice contrast to fish.

2. Pour ¼ cup fresh oil into strained frying oil to help cool it to gentle poaching temperature.

3. Add onion half to displace oil, so it comes up higher in pan—and so less oil is needed.

4. Poach in low oven (rather than on stovetop) for more even cooking.

5. Use flavorful poaching oil to create simple vinaigrette that adds brightness.

3. Return strained oil to skillet and add remaining ¼ cup oil. Place onion half in center of pan. Let oil cool until it registers about 180 degrees, 5 to 8 minutes. Arrange fish fillets, skinned side up, around onion (oil should come roughly halfway up fillets). Spoon a little oil over each fillet, cover skillet, transfer to middle oven rack, and cook for 15 minutes.

4. Remove skillet from oven. Using 2 spatulas, carefully flip fillets. Cover skillet, return to middle rack, and place plate with artichokes and garlic on lower-middle rack. Continue to cook fish until it registers 130 to 135 degrees, 9 to 14 minutes longer. Gently transfer fish to serving platter, reserving ½ cup oil, and tent fish loosely with aluminum foil. Turn off oven, leaving plate of artichokes in oven.

5. FOR THE VINAIGRETTE: Process cherry tomatoes, shallot, vinegar, ¾ teaspoon salt, and ½ teaspoon pepper with reserved ½ cup fish cooking oil in blender until smooth, 1 to 2 minutes. Add any accumulated fish juices from platter, season with salt to taste, and blend for 10 seconds. Strain sauce through fine-mesh strainer; discard solids.

6. To serve, pour vinaigrette around fish. Garnish each fillet with warmed crisped artichokes and garlic, tomato rounds, and parsley. Serve immediately.

VARIATIONS

Poached Fish Fillets with Crispy Scallions and Miso-Ginger Vinaigrette

For fish, substitute 8 scallion whites, sliced ¼ inch thick, for artichoke hearts; omit garlic; and reduce cornstarch to 2 teaspoons. For vinaigrette, process 6 scallion greens, 8 teaspoons lime juice, 2 tablespoons mirin, 4 teaspoons white miso paste, 2 teaspoons minced ginger, and ½ teaspoon sugar with ½ cup reserved fish cooking oil as directed in step 5. Garnish fish with 2 thinly sliced scallion greens and 2 halved and thinly sliced radishes.

Poached Fish Fillets with Jalapeño Vinaigrette

To make this dish spicier, add some of the reserved chile seeds to the vinaigrette in step 5. Serve with steamed white rice.

For fish, substitute 2 jalapeño chiles, stemmed, seeded, and cut into ⅛-inch-thick rings, for artichoke hearts and reduce cornstarch to 2 teaspoons. For vinaigrette, process 4 jalapeños, stemmed, halved, and seeded (seeds reserved); ½ small shallot, peeled; 6 sprigs fresh cilantro; 8 teaspoons lime juice; and ½ teaspoon kosher salt with ½ cup reserved fish cooking oil as directed in step 5. Garnish fish with 2 tablespoons fresh cilantro leaves and ½ avocado, cut into ¼-inch pieces.

SCIENCE DESK

WHY POACH IN OIL?

Poaching in oil allows fish to retain more of its juices than poaching in wine or broth, leading to remarkably moist, velvety results. This is because cooking in oil is inherently gentler than cooking in water. And while you might expect that fish poached in fat would be greasy, it actually absorbs very little oil. Why? In order for oil to penetrate the fish, moisture must exit first. But because oil and water repel each other, it's very difficult for moisture inside the fish to readily enter the oil. Hence, more of the juices stay in the fish. In fact, in our tests, oil-poached fish lost just 14 percent of its weight during cooking, while water-poached fillets lost 24 percent.

EASY SALMON CAKES

✔ WHY THIS RECIPE WORKS: Most salmon cakes are mushy and overly fishy, overtaken by heavy binders and too much seasoning. Our goal was a quick and simple recipe for salmon cakes that first and foremost tasted like salmon, with a moist, delicate texture. To simplify preparation, we broke out our food processor. Pulsing small pieces of salmon (raw was preferred over cooked, which turned fishy), allowed for more even chopping and resulted in small, discrete pieces of fish. We also found a way to ditch the egg and flour steps of the breading process. Instead, we coated the salmon cakes with panko, which we had also used as a binder.

WHILE WE HAVE A SOFT SPOT FOR THOSE STARCH-HEAVY cod and haddock cakes of our youth, we sometimes crave a more refined version, in which the fish itself isn't camouflaged by gluey binders (usually potatoes) and heavy-handed seasoning. Enter salmon cakes. When done well, these pan-fried patties are tender and moist on the inside, crisp and golden brown on the outside. The seasoning complements—rather than overpowers—the flavor of the fish, and there is just enough binder to hold the cakes together. Unfortunately, most salmon cakes we've tried stray far from this ideal. Their interiors are mushy and their flavor overly fishy. And then there's the fussy breading process.

With a lifetime of fish cake–eating experience, we knew we could do better. Our goal: salmon cakes that tasted first and foremost of salmon, with a moist, delicate texture. We'd dump the potatoes in favor of a less stodgy binder and keep it to a minimum. And although we'd make them from scratch, these cakes would be quick and simple to prepare.

Fish cakes have long been a mainstay of New England cuisine, designed for using up leftover fish and potatoes. But today, most of us buy and cook only as much fish as we plan to eat in one sitting. Which led us to our first question: Should we use cooked or raw fish? We were pretty sure raw would be the way to go if we wanted a moist cake. But to be sure, we tried both approaches.

We chopped both raw and cooked salmon fillets by hand into small pieces, then stirred in two typical binders (bread crumbs and mayonnaise), shaped the mixture into cakes, and coated them with all-purpose flour, egg, and bread crumbs. We fried the cakes on both sides in vegetable oil until they were crisp and golden brown.

Just as we'd expected, the cakes made with cooked salmon lacked moisture. Plus, they tasted noticeably "fishier" than the raw-fish batch. But making raw salmon cakes was no joy either. Chopping slippery raw fish by hand into ¼-inch pieces was messy, sticky, and tedious. Larger chunks weren't an option—with bigger salmon bits the cakes fell apart, even with strong binders. That said, our colleagues deemed the cakes made from raw salmon "pretty darn good." They were tender and moist inside and boasted pleasantly rich, almost creamy flavor with none of the "fishiness" of the twice-cooked samples. They just needed a bit of flavor enhancement and, for the sake of weeknight cooking, an easier method.

To that end, we took out our food processor. We cut a salmon fillet into 2-inch pieces, chucked them in, and let the processor whirl. This resulted in big chunks of salmon bound by finely ground fish paste. Processing the salmon in two batches yielded smaller pieces, but the mixture was still too pasty; when we formed it into rounds and fried them, the finished cakes had a ground-meat consistency that was dense rather than delicate.

But that ground-meat analogy gave us an idea. When we make burgers, we grind the meat ourselves using an easy three-step process: We cut the meat into 1-inch pieces, briefly freeze them to firm them up, and then batch-grind them into smaller chunks in the food processor. The method ensures small, discrete pieces rather than mush. We didn't have time for the freezer, but smaller pieces and smaller batches were both doable. We cut the salmon into 1-inch chunks and gently pulsed them in three batches. This approach—pulsing, rather than letting the processor run continuously—allowed for more even chopping. Some of the pieces were still a bit bigger than the ideal ¼-inch morsels and some were smaller, but they produced cakes very similar to those we'd made with tediously hand-minced fish.

Having succeeded in making the chopping easier, we now could address an issue that had been annoying us from the start: The raw cakes were so wet and sticky that dipping them in egg made them slippery and awkward. Adding more bread crumbs made the patties less goopy but masked the delicate sweetness of the fish. We had a radical thought: Was the three-step breading process really necessary for salmon cakes? In previous testing for crab cakes, we coated the cakes in bread crumbs alone. What if we followed suit here—ditching the egg and flour and simply coating the salmon cakes in bread crumbs before frying? This approach made the patties easier to handle, and the bread crumbs clung surprisingly well to the fish on their own, but the results weren't stellar. Without a little bit of flour to act as a buffer from the moisture in the cakes, the fresh bread crumbs came out too pale and soft. But when we traded the fresh crumbs for ultra-crisp Japanese panko, the salmon cakes emerged from the pan crisp and golden brown. For convenience, we decided to use panko for a binder as well.

Though this simple solution worked well, we wondered why the traditional breading procedure proved superfluous in this case. Our science editor explained that a typical breading process works because the egg contains sticky soluble proteins called ovalbumin that (along with the flour) help the mixture hold together. But it turns out that salmon also contains tacky soluble proteins, called myosins, that migrate to the surface with the moisture in the fish and help the bread crumbs stick. Salmon has more of these water-soluble proteins than many other kinds of fish, as well as chicken and shrimp, making it the perfect candidate for a nontraditional breading.

Now that we had settled on a technique, it was time to jazz up the plain cakes in a way that would enhance the fish flavor rather than disguise it. We added some finely chopped shallot for depth and both scallion and parsley for freshness. Lemon juice brightened the flavor and cut the richness of the salmon, and a teaspoon of mustard and a pinch of cayenne added punch.

Served with tartar sauce or simply with a wedge of lemon, these moist yet crisp salmon cakes managed to be both elegant fare and comfort food. What's more, we could easily whip them up for a weeknight dinner.

NOTES FROM THE TEST KITCHEN

THREE EASY STEPS TO CRISPY SALMON CAKES

1. Hand-chop fish into 1-inch pieces before adding them to food processor. Any bigger, and you'll end up with some large chunks and some finely ground paste.

2. To ensure that pieces grind evenly, pulse chopped fish in 3 batches into ¼-inch bits. (Be careful not to overprocess.) Mix with bread-crumb binder and flavorings.

3. Gently coat shaped cakes with coarse panko bread crumbs. Salmon's high concentration of tacky water-soluble proteins glues crumbs to patties without need for egg or flour.

EASY SALMON CAKES

Easy Salmon Cakes

SERVES 4

If buying a skin-on salmon fillet, purchase 1⅓ pounds fish. This will yield 1¼ pounds fish after skinning. When processing the salmon, it is OK to have some pieces that are larger than ¼ inch. It is important to avoid over-processing the fish. Serve the salmon cakes with lemon wedges and/or tartar sauce.

- 3 tablespoons plus ¾ cup panko bread crumbs
- 2 tablespoons minced fresh parsley
- 2 tablespoons mayonnaise
- 4 teaspoons lemon juice
- 1 scallion, sliced thin
- 1 small shallot, minced
- 1 teaspoon Dijon mustard
- ¾ teaspoon salt
- ¼ teaspoon pepper
  Pinch cayenne pepper
- 1 (1¼-pound) skinless salmon fillet, cut into 1-inch pieces
- ½ cup vegetable oil

1. Combine 3 tablespoons panko, parsley, mayonnaise, lemon juice, scallion, shallot, mustard, salt, pepper, and cayenne in bowl. Working in 3 batches, pulse salmon in food processor until coarsely chopped into ¼-inch pieces, about 2 pulses, transferring each batch to bowl with panko mixture. Gently mix until uniformly combined.

2. Place remaining ¾ cup panko in shallow dish. Using ⅓-cup measure, scoop level amount of salmon mixture and transfer to baking sheet; repeat to make 8 cakes. Carefully coat each cake with bread crumbs, gently patting into disk measuring 2¾ inches in diameter and 1 inch high. Return coated cakes to baking sheet.

3. Heat oil in 12-inch skillet over medium-high heat until shimmering. Place salmon cakes in skillet and cook without moving until bottoms are golden brown, about 2 minutes. Carefully flip cakes and cook until second side is golden brown, 2 to 3 minutes. Transfer cakes to paper towel–lined plate to drain for 1 minute. Serve.

RATING OYSTER CRACKERS

Many people enjoy oyster crackers simply for snacking, but most of the time they're intended to accompany soup. We wondered whether traditional or modern versions would perform both functions best. We evaluated four brands for their taste and texture, both alone and in tomato soup. The crackers ranged from small and hexagonal to large and almost spherical, with some featuring the typical crimped edges. Our tasters panned the largest and most traditional cracker for being too "dense," "bland," and even "raw"-tasting. The winning cracker, by contrast, was well suited for straight-from-the-box snacking, with its "tender," "flaky" texture and "wheaty" taste, plus it also held its crispness in soup. Brands are listed in order of preference. See AmericasTestKitchen.com for updates to this testing.

HIGHLY RECOMMENDED

SUNSHINE Krispy Soup & Oyster Crackers
PRICE: $3.49 for 11 oz
COMMENTS: Tasters repeatedly praised Sunshine's hexagonal crackers for their "addictive," "wheaty, toasty flavor." Although their texture "adds crunch to soup," their "flaky," "delicate," "melt-in-your-mouth" quality also made them a cracker that tasters could "nosh on all day."

OLDE CAPE COD All-Natural Soup & Chowder Oyster Crackers (also sold as Westminster Crackers)
PRICE: $2.69 for 8 oz
COMMENTS: Tasters enjoyed the "puffiness" and "mild, creamy" flavor of these round, pale crackers. Their traditionally "light," "floury" quality was deemed "just what an oyster cracker should be." In soup, the crackers "stayed crisp" and "held up well."

RECOMMENDED WITH RESERVATIONS

PREMIUM Soup & Oyster Crackers (by Nabisco)
PRICE: $3.59 for 9 oz
COMMENTS: Eaten plain, these round, crimped crackers were praised for their "toasty," "nutty" flavor and "nice crunch," but in soup we found that they quickly turned "mushy" and "soggy."

NOT RECOMMENDED

OTC Oyster Crackers
PRICE: $2.88 for 10 oz
COMMENTS: The "giant," "unwieldy" knob-shaped OTC crackers (for Original Trenton Cracker, made in New Jersey since the mid-19th century) prompted comparisons to "jaw breakers." Their "stale," "too-hard" texture and "raw" flavor also yielded comparisons to "dog biscuits."

RATING OYSTER KNIVES

You could wait for a night out to enjoy the briny pleasure of a fresh, raw oyster, but with the right tool and some practice you can shuck oysters at home for a fraction of restaurant prices. Regular knives are unsuitable for opening oysters because they're too sharp and flexible; the thick, dull blades of oyster knives function as levers to pry shells apart without cutting into them. To find the best all-purpose oyster knife, we tried out six different knives in four different styles (named for their region of origin), priced from $7.99 to $16.80, using them to open both large and small oysters. Handle design was important, since it takes a certain amount of pressure to shuck an oyster. Some handles felt clumsy and were too thick, slippery, or short to hold firmly. The best handles fit comfortably in our palms and had a nonslip surface that didn't send our hands sliding toward the blade. In the end, all testers gave top marks to a New Haven–style knife that had a flat blade with a slight upward bend at the tip. This bend gives excellent leverage when popping the hinge and can slip under the meat, curving along the inside of the shell to neatly sever the muscle and detach the oyster meat. Brands are listed in order of preference. See AmericasTestKitchen.com for updates to this testing.

HIGHLY RECOMMENDED

R. MURPHY New Haven Oyster Knife with Stainless Steel Blade

MODEL: NHYOS   **PRICE:** $16.65   **STYLE:** New Haven
COMFORT: ★★★   **FUNCTION:** ★★★   **DURABILITY:** ★★★
BLADE: ★★★   **HANDLE:** ★★★
COMMENTS: This oyster knife (we chose the model with a stainless steel blade) is well crafted, with a simple, comfortable wooden handle that never budged in our hands. A slightly upturned tip was helpful when inserting the point into the hinge and was able to slice oyster muscle without damaging the meat. It's the lightest knife that we tested; one shucker noted that it "seemed to disappear and become part of your hand."

DEXTER-RUSSELL 2¾-inch Oyster Knife

MODEL: 10843   **PRICE:** $10.83   **STYLE:** New Haven
COMFORT: ★★★   **FUNCTION:** ★★★   **DURABILITY:** ★★★
BLADE: ★★★   **HANDLE:** ★★½
COMMENTS: Restaurant professionals that we interviewed favor this sturdy knife, and we can see why. Its pointy, upturned tip easily maneuvers to pop hinges and slice muscles. The textured, nonslip polypropylene handle is longer than most of the others that we tested, with a rounded bulb at the end that fit comfortably in hands of all sizes. It performed just as well as our winner but is a bit heavier.

RECOMMENDED

DÉGLON Oyster Knife

MODEL: 59047   **PRICE:** $9.75   **STYLE:** French
COMFORT: ★★★   **FUNCTION:** ★★ ½   **DURABILITY:** ★★★
BLADE: ★★½   **HANDLE:** ★★★
COMMENTS: This deft little knife has an ergonomically shaped handle that nestled neatly into palms large and small. Its sharp blade allowed for adroit maneuvering, popping hinges with finesse and dexterously severing muscles. We downgraded it slightly only because it's less all-purpose than our winners: The tip is too sharp for beginners, and while it easily opened small-to-medium-size oysters, its stubby blade cracked a few large shells in half. Perfect for a more experienced shucker and smaller oysters.

RECOMMENDED WITH RESERVATIONS

VICTORINOX Boston-Style Oyster Knife, 3″ Narrow, SuperGrip Handle

MODEL: 44694   **PRICE:** $16.80   **STYLE:** Boston
COMFORT: ★★★   **FUNCTION:** ★½   **DURABILITY:** ★★★
BLADE: ★½   **HANDLE:** ★★★
COMMENTS: This knife had the same handle as our highly recommended Dexter-Russell: bulb-shaped and comfortable, with a great grip. But the blade was too long for some testers, who felt that they couldn't get proper leverage with their hands so far away from the oyster, especially with petite Kumamotos. "I don't trust myself with it," said one tester. The blade also wasn't as dexterous at severing muscles due to its lack of a curved tip.

OXO GOOD GRIPS Oyster Knife

MODEL: 35681   **PRICE:** $7.99   **STYLE:** New Haven
COMFORT: ★½   **FUNCTION:** ★★   **DURABILITY:** ★★★
BLADE: ★★   **HANDLE:** ★½
COMMENTS: This knife had all the right traits, but somehow they didn't add up to a great knife. It worked decently with large oysters, but its New Haven–style tip at the end of a thick, wide blade had us struggling to pop shell hinges. The handle was another problem: Large and clumsy, it was too broad to get a comfortable grip. Thin ridges in the handle didn't help—our thumbs still slipped toward the blade.

NOT RECOMMENDED

TRUDEAU Oyster Knife and Case Set

MODEL: 0991902   **PRICE:** $11.99   **STYLE:** Providence
COMFORT: ★   **FUNCTION:** ★   **DURABILITY:** ★
BLADE: ★   **HANDLE:** ★
COMMENTS: The only knife in our lineup equipped with a blade guard comes with a small plastic case for holding the oyster as you open it. But it was also the only blade judged unsafe by testers. The case didn't let us get a firm grip: Oysters of all sizes jiggled around inside. The flimsy blade bent in the first round of testing, and the handle was slippery and short; the plastic guard at its end just made it impossible to get a firm grip.

Indian Classics
MADE EASY

*Naan should be chewy
and moist with a charred,
flavorful exterior—we'll show
you how to make this classic
Indian flatbread in your own
kitchen.*

WHILE WE HAVE DEVELOPED RECIPES FOR A VARIETY OF INDIAN dishes, there are two that we hadn't really considered for the home cook, thinking they might be too challenging: *naan*, the Indian flatbread, and *saag paneer*, Indian-style spinach with fresh cheese.

Who could blame us for thinking naan shouldn't be attempted by the home cook? After all, traditionally, this light, tender flatbread is baked in a tandoor, where heat levels can reach more 1,000 degrees. A little investigation suggested we might be able to prepare naan with a preheated pizza stone. But we weren't making pizza—we wanted our naan as authentic as possible. This meant not only figuring out the right cooking method but also developing a dough that was moist enough to withstand blistering heat without drying out.

Many American adaptations of saag paneer rely on tofu as a stand-in for the cubes of fresh cheese. This is too much of a cheat in our book. Once we started reading about how easy it was to make paneer, it became clear that homemade paneer was essential. Luckily, the ingredients can all be found at the supermarket. As for the thick, pureed spinach sauce, we wanted real complexity in our dish but we were determined to stick with supermarket ingredients. (As much as we love visiting Indian markets, we're aware not every city or town has one.) Put away your takeout menu for today; we've got Indian classics you can make at home tonight.

NAAN

✔ **WHY THIS RECIPE WORKS:** Even in India, naan is considered "restaurant" bread. This may be because it calls for a traditional tandoor oven, which few home cooks own. We wanted an ideal version of this bread—light and airy, with a pliant, chewy crust—that we could easily make at home. We started with a moist dough with a fair amount of fat, which created a soft bread that was pleasantly chewy, but the real secret was the cooking method. While we thought a grill or preheated pizza stone would be the best cooking method, we discovered that they cooked the bread unevenly. A much better option was a covered skillet. The skillet delivers heat to the bottom and the top of the bread, producing loaves that are nicely charred but still moist.

WE'VE RE-CREATED PLENTY OF INDIAN CURRIES, biryanis, and chutneys in the test kitchen and in our home kitchens, but naan, the cuisine's famous leavened flatbread, is something we had yet to tackle. That might be because it's considered "restaurant" bread, even in India. To create the ideal version featuring a light, airy interior and a pliant, chewy crust, the dough is baked in the traditional barrel-shaped, charcoal- or wood-fired clay oven known as a tandoor. These vessels weigh upwards of 600 pounds and often top 1,000 degrees, which explains how the crust gets so beautifully blistered—and also why few home cooks own tandoors. At the same time, we've often wondered if we really have to venture out for something as simple as flatbread. We decided it was time to give home-baked naan a shot.

We scoured the test kitchen's collection of Indian cookbooks and came away feeling optimistic. The ingredient list would be no problem. Most of the recipes we found called for some combination of flour, yeast, water, salt, yogurt, and sugar. And though we'd worried that getting good char on the bread without a tandoor would be tricky, most sources seemed to suggest that it could be done in a conventional oven on a preheated baking stone.

Aiming for a dough that was wet enough to stay moist during cooking but not so hydrated that it was too sticky or soupy to handle, we mixed a few cups of all-purpose flour with a pinch of yeast, about ⅓ cup of low-fat yogurt, a little sugar, and some salt, along with enough water to make the dough pliable. We let the dough rise for a few hours, divided it into four balls, rolled them into thin disks, and slid them onto a baking stone that we'd preheated as hot as our oven would go (500 degrees).

Trouble started early, when we were rolling out the dough rounds and they snapped back like rubber bands. When we finally managed to get them flat, the loaves baked up dry and tough before they'd even had a chance to properly brown on the bottom, let alone develop any of those dark patchy blisters that, in our opinion, are the best part of naan. They also continued to rapidly lose more moisture as they cooled—a problem since, unlike in a restaurant, we couldn't exactly make each piece to order. Although we were still unsure whether the oven was the best stand-in for a tandoor, we decided the first order of business was to create a dough that was softer but still pleasantly chewy.

One change to make right off the bat: switching from low-fat yogurt to the whole-milk kind. The extra fat would coat the flour proteins, weakening gluten formation by preventing them from binding to each other too tightly, as well as hold in more moisture for a more tender bread. With this change, our next batch of dough was easier to roll out, but it baked up too soft; the inside was like sandwich bread. We wondered if the higher protein (as much as 14 percent) in bread flour might be a better bet. But bread flour created so much chew that the resulting bread was leathery. High-protein all-purpose flour, such as King Arthur brand, was a better choice, producing naan that boasted a near-ideal texture. As we pulled apart an oven-fresh piece, we couldn't help but admire its tender chew. But then the inevitable happened: The thin rounds cooled almost instantly and were tough by the time we pulled the next batch off the baking stone a few minutes later. To buy each piece some time, we needed to figure out a way to keep the dough from drying out.

The solution wasn't more water; that would just make the dough loose and sticky. More fat was a better idea, since besides impeding gluten formation it limits water evaporation from the starches during baking, minimizing moisture loss. To that end, we tried adding vegetable oil

INDIAN FLATBREAD (NAAN)

to the dough, 1 teaspoon at a time, discovering that the more we added, the more tender and capable of staying soft the breads became. The dough maxed out at 5 teaspoons per cup of flour; any more and the bread was greasy. But we had one more fat source in mind to boost moisture retention: an egg yolk. While unusual in naan recipes, egg yolks often turn up in other types of bread for just this reason. (We stayed away from whole eggs, knowing that the white's structure-enhancing proteins would toughen the dough.)

The last tweak we made before moving on to the cooking method was refrigerating the dough for several hours to keep it from snapping back during stretching. We learned this trick while developing a thin-crust pizza recipe: Cold fermentation encourages the relaxation of gluten strands so that the dough is more flexible. As an added bonus, preparing the dough the day before freed up time the next day for cooking the rest of the meal.

With the dough formula nailed down, we moved on to face the real challenge of making naan at home: getting good color and char without a tandoor. Since the oven wasn't browning the bread fast enough, we figured our best alternative was the hottest, most powerful heat source

NOTES FROM THE TEST KITCHEN

FINDING THE RIGHT HEAT TO REPLICATE A TANDOOR

We initially thought that a grill or preheated pizza stone would best approximate the intense heat of a tandoor, which cooks naan mainly by heat conducted through its walls. We were wrong. The best alternative? A trusty cast-iron skillet.

GRILL? NO

A grill's searing heat gets close to that of a tandoor. The problem: It only chars the bottom of the bread, while the top remains barely cooked. (Flipping only dries out the bread.)

PIZZA STONE IN OVEN? NO

Baked on a pizza stone in the oven, the bread encounters not only the conductive heat of the stone, which we wanted, but also the drying heat of the oven's air currents, which we didn't.

COVERED SKILLET? YES

A covered skillet delivers heat to the bottom and top of the bread, producing loaves that are nicely charred but still moist. To ensure a tender interior, we mist the dough with water.

we had: a grill. We fired up some charcoal, expecting to come away with beautifully grill-marked breads. To say our first attempt was a disaster would be an understatement. Like a poorly cooked piece of meat, the bottom blackened while the top remained practically raw. We thought the fire was just too hot so we downsized it on our next test, but even a smaller fire produced the same charred result. Flipping the dough midway through cooking also wasn't the answer—it merely dried out the bread.

We took a step back to consider what really happens when naan cooks in a tandoor. The shaped dough is slapped directly onto the tandoor's inside wall, where it sticks and cooks in minutes, without ever being flipped. While heat radiating from the coals at the bottom of the oven helps cook the bread's exposed side, more important is the heat conducted through its walls, which also trap moisture to keep the bread soft. We could see now that a grill wasn't the best substitute for a tandoor. But neither was a pizza stone in the oven, since that method also exposed the bread to drying air currents. Our choice became clear: a skillet on the stovetop.

So for our next test, we slipped our stretched and shaped dough into a preheated cast-iron skillet. It puffed up quickly, and after a few minutes the bottom had browned a bit; we flipped it to finish cooking the top side. The result was a dramatic improvement on anything we'd made so far—lightly browned and bubbled in spots and tender inside. It wasn't perfect, though. The bread ballooned as it baked, which made it cook unevenly when we flipped it; the crust was a bit floury; and the loaves still dried out too quickly as they sat.

None of these issues were hard to fix. We poked the dough with a fork before putting it in the pan to let steam escape and prevent puffing. Improving the crust and prolonging the optimal tender texture of the bread required a two-tiered approach. First, we misted the dough with water before cooking it to moisten the flour that coated it. We also covered the pan to trap steam around the bread as it baked.

Our simple approach created naan as good as any from a restaurant. Brushed with a little melted butter after cooking, it makes for a delicious edible utensil, perfect for tearing into bite-size pieces to dip into curries, chutneys, or even stew.

Indian Flatbread (Naan)

MAKES 4 BREADS

This recipe works best with a high-protein all-purpose flour such as King Arthur brand. Do not use nonfat yogurt in this recipe. A 12-inch nonstick skillet may be used in place of the cast-iron skillet. For efficiency, stretch the next ball of dough while each naan is cooking.

½ cup ice water

⅓ cup plain whole-milk yogurt

3 tablespoons plus 1 teaspoon vegetable oil

1 large egg yolk

2 cups (10 ounces) all-purpose flour

1¼ teaspoons sugar

½ teaspoon instant or rapid-rise yeast

1¼ teaspoons salt

1½ tablespoons unsalted butter, melted

1. In measuring cup or small bowl, combine water, yogurt, 3 tablespoons oil, and egg yolk. Process flour, sugar, and yeast together in food processor until combined, about 2 seconds. With processor running, slowly add water mixture; process until dough is just combined and no dry flour remains, about 10 seconds. Let dough stand for 10 minutes.

2. Add salt to dough and process until dough forms satiny, sticky ball that clears sides of workbowl, 30 to 60 seconds. Transfer dough to lightly floured counter and knead until smooth, about 1 minute. Shape dough into tight ball and place in large, lightly oiled bowl. Cover tightly with plastic wrap and refrigerate for 16 to 24 hours.

3. Adjust oven rack to middle position and heat oven to 200 degrees. Place heatproof plate on rack. Transfer dough to lightly floured counter and divide into 4 equal pieces. Shape each piece into smooth, tight ball. Place dough balls on lightly oiled baking sheet, at least 2 inches apart; cover loosely with plastic coated with vegetable oil spray. Let stand for 15 to 20 minutes.

4. Transfer 1 ball to lightly floured counter and sprinkle with flour. Using hands and rolling pin, press and roll piece of dough into 9-inch round of even thickness, sprinkling dough and counter with flour as needed to prevent sticking. Using fork, poke entire surface of round 20 to 25 times. Heat remaining 1 teaspoon oil in 12-inch cast-iron skillet over medium heat until shimmering. Wipe oil out of skillet completely with paper towels. Mist top of dough lightly with water. Place dough in pan, moistened side down; mist top surface of dough with water; and cover. Cook until bottom is browned in spots across surface, 2 to 4 minutes. Flip naan, cover, and continue to cook on second side until lightly browned, 2 to 3 minutes longer. (If naan puffs up, gently poke with fork to deflate.) Flip naan, brush top with about 1 teaspoon melted butter, transfer to plate in oven, and cover plate tightly with aluminum foil. Repeat rolling and cooking remaining 3 dough balls. Once last naan is baked, serve immediately.

VARIATION

Quicker Indian Flatbread

This variation, which can be prepared in about 2 hours, forgoes the overnight rest, but the dough may be a little harder to roll out.

After shaping dough in step 2, let dough rise at room temperature for 30 minutes. After 30 minutes, fold partially risen dough over itself 8 times by gently lifting and folding edge of dough toward middle, turning bowl 90 degrees after each fold. Cover with plastic wrap and let rise for 30 minutes. Repeat folding, turning, and rising 1 more time, for total of three 30-minute rises. After last rise, proceed with recipe from step 3.

SAAG PANEER

SAAG PANEER

✔ **WHY THIS RECIPE WORKS:** Saag paneer, soft cubes of creamy cheese in a spicy pureed spinach sauce is an Indian restaurant classic. We found that re-creating this dish at home wasn't so difficult. We made our own cheese by heating a combination of whole milk and buttermilk, squeezing the curds of moisture, then weighting the cheese down until it was firm enough to slice. As for the spinach sauce, instead of cooking the spinach in batches on the stovetop, we simply wilted it all in the microwave. The addition of mustard greens gave our sauce additional complexity that worked well with the dish's warm spices. Canned diced tomatoes brightened the dish. And buttery cashews—both pureed and chopped gave our Indian classic a subtle nutty richness.

SAAG PANEER IS RIGHT UP THERE WITH WILDLY popular chicken tikka masala and crispy fried samosa triangles—and for good reason. The paneer—lightly firm, milky cubes of fresh homemade cheese—is simmered in a creamy spinach sauce that's heady with garlic, ginger, chiles, and warm spices. Served with a scoop of fragrant basmati rice, it's one of the most satisfying main dishes we know of—in any cuisine.

But as much as we love ordering the dish at restaurants, we've never tried making it. Why? Well, for one thing, you have to make your own cheese—we'd always assumed that would be a lot of trouble. But then we paged through a couple of Indian cookbooks and discovered that the method is dead simple. In fact, the whole dish looked surprisingly approachable, the familiar vegetables and spices erasing our preconceived notion that this entrée would require a slew of specialty purchases. Feeling confident (and hungry), we decided to give it a whirl.

We weren't kidding when we said the cheese-making process was simple. According to most Indian cookbooks we consulted, all you need to do is heat some milk (about 3 quarts to make enough cheese for four to six people), add acid to curdle it, strain off the whey, and press the remaining curds into a sliceable "cake." The result looks

and tastes a bit like cottage cheese, but it's drier and firmer because much more of the water is pressed out. That said, there were some details to iron out—specifically, what kind of milk and acid to use. A dozen or so batches later we had our answers. First (and not surprisingly), whole milk made the creamiest, most full-flavored paneer by far. (Low-fat versions were passable.)

The other half of the equation—the acid—yielded a less predictable result. Plain old white vinegar and lemon juice are the most common coagulants used to curdle the milk, while some recipes called for buttermilk. The first two got the job done, but paneer made with buttermilk stood out as strikingly complex. One cup of buttermilk per quart of regular milk resulted in a cheese that was tender and creamy but still firm enough to hold its shape when simmered.

As for forming the curds into a cake, the method couldn't have been simpler: Drawing up the ends of the cheesecloth pouch, we squeezed the curds to wring out as much moisture as possible, then sandwiched the pouch between a pair of dinner plates and weighted the top with a Dutch oven. Forty-five minutes later—about the time that we guessed it would take us to put together the spinach sauce—we had a tender-firm block, which we sliced into tidy ½-inch cubes. (In subsequent tests, we discovered that the cheese could be made up to three days ahead.)

On to the sauce. According to most recipes, this is simply a thick puree of sautéed spinach (bunched mature spinach for now—we'd test other varieties later), aromatics, and spices, plus a little milk or cream. Exactly which aromatics and spices went into the pan distinguished one regional variation from another, but we started with a typical combination of minced onion, chiles, generous spoons of both garlic and ginger, whole cumin seeds, and ground coriander and cardamom, all sautéed in butter. Our tasters deemed the heady mixture bold and complex but just a bit unbalanced, with the pungent aromatics overshadowing the warm spices. We saw to their complaint with a dash of cinnamon and an unusual (but not unheard-of) hit of sweet, earthy paprika.

We also followed the lead of the recipes that we came across that called for brightening the sauce with tomatoes. Fresh (and almost always out-of-season) tomatoes were

been prewashed and stemmed) held its own against bunched spinach, so at least we could do away with all the cleaning.

That was one fussy spinach cookery step gone, but we had another to address: tediously sautéing the piles of spinach leaves in batches to drive off moisture and create a more manageable mass for pureeing. Hoping to streamline the process, we loaded the leaves into a large microwave-safe bowl and gave them a 3-minute zap. Sure enough, the once-fluffy pile had shrunk to a small flattened mound by the time the buzzer went off. We roughly chopped the wilted greens, which released more water, and into the blender they went with the sautéed aromatics.

Nobody disagreed that the recipe was getting close, but there was something missing—assertiveness, according to one taster, and maybe some texture to the sauce. We paged through some of the Indian cookbooks again and came across an intriguing idea. Apparently, some versions of saag paneer include a second, stronger-flavored green (saag, in fact, is a generic term for any leafy green), like kale, collards, or mustard greens. Intrigued, we paired each of these greens (also microwaved until wilted) with the spinach and were encouraged by the improved results. But it was the peppery bite of the mustard greens that best magnified the flavors of both the spinach and the spices. As for creating texture in the sauce, we chopped and reserved ⅓ cup of each green (along with some of the aromatics and tomatoes) to add directly to the skillet.

For the dairy component, we tried yogurt and cream, but buttermilk won out with its moderate richness and tang; plus, it was convenient, since we had leftovers from making the paneer. A brief simmer before adding the cheese tied all of the flavors together and tightened up the now-velvety sauce.

The texture of the sauce was just where we wanted it, but it didn't seem rich enough. A splash of cream added richness, but it also muffled the spices. Then, as we were casting about for ideas, we noticed that the final dish is sometimes garnished with buttery cashews. Thinking that perhaps cashews were just what our recipe needed, we stirred a handful of finely chopped nuts into the sauce. They added richness without dulling the flavors one bit, but the gritty texture was objectionable. The solution

dull and watery, while tomato paste deadened the sauté with its overly sweet, "cooked" flavors. We had better results with drained, diced canned tomatoes, which we added to the pan after the aromatics were brown and fragrant.

With the cheese and spices settled, we moved on to the meat—or, rather, vegetable—of the matter: the spinach. Because greens cook down a great deal, we needed nearly 2 pounds to make the sauce—but cleaning and stemming all that spinach was a pain. We'd hoped that frozen spinach would fit the bill, but no such luck. The defrosted leaves lacked the sweetness and depth of the fresh stuff. But bagged fresh curly spinach (which has proved as simple as pureeing the cashews into the sauce along with the other ingredients so that they added creaminess but went undetected.

With our final recipe, we can have an authentic-tasting rendition of our favorite Indian entrée within an hour—using supermarket staples. We've never been happier to have our assumptions proved wrong.

Indian-Style Spinach with Fresh Cheese (Saag Paneer)

SERVES 4 TO 6

To ensure that the cheese is firm, wring it tightly in step 2 and be sure to use two plates that nestle together snugly. Use commercially produced cultured buttermilk in this recipe. We found that some locally produced buttermilks didn't sufficiently coagulate the milk. Serve with basmati rice.

CHEESE

- 3 **quarts whole milk**
- 3 **cups buttermilk**
- 1 **tablespoon salt**

SPINACH SAUCE

- 1 **(10-ounce) bag curly-leaf spinach, rinsed**
- 12 **ounces mustard greens, stemmed and rinsed**
- 3 **tablespoons unsalted butter**
- 1 **teaspoon cumin seeds**
- 1 **teaspoon ground coriander**
- 1 **teaspoon paprika**
- ½ **teaspoon ground cardamom**
- ¼ **teaspoon ground cinnamon**
- 1 **onion, chopped fine**
   Salt and pepper
- 3 **garlic cloves, minced**
- 1 **tablespoon grated fresh ginger**
- 1 **jalapeño chile, stemmed, seeded, and minced**
- 1 **(14.5-ounce) can diced tomatoes, drained and chopped coarse**
- ½ **cup roasted cashews, chopped coarse**
- 1 **cup water**
- 1 **cup buttermilk**
- 3 **tablespoons chopped fresh cilantro**

1. FOR THE CHEESE: Line colander with triple layer of cheesecloth and set in sink. Bring milk to boil in Dutch oven over medium-high heat. Whisk in buttermilk and salt, turn off heat, and let stand for 1 minute. Pour milk mixture through cheesecloth and let curds drain for 15 minutes.

2. Pull edges of cheesecloth together to form pouch. Twist edges of cheesecloth together, firmly squeezing out as much liquid as possible from cheese curds. Place taut, twisted cheese pouch between 2 large plates and weigh down top plate with heavy Dutch oven. Set aside at room temperature until cheese is firm and set, at least 45 minutes. Remove cheesecloth and cut cheese into ½-inch pieces. (Left uncut, cheese can be wrapped in plastic wrap and refrigerated for up to 3 days.)

3. FOR THE SPINACH SAUCE: Place spinach in large bowl, cover, and microwave until wilted, about 3 minutes. When cool enough to handle, chop enough spinach to measure ⅓ cup and set aside. Transfer remaining spinach to blender and wipe out bowl. Place mustard greens in now-empty bowl, cover, and microwave until wilted, about 4 minutes. When cool enough to handle, chop enough mustard greens to measure ⅓ cup and transfer to

bowl with chopped spinach. Transfer remaining mustard greens to blender.

4. Meanwhile, melt butter in 12-inch skillet over medium-high heat. Add cumin seeds, coriander, paprika, cardamom, and cinnamon and cook until fragrant, about 30 seconds. Add onion and ¾ teaspoon salt; cook, stirring frequently, until softened, about 3 minutes. Add garlic, ginger, and jalapeño; cook, stirring frequently, until lightly browned and just beginning to stick to pan, 2 to 3 minutes. Stir in tomatoes and cook mixture until pan is dry and tomatoes are beginning to brown, 3 to 4 minutes. Remove skillet from heat.

5. Transfer half of onion mixture to blender with greens. Add ¼ cup cashews and water; process until smooth, about 1 minute. Return puree to skillet.

6. Return skillet to medium-high heat, stir in chopped greens and buttermilk, and bring to simmer. Reduce heat to low, cover, and cook until flavors have blended, 5 minutes. Season with salt and pepper to taste. Gently fold in cheese cubes and cook until just heated through, 1 to 2 minutes. Transfer to serving dish, sprinkle with remaining ¼ cup cashews and cilantro, and serve.

RATING JUICERS

Freshly made juice has no comparison, but if you're looking for more than fresh-squeezed orange or grapefruit juice, you'll need a juicer. While citrus reamers tackle oranges and the like, juice extractors expand the options to almost any fruit or vegetable. These machines extract liquid in one of two ways: Masticating juicers use an augur that grinds the produce and presses it against a strainer; centrifugal juicers shred and spin the food on a serrated disk. We tested six models, including four centrifugal and two masticating, looking for the best one. Noise level and ease of use were two important considerations. Centrifugal juicers operate at higher rpm, so they tend to be louder—two were even comparable to a motorcycle. As for usability, a few models made us work harder than others—it didn't matter which style they were. Juicers with narrow tubes had us dicing apples and cutting pineapples into skinny strips. Several juicers lacked stability, and lurched and scooted on the counter. Some had several parts, making them harder to assemble and clean. Only one model excelled across the board, breezing through various produce. Although it used centrifugal technology, it was not overly loud. Brands are listed in order of preference. See AmericasTestKitchen.com for updates to this testing.

HIGHLY RECOMMENDED

BREVILLE Juice Fountain Plus
MODEL: JE98XL   **PRICE:** $149.99   **TYPE:** Centrifugal
WEIGHT: 8 lb   **NOISE LEVEL:** 82 dB (comparable to a dishwasher)
PERFORMANCE: ★★★   **EASE OF USE:** ★★★   **CLEANUP:** ★★★
COMMENTS: This surprisingly quiet centrifugal juicer whipped through fruits and vegetables with ease on high and low speeds, and its 3-inch-wide feed chute accommodated large apple quarters or multiple carrots at a time. It was easy to assemble and its smooth surfaces (with fewer nooks and crannies than other models) proved easy to clean. Its stiff cleaning brush made a clean sweep of pulpy bits in the fine-mesh strainer basket. All parts except the food pusher are top-rack dishwasher-safe.

RECOMMENDED WITH RESERVATIONS

OMEGA VRT Low Speed Juicing System
MODEL: VRT350   **PRICE:** $379.99   **TYPE:** Masticating
WEIGHT: 10 lb   **NOISE LEVEL:** 64 dB
(same as a conversation)
PERFORMANCE: ★★★   **EASE OF USE:** ★★   **CLEANUP:** ★
COMMENTS: This masticating model juiced everything—but only if we inserted produce slowly. (Using the reverse mode helped dislodge food.) Plus, its small feed tube hindered efficiency, the parts were tricky to reassemble, and the spout that offloads pulp frequently clogged.

CHAMPION Commercial Juicer
MODEL: G5-PG-710   **PRICE:** $259   **TYPE:** Masticating
WEIGHT: 20 lb   **NOISE LEVEL:** 76 dB (same as a vacuum cleaner)
PERFORMANCE: ★★   **EASE OF USE:** ★   **CLEANUP:** ★★
COMMENTS: This commercial-level juicer came with a few perks: an additional fine-mesh strainer for holding back foam and a grinding plate for making nut butters. But its 2-inch-wide feed tube forced us to precut the produce, and its 20-pound frame was uncomfortably heavy to move. Removing the mesh screen for cleaning was tricky, and the small "teeth" of its serrated augur didn't take on kale and beets unless we pressed hard with the plunger.

RECOMMENDED WITH RESERVATIONS (cont.)

HAMILTON BEACH Big Mouth Juice Extractor
MODEL: 67601   **PRICE:** $69.99   **TYPE:** Centrifugal
WEIGHT: 5 lb   **NOISE LEVEL:** 92 dB
(same as a motorcycle)
PERFORMANCE: ★★   **EASE OF USE:** ★★
CLEANUP: ★
COMMENTS: The good news: This centrifugal juicer's large feed tube made for short prep work, and it juiced apples with ease. The bad: It whined loudly and struggled with tougher foods like kale and beets, scooting on the counter. There was a juice collection carafe, but the tight seam surrounding the cutting disk trapped pulp and made cleaning a chore.

JUICEMAN All-in-One Juice Extractor
MODEL: JM480S   **PRICE:** $80.99   **TYPE:** Centrifugal
WEIGHT: 7 lb   **NOISE LEVEL:** 87 dB
(same as a garbage disposal)
PERFORMANCE: ★½   **EASE OF USE:** ★   **CLEANUP:** ★★
COMMENTS: This centrifugal juicer's citrus reamer attachment seemed like a plus until it required brute force to use and made a deafening screech. It was also the only model that didn't offload the pulp, which hampered efficiency. The silver lining: The juice spout was adjustable, allowing us to stop the flow if we'd left the collection carafe out of place, and the parts proved easy to reassemble after cleaning.

NOT RECOMMENDED

OSTER 400-Watt Single-Speed Juice Extractor
MODEL: 3157   **PRICE:** $106.48   **TYPE:** Centrifugal
WEIGHT: 3 lb   **NOISE LEVEL:** 90 dB (same as a motorcycle)
PERFORMANCE: ★   **EASE OF USE:** ★   **CLEANUP:** ★
COMMENTS: The smallest juicer in our lineup lurched on the counter as it struggled on carrots, and its 400-watt motor juiced everything at a loud continuous whine. Thin slices of apple and leaves of kale slipped past its serrated base unprocessed. Its tiny feed chute forced us to pare apples into eighths and pineapples into skinny strips. It was the only juicer that didn't include a brush for cleaning.

ASIAN TAKEOUT *Favorites*

It takes more than a few tries to toss hot stir-fried noodles as well as test cook Andrea Geary.

STIR-FRIES ARE AMONG THE EASIEST AND QUICKEST DISHES TO MAKE at home, so why do we so often resort to takeout versions? We admit that convenience has a lot to do with it. But honestly, restaurants often do a better job. We set out to find out how we could bring two favorites up to speed for the home cook: *yu xiang* (Sichuan stir-fried pork in garlic sauce) and *pad see ew* (Thai-style stir-fried noodles with chicken and broccolini).

Sichuan stir-fried pork in garlic sauce is a mix of strips of juicy pork and crisp-tender vegetables in a glossy, garlicky sauce seasoned with a splash of tangy black vinegar. The flavors in this sauce are multiple: salty, sour, sweet, and spicy. The problem with recipes we prepared from a variety of sources was that the sauces were wildly unbalanced. And these subpar sauces couldn't hide the fact that the pork often turned out tough and chewy. We decided to tackle the problem of the pork first and then sort out the sauce for a home version of this Sichuan classic that wouldn't be a pale imitation of those found in our favorite Chinese restaurants.

These days, Thai stir-fries are just as popular as their Chinese cousins. Take pad see ew: This tangle of thick rice noodles, tender chicken, broccolini, and egg in a sweet and salty soy-based sauce is addictive. But fresh wide rice noodles, sweet Thai soy sauce, and leafy Chinese broccoli can be hard to find. We wanted to replicate this dish at home using supermarket ingredients—and have it be just as appealing as authentic versions. Join us as we stay home to enjoy two takeout favorites.

SICHUAN STIR-FRIED PORK IN GARLIC SAUCE

✔ **WHY THIS RECIPE WORKS:** Recipes for this Sichuan staple are imbalanced; some taste cloyingly sweet, while others overdo it on the vinegar. And the pork is usually dry, chewy, and stringy. We wanted a version as good as anything we'd order in a Sichuan restaurant. To re-create the succulent pork found in the best restaurant stir-fries (usually achieved by low-temperature deep frying), we soaked the pork in a baking soda solution, which tenderizes and moisturizes the meat, and then coated it in a velvetizing cornstarch slurry, which helps it retain moisture as it cooks. And the secret to the sauce's rich flavor? Ketchup and fish sauce, both high in flavor-enhancing glutamates.

WITH THIN-CUT STRIPS OF PORK, A SOY-BASED SAUCE, and plenty of garlic, the Sichuan staple, yu xiang, boasts loads of appeal. Yu xiang translates literally as "fish-fragrant," but the sauce isn't the least bit fishy. (The name refers to its origins as a condiment for seafood.) Rather, it's a mix of salty, sweet, hot, and—thanks to a healthy splash of Chinese black vinegar—sour flavors that, when prepared well, balance out into a bold-tasting, silky sauce that coats the super-tender meat and accompanying vegetables. These usually feature a crunchy element like celery, bamboo shoots, or water chestnuts, plus dark, wrinkly wood ear mushrooms.

That's what it tastes like in a restaurant, anyway. But since we'd found plenty of recipes for yu xiang pork in Chinese cookbooks, we figured we'd make it ourselves. The method looked easy enough: Gently parcook the meat in oil, drain it, and set it aside; turn up the heat and add aromatics and Asian broad-bean chili paste, followed by the vegetables; return the meat to the pan along with the sauce ingredients and simmer until thickened.

But our attempts were all disappointments. None achieved the requisite balance of yu xiang; one tasted cloyingly sweet, and another overdid it on the vinegar and left tasters puckering. Some were thin and watery, others slick and greasy. The biggest problem of all, however, was the pork itself. In most cases, its texture was dry, chewy, and stringy, and the sauce didn't sufficiently camouflage those flaws.

Figuring we'd tackle the meat itself first, we spread our test recipes out in front of us and discovered the common problem: Almost all of them called for pork loin, a lean, notoriously unforgiving cut that tends to cook up dry and fibrous. Switching to another cut was an obvious move, so we surveyed the butcher case and came back with two fattier cuts that promised more flavor and tenderness—pork shoulder and country-style ribs. Both cuts tasted markedly richer and juicier, but shoulder meat came with its own set of challenges. Not only was it hard to find in quantities small enough for stir-fry purposes (we needed only about 12 ounces), but it required quite a bit of knife work to trim out the excess fat and pare it down to matchstick-size pieces. Country-style ribs, cut from the shoulder end of the loin, were a lot easier to butcher, so we went with them.

Now that we were using a fattier cut, we wondered if the low-temperature fat bath was actually necessary. It seemed to us that the only purpose of that step was to ensure that the lean tenderloin emerged moist and silky. But when we tried to eliminate the step, even this more marbled cut didn't cook up as supple as the best yu xiang pork we've eaten in restaurants. If we wanted supremely tender, juicy pork without the mess of all that oil, we'd have to look for another way.

Fortunately, there's a far simpler technique from Chinese cookery that tackles the problem of meat drying out in a stir-fry: velveting. This approach involves coating the meat in a cornstarch slurry to provide an insulating barrier that shields the meat from the pan's high temperatures. We gave it a whirl, mixing 2 teaspoons of cornstarch with an equal amount of rice wine and tossing it with the pork before proceeding with the recipe. Though this was a definite improvement, the leaner pieces of meat were still less tender and juicy than we wanted. For the results that we were after, we needed a technique that offered more than just a starch overcoat; it would have to actually tenderize the meat, too.

As it happens, we learned an interesting fact about meat texture during a recent tasting: Tenderness, especially in pork, is highly dependent on the pH of the meat; the

SICHUAN STIR-FRIED PORK IN GARLIC SAUCE

higher the pH, the more tender it will be. If we could find a way to artificially boost the pH of the meat, it might just soften up a bit. And we had just the ingredient in mind to help: alkaline baking soda.

Our plan was to soak the pork in a solution of 1 tablespoon baking soda and ½ cup water for an hour or so and then proceed with velveting. And the results were promising; even the leaner strips of meat were considerably more tender. Too tender, in fact, and also soapy-tasting. We'd overcompensated a bit, so in the next batch we cut back to 1 teaspoon of baking soda and soaked the meat for just 15 minutes. We also rinsed the pork afterward, to remove any residual soda. This time the pork was perfect: marvelously juicy and supple. Even better, we needed only a few tablespoons of oil to cook the meat.

Meanwhile, the other half of the equation—the sauce—needed adjusting to achieve just the right balance of salty, sour, sweet, and spicy flavors. Starting with a base of equal parts soy sauce and rice wine, plus 4 teaspoons of tangy Chinese black vinegar and a tablespoon of sesame oil, we diluted the mixture with enough chicken broth to amply coat the meat and vegetables and stirred in 2 teaspoons of cornstarch for thickening. Then we

fried up some minced garlic and scallion whites and a few teaspoons of broad-bean chili paste in a nonstick skillet, poured in the sauce mixture, and simmered it until it turned glossy. Not bad, tasters said, but they wanted more—particularly more sweetness and more savory depth.

The first request was easy to fulfill with a couple of tablespoons of sugar. It was boosting the savoriness of the dish that was more challenging. We spent more than 30 subsequent tests tinkering with the ratios of sesame oil, vinegar, garlic, and bean paste, but each batch still lacked a certain full-bodied depth that we remembered in the restaurant versions we'd tried. Two likely reasons: Many restaurants build the sauce from a base of homemade stock (instead of store-bought chicken broth), and some also add monosodium glutamate to punch up the savoriness. Neither of those ingredients would be in our recipe, so we started rooting through our pantry for ingredients that we thought might do the trick and came away with two successful (albeit untraditional) additions: fish sauce and ketchup, both of which are naturally packed with flavor-enhancing glutamates. Just 2 teaspoons of each rounded out the savory flavor we were looking for. As an added bonus, the ketchup also contributed to the smooth viscosity of the sauce.

A few last substitutions were necessary. Instead of hard-to-find wood ear mushrooms, we used shiitakes. We also settled on readily available celery over water chestnuts for a contrasting crunch. Though Chinese black vinegar and Asian broad-bean chili paste are popping up in more and more supermarkets, we found that equal parts balsamic and rice vinegars provided a fine alternative to the former, and either Asian chili-garlic paste or Sriracha sauce made a good sub for the latter (but in smaller amounts).

At last, we had a version of yu xiang pork as good as anything we'd find in a Sichuan restaurant.

Sichuan Stir-Fried Pork in Garlic Sauce

SERVES 4 TO 6

If Chinese black vinegar is unavailable, substitute 2 teaspoons balsamic vinegar and 2 teaspoons rice vinegar. If Asian broad-bean chili paste is unavailable, substitute 2 teaspoons Asian chili-garlic paste or Sriracha sauce. Serve with steamed white rice.

SCIENCE DESK

BAKING SODA AS MEAT TENDERIZER

Meat soaked in a solution of baking soda and water? We admit it sounds pretty unappetizing, but there's a good reason we worked this step into our recipe for Sichuan Stir-Fried Pork in Garlic Sauce. Simply put, alkaline baking soda makes the meat more tender by raising its pH. As this happens, enzymes in the meat called calpains become more active and cut the meat's muscle fibers. The tenderizing effect is twofold. First, as the meat's fibers break down, its texture softens. Second, since the meat's looser consistency retains water better, it's less likely to contract and expel moisture when heated, ensuring that the meat stays juicy throughout. The succulent results are well worth it. And don't worry; the baking soda solution gets washed off before cooking.

SAUCE

- ½ cup low-sodium chicken broth
- 2 tablespoons sugar
- 2 tablespoons soy sauce
- 4 teaspoons Chinese black vinegar
- 1 tablespoon toasted sesame oil
- 1 tablespoon Chinese rice wine or dry sherry
- 2 teaspoons ketchup
- 2 teaspoons fish sauce
- 2 teaspoons cornstarch

PORK

- 12 ounces boneless country-style pork ribs, trimmed
- 1 teaspoon baking soda
- 2 teaspoons Chinese rice wine or dry sherry
- 2 teaspoons cornstarch

STIR-FRY

- 2 scallions, white parts minced, green parts sliced thin
- 4 garlic cloves, minced
- 2 tablespoons Asian broad-bean chili paste
- ¼ cup vegetable oil
- 6 ounces shiitake mushrooms, stemmed and sliced thin
- 2 celery ribs, cut on bias into ¼-inch slices

1. FOR THE SAUCE: Whisk all ingredients together in bowl; set aside.

2. FOR THE PORK: Cut pork into 2-inch lengths, then cut each length into ¼-inch matchsticks. Combine pork with ½ cup cold water and baking soda in bowl. Let sit at room temperature for 15 minutes.

3. Rinse pork in cold water. Drain well and pat dry with paper towels. Whisk rice wine and cornstarch together in bowl. Add pork and toss to coat.

4. FOR THE STIR-FRY: Combine scallion whites, garlic, and chili paste in bowl.

5. Heat 1 tablespoon oil in 12-inch nonstick skillet over high heat until just smoking. Add mushrooms and cook, stirring frequently, until tender, 2 to 4 minutes. Add celery and continue to cook until celery is crisp-tender, 2 to 4 minutes. Transfer vegetables to separate bowl.

6. Add remaining 3 tablespoons oil to now-empty skillet and place over medium-low heat. Add scallion-garlic mixture and cook, stirring frequently, until fragrant, about 30 seconds. Transfer 1 tablespoon scallion-garlic oil to small bowl and set aside. Add pork to skillet and cook, stirring frequently, until no longer pink, 3 to 5 minutes. Whisk sauce mixture to recombine and add to skillet. Increase heat to high and cook, stirring constantly, until sauce is thickened and pork is cooked through, 1 to 2 minutes. Return vegetables to skillet and toss to combine. Transfer to serving platter, sprinkle with scallion greens and reserved scallion-garlic oil, and serve.

THAI-STYLE STIR-FRIED NOODLES WITH CHICKEN AND BROCCOLINI

✔ **WHY THIS RECIPE WORKS:** We wanted to create a version of pad see ew—the traditional Thai dish of chewy, lightly charred rice noodles, with chicken, crisp broccoli, and moist egg, bound with a sweet and salty soy-based sauce—that would work in the American home kitchen. We substituted supermarket ingredients for hard-to-find fresh rice noodles, Chinese broccoli, and sweet Thai soy sauce, but it was simulating the high heat of a restaurant wok burner on a lower-output home stovetop that was the real challenge. Since we were already using maximum heat, we increased the surface area by using a 12-inch nonstick skillet, and we cooked the dish in batches, combining all of the components right before serving. Most important, we found that eliminating much of the stirring in our stir-fry helped us achieve the all-important char that characterizes pad see ew.

THE AMAZINGLY VARIED AND INVENTIVE STREET FOOD of Thailand is a big reason that Bangkok is a dream destination for those of us in the test kitchen. Until we get there, though, we're happy to console ourselves with frequent visits to local Thai restaurants, which specialize in the same kinds of stir-fries that are offered on the streets of Bangkok. And maybe call it research.

Many of us like to order pad see ew, which is a soft tangle of chewy, lightly charred rice noodles, studded with tender slices of chicken breast, crisp Chinese broccoli, and moist egg, all very lightly coated with a beautifully balanced sweet and salty soy-based sauce. It's a simple dish, but that subtle browning of the noodles is like a secret ingredient that elevates pad see ew above other more elaborate stir-fries. Unlike a lot of Thai dishes, it is not inherently fiery, though each serving is usually seasoned to taste with chile vinegar.

THAI-STYLE STIR-FRIED NOODLES WITH CHICKEN AND BROCCOLINI

The delicious simplicity of pad see ew makes it a natural choice for weeknight dinners at home, so we decided to figure out how to translate this dish for the weeknight repertoire. We knew we'd have to find substitutes for some of the more exotic ingredients—fresh wide rice noodles, sweet Thai soy sauce, and leafy Chinese broccoli—and we knew it would take a bit longer to make than it does at the local Thai place. After all, we would be cooking four servings at one time on a domestic stove, not one or two servings on an insanely hot burner as they do at a restaurant or street food cart. But anything less than 45 minutes seemed reasonable.

Authentic pad see ew calls for fresh thick rice noodles, which require no precooking or soaking. However, since they only have a shelf life of about 24 hours, they're virtually impossible to find. For our home version of pad see ew, we'd stick with the dried rice noodles available at any supermarket; the flat, ¼-inch-wide noodles called rice sticks that are used for Thailand's most famous dish, pad thai.

Unlike Italian pasta, rice sticks are meant to absorb a good bit of the sauce they're cooked with and when

properly prepared are soft and delicately chewy throughout. To get them to this state, you merely soak them in water to make them pliable before cooking. Sounds easy enough, for sure, but recommended soaking times and water temperatures vary. Many Thai cookbooks say that rice sticks should be covered with room-temperature water for about 30 minutes, but other sources advise covering them with hot tap water, which reduces the soaking time to 20 minutes. We find such directions maddeningly vague: How warm is "room temperature"? How hot is "hot tap water"? And anyway, given the time constraints of a weeknight supper, 20 to 30 minutes before we could even start heating our pan was too long.

The advantage of the traditional cool-water soak is that it gives the cook a little wiggle room as far as timing is concerned—an extra 5 minutes in cool water will not harm your noodles; however, in very hot water it can turn them into a soggy mess. But the hotter the water the shorter the time, and since we were willing to be diligent if it meant a much shorter soaking time, we devised the following method: We placed ½ pound of dried noodles in a large bowl, poured 6 cups of boiling water over them, and let them sit for exactly 8 minutes, stirring them well when the water went in and once again during the soaking time to prevent them from sticking together. Then we drained them thoroughly, rinsed them with cold water to remove the loose surface starch that would otherwise cause them to fuse together into one big clump, and tossed them with a little bit of oil for some extra antistick insurance. Noodles sorted, we moved on to the other components: chicken, broccoli, eggs, and sauce.

The ubiquitous boneless, skinless chicken breast is the traditional cut in pad see ew, but it is notoriously tricky to cook properly, especially in a fast-paced stir-fry scenario. We often worry that—given the brief cooking time in a crowded pan—our stir-fried chicken will be undercooked, so we admit that we sometimes give the meat a little extra time over the heat, which makes it dry and fibrous. To keep the meat tender, we employed a technique we had developed recently for another stir-fry recipe: we raised the meat's pH by soaking it briefly in a baking soda and water solution. This prevented the proteins in the meat from bonding together as tightly as they otherwise would, enabling us to cook the meat thoroughly without fear of its being chewy.

We whizzed through the next components in quick succession. Chinese broccoli is rarely sold in mainstream supermarkets, so we settled on broccolini (which is actually a hybrid of Chinese and conventional broccoli) as a more accessible substitute. After a few egg tests, we found that dumping unbeaten eggs straight into the pan gave us the denser, variegated curds that usually feature in Asian stir-fries instead of fluffy, American-style scrambled eggs. And we replicated the sweet, salty sauce that is usually used in pad see ew by mixing up a cocktail of ingredients we had on hand: oyster sauce, brown sugar, molasses, fish sauce, garlic (which we browned much more deeply than we typically do in American cooking), and—of course—soy sauce. With all our components in place, we were ready to refine our cooking technique. And that's where it started to go horribly wrong.

In developing previous stir-fry recipes, we'd found that the tapered shape of a wok doesn't absorb as much heat on a flat Western burner as a flat-bottomed skillet, whose design allows more of its surface area to come in direct contact with the heat. So we reached instead for a 12-inch skillet, choosing stainless steel over nonstick because we figured the latter's slick surface wouldn't deliver enough char. We poured in 2 tablespoons of oil and placed the skillet over high heat until it was smoking hot. Then we added our ingredients: chicken first, then eggs, followed by broccoli, and noodles last, with splashes of sauce added throughout the process.

But 2 tablespoons of oil were not enough to keep our stir-fry from sticking. Three tablespoons were not enough. Four and even 5 tablespoons were not enough (those eggs are tough!). In the end it took nearly ½ cup of oil to keep our ingredients from fusing themselves permanently to the surface of our stainless steel skillet. Our stir-fry was limp, greasy, and thoroughly unappetizing. We would have to go with nonstick.

Now we were able to cut the amount of oil in our recipe in half without our ingredients sticking, but crowded into that pan the noodles achieved even less of the smoky char that makes this simple dish interesting than they had

in the stainless pan. So instead of gradually adding ingredients to our skillet, we tried cooking them in batches to maximize the heat, stirring frantically, adding a bit of sauce to everything, and transferring each batch to a bowl when it was cooked. But even with this batch-cooking method the all-important char continued to elude us, and without it the stir-fry was insipid.

In the end, we stumbled on the key to proper browning quite by accident. We had transferred everything back to the skillet for a final warm-through when we realized we had forgotten to prepare a platter for serving. Leaving the pan on the heat, we rushed to find a platter. When we returned, we could smell the contents of the skillet just beginning to burn, so we quickly flipped our stir-fry out onto the awaiting platter. And there, crowning our creation, was the burnished brown color we had been chasing. All we had to do to get it was . . . nothing. Ultimately, the key to adapting pad see ew to a quick and satisfying weeknight meal wasn't emulating the vibrant energy of a Thai street chef; it was all about standing back and letting the magic happen. We call it "Zen and the Art of Stir-Frying."

Thai-Style Stir-Fried Noodles with Chicken and Broccolini

SERVES 4

The flat pad thai–style rice noodles that are used in this recipe can be found in the Asian section of most supermarkets. If you can't find broccolini, you can substitute an equal amount of conventional broccoli, but be sure to trim and peel the stalks before cutting.

CHILE VINEGAR

⅓ cup white vinegar
1 serrano chile, stemmed and sliced into thin rings

STIR-FRY

2 (6-ounce) boneless, skinless chicken breasts, trimmed and cut against grain into ¼-inch-thick slices
1 teaspoon baking soda
8 ounces (¼-inch-wide) rice noodles
¼ cup vegetable oil
¼ cup oyster sauce
1 tablespoon plus 2 teaspoons soy sauce
2 tablespoons packed dark brown sugar
1 tablespoon white vinegar
1 teaspoon molasses
1 teaspoon fish sauce
3 garlic cloves, sliced thin
3 large eggs
10 ounces broccolini, florets cut into 1-inch pieces, stalks cut on bias into ½-inch pieces (5 cups)

1. FOR THE CHILE VINEGAR: Combine vinegar and serrano in bowl. Let stand at room temperature for at least 15 minutes.

2. FOR THE STIR-FRY: Combine chicken with 2 tablespoons cold water and baking soda in bowl. Let sit at room temperature for 15 minutes. Rinse chicken in cold water and drain well.

3. Bring 6 cups water to boil. Place noodles in large bowl. Pour boiling water over noodles. Stir, then soak until noodles are almost tender, about 8 minutes, stirring once halfway through soaking. Drain and rinse with cold water. Drain well and toss with 2 teaspoons oil.

4. Whisk oyster sauce, soy sauce, sugar, vinegar, molasses, and fish sauce together in bowl.

5. Heat 2 teaspoons oil and garlic in 12-inch nonstick skillet over high heat, stirring occasionally, until garlic is deep golden brown, 1 to 2 minutes. Add chicken and 2 tablespoons sauce mixture, toss to coat, and spread chicken into even layer. Cook, without stirring, until chicken begins to brown, 1 to 1½ minutes. Flip chicken and cook, without stirring, until second side begins to brown, 1 to 1½ minutes. Push chicken to 1 side of skillet. Add 2 teaspoons oil to cleared side of skillet. Add eggs to clearing. Using rubber spatula, stir eggs gently and cook until set but still wet. Stir eggs into chicken and continue to cook, breaking up large pieces of egg, until eggs are fully cooked, 30 to 60 seconds. Transfer chicken mixture to bowl.

6. Heat 2 teaspoons oil in now-empty skillet until smoking. Add broccolini and 2 tablespoons sauce and toss to coat. Cover skillet and cook for 2 minutes, stirring once halfway through cooking. Remove lid and continue to cook until broccolini is crisp and very brown in spots, 2 to 3 minutes, stirring once halfway through cooking. Transfer broccolini to bowl with chicken mixture.

7. Heat 2 teaspoons oil in now-empty skillet until smoking. Add half of noodles and 2 tablespoons sauce and toss to coat. Cook until noodles are starting to brown in spots, about 2 minutes, stirring halfway through cooking. Transfer noodles to bowl with chicken mixture. Repeat with remaining 2 teaspoons oil, noodles, and sauce. When second batch of noodles is cooked, add contents of bowl back to skillet and toss to combine. Cook, without stirring, until everything is warmed through, 1 to 1½ minutes. Transfer to platter and serve immediately, passing chile vinegar separately.

RATING BLENDERS

A good blender needs to tackle a variety of tasks—from crushing ice and making frozen drinks to blending lump-free smoothies, milkshakes, and even making hummus—quickly and easily. To find the best one, we gathered nine models and put them through their paces, using them not only on the aforementioned tasks, but also pressing them into service every day for a month to make thick smoothies with fibrous frozen pineapple and stringy raw kale. We identified three key features that can make or break a blender's performance: long blades, each set at a different position and angle; a jar with a bowl-shaped bottom; and a relatively powerful (at least 750-watt) motor. In the end, two blenders clearly outperformed the others. Our top-rated blender is a long-time test kitchen favorite thanks to its durability, long-armed, well-configured blades, and souped-up (1,300-watt) motor—but it costs $449. Fortunately, there's a runner-up; it sports all three key blender features and sailed through all of our tests. Plus, it costs less than half the price of our winner. Brands are listed in order of preference. See AmericasTestKitchen.com for updates and further information on this testing.

HIGHLY RECOMMENDED

VITAMIX 5200

MODEL: 5200   PRICE: $449
DURABILITY: ★★★   SPEED: ★★½   NOISE: ★★½
HUMMUS: ★★½   FRUIT SMOOTHIE: ★★★
KALE SMOOTHIE: ★★★   MILKSHAKE: ★★½
MARGARITA: ★★★   ICE CRUSHING: ★★★
COMMENTS: Years of hard-core test kitchen use have not compromised this blender's superior performance. Its hummus and milkshakes weren't as silky-smooth as others, but its 1,380-watt motor propelled it through most tasks with ease.

BREVILLE The Hemisphere Control

MODEL: BBL605XL   PRICE: $200
DURABILITY: ★★★   SPEED: ★★½   NOISE: ★★★
HUMMUS: ★★★   FRUIT SMOOTHIE: ★★★
KALE SMOOTHIE: ★★½   MILKSHAKE: ★★
MARGARITA: ★★★   ICE CRUSHING: ★★★
COMMENTS: With a curved jar, six blades, and a 750-watt motor, this blender excelled at almost every task—and at less than half the cost of our cowinner. If it stands the test of time, we may eventually make it our sole winner.

RECOMMENDED WITH RESERVATIONS

NINJA Professional Blender

MODEL: NJ600   PRICE: $100
DURABILITY: ★★   SPEED: ★★★   NOISE: ★½
HUMMUS: ★★★   FRUIT SMOOTHIE: ★★½
KALE SMOOTHIE: ★   MILKSHAKE: ★★½
MARGARITA: ★★   ICE CRUSHING: ★★
COMMENTS: This 1,000-watt blender, with a central shaft bearing three sets of food processor–like blades, crushed ice in 7 seconds. Unfortunately, it left margaritas crunchy and couldn't fully break down tough, fibrous kale.

HAMILTON BEACH Rio Commercial Bar Blender

MODEL: HBB250R   PRICE: $106.99
DURABILITY: ★★★   SPEED: ★★   NOISE: ★
HUMMUS: ★★★   FRUIT SMOOTHIE: ★★★
KALE SMOOTHIE: ★★   MILKSHAKE: ★
MARGARITA: ★★½   ICE CRUSHING: ★
COMMENTS: This moderately powered 430-watt blender was a whiz with hummus and fruit smoothies, but its fluted jar trapped ice cubes.

RECOMMENDED WITH RESERVATIONS (*cont.*)

CUISINART Blend and Cook Soup Maker

MODEL: SBC-1000   PRICE: $200
DURABILITY: ★★   SPEED: ★½   NOISE: ★★
HUMMUS: ★★★   FRUIT SMOOTHIE: ★★
KALE SMOOTHIE: ★★   MILKSHAKE: ★
MARGARITA: ★★   ICE CRUSHING: ★★
COMMENTS: While it had six blades and a 900-watt motor, the large, flat bottom of the jar was a drawback. It made excellent hummus but failed to blend a shake, emitting a burning smell as it tried.

NOT RECOMMENDED

OSTER 7-Speed Reversing Motor Blender

MODEL: BVCB07-Z   PRICE: $59.99
DURABILITY: ★   SPEED: ★   NOISE: ★
HUMMUS: ★   FRUIT SMOOTHIE: ★★★
KALE SMOOTHIE: ★½   MILKSHAKE: ★★
MARGARITA: ★★★   ICE CRUSHING: ★½
COMMENTS: This model had six blades and a 600 watt-motor, but the jar tapered so dramatically that large chunks and thick food couldn't reach the blades.

HAMILTON BEACH Wave Maker 2-Speed Blender

MODEL: 53205   PRICE: $39.99
DURABILITY: ★★   SPEED: ★½   NOISE: ★★★
HUMMUS: ★★   FRUIT SMOOTHIE: ★★
KALE SMOOTHIE: ★   MILKSHAKE: ★★
MARGARITA: ★½   ICE CRUSHING: ★
COMMENTS: Thanks to its flat-bottomed jar and four very short blades that were not only symmetrical but also set directly atop one another, this 360-watt blender either struggled or flat-out failed to perform most tasks.

WARING PRO Professional Food and Beverage Blender

MODEL: PBB201   PRICE: $99.95
DURABILITY: ★   SPEED: ★   NOISE: ★
HUMMUS: ★   FRUIT SMOOTHIE: ★
KALE SMOOTHIE: ★   MILKSHAKE: ★
MARGARITA: ★½   ICE CRUSHING: ★
COMMENTS: Given its four short blades, a cramped jar with a flat bottom, and a weak motor, it was no surprise that this 360-watt blender failed at most tasks. Furthermore, it began emitting a noxious odor and making an awful rattling noise almost immediately.

A TASTE OF *Spain*

Bowls of toasted noodles and containers of chopped herbs are ready for cooking on set.

WHY DON'T WE COOK SPANISH FOOD MORE OFTEN? GOOD QUESTION! Spanish cuisine boasts complex layers of flavor usually starting with a *sofrito,* a slow-cooked mixture of aromatics like onions and garlic. We set out to explore two Spanish classics that begin with sofrito: Catalan beef stew and *fideuà,* Spanish-style pasta with shrimp.

The meat stews of Catalonia are unlike any stews we'd run across. In addition to the sofrito of aromatics along with tomatoes, recipes often include cinnamon, smoked paprika, and a *picada,* a pestolike mixture of bread crumbs, nuts, and herbs. While game, boar, or sausage are more common in their stews than beef, we were set on beef. First, we'd need to determine the right cut. Next we'd refine the sofrito-making process—was there any way to speed this time-consuming step? And what about vegetables? American beef stews typically include peas, carrots, and potatoes. Would we want to bulk up our Spanish stew in a similar fashion?

Fideuà is a cousin to perhaps Spain's most famous dish, paella. It features briny shrimp and other seafood such as clams, and sometimes spicy chorizo sausage. The rice is replaced with toasted pasta. The steps to making fideuà are many, starting with building a seafood stock, then toasting the pasta, cooking the sofrito, and finally, combining these components with seafood until it's all cooked through. We wanted to simplify these steps without skimping on flavor. Join us as we bring the flavors of Spain into the test kitchen.

CATALAN-STYLE BEEF STEW

✓ **WHY THIS RECIPE WORKS:** Supremely meaty and complexly flavored, Spanish beef stew is a little different than its American counterpart. It starts with a sofrito, a slow-cooked jamlike mixture of onions, spices, and herbs that builds a flavor-packed base. We normally use chuck eye for stew, but swapped it out for boneless beef short ribs, feeling that they gave us a beefier-tasting stew. We finished the stew with a mixture of toasted bread, toasted almonds, garlic, and parsley. This mixture, called a picada, brightened the stew's flavor and thickened the broth.

FEW CUISINES CAN RIVAL THE COMPLEXITY OF SPANISH food, with its influences from ancient Greece and Rome, North Africa, and even the Americas. This multilayering of flavors and textures is particularly apparent in the meat stews from the country's easternmost region of Catalonia. Almost all begin with a slow-cooked jam of onions and tomatoes known as sofrito and end with the stirring in of picada, a pestolike paste that includes fried bread, herbs, and ground nuts and gives the stew body and even more dimension. Cinnamon and smoked paprika are also common, along with a sherrylike fortified wine known as *vi ranci*. Though stews made from game, boar, or sausage are most typical in Catalonia, we were intent on investigating beef stew. When a search turned up only a handful of recipes, we consulted the renowned Spanish chef José Andrés, whose restaurants include Jaleo in Washington, D.C. Andrés explained the scarcity: Because Catalonia has little pastureland, beef stews are a special indulgence. We love beef, so there was no question that any Catalan-style stew we came up with would feature it. After jotting down a few pointers from Andrés, we set out to build our own recipe.

While most American beef stews are made with chuck roast, Spanish cooks employ a variety of cuts, including flank or skirt steak, blade steak, and short ribs. We tested all of these, comparing each one to chuck. The long, fibrous muscles of flank and skirt steak led to stringy results, and blade steak was flavorful but tended to dry out due to its lower fat content. We settled on boneless beef short ribs. Not only were these easier to butcher than a chuck roast, which is full of intramuscular fat and sinew, but they boasted outstanding beef flavor and became supremely tender and moist after a long, slow simmer. We seared chunks of short ribs in batches in a Dutch oven and then transferred them to a plate so we could prepare the foundation of our stew: the sofrito.

This flavor base is the cornerstone of not only Catalan cooking but also much of Spanish cuisine, lending remarkable depth to countless recipes. A traditional sofrito consists of finely chopped onions browned slowly over low heat and brightened with tomatoes (and sometimes herbs, spices, and aromatics). We've discovered that adding a small amount of salt and sugar to the onions helps draw out their moisture, both hastening and deepening the level of caramelization, so we sprinkled a bit of each onto two minced onions as they cooked over the traditional very low heat in olive oil. Once the onions were soft and dark brown we added tomatoes.

We experimented with canned and fresh tomatoes, preferring the latter for their greater acidity and brightness. We found, however, that fresh tomatoes had to be peeled or the skins made the stew stringy. Our standard method of blanching tomatoes before peeling seemed too fussy, particularly since we were using only two plum tomatoes. We decided to try a simpler method we'd seen in a Spanish cookbook: scraping the pulpy flesh of the tomatoes over the large holes of a box grater and then discarding the leathery skin. This worked beautifully. Along with the tomatoes, we stirred a bay leaf and a teaspoon of heady smoked paprika into the onions.

After 10 minutes more of cooking, the sweet and savory flavors of the sofrito had fully melded, and its texture was sticky and jamlike. But nearly 45 minutes had passed, and we couldn't help but wonder if we could cut back on some of the cooking time. When we sampled sofritos cooked for 15 and 30 minutes alongside a 45-minute flavor base, we had our answer: The long-cooked sample had a significantly richer, more developed taste; the shorter versions simply didn't have enough time to thoroughly caramelize. There would be no shortcuts taken here.

CATALAN-STYLE BEEF STEW WITH MUSHROOMS

We nestled several batches of seared short-rib chunks atop the slow-cooked sofrito and poured in cooking liquids, experimenting with various combinations of chicken broth, beef broth, and water. Surprisingly, the broths actually detracted from the flavor of the beef and sofrito. Tasters preferred the cleanness of a stew made with water alone, which allowed more of the beef, onion, and tomato flavors to dominate.

As for the sherry that is typically added, the sofrito was already providing mild sweetness, and tasters thought that vi ranci (as well as American-made sherries) rendered the sauce too cloying. Instead, we turned to wine. We remembered a tip from Andrés that less-assertive white wine is often preferred to red wine in stew as it complements, rather than overpowers, the flavor of the meat. We selected a dry Spanish white (Albariño), which our tasters agreed worked far better in the stew than red wine. In the end, we simmered the beef in just 1½ cups each of water and wine. To capture the warm spice flavor typical of Catalan stew, we also stirred a touch of cinnamon along with a sprig of fresh thyme into the pot.

Our stew was coming along nicely, but after searing the short ribs and cooking the sofrito, we were an hour into our recipe, and hadn't even started simmering the beef. We wondered whether searing the meat (a step that took about 15 minutes) was absolutely necessary. Spanish stews are usually simmered covered, but we had an idea.

In past test kitchen work for Hungarian beef stew, we were able to do away with searing since the meat was cooked on a bed of onions with no added liquid. Any portion of meat sitting above the liquid released by the onions was exposed to the heat of the oven and browned nearly as well as it would if it were seared, developing thousands of new flavor compounds. To see if we could eliminate searing in this recipe, we set the oven to a moderate 300 degrees and prepared a comparison of stews made with seared and unseared meat, leaving the unseared batch uncovered to fully expose it to the heat of the oven. When the stews emerged from the oven 2½ to 3 hours later, they tasted remarkably similar. We concluded that we could eliminate searing. An added benefit of this move was that the gentle, ambient heat of a low oven provided more reliable results than the stove, which runs the risk of scorching the meat on the bottom of the pot.

Now that we had achieved tender, intensely flavored beef, it was time for the critical final flourish: the picada. Some experts estimate that this bracing mixture of fried bread, nuts (most often almonds or hazelnuts), garlic, olive oil, and herbs (typically parsley) ground together has been used in Catalan cooking since the 13th century. In stews, the nuts and bread bulk up the braising liquid, and the garlic and parsley add flavor and freshness.

Opting for blanched almonds, which, unlike hazelnuts, require no fussy skinning, we sautéed ¼ cup of nuts with chunks of bread and a couple of cloves of minced garlic in olive oil before processing the whole lot with the parsley in a food processor. Stirred into the finished stew, the picada gave the dish a jolt of bright flavor, but we wondered if it would be even better if we left the garlic raw. Sure enough, a subsequent batch with raw garlic imparted a pungency to the stew that tasters loved. And although a food processor proved faster and more convenient than a mortar and pestle, its whizzing blade muddied the grassy flavor of the parsley, so we minced it with a knife before combining it with the ground ingredients.

So far, our stew contained no vegetables, and although we didn't plan on loading it up with carrots, peas, and potatoes like a typical American stew, some additional element seemed appropriate. It only made sense to feature a popular Catalan ingredient: oyster mushrooms. Rather than cook them directly in the stew, which spoiled their delicate flavor and texture, we sautéed them separately. The mushrooms went into the finished stew along with the picada and a shot of sherry vinegar. Here was a beef stew rich and fragrant with the flavors of Catalonia that employed classic Spanish techniques, plus a few of our own.

Catalan-Style Beef Stew with Mushrooms
SERVES 4 TO 6

While we developed this recipe with Albariño, a dry Spanish white wine, you can also use a Sauvignon Blanc. Remove the woody base of the oyster mushroom stems before cooking. An equal amount of quartered button mushrooms may be substituted for the oyster mushrooms. Serve the stew with boiled or mashed potatoes or rice.

STEW

- 2 tablespoons olive oil
- 2 large onions, chopped fine
- ½ teaspoon sugar
  Kosher salt and pepper
- 2 plum tomatoes, halved lengthwise, pulp grated on large holes of box grater, and skins discarded
- 1 teaspoon smoked paprika
- 1 bay leaf
- 1½ cups dry white wine
- 1½ cups water
- 1 large sprig fresh thyme
- ¼ teaspoon ground cinnamon
- 2½ pounds boneless beef short ribs, trimmed and cut into 2-inch cubes

PICADA

- ¼ cup whole blanched almonds
- 2 tablespoons olive oil
- 1 slice hearty white sandwich bread, crusts removed, torn into 1-inch pieces
- 2 garlic cloves, peeled
- 3 tablespoons minced fresh parsley
- 8 ounces oyster mushrooms, trimmed
- 1 teaspoon sherry vinegar

NOTES FROM THE TEST KITCHEN

SHAKING UP STEW STANDARDS
To achieve the supremely beefy and complex flavor profile of Spanish beef stew, we learned a few new tricks—and gave up some long-held notions.

START WITH SOFRITO
A slow-cooked mixture of onions, tomatoes, spices, and herbs—known as sofrito in Spain—forms a flavor-packed base for the stew.

GO FOR WHITE WINE
We typically use red wine in beef stew. Here, we agreed with Spanish cooks that red wine competes with beefy flavor, so we reached for white instead.

SWAP THE ROAST FOR RIBS
Most stew recipes (including many of ours) call for chuck-eye roast. Boneless beef short ribs are even beefier tasting and are easier to break down.

SKIP THE SEAR
When the stew is cooked in the oven and the pot is left uncovered, any part of the beef not submerged in liquid can brown, making searing unnecessary.

END WITH PICADA
A mixture of ground toasted bread, almonds, garlic, and parsley—the picada—stirred in before serving brightens the stew's flavor and thickens the broth.

1. **FOR THE STEW:** Adjust oven rack to middle position and heat oven to 300 degrees. Heat oil in Dutch oven over medium-low heat until shimmering. Add onions, sugar, and ½ teaspoon salt; cook, stirring often, until onions are deeply caramelized, 30 to 40 minutes. Add tomatoes, smoked paprika, and bay leaf; cook, stirring often, until darkened and thick, 5 to 10 minutes.

2. Add wine, water, thyme, and cinnamon to pot, scraping up any browned bits. Season beef with 1½ teaspoons salt and ½ teaspoon pepper and add to pot. Increase heat to high and bring to simmer. Transfer to oven and cook, uncovered. After 1 hour stir stew to redistribute meat, return to oven, and continue to cook, uncovered, until meat is tender, 1½ to 2 hours longer.

3. **FOR THE PICADA:** While stew is in oven, heat almonds and 1 tablespoon oil in 10-inch skillet over medium heat; cook, stirring often, until almonds are golden brown, 3 to 6 minutes. Using slotted spoon, transfer almonds to food processor. Return now-empty skillet to medium heat, add bread, and cook, stirring often, until toasted, 2 to 4 minutes; transfer to food processor with almonds. Add garlic and process until mixture is finely ground, about 20 seconds, scraping down bowl as needed. Transfer mixture to bowl, stir in parsley, and set aside.

4. Return again-empty skillet to medium heat. Heat remaining 1 tablespoon oil until shimmering. Add mushrooms and ½ teaspoon salt; cook, stirring often, until tender, 5 to 7 minutes. Transfer to bowl and set aside.

5. Remove bay leaf and thyme sprig. Stir picada, mushrooms, and vinegar into stew. Season with salt and pepper to taste and serve.

SPANISH-STYLE PASTA WITH SHRIMP

✓ **WHY THIS RECIPE WORKS:** Traditional recipes for *fideuà*, a dish similar to paella, where toasted pasta stands in for rice, can take several hours to prepare. We wanted to speed up the process but keep the deep flavors of the classic. To replace the fussy fish stock, we made a quick shrimp stock using the shrimp's shells, a combination of chicken broth and water, and a bay leaf. We also streamlined the sofrito, the aromatic base common in Spanish cooking, by finely mincing the onion and using canned tomatoes (instead of fresh), which helped the recipe components soften and brown more quickly. And we boosted the flavor of the shrimp by quickly marinating them in olive oil, garlic, salt, and pepper.

THE BIGGEST STAR OF TRADITIONAL SPANISH COOKING is arguably paella, but there's another closely related dish equally deserving of raves: *fideuà*. This richly flavored dish swaps the rice for thin noodles that are typically toasted until nut-brown before being cooked in a garlicky, tomatoey stock loaded with seafood and sometimes chorizo sausage. As with the rice in paella, the noodles (called fideos) should be tender but not mushy. But whereas paella tends to be moist but not soupy, fideuà is often a little brothy.

One thing that paella and fideuà have in common: a lengthy and involved cooking process. Almost all of the recipes we tried called for the same series of steps: Simmer fish and shellfish scraps to create stock. Toast the fideos and put together a flavorful base (the sofrito) by slowly reducing fresh tomatoes with aromatics and seasonings. Combine the sofrito with the stock and then simmer the toasted noodles and seafood in this rich-tasting liquid until cooked. Finally, put the whole thing in the oven to create a crunchy layer of pasta on top.

Just as with paella, tinkering with fideuà is part of the art. We decided that our tweaks would be aimed at streamlining a recipe but leaving it every bit as deeply flavorful as the more time-consuming versions.

SPANISH-STYLE TOASTED PASTA WITH SHRIMP

Our first decision was to keep things simple in the seafood department and go with shrimp alone. Our next step was to make a stock without even dirtying a pot. We knew that shrimp shells can build a surprisingly flavorful broth without much help, so we combined the shells from 1½ pounds of shrimp in a bowl with some water and a bay leaf and microwaved until the shells turned pink and the water was hot. The resulting broth wasn't bad for something that took such little effort, but its taste improved when we replaced a portion of the water with chicken broth and added a small measure of white wine for brightness.

Fideos come in varying thicknesses and shapes, including short, straight strands and coiled nests of thin, vermicelli-like noodles. We found that snapping spaghettini (more widely available than fideos) into pieces gave us a fine approximation of the first type of fideos. Not all fideuà recipes call for toasting the pasta, but skipping that step led to a dish that tasted weak and washed out. So what was the best way to toast? The oven provided controlled heat but required repeatedly moving a baking sheet in and out in order to stir the noodles. Toasting on the stovetop in a skillet—the same skillet in which the dish would be cooked and served—also required stirring, but this was much easier to monitor.

Next we examined the sofrito. This flavor base shows up in a variety of forms in Spanish dishes but always features some combination of aromatics—onion, garlic, celery, and bell pepper are common—slow-cooked in oil to soften and concentrate their flavors. In fideuà, onion and garlic are typical, along with tomato. In the interest of efficiency, we ruled out preparing the sofrito separately, in another skillet. We also finely chopped our onion so that it would cook quickly and added ¼ teaspoon of salt to help draw out moisture so that the onion softened and browned even faster in the oil.

Fresh tomatoes would take time to cook down, so we opted for canned diced tomatoes that we drained well and chopped fine. Added to the skillet with the softened onion, they reduced to a thick paste in a matter of minutes. Then we introduced minced garlic and cooked the mixture for a minute to bloom the flavors. When we pitted fideuà made with our abbreviated sofrito against a traditional slow-cooked version, tasters were hard-pressed to taste any difference. Our next task: getting the right proportion of liquid to pasta. For 8 ounces of pasta, 3¾ cups of liquid was the perfect amount. It allowed the pasta to soak up enough liquid to become tender while leaving just a little behind in the skillet.

It was time to fine-tune the flavors. A mixture of sweet and Spanish smoked paprikas won praise for its balance of smokiness and earthy sweetness, and while we liked the distinctly Spanish flavor of saffron, it wasn't worth the exorbitant cost, so we left it out. We added ½ teaspoon of anchovy paste, a go-to flavor booster in the test kitchen, to the sofrito along with the garlic and paprika; it offered depth and its flavor blended seamlessly with the shrimp.

Speaking of the shrimp, we found that simmering them in the stock with the pasta rendered them rubbery. Adding them during the last 5 minutes of cooking and covering the skillet improved their texture but not their wan flavor. A quick soak in olive oil, garlic, salt, and pepper took care of that problem.

Some recipes finish fideuà in the oven, turning the surface of the pasta crisp and brown—a nice contrast with the tender noodles and seafood underneath. The broiler seemed ideal for achieving such a crust, but when its intense heat toughened up the shrimp, we decided to make a small change: We gently stirred the raw shrimp into the noodles to partially submerge them and protect them from the heat.

NOTES FROM THE TEST KITCHEN

IT'S A SNAP

Since traditional short fideos noodles are hard to find, we came up with an easy way to break long strands into even lengths.

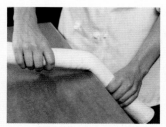

Loosely fold 4 ounces of spaghettini in dish towel, keeping pasta flat, not bunched. Position so that 1 to 2 inches of pasta rests on counter and remainder of pasta hangs off edge. Pressing bundle against counter, press down on long end of towel to break strands into pieces, sliding bundle back over edge after each break.

Finally, we accompanied our fideuà with two traditional condiments: lemon wedges and a spoonful of aïoli, a garlic mayonnaise that adds richness. What had our tweaks accomplished? A recipe for Spanish-style fideuà that delivered terrific flavor, in far less time and with far less effort.

Spanish-Style Toasted Pasta with Shrimp

SERVES 4

In step 5, if your skillet is not broiler-safe, once the pasta is tender transfer the mixture to a broiler-safe 13 by 9-inch baking dish lightly coated with olive oil; scatter the shrimp over the pasta and stir them in to partially submerge. Broil and serve as directed. Serve this dish with lemon wedges and Aïoli (recipe follows), stirring it into individual portions at the table.

- 3 tablespoons plus 2 teaspoons extra-virgin olive oil
- 3 garlic cloves, minced
  Salt and pepper
- 1½ pounds extra-large shrimp (21 to 25 per pound), peeled and deveined, shells reserved
- 2¾ cups water
- 1 cup low-sodium chicken broth
- 1 bay leaf
- 8 ounces spaghettini or thin spaghetti, broken into 1- to 2-inch lengths
- 1 onion, chopped fine
- 1 (14.5-ounce) can diced tomatoes, drained and chopped fine
- 1 teaspoon paprika
- 1 teaspoon smoked paprika
- ½ teaspoon anchovy paste
- ¼ cup dry white wine
- 1 tablespoon chopped fresh parsley
  Lemon wedges
- 1 recipe Aïoli (optional) (recipe follows)

1. Combine 1 tablespoon oil, 1 teaspoon garlic, ¼ teaspoon salt, and ⅛ teaspoon pepper in medium bowl. Add shrimp, toss to coat, and refrigerate until ready to use.

2. Place reserved shrimp shells, water, chicken broth, and bay leaf in medium bowl. Cover and microwave until

NOTES FROM THE TEST KITCHEN

WEEKNIGHT SPANISH-STYLE PASTA WITH SHRIMP
A series of shortcuts allowed us to create this traditionally labor-intensive, paella-like dish in a single skillet in just an hour.

1. SEASON SHRIMP
Marinating the shrimp in olive oil, garlic, salt, and pepper infuses them with flavor as we prepare the other ingredients.

2. MAKE INSTANT STOCK
Microwaving the shrimp shells with diluted chicken broth and a bay leaf creates a quick, surprisingly rich-tasting stock.

3. TOAST NOODLES
Cooking the pasta (broken into pieces) in a skillet with olive oil until well browned develops deep, nutty flavor.

4. COOK IN BROTH
Simmering the noodles in stock and a quick sofrito of sautéed onion, garlic, and tomatoes lets them soak up lots of flavor.

5. ADD SHRIMP; BROIL
Partially submerging the shrimp under the pasta and then transferring the skillet to the broiler creates a crisp, browned crust.

liquid is hot and shells have turned pink, about 6 minutes. Set aside until ready to use.

3. Toss spaghettini and 2 teaspoons oil in broiler-safe 12-inch skillet until spaghettini is evenly coated. Toast spaghettini over medium-high heat, stirring frequently, until browned and nutty in aroma (spaghettini should be color of peanut butter), 6 to 10 minutes. Transfer spaghettini to bowl. Wipe out skillet with paper towel.

4. Heat remaining 2 tablespoons oil in now-empty skillet over medium-high heat until shimmering. Add onion and ¼ teaspoon salt; cook, stirring frequently, until onion is softened and beginning to brown around edges, 4 to 6 minutes. Add tomatoes and cook, stirring occasionally, until mixture is thick, dry, and slightly darkened in color, 4 to 6 minutes. Reduce heat to medium and add remaining garlic, paprika, smoked paprika, and anchovy paste. Cook until fragrant, about 1½ minutes. Add spaghettini and stir to combine. Adjust oven rack 5 to 6 inches from broiler element and heat broiler.

5. Pour broth through fine-mesh strainer into skillet. Add wine, ¼ teaspoon salt, and ½ teaspoon pepper and stir well. Increase heat to medium-high and bring to simmer. Cook uncovered, stirring occasionally, until liquid is slightly thickened and spaghettini is just tender, 8 to 10 minutes. Scatter shrimp over spaghettini and stir shrimp into spaghettini to partially submerge. Transfer skillet to oven and broil until shrimp are opaque and surface of spaghettini is dry with crisped, browned spots, 5 to 7 minutes. Remove from oven and let stand, uncovered, for 5 minutes. Sprinkle with parsley and serve immediately, passing lemon wedges and aïoli, if using, separately.

VARIATION

Spanish-Style Toasted Pasta with Shrimp and Clams

Reduce amount of shrimp to 1 pound and water to 2½ cups. In step 5, cook pasta until almost tender, about 6 minutes. Scatter 1½ pounds scrubbed littleneck or cherrystone clams over pasta, cover skillet, and cook until clams begin to open, about 3 minutes. Scatter shrimp over pasta, stir to partially submerge shrimp and clams, and proceed with recipe as directed.

Aïoli

MAKES ¾ CUP

1 garlic clove, grated fine
2 large egg yolks
4 teaspoons lemon juice
¼ teaspoon salt
⅛ teaspoon sugar
  Ground white pepper
¾ cup olive oil

In large bowl, combine garlic, egg yolks, lemon juice, salt, sugar, and pepper to taste until combined. Whisking constantly, very slowly drizzle oil into egg mixture until thick and creamy. Season with salt and pepper to taste.

RATING SPAGHETTI

Spaghetti is usually made of just semolina (coarsely milled durum wheat) and maybe added vitamins, yet when it comes to supermarket brands, texture and flavor can vary tremendously. We sampled eight brands, dressed with olive oil and with tomato sauce, looking for one that delivered clean, wheaty flavor and a firm, nutty chew. The best brands stood out for their great texture, while the worst ones cooked up sticky or mushy; cloudier cooking water indicated which brands had a weak structure and broke down during boiling. Some brands include durum flour, a finer, cheaper grind of durum wheat that can lead to gummy noodles. The dies used to make the pasta and drying temperature can affect texture, too. Poorly maintained machines, no matter if the dies are traditional bronze or more modern Teflon-coated, cannot produce perfectly compact strands of spaghetti, and the texture can suffer. Also, ultra-high temperatures (190 degrees or higher) can speed up the process but may end up cooking out some of the flavor. Brands are listed in order of preference. See AmericasTestKitchen.com for updates and further information on this testing.

RECOMMENDED

DE CECCO Spaghetti No. 12
PRICE: $1.39 for 16 oz   **SOURCE:** Italy
INGREDIENTS: Durum wheat semolina, niacin, ferrous lactate, thiamine mononitrate, riboflavin, folic acid
PROCESSING METHOD: Pressed through bronze dies; dried at 158°F
COMMENTS: This Italian import boasted "clean wheat flavor" and a "firm, ropy quality"; in fact, the lab confirmed these strands as the strongest of the samples. The texture was just as good with sauce; tasters found it "firm," with "good chew."

RUSTICHELLA D'ABRUZZO Pasta Abruzzese di Semola di Grano Duro
PRICE: $4.56 for 17.5 oz ($4.17 for 16 oz)   **SOURCE:** Italy
INGREDIENTS: Durum wheat semolina
PROCESSING METHOD: Pressed through bronze dies; dried at 95°F
COMMENTS: Even though these noodles were dried at a fairly low 95 degrees, they retained a nice "firm" bite and chew. We also appreciated this pricey Italian brand's "nutty," "toasty" taste.

GAROFALO Spaghetti
PRICE: $2.49 for 16 oz   **SOURCE:** Italy
INGREDIENTS: Durum wheat semolina, niacin, iron lactate, thiamine mononitrate, riboflavin, folic acid
PROCESSING METHOD: Pressed through bronze dies; dried at 176°F
COMMENTS: Tossed with olive oil, this Italian pasta ranked highest for flavor that was "buttery" and "rich-tasting" and had a "roughness" to the exterior. However, that pleasant coarseness was obscured by the sauce, which made the noodles slightly "gummy."

DELALLO Spaghetti No. 4
PRICE: $2.81 for 16 oz   **SOURCE:** Italy Ingredients: Semolina, ferrous lactate (iron), niacin, thiamine mononitrate, riboflavin, folic acid
PROCESSING METHOD: Pressed through bronze dies; dried at 167°F
COMMENTS: In general, tasters found this spaghetti to be "middle-of-the-road." It didn't stand out for having major flaws, and it didn't elicit raves. Its taste was "light" but still "wheaty," while its texture was deemed "fine."

RECOMMENDED

RONZONI Spaghetti
PRICE: $1.39 for 16 oz   **SOURCE:** USA
INGREDIENTS: Semolina (wheat), durum flour, niacin, iron (ferrous sulfate), thiamine mononitrate, riboflavin, folic acid
PROCESSING METHOD: Pressed through Teflon-coated dies; dried at 190°F
COMMENTS: Overall, this brand passed muster. But perhaps due in part to ultra-high-temperature drying, which cooks out flavor, some tasters thought this mass-market American spaghetti "lacked nuttiness." The inclusion of fine-ground durum flour may have accounted for why some tasters found the texture "mealy."

BARILLA Spaghetti
PRICE: $1.67 for 16 oz   **SOURCE:** USA
INGREDIENTS: Semolina (wheat), durum flour, niacin, iron (ferrous sulfate), thiamine mononitrate, riboflavin, folic acid
PROCESSING METHOD: Pressed through Teflon-coated dies; dried at ultra-high temperature (company would not provide exact data)
COMMENTS: "There is something a little flat about the flavor of this," said one taster about this American bestseller, which we speculated must have been dried at a temperature high enough to make it taste less wheaty than some. Overall, though, tasters found the strands "OK" but "unremarkable."

RECOMMENDED WITH RESERVATIONS

MONTEBELLO Organic Spaghetti
PRICE: $2.99 for 16 oz   **SOURCE:** Italy
INGREDIENTS: Organic durum wheat semolina
PROCESSING METHOD: Pressed through bronze dies; dried at 130–150°F
COMMENTS: It wasn't flavor criticisms that sank this imported spaghetti to the lower rungs of the chart; most tasters praised the "clean," "bright," "almost nutty" taste. These strands lost the most starch during cooking, for a "mushy," "crumbly" texture.

Ultimate
ITALIAN

Chris learned in the test kitchen that when draining pasta, always reserve some of the cooking water in case you need to thin the sauce. (Placing a measuring cup inside the colander before you drain is a good reminder.)

IN OUR OPINION, EVERYONE SHOULD HAVE AN ITALIAN GRANDmother—preferably one who cooks well and all day long! We never tire of Italian food, and when it's done right, few cuisines can touch it. Since most of us need to make do on our own, we wanted to develop recipes for the ultimate versions of two Italian favorites: fresh pasta and *ragu alla bolognese.*

Some of us in the test kitchen frequently make pasta at home while others rely instead on fresh pasta from an Italian market. What's their excuse? They don't have a pasta machine. Few people do. What if we could find a way to make pasta by hand—without apprenticing to an Italian master? We wouldn't settle for anything less than eggy rich ribbons with a springy yet delicate chew. And our only piece of equipment would be a simple rolling pin.

If there's one pasta sauce that can make us swoon, it's ragu alla bolognese. This quintessential meat sauce is remarkably velvety, thick, and rich. We could almost eat a bowl of it without the pasta. We wanted to make a bolognese truly worth the effort. Because the choice of meat is central to the success of this sauce, that's where we'd start. We would also examine whether dairy should be included. Some recipes insist on milk or cream and others leave it out altogether. Wine is another factor recipes can't seem to agree on: red or white? Let's clear the decks and start with a bolognese cook–off to narrow down what makes the best pot of sauce.

FRESH PASTA

✔ **WHY THIS RECIPE WORKS:** Not everyone has a pasta machine and rolling out pasta dough by hand is no easy task. For an easy-to-roll pasta dough (that would still cook up into delicate, springy noodles), we added six extra egg yolks and a couple tablespoons of olive oil to our dough. In addition, we incorporated an extended resting period to allow the gluten network to relax. To roll and cut the pasta, we first divided the pasta into smaller manageable pieces, then used a rolling pin to roll the dough and a sharp knife to cut the dough into noodles.

WE'VE ALWAYS WANTED TO FIGURE OUT HOW TO MAKE pasta with nothing more than dough, a rolling pin, and some elbow grease. While mechanical pasta rollers aren't all that expensive, many home cooks don't own them. But as anyone who has ever attempted to roll out a block of hard pasta dough by hand knows, it's no easy task. The dough has a tendency to spring back, and if it isn't rolled out gossamer thin, the pasta will never achieve the right al dente texture when cooked. So how do Italian cooks manage to pull off this feat? One answer: years of perseverance.

In her *Essentials of Classic Italian Cooking,* Marcella Hazan devotes no fewer than six pages to the classic hand-rolling technique perfected in the Emilia-Romagna region of Italy. Employing extra-thin, super-long rolling pins measuring 1½ inches in diameter and 32 inches in length, Italians in this part of the country have developed a series of stretching movements that can transform a lump of firm dough into a thin, delicate sheet. Besides the obvious drawback of needing a generous work surface to accommodate the pin, Hazan is the first to admit that this traditional technique must be exhaustively practiced "until the motions are performed through intuition rather than deliberation."

While we're typically game for a hard-won lesson in authenticity, even we have limits. We wanted a dough that any cook could roll out with ease on the first try and that would cook up to that incomparably tender yet slightly chewy texture that makes fresh pasta so worth making.

In addition to centuries of experience, Italians have another hand-rolling advantage—the best kind of flour for the job: *doppio zero*, or 00. The name denotes the fine talcumlike grind that gives pasta an almost creamy texture. Also important is its protein content (around 9 percent). To see what we were missing, we mail-ordered some and mixed up a typical batch of dough. Sure enough, the 00 flour produced a malleable dough that was far easier to work with than dough made from all-purpose flour.

To achieve similarly soft dough without the specialty flour, our first inclination was to dilute the protein content of all-purpose flour (which boasts 10 to 12 percent protein) by cutting it with cake flour (which has 6 to 8 percent protein). We substituted increasing amounts of cake flour for all-purpose and saw a dramatic impact. With just 25 percent cake flour in the mix, our dough was much softer, less elastic, and easier to roll out. Unfortunately, the cooked strands, which released a lot of starch into the cooking water, emerged with a pitted, pebbly surface. Our science editor explained why: For noodles to remain intact and leach only a little starch into the cooking water, the starch granules in the flour need to be fully surrounded by a strong network of proteins. But the bleach in cake flour weakens the proteins and makes the starch more absorbent and prone to bursting—a good thing when you want a tender cake but not when you're making pasta. Clearly, we needed a different strategy, so we turned our attention to the amount of liquid in the recipe.

Traditional pasta dough is about 30 percent water (compared with around 55 percent water for a basic sandwich loaf), all of which comes from the eggs. We figured that simply upping the hydration level would create a softer dough that would be easier to roll out, so we experimented with adding plain water to one batch of dough and an extra egg white to another. Just as we'd hoped, these more hydrated doughs were softer, but the wetter surface of the dough caused considerable sticking, which required more flour during rolling and led to cooked pasta with a starchy, gummy surface. Still, we felt we were on to something by increasing the liquid in our recipe. Olive oil is a common addition to many fresh pasta recipes. What if we used it instead of water?

FRESH PASTA WITH WALNUT CREAM SAUCE

We mixed up a few more batches of dough, adding increasing amounts of olive oil. As the oil amount increased, the dough became more supple and easier to roll out. But because fat coats the proteins, inhibiting gluten formation, too much oil once again weakened the dough's structure, leading to excess starch loss in the water and a compromised texture. We found our upper limit at 2 tablespoons of oil. We were finally getting somewhere, but this dough was still far from user-friendly.

In many pasta doughs yolks are substituted for some of the whole eggs, and for good reason. While yolks still contain about 50 percent water, they are also loaded with fat and emulsifiers, both of which limit gluten development. However, unlike doughs made with cake flour or excessive amounts of oil, dough made with extra yolks still has plenty of structure thanks to the coagulation of the egg proteins. We tried adding more yolks until we had a truly soft, easy-to-work dough that also boiled up nice and tender. The magic number proved to be six extra yolks. This dough took on a beautiful yellow hue, yielded to gentle pressure with a rolling pin, and cooked up into delicate ribbons with a springy bite.

We had cleared some big hurdles, but we weren't finished. We turned our attention to finding the best way to rest, roll, and cut the pasta. After being mixed, pasta dough is often rested for 20 to 30 minutes to allow the flour to fully hydrate and the newly formed gluten to cross-link into a network and then relax. Given that 30 minutes makes for friendlier dough, would longer be even better? To find out, we made a batch and let the dough sit at room temperature for an extended period of time, cutting and rolling out pieces every 30 minutes. As we suspected, after an hour, our dough was significantly more malleable—and it continued to soften over the next 3 hours (we found 4 hours of resting time to be ideal, though not critical for success). All we had to do now was divide the dough into manageable pieces and grab a heavy rolling pin—right?

Well, almost. This dough was better than the dense blocks we'd struggled with in the past, but it still required a bit of technique. We knew we needed to avoid using too much flour on the counter; a little stickiness is a good thing, as it prevents the dough from springing back too easily. Plus, as we'd already learned, the excess flour turns the surface of the pasta coarse and gummy once cooked.

With that in mind, we first cut the dough into six manageable pieces. Working with one at a time, we dusted each piece lightly with flour and used our fingers to flatten it into a 3-inch square. From there we switched to a rolling pin and doubled it to a 6-inch square. After another light dusting of flour, we began working the dough. Starting with the pin in the middle of the dough, we first rolled it away from us, then returned it to the middle and rolled it toward us. When the dough reached 6 by 12 inches, we gave it another dusting of flour and then repeated the rolling process until the dough measured roughly 6 by 20 inches.

From here, the possibilities were limitless. For ribbon-style pasta, we let the sheets dry on clean dish towels until firm around the edges (a step that enabled us to avoid dusting with more flour) before folding them up at 2-inch intervals and slicing crosswise to the desired thickness. With dough that rolls out this easily and cooks up into such wonderfully springy, delicate noodles, we'd wager that even cooks with pasta machines might be tempted to leave them in the cabinet.

Fresh Pasta without a Machine

MAKES 1 POUND; SERVES 4 TO 6

If using a high-protein all-purpose flour like King Arthur brand, increase the number of egg yolks to 7. The longer the dough rests in step 2, the easier it will be to roll out. When rolling out the dough, avoid adding too much flour, which may result in excessive snapback.

- 2 **cups (10 ounces) all-purpose flour**
- 2 **large eggs plus 6 large yolks**
- 2 **tablespoons olive oil**
- 1 **tablespoon salt**
- 1 **recipe sauce (recipes follow)**

1. Process flour, eggs and yolks, and oil together in food processor until mixture forms cohesive dough that feels soft and is barely tacky to touch, about 45 seconds. (If dough sticks to fingers, add up to ¼ cup flour, 1 tablespoon at a time, until barely tacky. If dough doesn't become cohesive, add up to 1 tablespoon water,

TROUBLESHOOTING FRESH PASTA

This dough is designed to be tacky enough to stick lightly to the counter, giving it traction to be stretched ultra-thin, but not so sticky that it wrinkles when rolled out. Variables such as flour brand, measuring technique, and size of the eggs may lead to slight differences in consistency. Here are tips on how to address texture-related problems and other issues that may arise.

PROBLEM: Dough doesn't come together in food processor.
SOLUTION: Add up to 1 tablespoon water, 1 teaspoon at a time, until dough forms cohesive mass that's barely tacky to touch.

PROBLEM: Dough is too sticky.
SOLUTION: Add up to ¼ cup flour, 1 tablespoon at a time, until dough is barely tacky.

PROBLEM: Dough wrinkles when rolled out.
SOLUTION: Lift dough from counter; dust both sides lightly with flour.

PROBLEM: Dough has too much extra flour, doesn't stick to counter, and snaps back when rolled.
SOLUTION: Use pastry brush to dust off excess flour from dough.

PROBLEM: Dough sheet is too dry and cracks when folded.
SOLUTION: Mist sheet lightly with water; let sit for few minutes to allow dough to absorb water before folding again.

PROBLEM: Dough pieces aren't same size.
SOLUTION: When rolling out, pay more attention to visual cue provided—dough should be rolled thin enough that outline of fingers is visible through it—than to final dimensions.

1 teaspoon at a time, until it just comes together; process 30 seconds longer.)

2. Turn dough ball out onto dry counter and knead until smooth, 1 to 2 minutes. Shape dough into 6-inch-long cylinder. Wrap with plastic wrap and set aside at room temperature to rest for at least 1 hour or up to 4 hours.

ROLLING AND CUTTING PASTA DOUGH BY HAND

What's the trick to turning a lump of pasta dough into long, silky strands—without a pasta roller? Starting with a soft, malleable dough is half the battle. The other half: dividing the dough into small, manageable pieces and working with them one at a time.

1. Shape dough into 6-inch cylinder; wrap in plastic wrap and let rest for at least 1 hour. Divide into 6 equal pieces. Reserve 1 piece; rewrap remaining 5.

2. Working with reserved piece, dust both sides with flour, then press cut side down into 3-inch square. With rolling pin, roll into 6-inch square, then dust both sides again with flour.

3. Roll dough to 12 by 6 inches, rolling from center of dough 1 way at a time, then dust with flour. Continue rolling to 20 by 6 inches, lifting frequently to release from counter. Transfer dough to dish towel and air-dry for about 15 minutes.

4. Starting with short end, gently fold dried sheet at 2-inch intervals to create flat, rectangular roll.

5. With sharp knife, cut into ³⁄₁₆-inch-wide noodles.

6. Use fingers to unfurl pasta; transfer to baking sheet.

3. Cut cylinder crosswise into 6 equal pieces. Working with 1 piece of dough (rewrap remaining dough), dust both sides with flour, place cut side down on clean counter, and press into 3-inch square. Using heavy rolling pin, roll into 6-inch square. Dust both sides of dough lightly with flour. Starting at center of square, roll dough away from you in 1 motion. Return rolling pin to center of dough and roll toward you in 1 motion. Repeat steps of rolling until dough sticks to counter and measures roughly 12 inches long. Lightly dust both sides of dough with flour and continue rolling dough until it measures roughly 20 inches long and 6 inches wide, frequently lifting dough to release it from counter. (You should be able to easily see outline of your fingers through dough.) If dough firmly sticks to counter and wrinkles when rolled out, dust dough lightly with flour.

4. Transfer pasta sheet to dish towel and let stand, uncovered, until firm around edges, about 15 minutes; meanwhile, roll out remaining dough. Starting with 1 short end, gently fold pasta sheet at 2-inch intervals until sheet has been folded into flat, rectangular roll. With sharp chef's knife, slice crosswise into ³⁄₁₆-inch-wide noodles. Use fingers to unfurl pasta and transfer to baking sheet. Repeat folding and cutting remaining sheets of dough. Cook noodles within 1 hour.

5. Bring 4 quarts water to boil in large pot. Add pasta and salt and cook, stirring often, until al dente, about 3 minutes. Reserve 1 cup pasta cooking water, then drain pasta. Toss with sauce; serve immediately.

TO MAKE AHEAD: Follow recipe through step 4, transfer baking sheet of pasta to freezer, and freeze until pasta is firm. Transfer to zipper-lock bag and store for up to 2 weeks. Cook frozen pasta straight from freezer as directed in step 5.

Olive Oil Sauce with Anchovies and Parsley

MAKES 1 CUP; ENOUGH FOR 1 POUND PASTA

Mincing the anchovies ensures that their flavor gets evenly distributed. Use a high-quality extra-virgin olive oil in this recipe; our preferred brand is Columela.

⅓ cup extra-virgin olive oil

2 garlic cloves, minced

2 anchovy fillets, rinsed, patted dry, and minced
   Salt and pepper

4 teaspoons lemon juice

2 tablespoons minced fresh parsley

1. Heat oil in 12-inch skillet over medium-low heat until shimmering. Add garlic, anchovies, ⅛ teaspoon salt, and ½ teaspoon pepper; cook until fragrant, about 30 seconds. Remove pan from heat and cover to keep warm.

2. To serve, return pan to medium heat. Add pasta, ½ cup reserved cooking water, lemon juice, and parsley; toss to combine. Season with salt and pepper to taste and add remaining cooking water as needed to adjust consistency. Serve immediately.

Tomato and Browned Butter Sauce

MAKES 3 CUPS; ENOUGH FOR 1 POUND PASTA

1 (28-ounce) can whole peeled tomatoes

4 tablespoons unsalted butter, cut into 4 pieces

2 garlic cloves, minced

½ teaspoon sugar
   Salt and pepper

2 teaspoons sherry vinegar

3 tablespoons chopped fresh basil
   Grated Parmesan cheese

1. Process tomatoes and their juice in food processor until smooth, about 30 seconds. Melt 3 tablespoons butter in 12-inch skillet over medium-high heat, swirling occasionally, until butter is dark brown and releases nutty aroma, about 1½ minutes. Stir in garlic and cook for 10 seconds. Stir in processed tomatoes, sugar, and ½ teaspoon salt and simmer until sauce is slightly reduced, about 8 minutes. Remove pan from heat; whisk in remaining 1 tablespoon butter and vinegar. Season with salt and pepper to taste; cover to keep warm.

2. To serve, return pan to medium heat. Add pasta, ¼ cup reserved cooking water, and basil; toss to combine. Season with salt and pepper to taste and add remaining cooking water as needed to adjust consistency. Serve immediately, passing Parmesan separately.

Walnut Cream Sauce

MAKES 2 CUPS; ENOUGH FOR 1 POUND PASTA

1½ cups (6 ounces) walnuts, toasted

¾ cup dry white wine

½ cup heavy cream

1 ounce Parmesan cheese, grated (½ cup)
   Salt and pepper

¼ cup minced fresh chives

1. Process 1 cup walnuts in food processor until finely ground, about 10 seconds. Transfer to small bowl. Pulse remaining ½ cup walnuts in food processor until coarsely chopped, 3 to 5 pulses. Bring wine to simmer in 12-inch skillet over medium-high heat; cook until reduced to ¼ cup, about 3 minutes. Whisk in cream, ground and chopped walnuts, Parmesan, ¼ teaspoon salt, and ½ teaspoon pepper. Remove pan from heat and cover to keep warm.

2. To serve, return pan to medium heat. Add pasta, ½ cup reserved cooking water, and chives; toss to combine. Season with salt and pepper to taste and add remaining cooking water as needed to adjust consistency. Serve immediately.

RAGU ALLA BOLOGNESE

RAGU ALLA BOLOGNESE

✔ **WHY THIS RECIPE WORKS:** There are many different ways to interpret what "real" bolognese sauce is. But no matter what the ingredients are, the sauce should be hearty and rich, but not cloying, with a velvety texture that lightly clings to the noodles. For our version we used six different types of meats: ground beef, pork, and veal; pancetta; mortadella (bologna-like Italian deli meat); and chicken livers. These meats and the combination of red wine and tomato paste gave us a rich, complex sauce with balanced acidity. The final addition of gelatin lent the sauce an ultra-silky texture.

RAGU ALLA BOLOGNESE, THE HEARTY MEAT SAUCE native to the northern Italian city for which it is named, has always been a simple concept—but with a lot of complications to hamper its simplicity. Despite its undisputed Bolognese pedigree, there are countless "authentic" interpretations on record. While ground beef is the common starting point, many versions include ground pork and often veal as well. In others the ground meat is supplemented with finely chopped *salumi*, usually pancetta or prosciutto. Some recipes call for brightening the ragu with crushed tomatoes; others lean toward the drier, more concentrated depth of tomato paste. One version may call for white wine, another for red; some call for no wine at all. Cooking times range from 90 minutes to 3 hours.

But the most controversial point of all? Dairy. Depending on which source you consult, milk and/or cream either is an essential component, lending further richness and tenderizing the long-cooked meat, or it has no place in the sauce whatsoever. In other words, what constitutes "real" ragu alla bolognese is largely a matter of interpretation. The only thing that all Italian cooks seem to agree on is this: The end product should be hearty and rich but not cloying, with a velvety texture that lightly clings to the noodles—and tomatoes should be a bit player in this show. The true star is the meat.

We'd never felt strongly about the dairy issue until recently, when we sampled a bolognese sauce made by

Dante de Magistris, an Italian chef in Boston with a big following. His version was by far the meatiest, most complex version we'd ever had. We were so taken with it that we asked him for a breakdown of the recipe. Two points stood out. First, he used a whopping six meats: ground beef, pork, veal, pancetta, mortadella (bologna-like Italian deli meat), and, to our surprise, chicken livers. Second, de Magistris stood squarely in the no-dairy camp, saying that when he learned to make the dish in Bologna, milk and cream were definitely not included.

Those clues—plus the test kitchen's library of Italian cookbooks—were enough to get us started on our own dairy-free bolognese. We were determined to make our version home cook–friendly and yet satisfying to even the most discriminating Italian palate.

We started with a test batch that we cobbled together based on de Magistris's version, loading up the pot with the components of the flavor base, or *soffritto* (chopped carrot, celery, and onion), followed by five different meats. (We weren't sure we really needed the chicken livers, so we left them out for the time being.) We then stirred in crushed tomatoes. We let it all simmer, covered, for a couple of hours. The result was acceptably rich and flavorful, but it still needed a good bit of tweaking, to both the ingredient list and the technique.

We made several more batches, adding a fistful of minced sage to the meat—considered an essential component by some sources—and trying various proportions of all five meats until we landed on equal amounts of the ground beef, pork, and veal and 4 ounces each of pancetta and mortadella. Some of the other classic bolognese recipes we'd consulted specified that the ground meat should be cooked only until it loses its pink color, lest the browning lead to toughness. But we found the textural compromise in the finished sauce to be far subtler than the flavor benefit of a good sear. We also decided to ignore tradition and add the meat to the pot before the soffritto. Without the interference of moisture from the vegetables, we could get a much better sear on the meat, and sautéing the veggies in the rendered fat built up even richer flavor.

What gave us pause was a more minor complaint: finely chopping the pancetta and mortadella. It was tedious work, so we called on our food processor to take over.

The job was literally done with the push of a button. In fact, the appliance worked so efficiently that we also pulsed the soffritto components before sautéing them.

We moved on to the next major decision: the best kind of tomato product to use. The recipes we'd read didn't help narrow things down—we'd seen everything from the crushed tomatoes we had been using to tomato sauce to paste. One source we consulted even suggested that tomatoes were not originally part of the sauce. That reminded us that we had liked the unobtrusive texture of tomato paste in de Magistris's version, so we added a healthy dollop to the pot. Once the fond had taken on a deep rust tone, we poured in a few big glugs of red wine, deglazed the pan by scraping up the browned bits with a wooden spoon, and let the sauce simmer gently for the better part of 2 hours. When the sauce was nearly done, we boiled some pasta and tossed the noodles with the ragu.

Flavor-wise, the sauce was in good shape: rich and complex and, thanks to the wine and tomato paste, balanced with just enough acidity. But as our tasters noted, this ragu had a textural flaw: Its consistency was pebbly, dry, and not particularly saucelike.

There was one element of de Magistris's recipe that we had overlooked in our earlier attempts: Just before the long simmering step, he ladled some homemade *brodo* (or broth) into the ragu, repeating the step twice more during cooking to moisten the reduced sauce. We suspected that the brodo—and the technique of adding the brodo in stages—had an important effect on the texture of the bolognese. Besides boosting the meaty flavor, the bones used to make the broth give up lots of gelatin as they simmer, which renders the liquid glossy and viscous. The more the broth reduced in the bolognese, the more savory and satiny it became. But homemade broth was out of the question for us. Simmering bones for hours on top of making the ragu was just too much fuss; we'd have to make do with commercial broth.

No surprise here: The ragus we made with store-bought broth didn't measure up to bolognese made with homemade broth—especially in regard to texture. We started brainstorming other ways to mimic the velvetiness contributed by the gelatin in real brodo—and realized that the answer was simple: powdered gelatin. It's a trick we've used to lend suppleness to all-beef meatloaf and viscosity to beef stew—two qualities that we were looking for in our ragu. We prepped multiple batches of the sauce, blooming varying amounts of gelatin—from 1 teaspoon all the way up to a whopping 8 teaspoons—in a combination of store-bought beef and chicken broths before proceeding with the recipe. Every batch was an improvement over the gelatin-free version, but the effect was relatively subtle until we got up into the higher amounts of gelatin, which rendered the sauce ultra-silky. That settled it: Eight teaspoons it was.

We had one more thought about the store-bought broth: Since the flavor and body of the store-bought stuff hardly equaled that of a real brodo, we wondered if the reduction step was really doing that much for the sauce. One side-by-side test gave us our answer: The batch to which we'd added all the broth at once boasted just as much meatiness and body as the one with the staggered additions. It also finished cooking in about 90 minutes.

And yet while store-bought broth plus gelatin nicely solved the texture problem, the sauce still lacked a certain depth and roundness of flavor. Fortunately, we still had one card left to play: chicken livers. They'd seemed superfluous to us at first, but we wondered if finely chopping them and tossing them in at the end might get at the complexity we were after. That they did—but according to our tasters, their effect was a bit too strong. Pureeing them in the food processor worked much better; this way, their rich, gamy flavor incorporated seamlessly into the sauce.

Though our sauce could hardly get any more perfect, we just couldn't push away the thought that kept sneaking into our heads: What would happen if the sauce included a little dairy? We made one last batch, adding 1 cup of milk along with the broth. But when our tasters sampled this latest version, the consensus was unanimous: Dairy muted its meaty flavor, and they liked it better without.

Without dairy, we knew that some Italian cooks out there would not consider our recipe authentic. But no matter: The sauce was undeniably complex, rich-tasting, and lusciously silky. And besides, how could any version be bolognese without a little controversy?

Ragu alla Bolognese

MAKES ABOUT 6 CUPS

This recipe makes enough sauce for 2 pounds of pasta. Eight teaspoons of gelatin is equivalent to one (1-ounce) box of gelatin. If you can't find ground veal, use an additional ¾ pound of ground beef.

- 1 cup low-sodium chicken broth
- 1 cup beef broth
- 8 teaspoons unflavored gelatin
- 1 onion, chopped coarse
- 1 large carrot, peeled and chopped coarse
- 1 celery rib, chopped coarse
- 4 ounces pancetta, chopped
- 4 ounces mortadella, chopped
- 6 ounces chicken livers, trimmed
- 3 tablespoons extra-virgin olive oil
- ¾ pound 85 percent lean ground beef
- ¾ pound ground veal
- ¾ pound ground pork
- 3 tablespoons minced fresh sage
- 1 (6-ounce) can tomato paste
- 2 cups dry red wine
  Salt and pepper
- 1 pound pappardelle or tagliatelle
  Grated Parmesan cheese

NOTES FROM THE TEST KITCHEN

BUILDING A MEATY, SATINY-TEXTURED BOLOGNESE

1. Cook ground meats, then add depth by sautéing chopped mortadella, pancetta, and sage in rendered fat.

2. Add soffritto and sweat it until softened, then add concentrated tomato flavor with tomato paste.

3. Deglaze pot with wine; stir in broth plus bloomed gelatin to develop luxurious silky texture.

4. Stir in pureed chicken livers for subtle but rich taste.

1. Combine chicken broth and beef broth in bowl; sprinkle gelatin over top and set aside. Pulse onion, carrot, and celery together in food processor until finely chopped, about 10 pulses, scraping down bowl as needed; transfer to separate bowl. Pulse pancetta and mortadella together in now-empty food processor until finely chopped, about 25 pulses, scraping down bowl as needed; transfer to second bowl. Process chicken livers in now-empty food processor until pureed, about 5 seconds; transfer to third bowl.

2. Heat oil in Dutch oven over medium-high heat until shimmering. Add beef, veal, and pork; cook, breaking up pieces with wooden spoon, until all liquid has evaporated and meat begins to sizzle, 10 to 15 minutes. Add pancetta mixture and sage; cook, stirring frequently, until pancetta is translucent, 5 to 7 minutes, adjusting heat as needed to keep fond from burning. Add chopped vegetables and cook, stirring frequently, until softened, 5 to 7 minutes. Add tomato paste and cook,

stirring constantly, until rust-colored and fragrant, about 3 minutes.

3. Stir in wine, scraping up any browned bits. Simmer until sauce has thickened, about 5 minutes. Stir in broth mixture and return to simmer. Reduce heat to low and cook at bare simmer until thickened (wooden spoon should leave trail when dragged through sauce), about 1½ hours.

4. Stir in pureed chicken livers, bring to boil, and remove from heat. Season with salt and pepper to taste; cover and keep warm.

5. Bring 4 quarts water to boil in large pot. Add pasta and 1 tablespoon salt and cook, stirring often, until al dente. Reserve ¾ cup cooking water, then drain pasta and return it to pot. Add half of sauce and cooking water to pasta and toss to combine. Transfer to serving bowl and serve, passing Parmesan separately. (Leftover sauce may be refrigerated for up to 3 days or frozen for up to 1 month.)

RATING MOZZARELLA

A staple in many Italian (and non-Italian) kitchens, mozzarella offers mellow flavor that blends seamlessly with bolder ingredients in baked pasta dishes and melts nicely in everything from lasagna to pizza. To find the best brand, we sampled nine different low-moisture mozzarellas, both block-style and preshredded, made with whole or part-skim milk, plain and on pizza. Preshredded cheeses quickly fell to the bottom of the heap; these are tossed with powdered cellulose (and sometimes potato starch) to absorb moisture, which prevents clumping and slows spoilage—but it also dulls the flavor of the cheese. As for the block-style cheeses, we preferred brands with more fat that were made from whole milk, not a cheaper alternative, such as condensed skim milk or nonfat dry milk, which can result in oddly sweet off-flavors and overbrowning when the cheese is melted. Also, tasters gave a thumbs-down to aged cheeses; they found the age-related tang and sharpness to be distracting. Fat is per 28-gram serving. Brands are listed in order of preference. See AmericasTestKitchen.com for updates to this testing.

RECOMMENDED

SORRENTO Whole-Milk Mozzarella
(sold as Precious on the West Coast)
PRICE: $5.29 for 16 oz (33 cents per oz)
STYLE: Block **FAT:** 6.5 g
COMMENTS: Tasters raved that our favorite mozzarella's flavor was so "clean," "mellow," and "buttery" that it was "practically like drinking milk." Even better, its "smooth" texture boasted just a hint of "nice chew" that was great both eaten out of hand and melted on pizza.

KRAFT Low-Moisture Part-Skim Mozzarella
PRICE: $3.68 for 8 oz (46 cents per oz)
STYLE: Block **FAT:** 6 g
COMMENTS: The "creamy," "milky," "fresh-tasting" flavors that tasters praised when sampling this cheese plain turned up again when the cheese had been melted on pizza. There, it earned points for its "stretchy," "gooey" texture.

BOAR'S HEAD Whole-Milk Low-Moisture Mozzarella
PRICE: $7.49 for 16 oz (47 cents per oz)
STYLE: Block **FAT:** 7 g
COMMENTS: Though a few of us found this cheese's texture a bit too "chewy" on pizza, its flavor made up for it. Tasters noted that its balance of "creamy" and "milky" overtones, with "a touch of tang," made it ideal as a pizza topper.

RECOMMENDED WITH RESERVATIONS

KRAFT Low-Moisture Part-Skim Mozzarella
PRICE: $4.29 for 8 oz (54 cents per oz)
STYLE: Shredded **FAT:** 6 g
COMMENTS: Our favorite among the shredded cheeses, this sample's "creamy," "milky" flavor came through particularly well on pizza, where the dusty coating dissolved and gave way to a "smooth" texture.

ORGANIC VALLEY Low-Moisture Part-Skim Organic Mozzarella
PRICE: $6.99 for 8 oz (87 cents per oz)
STYLE: Block **FAT:** 6 g
COMMENTS: Most tasters thought that this sample's "sharp," "cheddar"-like flavors, which stood out in the plain tasting, became "nice" and "milky" on pizza. As for texture, some found it "rubbery," but others liked its "moderate chew."

RECOMMENDED WITH RESERVATIONS *(cont.)*

SORRENTO Part-Skim Mozzarella
PRICE: $5.29 for 16 oz (33 cents per oz)
STYLE: Block **FAT:** 5.6 g
COMMENTS: Almost everyone noted that this cheese was comparatively "damp," even "wet," and "a bit spongy," but that meant different things to different tasters. Many happily compared it to "fresh mozzarella"; others panned it as "limp," particularly when it was melted on pizza.

HORIZON Organic Low-Moisture Part-Skim Mozzarella
PRICE: $3.99 for 6 oz (67 cents per oz)
STYLE: Shredded **FAT:** 5 g
COMMENTS: One of the two leanest cheeses of the bunch, this sample—our least favorite in the plain tasting—was nothing you'd want to snack on. Many found it "dry" and "bland." Some picked up on "pungent" flavors. On pizza, however, those harsh notes faded to a "creamy," "milky tang."

ORGANIC VALLEY Low-Moisture Part-Skim Mozzarella
PRICE: $4.29 for 6 oz (72 cents per oz)
STYLE: Shredded **FAT:** 6 g
COMMENTS: "Looks like cheap grated Parm—and kinda tastes like it, too," said one taster about these wispy shreds. Others agreed, citing "sharper, tangier" flavor than you'd expect from mozzarella. Its pizza performance redeemed it—but only slightly: Its higher fat content rendered it "stretchier" and "creamier" than other low-ranking samples.

NOT RECOMMENDED

SARGENTO Classic Mozzarella
PRICE: $3.49 for 8 oz (44 cents per oz)
STYLE: Shredded **FAT:** 5 g
COMMENTS: Though "void of flavor" to some, most found this cheese "overly sweet." The anticaking residue made it "super-dry," "like there's a packet of mac and cheese powder dumped over it." On pizza, it was "dry and leathery," even "crunchy," with an odd "sweet" flavor.

KNIVES

Skewered
AND WRAPPED

Beef is threaded onto skewers and ready to hit the grill for the Thai classic, satay.

DITCH YOUR KNIFE AND FORK, WE'VE GOT A COUPLE OF ASIAN-inspired fun-to-eat dishes for you to try: beef satay and chicken lettuce wraps.

If you haven't been lucky enough to enjoy satay on its home turf in Thailand, surely you've eaten it at a restaurant or nibbled on a skewer at a cocktail party. This classic street food should boast charred, tender, flavor-packed meat. So why do so many recipes turn out versions that are mealy and tough? Street-food vendors rely on a trough-shaped grill to cook satay. Was there some way we could rig an American-style grill to mimic this setup? What cut of meat is best for satay and how would we ensure tender, not mealy meat—could the answer lie in the marinade? We had a host of questions to answer before we could bring a foolproof version of satay home.

Chicken lettuce wraps, called *sung choy bao,* have been popularized in this country by chain restaurants. If you aren't familiar with them, simply think of the wraps as Asian-style tacos. Lettuce stands in for the tortilla and the filling is composed of tender pieces of stir-fried chicken in a salty-sweet sauce. Too many recipes we tried produced dry chicken and flat-tasting sauces. Not to mention that these recipes called for the painstaking step of finely dicing the raw chicken before stir-frying it. We wanted to find an easier way. Get ready to learn how to translate a Chinese classic for the American kitchen and perfect a Thai favorite.

GRILLED BEEF SATAY

✔ **WHY THIS RECIPE WORKS:** In the hands of American cooks, satay often comes out thick and chewy or overly marinated and mealy. To return this dish to its Thai roots, we sliced beefy-flavored flank steak thin across the grain and threaded it onto bamboo skewers. To add flavor, we used an aromatic basting sauce consisting of authentic Thai ingredients, rather than the overtenderizing marinade used in many recipes. And to ensure that the quick-cooking beef achieved a burnished exterior, we corralled the coals in an aluminum pan in the center of the grill to bring them closer to the meat.

IN BANGKOK'S OUTDOOR MARKETS, THE PUNGENT fragrance of charring meat hovers in the air. It's grilled satay—Southeast Asia's most famous street fare, featuring tender swaths of assertively flavored pork, chicken, or beef that have been marinated for hours, threaded onto bamboo skewers, and then cooked over charcoal to achieve a lightly burnished crust.

But something funny happened on satay's journey from Thai food stall to stateside sit-down restaurant: The magic got lost. And the worst offender, hands down, is the beef version. Whether the meat is cut too thick and overcooked (making it chewy like leather) or "tenderized" by a lengthy marinade (giving it a mealy exterior), the texture is unappealing—to say nothing of the meat's lackluster flavor, which relies far too much on the chile-spiked peanut sauce served on the side. How hard could it be to bring beef satay back to its streetwise roots? We headed to the test kitchen to find out.

Figuring out the best cut of beef—and how to slice it—would go far toward improving the situation, so we started there. We ruled out luxury cuts from the outset and narrowed the field to less expensive flank, skirt, top round, and top sirloin steaks, all of which have good flavor and can be tender, too, if treated right.

We cut each of these steaks into pieces small enough to thread onto skewers, taking care to slice the flank and skirt against the grain (a tenderizing trick we use for heavily striated cuts of beef). We soaked the meat for 30 minutes in a simple coconut milk–based marinade before skewering it and throwing it onto the grill.

Top round was the loser, coming out tough with liver-y off-notes. Sirloin had great flavor but inconsistent texture. Skirt and flank ended up in a dead heat for first place, thanks to plenty of evenly distributed fat. We went with symmetrical flank, which would be far easier to prep than tapered skirt.

Experimenting with butchering methods, we found that halving the flank steak lengthwise first, and then slicing the two long, thin portions on a slight bias, about ¼ inch thick, yielded the optimal size and shape for skewering—and for consuming in a bite or two.

Small pieces of flank steak cook in a matter of minutes, and it's a race to get the exterior adequately crusted before the interior overcooks—a chronic problem in the satay recipes we'd tested. The solution seemed easy enough: Just make the fire hotter. Piling the coals on one side of the grill gave us the firepower we wanted but required seriously nimble work with tongs to keep every morsel on the 12-inch skewers directly over this more contained fire. Add basting, which we did right as we put the meat on the grill, again when we flipped the skewers, and once more right before we took them off, and the whole process became more trouble than it was worth.

Trolling the Internet for a better idea, we happened upon videos of satay vendors in action and were reminded of the unique style of grill they use for the job. Instead of a kettle with grates, the street vendors cook over a trough-shaped grill, about as wide as the skewers are long, which allows them to suspend the meat mere inches above the coals. To mimic this setup, we used a 13 by 9-inch disposable aluminum roasting pan as a makeshift "trough," poking several holes in the bottom of it (to allow for air circulation), positioning it atop the cooking grate of our kettle grill, and filling it with hot coals. We strategically threaded the steak onto only the middle 9 inches of each skewer—so the ends could rest on the edge of the pan—and positioned them just above the coals, Thai-style. We imagined street vendors in Bangkok giving us the thumbs-up for our ingenuity—until reality set in. The meat was now so close to the fire that we needed to flip it as constantly and frenetically as they did in the videos, and doing so still didn't prevent us from overcooking it.

Maybe what we needed to do was mimic the setup but introduce a little more space between the coals and the meat. This time we positioned the pan inside the kettle, poured the hot coals inside, and replaced the cooking grate. We then lined up the skewers over the pan. This method worked like a charm. When we basted the satay, the coals smoldered just enough to impart a subtle smokiness, and with the coals corralled in the center of the grill, the heat was sufficiently powerful to yield a lovely burnished exterior—but not so hot that we had to flip the skewers more than once.

Finally, we turned our attention back to the marinade. The test kitchen has spent years determining what works and what doesn't, so it was with a touch of hubris that we picked off ingredients we knew would be problematic. Acids—gone. We've found that they do nothing but weaken the surface of the meat, giving it a mushy texture. Likewise, enzyme-rich juices like pineapple and papaya were sent packing. Though many recipes incorporate them to help "tenderize" tough cuts of meat, our tests have shown that all they do is break down the exterior. Besides, our choice of cut and cooking method yielded ample tenderness; what we needed now was big flavor.

From the ingredients left standing, we assembled the marinade: oil, to facilitate the transfer of oil-soluble flavorings; salty fish sauce, for its brining and flavor-boosting qualities; brown sugar, for complexity and enhanced browning; plus coconut milk, a smattering of dried spices, and a generous amount of minced fresh lemon grass, shallots, and ginger.

Confidently, we tossed the sliced flank steak with the marinade, letting it chill in the refrigerator for an hour. (We've found that there is little benefit to longer marinating times.) We skewered the slices, grilled them, and dug in. As expected, the flavor was terrific. The problem was the texture: The exterior suffered from the mealiness we thought we'd taken every precaution to avoid. Cutting the marinating time in half, we tried again. The flavor was every bit as good, but the texture was just as mealy.

Puzzled, we went down the ingredient list, omitting each component of the marinade one by one in subsequent batches. It was only when we eliminated the ginger that we fingered the culprit—without this root, the meat wasn't mealy in the least. Additional research revealed that ginger contains zingibain, an enzyme that aggressively breaks down protein. And our recipe had called for 2 tablespoons of the stuff. We hated to remove such a key flavoring, but what could we do?

Then it occurred to us: What if we kept the marinade very simple and ramped up the basting sauce with ginger and most of the other flavorings instead? We cooked one more batch, this time marinating the steak in just fish sauce, oil, and sugar. During grilling, we basted the meat heavily with the coconut milk mixture, redolent with ginger, lemon grass, and spices. This was our breakthrough: The texture was flawless, and the flavors from the basting sauce really stuck to the meat, so no one missed them in the marinade.

Finally, we focused on the peanut sauce. Using chunky peanut butter as a base, we spiced things up with Thai red curry paste and garlic. Coconut milk contributed body, and chopped roasted peanuts offered additional texture. A final hit of lime juice, coupled with soy and fish sauces, lent brightness.

Served with the peanut sauce, this beef satay was as good as it gets. And who knows? Maybe one day a Thai street vendor will look to our method for tips.

Grilled Beef Satay

SERVES 6

Bamboo skewers soaked in water for 30 minutes can be substituted for metal skewers. The aluminum pan used for charcoal grilling should be at least 2¾ inches deep; you will not need the pan for a gas grill. Kitchen shears work well for punching the holes in the pan. Unless you have a very high-powered gas grill, these skewers will not be as well seared as they would be with charcoal. Serve with Peanut Sauce (recipe follows). To make it a meal, serve this dish with steamed white rice.

BASTING SAUCE

- ¾ cup regular or light coconut milk
- 3 tablespoons packed dark brown sugar
- 3 tablespoons fish sauce
- 2 tablespoons vegetable oil
- 3 shallots, minced
- 2 lemon grass stalks, trimmed to bottom 6 inches and minced
- 2 tablespoons grated fresh ginger
- 1½ teaspoons ground coriander
- ¾ teaspoon red pepper flakes
- ½ teaspoon ground cumin
- ½ teaspoon salt

BEEF

- 2 tablespoons vegetable oil
- 2 tablespoons packed dark brown sugar
- 1 tablespoon fish sauce
- 1 (1½- to 1¾-pound) flank steak, halved lengthwise and sliced on slight angle against grain into ¼-inch-thick slices
  Disposable aluminum deep roasting pan

1. FOR THE BASTING SAUCE: Whisk all ingredients together in bowl. Reserve one-third of sauce in separate bowl.

2. FOR THE BEEF: Whisk oil, sugar, and fish sauce together in medium bowl. Toss beef with marinade and let stand at room temperature for 30 minutes. Weave beef onto 12-inch metal skewers, 2 to 4 pieces per skewer, leaving 1½ inches at top and bottom of skewer exposed. You should have 10 to 12 skewers.

3A. FOR A CHARCOAL GRILL: Punch twelve ½-inch holes in bottom of disposable roasting pan. Open bottom vent completely and place roasting pan in center of grill. Light large chimney starter mounded with charcoal briquettes (7 quarts). When top coals are partially covered with ash, pour into roasting pan. Set cooking grate over coals with grates parallel to long side of roasting pan, cover, and open lid vent completely. Heat grill until hot, about 5 minutes.

3B. FOR A GAS GRILL: Turn all burners to high, cover, and heat grill until hot, about 15 minutes. Leave all burners on high.

4. Clean and oil cooking grate. Place beef skewers on grill (directly over coals if using charcoal) perpendicular to grate. Brush meat with reserved one-third of basting sauce and cook (covered if using gas) until browned, about 3 minutes. Flip skewers, brush with half of remaining basting sauce, and cook until browned on second side, about 3 minutes. Brush meat with remaining basting sauce and cook 1 minute longer. Transfer to large platter and serve with Peanut Sauce.

Peanut Sauce

MAKES ABOUT 1½ CUPS

- 1 tablespoon vegetable oil
- 1 tablespoon Thai red curry paste
- 1 tablespoon packed dark brown sugar
- 2 garlic cloves, minced
- 1 cup regular or light coconut milk
- ⅓ cup chunky peanut butter
- ¼ cup dry-roasted unsalted peanuts, chopped
- 1 tablespoon lime juice
- 1 tablespoon fish sauce
- 1 teaspoon soy sauce

Heat oil in small saucepan over medium heat until shimmering. Add curry paste, sugar, and garlic; cook, stirring constantly, until fragrant, about 1 minute. Add coconut milk and bring to simmer. Whisk in peanut butter until smooth. Remove from heat and stir in peanuts, lime juice, fish sauce, and soy sauce. Cool to room temperature.

NOTES FROM THE TEST KITCHEN

HOW TO PREP LEMON GRASS

When buying lemon grass, look for green (not brown) stalks that are firm and fragrant.

1. Trim dry leafy top (this part is usually green) and tough bottom of each stalk.

2. Peel and discard dry outer layer until moist, tender inner stalk is exposed.

3. Smash peeled stalk with bottom of heavy saucepan to release maximum flavor from fibrous stalk.

4. Cut smashed stalk into long, thin strips; cut crosswise to mince.

CHINESE CHICKEN LETTUCE WRAPS

✔ **WHY THIS RECIPE WORKS:** This dish, popularized by chain restaurants, is based on a Cantonese dish called sung choy bao. Most recipes for this dish suffer from a similar fate—stringy, tasteless meat drowned in a bland sauce. To remedy this, we started with flavorful chicken thighs and marinated them in soy sauce and rice wine. To keep the meat from drying out when stir-fried, we coated it in a velvetizing cornstarch slurry, which helped it retain moisture as it cooked.

THERE AREN'T MANY CHAIN RESTAURANT DISHES that are worth making at home, but Chinese chicken lettuce wraps is one exception. Originally part of Cantonese banquet spreads, this dish (known as sung choy bao) was popularized in this country by places like P.F. Chang's and the Cheesecake Factory. At its best it offers tender morsels of chicken and crunchy vegetables stir-fried in a salty-sweet sauce and served in crisp lettuce cups—ideal either as an appetizer or as a light meal.

The recipes we found shared more or less the same technique: Stir-fry the chicken over high heat, add chopped vegetables, pour in the sauce and toss to coat, and spoon the mixture into Bibb lettuce leaves. We didn't bother trying recipes that called for ground chicken, since commercial ground meat is often processed so fine that it cooks up stringy and chalky. But even when we painstakingly diced the chicken breast by hand, the meat cooked up dry and bland; plus, all the sauces we tried needed a little punching up, too.

To introduce more flavor and juiciness, we soaked the chopped chicken in soy sauce and rice wine. When this step didn't do enough, we switched to chicken thighs, which boast more intramuscular fat, making them less prone to drying out when stir-fried and giving them richer, meatier flavor.

We also wondered if instead of finely (and fussily) dicing the meat by hand, we could use the test kitchen's food-processor method for grinding meat. This involved

CHINESE CHICKEN LETTUCE WRAPS

briefly freezing the thighs to firm them up and then pulsing them until coarsely chopped. The results? Not bad—and way faster than hand chopping. But the machine invited a new problem: Even after we froze the meat, a small amount of the chicken inevitably became overprocessed, releasing sticky meat proteins that glued the larger pieces together into chewy clumps during cooking. Tossing the chopped pieces with oil before cooking helped but also turned the dish greasy.

The idea of coating the pieces wasn't a bad one, though, and reminded us that a handful of the more traditional recipes we'd come across called for "velveting" the chicken. In this common Chinese technique, the meat is dipped into a cornstarch slurry that forms a barrier against clumping and also helps it retain moisture. We gave it a whirl, whisking a couple of teaspoons of cornstarch and a little sesame oil into the soy-wine mixture

and tossing it with the processor-chopped chicken before stir-frying. This was the breakthrough we'd been hoping for. Our tasters raved about these tender, juicy, distinct bits of chicken.

The other major components—the vegetables and the aromatics—were much simpler to nail down. Most recipes include either water chestnuts or celery for crunch, but tasters agreed that using both was ideal. We also added a handful of sliced shiitake mushrooms for earthy depth and chew, along with garlic and scallions.

As for the sauce, we built complexity into the traditional mixture of oyster sauce, soy sauce, and rice wine by adding toasted sesame oil, sugar, and red pepper flakes. (Per tradition, we'd also be passing salty-sweet hoisin sauce as a tableside condiment.) Spooned into the tender Bibb cups, this stir-fry was as bold and complex as it was light, and it came together in less than an hour.

Chinese Chicken Lettuce Wraps

SERVES 4 AS A MAIN DISH OR 6 AS AN APPETIZER

To make an entrée, serve this dish with steamed white rice.

CHICKEN

- 1 pound boneless, skinless chicken thighs, trimmed and cut into 1-inch pieces
- 2 teaspoons Chinese rice wine or dry sherry
- 2 teaspoons soy sauce
- 2 teaspoons toasted sesame oil
- 2 teaspoons cornstarch

SAUCE

- 3 tablespoons oyster sauce
- 1 tablespoon Chinese rice wine or dry sherry
- 2 teaspoons soy sauce
- 2 teaspoons toasted sesame oil
- ½ teaspoon sugar
- ¼ teaspoon red pepper flakes

STIR-FRY

- 2 tablespoons vegetable oil
- 2 celery ribs, cut into ¼-inch pieces
- 6 ounces shiitake mushrooms, stemmed and sliced thin
- ½ cup water chestnuts, cut into ¼-inch pieces
- 2 scallions, white parts minced, green parts sliced thin
- 2 garlic cloves, minced
- 1 head Bibb lettuce (8 ounces), washed and dried, leaves separated and left whole
  Hoisin sauce

1. FOR THE CHICKEN: Place chicken pieces on large plate in single layer. Freeze meat until firm and starting to harden around edges, about 20 minutes.

2. Whisk rice wine, soy sauce, oil, and cornstarch together in bowl. Pulse half of meat in food processor until coarsely chopped into ¼- to ⅛-inch pieces, about 10 pulses. Transfer meat to bowl with rice wine mixture and repeat with remaining chunks. Toss chicken to coat and refrigerate for 15 minutes.

3. FOR THE SAUCE: Whisk all ingredients together in bowl; set aside.

4. FOR THE STIR-FRY: Heat 1 tablespoon oil in 12-inch nonstick skillet over high heat until smoking. Add chicken and cook, stirring constantly, until opaque, 3 to 4 minutes. Transfer to bowl and wipe out skillet.

5. Heat remaining 1 tablespoon oil in now-empty skillet over high heat until smoking. Add celery and mushrooms; cook, stirring constantly, until mushrooms have reduced in size by half and celery is crisp-tender, 3 to 4 minutes. Add water chestnuts, scallion whites, and garlic; cook, stirring constantly, until fragrant, about 1 minute. Whisk sauce to recombine. Return chicken to skillet; add sauce and toss to combine. Spoon into lettuce leaves and sprinkle with scallion greens. Serve, passing hoisin sauce separately.

RATING SAUTÉ PANS

Despite their name, sauté pans, which have a flat bottom and relatively high, straight sides, are not the best pans for sautéing or searing—for these tasks, we reach for a skillet, with low, sloping walls that encourage evaporation and browning. But they are ideal for cooking down heaps of greens, for shallow-frying, and for certain braises. To find the best sauté pan on the market, we tested nine models, making fried chicken, braised cabbage, Mexican rice, Swedish meatballs, and crêpes (to gauge even browning) in each. Midsize (9½- to 10½-inch) pans performed best; larger pans tended to heat unevenly, and smaller pans didn't provide adequate surface area, so we had to fry our chicken in two batches. Pans that were moderately thick and heavy were substantial enough to modulate heat but not so bulky that they retained too much of it and risked scorching our food. Also, pans that had a helper handle were much easier to move when full. Brands are listed in order of preference. See AmericasTestKitchen.com for updates and further information on this testing.

HIGHLY RECOMMENDED

VIKING Stainless 7-Ply 3-Quart Sauté Pan
MODEL: VSC0303   **PRICE:** $219.95
WEIGHT (WITHOUT LID): 4.6 lb
DIMENSIONS: 10½ in by 2¼ in; 3.88 mm thick
MATERIAL: Stainless with aluminum core; metal lid
OVENSAFE TEMPERATURE: 600°F
PERFORMANCE: ★★★   **EASE OF USE:** ★★★
COMMENTS: This midsize pan's heft was a boon to steady heating and even browning, and it's so well proportioned that the weight didn't bother us. The handle sported a ridge for a secure grip and stayed cool on the stove; the heavy, sturdy lid fit securely.

ALL-CLAD Stainless 3-Quart Tri-Ply Sauté Pan
MODEL: 16711   **PRICE:** $224.95
WEIGHT (WITHOUT LID): 3.1 lb
DIMENSIONS: 9¾ in by 2 in; 2.8 mm thick
MATERIAL: Stainless with aluminum core; metal lid
OVENSAFE TEMPERATURE: 500°F
PERFORMANCE: ★★★   **EASE OF USE:** ★★★
COMMENTS: Our previous favorite is back in an updated induction-compatible version. The price hike is disappointing, but it cooks steadily, browns evenly, has a stay-cool handle, and is well balanced and relatively lightweight.

RECOMMENDED

CUISINART MultiClad Pro Triple-Ply 3½-Quart Sauté Pan with Lid
MODEL: MCP33-24H   **PRICE:** $79.95   `BEST BUY`
WEIGHT (WITHOUT LID): 3.4 lb
DIMENSIONS: 9 in by 3 in; 3.7 mm thick
MATERIAL: Stainless with aluminum core; metal lid
OVENSAFE TEMPERATURE: 550°F
PERFORMANCE: ★★★   **EASE OF USE:** ★★½
COMMENTS: Although its cooking surface is small, causing some crowding, this pan browned food evenly. Its well-balanced body made for easy lifting and pouring, and its handle stayed cool on the stove.

RECOMMENDED *(cont.)*

CALPHALON Tri-Ply Stainless 3-Quart Sauté Pan
MODEL: 1767729   **PRICE:** $124.95
WEIGHT (WITHOUT LID): 3.2 lb
DIMENSIONS: 9½ in by 2¼ in; 3.43 mm thick
MATERIAL: Stainless with aluminum core; glass lid
OVENSAFE TEMPERATURE: 450°F
PERFORMANCE: ★★½   **EASE OF USE:** ★★★
COMMENTS: Even though this model fried chicken and braised meatballs just as well as our Best Buy—and offered slightly more surface area—it dropped a notch for costing roughly 50 percent more. It's light enough to lift easily, and the handle stayed cool.

RECOMMENDED WITH RESERVATIONS

LE CREUSET Tri-Ply Stainless 3-Quart Sauté Pan
MODEL: SSC5100-24   **PRICE:** $154.95
WEIGHT (WITHOUT LID): 2.9 lb
DIMENSIONS: 9 in by 2¼ in; 2.32 mm thick
MATERIAL: Stainless with aluminum core; metal lid
OVENSAFE TEMPERATURE: 425°F
PERFORMANCE: ★★   **EASE OF USE:** ★★½
COMMENTS: This was the lightest pan and also one of the thinnest; it ran hot, scorching braised cabbage. Its small surface accommodated only half a batch of chicken. The good news: Its light body and stay-cool handle made it comfortable to maneuver.

TRAMONTINA Tri-Ply Clad 12-Inch Stainless Steel Jumbo Cooker with Lid
MODEL: 80116/510   **PRICE:** $64
WEIGHT (WITHOUT LID): 4.7 lb
DIMENSIONS: 11¼ in by 2⅝ in; 3.71 mm thick
MATERIAL: Stainless with aluminum core; metal lid
OVENSAFE TEMPERATURE: 450°F
PERFORMANCE: ★★   **EASE OF USE:** ★★
COMMENTS: A lot of bang for your buck when it comes to surface area. However, its extra-broad surface browned unevenly and required extra cooking oil. It was also one of the heaviest pans in the lineup, requiring two hands to lift. Fortunately, it features a helper handle.

Turkey
ON THE GRILL

Test cook Dan Zuccarello uses a pair of tongs to help move Simple Grill-Roasted Turkey off the hot fire.

IT'S NOT THANKSGIVING WITHOUT A TURKEY, AND THE SAME COULD be said for the cranberry sauce. Interestingly, these dishes are at the opposite ends of the spectrum when it comes to level of difficulty—and angst. Ever hear anyone fret about their cranberry sauce?

Turkey is the diva of the Thanksgiving table. The turkey takes up all, or most, of the oven space (not to mention fridge space the day or so before). On the big day, once the turkey is finally done and can be moved out of the oven to rest, the cook bursts into a final frenzy of activity, with the aim of finishing up the sides so everything can make it to the table piping hot. What's a harried cook to do? A second oven is a pipe dream for most of us, but what about calling the grill up for Thanksgiving duty? Our goal: Develop a recipe for grill-roasted turkey, one that would deliver juicy meat and crisp skin and, most importantly, a turkey that would taste oven-roasted to fit in with all the traditional sides we planned on cooking indoors.

While we never worry about cranberry sauce, we do get tired of the simplicity of the sweet-tart holiday classic. Sometimes we crave a cranberry sauce with some sass. We had in mind a chunky savory sauce that tasted bold and complex; a sauce along the lines of an Indian chutney, which typically relies on aromatics, vinegar, and spices to deliver bright flavor. Let's head into the test kitchen to learn how to upgrade cranberry sauce as well as give the star of the show—turkey—the grill treatment.

GRILL-ROASTED TURKEY

✔ **WHY THIS RECIPE WORKS:** Besides freeing up your oven for other dishes, roasting your turkey out on the grill also means that you needn't worry about constantly monitoring the bird to ensure a perfectly juicy, tender turkey. To make grilling turkey foolproof, we divided our coals into two piles on either side of the grill so that the turkey thighs would receive the highest heat. A combination of lit coals and unlit briquettes yielded a longer-burning fire, making replenishing coals unnecessary. The addition of a pan of water stabilized the temperature inside the grill for even cooking and a quick salt rub before grilling yielded seasoned meat and crispy skin.

EVERY THANKSGIVING WE FIND OURSELVES IN THE same predicament. At the 11th hour, while the turkey roasts away in the oven, countless foil-wrapped side dishes wait (and wait) for their turn to cook or reheat. All we can do is hope that our families won't notice that the holiday dinner is late . . . again.

Moving the turkey out to the grill would be a great solution to our holiday conundrum, and the test kitchen has developed recipes for grill-roasted turkey with deep, smoky flavor. But for staunch traditionalists who insist on classic, clean-tasting turkey, we'd have to find a way to grill-roast the bird so it emerged tasting pretty much as if it had been roasted in the oven—that means no smoky or sooty flavors. If we could pull it off, we'd be well on our way to a low-stress holiday.

We wanted a recipe that would work on both gas and charcoal grills, and since it would be more of a challenge to get pure, smoke-free flavor on a charcoal grill, we tackled that scenario first.

As we formulated a plan, we realized that the grill is potentially even better than the oven for roasting a turkey since it could eliminate a perennial turkey-roasting problem: The lean white meat cooks faster than the fattier legs and thighs. In an oven, the bird is bombarded with heat from all angles, so to prevent the breast from drying out while the legs and thighs finish cooking, we have always taken extra steps such as flipping the turkey during roasting, chilling the breast with ice before cooking, or shielding the breast with aluminum foil. On a grill, however, almost all of the heat comes from below the bird (even when the lid is on), plus there is no roasting pan in the way. This means that as long as the bird is placed breast side up on the cooking grate, the fatty leg quarters are guaranteed to be exposed to more heat than the delicate breast, eliminating the need for flipping, shielding, or other tricks and ensuring that all parts of the bird emerge evenly cooked.

Inspired by the prospect of a super-simple approach, we perused recipes for charcoal grill–roasted turkey and found three recommended grill setups: banked, split, or "ring." Banked fires call for piling lit coals on one side of the grill and then placing the bird on the grate opposite the coals, while a split fire divides the coals into two piles, one on either side of the bird. The unusual ring-shaped setup involves inverting a disposable aluminum roasting pan in the center of the kettle and encircling it with coals; this supposedly cooks the bird evenly from all sides. On paper, the ring setup sounded promising. In reality, the fat dripping from the turkey ran down the sloped sides of the aluminum pan and straight into the hot coals, where it ignited, engulfing the bird in a ring of flames. Next.

Of the two remaining options, a banked fire was more laborious—it would require rotating the bird since only one side could be exposed to the hot coals at a time. A split fire requires no rotating and was thus the way to go.

To season the turkey and keep it moist during cooking, we had two options: salting or brining. Salting was more appealing since it eliminates the hassle of finding enough space in a jam-packed fridge for a container large enough to hold both the brine and the bird. It is also easier to crisp the skin if it doesn't start out waterlogged from a brine.

SIMPLE GRILL-ROASTED TURKEY

With that decision made, we loosened the skin on a turkey, applied kosher salt directly on the meat and in the cavity, wrapped the turkey in plastic wrap, and put it in the refrigerator. The next day, we lightly coated the skin with oil to help it brown, lit a full chimney of charcoal, and dumped half on each side of the kettle. After positioning the turkey breast side up on the grate between the coals, we set our timer since we knew we'd have to add briquettes at specific intervals to maintain the fire. Two hours later, we'd gone through an additional 2 quarts of charcoal and were trying to figure out how much more we'd need to light before the bird was cooked through. We were losing our patience: Repeatedly replenishing a fire is OK on a balmy summer day, but late November can be bitterly cold. And we certainly didn't want to have to babysit the grill on one of the busiest cooking days of the year. To add insult to injury, a few colleagues asked how we'd managed to impart a smoky taste without using wood chips. What was going on?

According to our science editor, the smoky flavor that we associate with grilling comes mostly from tiny soot particles in the kettle that are stirred up and land on the food when the grill lid is lifted. Even more of that trademark grilled taste is imparted when flare-ups occur, creating additional soot particles. (For more information, see "Smoky Flavor [and How to Prevent It]" on page 186.) This information led us to two new goals: First, find a way to leave the lid on the grill for the entire cook time. Second, roast the bird more gently, so there will be fewer smoke-generating flare-ups.

If we weren't going to open the lid during grilling, we'd have to build a longer-lasting fire. It only made sense to use a technique we've used when grill-roasting other meats: Simply arrange some unlit coals in the kettle with hot coals piled on top. The unlit coals slowly ignite and start to produce some real heat just as the top layer of coals disintegrates into ash.

To lower the overall temperature of the grill (and thus prevent flare-ups), we took a cue from a test kitchen recipe for barbecued spareribs and experimented with placing a disposable pan partially filled with water between the two piles of coals. It was intended to absorb heat, decreasing the overall temperature of the grill. We checked the efficacy of the setup by sticking an instant-read thermometer into the lid vent, happily finding that it brought the overall temperature of the grill from 400 degrees down to a moderate 325 degrees.

It was time to try our newfangled approach using an actual turkey. We prepped a bird; placed a disposable pan filled with 3 cups of water in the center of the kettle; arranged 1½ quarts of unlit coals topped with 2 quarts of lit coals on each side; added the turkey; replaced the lid; and let it go, untouched, for about 3 hours. We let the turkey rest for 45 minutes and then anxiously carved samples for our colleagues. Bingo—they reported that the grill flavor was no longer detectable.

Having achieved juicy, clean-tasting meat, we were ready to address the skin—it was browning nicely but it was just not crisp enough. No problem. We simply pulled out the test kitchen's arsenal of crisp-skin techniques: patting the skin dry with paper towels, pricking it and placing slits along the backbone to speed up the rendering of excess fat, and rubbing the skin with baking powder to help break down its proteins. Sure enough, these tricks worked like a charm, and we now had a beautifully bronzed, crisp-skinned turkey that looked and tasted every bit as though we'd pulled it from the oven.

The only thing left to do was to adapt our recipe for a gas grill, which required a couple of modifications. Since many models only have two burners, it was impossible to mimic the split fire setup by placing the turkey on a cooler area between two lit burners. Instead, we would have to leave one burner on high as the main heat source and grill-roast the turkey alongside it. This meant that we had no choice but to rotate the turkey halfway through grill-roasting. And since a large disposable roasting pan wouldn't fit on all gas grills, we put the water in two disposable pie plates placed directly on the burners. Now that our oven is freed up and roasting the turkey is as simple as striking a match, next Thanksgiving is sure to be far less stressful.

Simple Grill-Roasted Turkey

SERVES 10 TO 12

Table salt is not recommended for this recipe because it is too fine. If using a kosher or self-basting turkey (such as a frozen Butterball), do not salt it in step 1. Check the wings halfway through roasting; if they are getting too dark, fold a 12 by 8-inch piece of foil in half lengthwise and then again crosswise and slide the foil between the wing and the cooking grate to shield the wings from the flame. As an accompaniment, try our Gravy for Simple Grill-Roasted Turkey (recipe follows).

1 (12- to 14-pound) turkey, neck and giblets removed and reserved for gravy
Kosher salt and pepper
1 teaspoon baking powder
1 tablespoon vegetable oil
Large disposable aluminum roasting pan (if using charcoal) or 2 disposable aluminum pie plates (if using gas)

1. Place turkey breast side down on work surface. Make two 2-inch incisions below each thigh and breast along back of turkey (4 incisions total). Using fingers or handle of wooden spoon, carefully separate skin from thighs and breast. Rub 4 teaspoons salt evenly inside cavity of turkey, 1 tablespoon salt under skin of each side of breast, and 1 teaspoon salt under skin of each leg.

2. Combine 1 teaspoon salt, 1 teaspoon pepper, and baking powder in small bowl. Pat turkey dry with paper towels and evenly sprinkle baking powder mixture all over. Rub in mixture with hands, coating entire surface evenly. Wrap turkey tightly with plastic wrap; refrigerate for 24 to 48 hours.

3. Remove turkey from refrigerator and discard plastic. Tuck wings underneath turkey. Using hands, rub oil evenly over entire surface.

4A. FOR A CHARCOAL GRILL: Open bottom vent halfway and place disposable pan filled with 3 cups water in center of grill. Arrange 1½ quarts unlit charcoal briquettes on either side of pan in even layer. Light large chimney starter two-thirds filled with charcoal briquettes (4 quarts). When top coals are partially covered with ash, pour 2 quarts of lit coals on top of each pile of unlit coals. Set cooking grate in place, cover, and open lid vent halfway. Heat grill until hot, about 5 minutes.

4B. FOR A GAS GRILL: Place 2 disposable pie plates with 2 cups water in each directly on 1 burner over which turkey will be cooked. Turn all burners to high, cover, and heat grill until hot, about 15 minutes. Turn primary burner (burner opposite pie plates) to medium and turn other burner(s) off. Adjust primary burner as needed to maintain grill temperature of 325 degrees.

5. Clean and oil cooking grate. Place turkey, breast side up, in center of charcoal grill or on cooler side of gas grill, making sure bird is over disposable pans and not over flame. Cover (placing vents over turkey on charcoal grill) and cook until breasts register 160 degrees and thighs/drumsticks register 175 degrees, 2½ to 3 hours, rotating turkey after 1¼ hours if using gas grill.

6. Transfer turkey to carving board and let rest, uncovered, for 45 minutes. Carve turkey and serve.

Gravy for Simple Grill-Roasted Turkey

MAKES 6 CUPS

- 1 **tablespoon vegetable oil**
  Reserved turkey neck and giblets
- 1 **pound onions, chopped coarse**
- 4 **cups low-sodium chicken broth**
- 4 **cups beef broth**
- 2 **small carrots, peeled and chopped coarse**
- 2 **small celery ribs, chopped coarse**
- 3 **tablespoons unsalted butter**
- ½ **cup all-purpose flour**
- 2 **bay leaves**
- ½ **teaspoon dried thyme**
- 10 **whole black peppercorns**
  Salt and pepper

1. Heat oil in Dutch oven over medium-high heat until shimmering. Add turkey neck and giblets; cook, stirring occasionally, until browned, about 5 minutes. Add half of onions and cook, stirring occasionally, until softened, about 3 minutes. Reduce heat to low; cover and cook, stirring occasionally, until turkey parts and onions release their juices, about 20 minutes.

2. Add chicken broth and beef broth; increase heat to high and bring to boil. Reduce heat to low and simmer, uncovered, skimming any scum that rises to surface, until broth is rich and flavorful, about 30 minutes. Strain broth into large bowl (you should have about 8 cups), reserving giblets, if desired; discard neck. Reserve broth. If using, when cool enough to handle, remove gristle from gizzard;

dice giblets and set aside. (Broth can be refrigerated for up to 2 days.)

3. Pulse carrots in food processor until broken into rough ¼-inch pieces, about 5 pulses. Add celery and remaining onions; pulse until all vegetables are broken into ⅛-inch pieces, about 5 pulses.

4. Melt butter in now-empty Dutch oven over medium-high heat. Add vegetables and cook, stirring frequently, until softened and well browned, about 10 minutes. Reduce heat to medium; stir in flour and cook, stirring constantly, until thoroughly browned and fragrant, 5 to 7 minutes. Whisking constantly, gradually add reserved broth; bring to boil, skimming off any foam that forms on surface. Reduce heat to medium-low and add bay leaves, thyme, and peppercorns; simmer, stirring occasionally, until thickened and reduced to 6 cups, 30 to 35 minutes.

5. Strain gravy through fine-mesh strainer into clean saucepan, pressing on solids to extract as much liquid as possible; discard solids. Stir in diced heart and gizzard, if using. Season with salt and pepper to taste. Serve hot.

SCIENCE DESK

SMOKY FLAVOR (AND HOW TO PREVENT IT)

Using the grill to produce a bird that tasted as if it had been oven-roasted presented a unique hurdle: Just how do you keep the turkey from picking up smoky flavor? To find out, we had to consider the origin of that trademark grilled taste. One source is the convection currents that circulate through the grill and lid vents. These air drifts carry microscopic soot particles that adhere to food as it cooks, giving it that signature smoky flavor. Even more particles are stirred up on a breezy day or if the grill lid is lifted. Additionally, any fatty drippings that land in the coals will burn, vaporize, and contribute to this effect.

Eliminating as much of the telltale grill flavor as possible required a two-pronged approach. First, we used a combination of lit and unlit coals to create a long-lasting fire so we wouldn't have to lift the lid to replenish coals—and stir up the ashes—as the bird grill-roasted. Second, we cut down on soot-producing flare-ups by lowering the overall temperature of the grill with a makeshift heat sink—a cooling pan of water placed in the kettle between the coals.

HOLIDAY CRANBERRY CHUTNEY

✔ **WHY THIS RECIPE WORKS:** There's nothing wrong with the simplicity of a plain old sweet-tart cranberry sauce made with back-of-the-bag instructions, but sometimes we want more. To create a more complexly flavored sauce, we looked to Indian chutneys. Adding vinegar, aromatics, and spices to slow-cooked cranberries and fruit yielded a jammy relish with kick and savor.

THERE WILL ALWAYS BE A PLACE AT OUR THANKSGIVING table for back-of-the-bag cranberry sauce made with just cranberries, water, and granulated sugar. With its sweet-tart flavor and soft jelled texture, this no-fuss condiment is a fine way to cut the richness of the roast turkey, mashed potatoes, and gravy. But when we want a sauce with more dimension and sharpness—whether as an accompaniment for turkey or for more robustly flavored, fattier cuts of pork, lamb, or game—we find the options for a dressed-up sauce disappointing. Usually these sauces incorporate just one more flavor note, and typically it's sweet—not what we had in mind.

As we cast about for ideas, we realized that we wanted something with the complexity of an Indian chutney, which, in addition to slow-cooked fruits, boasts vinegar, aromatics, and spices that give the jammy relish kick and savor. We began by thinking of an aromatic element that would add that subtle savory quality to the sauce. Garlic and red onion, both common additions in Indian chutneys, seemed too potent. We settled on milder shallot instead. For an assertive fruit to pair with cranberries, we chopped up tart Granny Smith apples. Fresh ginger was the perfect choice for incorporating spiciness. We mixed all of these ingredients in a pot with the cranberries, sugar, and a little salt. Because we didn't want an overly strong mixture, it seemed unwise to introduce the vinegar typically added to chutney to the two tart fruits. We opted instead for water as the only liquid, simmering the mixture until the cranberries and apples had completely broken down, about 20 minutes.

The resulting chutney wasn't terrible, but overall, it lacked complexity. Also, the shallot and ginger were a little too prominent.

We wanted to keep our recipe relatively short, so developing depth via a bunch of additional ingredients was out. But what about our decision to omit vinegar? Indian cooks must have a good reason for its inclusion in chutney. Hoping that fruity cider vinegar would enliven the cranberry-apple mixture, we experimented with using it to replace some of the water, finally settling on swapping ⅓ cup of the water for ¼ cup of cider vinegar. To our surprise, rather than making the sauce overly sour, the cider vinegar lent both brightness and depth, helping to pull the flavors back into balance. After consulting our science editor, we learned that the acetic acid in vinegar reacts with pectin in the cranberries during cooking, reducing the vinegar's potency while preserving its lively taste.

For even more depth, we traded the granulated sugar for molasses-flavored brown sugar. Finally, we softened the shallot and ginger in oil along with some salt before adding the other ingredients, which drew out more of their flavor nuances while simultaneously toning down their harsh edges.

Now we were close to the chunky sauce that we had imagined, but we had inadvertently created a problem. While tasters appreciated the concentrated flavors of the sauce, many missed the fresh pop of the back-of-the-bag version, which cooks for just 10 minutes. We solved the problem by simmering half of the cranberries with the other ingredients for the full 20 minutes and reserving the other half until the last 5 minutes of cooking. This created a jamlike base dotted with soft but still intact berries that retained their zing. The textural contrast gave us the idea for one last tweak: We mixed ⅓ cup of minced crystallized ginger into the chutney along with the cranberries at the end of cooking, which added a slight, pleasing chewiness.

We used this concept to create four more versions. In addition to sweet-tart flavors, they all had a bit of punch, a bit of slow-cooked savor, a bit of fresh zing—and a whole lot of complexity.

Cranberry Chutney with Apples and Crystallized Ginger

MAKES ABOUT 3 CUPS

If using frozen cranberries, thaw them before cooking.

1 teaspoon vegetable oil

1 shallot, minced

2 teaspoons finely grated fresh ginger

½ teaspoon salt

⅔ cup water

¼ cup cider vinegar

1 cup packed brown sugar

12 ounces (3 cups) fresh or frozen cranberries

2 Granny Smith apples, peeled, cored, and cut into ¼-inch pieces

⅓ cup minced crystallized ginger

1. Heat oil in medium saucepan over medium heat until shimmering. Add shallot, fresh ginger, and salt; cook, stirring occasionally, until shallot has softened, 1 to 2 minutes.

2. Add water, vinegar, and sugar. Increase heat to high and bring to simmer, stirring to dissolve sugar. Add 1½ cups cranberries and apples; return to simmer. Reduce heat to medium-low and simmer, stirring occasionally, until cranberries have almost completely broken down and mixture has thickened, about 15 minutes.

3. Add remaining 1½ cups cranberries and crystallized ginger; continue to simmer, stirring occasionally, until cranberries just begin to burst, 5 to 7 minutes. Transfer to serving bowl and cool for at least 1 hour before serving. (Sauce can be refrigerated for up to 3 days.)

VARIATIONS

Spicy Cranberry Chutney

Increase oil to 2 teaspoons and substitute 1 stemmed and seeded red bell pepper cut into ¼-inch pieces and 2 seeded and minced jalapeño chiles for fresh ginger in step 1. Increase cooking time in step 1 to 5 minutes. Increase water to ¾ cup and omit apples and crystallized ginger.

Cranberry Chutney with Fennel and Golden Raisins

Increase oil to 2 teaspoons and substitute 1 cored fennel bulb cut into ¼-inch pieces and ½ teaspoon fennel seeds for fresh ginger in step 1. Increase cooking time in step 1 to 5 minutes. Increase water to 1 cup, omit apples, and substitute ⅓ cup golden raisins for crystallized ginger.

Cranberry-Orange Chutney

Starting with 2 oranges, remove four 2-inch-wide strips zest from 1 orange, then peel both oranges and remove segments. Set aside zest and segments. Increase fresh ginger to 4 teaspoons and add 1 teaspoon yellow mustard seeds to oil together with fresh ginger in step 1. Increase water to ¾ cup and add orange zest and segments to pot with cranberries in step 2. Omit apples and crystallized ginger.

Cranberry Chutney with Pear, Lemon, and Rosemary

Remove two 2-inch-wide strips zest from 1 lemon, then peel and remove segments. Set aside zest and segments. Substitute 2 teaspoons chopped fresh rosemary for fresh ginger. Substitute 2 peeled Bosc pears cut into ¼-inch pieces for apples; omit crystallized ginger. Add lemon zest and segments to pot with cranberries in step 2.

RATING ALL-PURPOSE CLEANERS

When it's time to clean grease, grime, and food splatters from your kitchen, a spray cleaner is a great solution. But store shelves teem with options, from all-purpose sprays to antibacterial products to "green" cleaning sprays, so how do you know which one to choose? We tested nine cleaning sprays, five labeled antibacterial and four billed as green or natural, on countertops and kitchen cabinets dirtied with vegetable oil. We also used them to tackle greasy stovetops, tomato sauce–splattered microwave interiors, and the grime on stainless steel range hoods. Finally, we rated the cleaners on their fragrances. Brands are listed in order of preference. See AmericasTestKitchen.com for updates and further information on this testing.

HIGHLY RECOMMENDED

METHOD All-Purpose Natural Surface Cleaner
(French Lavender)
PRICE: $3.79 for 28 oz (14 cents per oz)
SPRAYS TO CLEAN STOVETOP: 8   **CLEANING:** ★★★
STREAKING: ★★★   **SCENT:** ★★★
COMMENTS: This spray embodies the winning combination of being pleasant to use and cleaning thoroughly and effectively with a minimum number of squirts. It cut grease, lifted stuck-on messes, and left surfaces shining.

RECOMMENDED

LYSOL Antibacterial Kitchen Cleaner (Citrus Scent)
PRICE: $2.99 for 22 oz (14 cents per oz)
ANTIBACTERIAL CLAIMS: Kills 99.9% of *E. coli* and *Salmonella enterica*
WARNINGS: Rinse food contact surfaces after use. Do not get in eyes, on skin, or on clothing. Wash thoroughly after handling.
SPRAYS TO CLEAN STOVETOP: 8   **CLEANING:** ★★★
STREAKING: ★★★   **SCENT:** ★★
COMMENTS: Three stars for completely cleaning grease off the range hood in one swipe—and for leaving no streaks. It did fairly well with the splattered microwave, but we needed to rinse with water afterward. It cut grease on countertops and its smell was not bad.

RECOMMENDED WITH RESERVATIONS

SEVENTH GENERATION Natural All Purpose Cleaner, Free & Clear
PRICE: $5.49 for 32 oz (17 cents per oz)
SPRAYS TO CLEAN STOVETOP: 10   **CLEANING:** ★★
STREAKING: ★★   **SCENT:** ★★★
COMMENTS: Some testers appreciated this product as the only unscented cleaner in the lineup; others preferred some scent, if only as an indicator that cleaning was going on. Its cleaning power was fair but it left some streaks.

FANTASTIK Antibacterial All Purpose Cleaner Heavy Duty
PRICE: $2.99 for 32 oz (9 cents per oz)
ANTIBACTERIAL CLAIMS: Kills 99.9% of *E. coli* and *Salmonella choleraesuis*
WARNINGS: Rinse all food-contact surfaces after use. Avoid contact with eyes, skin, or clothing.
SPRAYS TO CLEAN STOVETOP: 9   **CLEANING:** ★★
STREAKING: ★★   **SCENT:** ★
COMMENTS: This product claims to kill household bacteria in as few as 10 seconds, and its spraying action has particularly good coverage. Unfortunately, it smells terrible, reminding one tester of Raid insect spray.

RECOMMENDED WITH RESERVATIONS *(cont.)*

FORMULA 409 Antibacterial Kitchen All-Purpose Cleaner
(Lemon Fresh)
PRICE: $3.49 for 22 oz (16 cents per oz)
ANTIBACTERIAL CLAIMS: Kills *Salmonella choleraesuis*
WARNINGS: Rinse food-contact surfaces with water. Avoid contact with eyes, skin, or clothing.
SPRAYS TO CLEAN STOVETOP: 14   **CLEANING:** ★★
STREAKING: ★★   **SCENT:** ★★
COMMENTS: Despite being antibacterial, this spray doesn't claim to kill *E. coli*, and it must stand for 10 minutes to kill any germs. It required extra sprays to clean the splattered microwave and greasy stovetop, and left streaks on stainless steel, although it did an adequate cleaning job.

CLOROX GREEN WORKS 97% Naturally Derived All-Purpose Cleaner
PRICE: $3.29 for 32 oz (10 cents per oz)
SPRAYS TO CLEAN STOVETOP: 12   **CLEANING:** ★★
STREAKING: ★½   **SCENT:** ★★
COMMENTS: A decent performer when it came to cleaning the countertops, greasy range hood, and stovetop, but it required extra sprays and wiping.

NOT RECOMMENDED

MR. CLEAN with Febreze Freshness Antibacterial Spray
(Citrus & Light)
PRICE: $2.99 for 32 oz (9 cents per oz)
ANTIBACTERIAL CLAIMS: Kills 99.9% of *E. coli*
WARNINGS: Rinse all food-contact surfaces after use. Avoid contact with eyes or clothing.
SPRAYS TO CLEAN STOVETOP: 10   **CLEANING:** ★
STREAKING: ★   **SCENT:** ★
COMMENTS: Its cleaning power was only so-so, it does not claim to kill salmonella, and it left plenty of streaks. In other words, this orange-tinted spray was a bust. Its scent was sickeningly sweet and chemical-y.

PERFECTING
Summer Classics

A RICH, JUICY STEAK HOT OFF THE GRILL, FOLLOWED BY A BRACING cold scoop of sorbet, is our kind of Saturday night summer supper, especially when we entertain. But when we get enough steaks for six to eight people rung up at the supermarket, reality swiftly sets in. It's how much?!

Call us cheapskates, but we just can't afford to spend upwards of $40 on steak unless it's a very special occasion. We wanted to grill a more affordable steak. While pricey porterhouse and rib eye need little more than salt and pepper to enhance their flavor, less expensive steaks could use a flavor boost. Therefore, once we determined just what cut of steak we'd be grilling (they're not all created equal; some are downright liver-y and tough), we'd be developing a spice rub to add flavor and help develop a savory crust. And we wanted our spice rub to stick to the steak—too often, rubs end up stuck to the cooking grate or down in the coals.

Once we had our main course down, we'd turn to our dessert. Sure, you can buy sorbet at the supermarket, but making it yourself with fresh summer fruit really can be so much better. Our ideal sorbet is creamy, not grainy, and its flavor is refreshing, not cloying. Join us as we figure out how to churn up the sorbet of our dreams and grill great-tasting steaks that leave room in our wallets for lots more summer entertaining.

Becky strains out the seeds from raspberry puree for a creamy, smooth sorbet.

SPICE-RUBBED STEAK ON THE GRILL

✔ **WHY THIS RECIPE WORKS:** In this recipe, we use a two-stage rub to make the most of a comparatively inexpensive steak, the shell sirloin. We started with a savory rub of salt, onion powder, garlic powder, fish sauce, and tomato paste. This *umami*-rich rub made the steaks more savory and enhanced juiciness. For the second stage, we made our own coarsely ground rub based on toasted whole spices and dried chiles. By grinding our own spices, instead of using store-bought ground spices, we created a rub with much deeper flavor.

AS DEDICATED AND RELENTLESS PRACTITIONERS OF the silk-purse-out-of-a-sow's-ear approach to cooking, we enjoy the challenge of transforming inexpensive ingredients into a memorable meal. But we've always conceded that when it comes to grilled steaks, you get what you pay for.

With their tender texture and big-time beef flavor, pricey cuts from the middle of the steer (like rib eyes and T-bones) need little more than salt, pepper, and a few minutes over a hot fire. Try that technique on cheaper steaks from farther down the animal (like the sirloin and the round) and you get meat that's chewy and dry, with flavors that veer toward liver-y and gamy. It's probably these flavor and texture challenges that inspire cooks to take a page from the barbecue manual and apply spice rubs to less expensive steaks. Unfortunately, in our experience that approach doesn't really work. Because cheap steaks exude little fat to bond with the spices, the rub tends to fall off in chunks. If by some stroke of luck the rub remains intact, it usually tastes dry and dusty, plus nuances of flavor can vaporize over the fire.

Still, our skinflint tendencies aren't easily subdued. Surely there was a way to create a recipe for inexpensive grilled steak that was also tender and juicy, with a flavorful, crunchy crust that stayed in place.

First we had to find a steak that provided the best taste and texture for the money, so we looked to the sirloin and the round, settling on what we here in New England call the shell sirloin steak. Tasters described the shell steak as having a relatively beefy taste, unlike cuts from the round, which were liver-y.

Salting the shell steaks before cooking was a given. Salt sprinkled liberally on the surface of the meat draws moisture from inside, which over time is then reabsorbed as the meat sits, seasoning it and changing the structure of the muscle fibers so that they hold on to more juices. But we'd have to do more than that to boost flavor. Some recipes suggest that allowing a spice rub to sit on the meat for a period of time enables its flavors to be absorbed for more complex-tasting results. Science, however, refutes this: Most flavor compounds in spices are fat-soluble rather than water-soluble, so they can't penetrate below the surface of the steak. Furthermore, in tests of marinades, we've found that, other than salt, the only water-soluble flavor compounds that can travel deep into the meat are glutamates.

So, what about glutamates? Scanning the pantry, we singled out two of the most potent sources of these compounds: tomato paste and—odd as it may sound—fish sauce, a condiment that we've called upon in other unlikely applications to amp up savory taste. We applied a rub made with kosher salt and a couple of teaspoons each of these two ingredients and applied it to a set of steaks an hour before grilling. The difference in these steaks was remarkable: They boasted a much deeper flavor without any trace of our secret enhancements. Spurred by this success, we decided to add ½ teaspoon each of garlic powder and onion powder to the rub. Though neither substance contains significant levels of glutamates, their water-soluble flavors are potent enough (especially in concentrated powdered form) that even if they penetrated only ¼ inch into the meat, they might make a difference in the overall flavor. Tasters confirmed that our hunch was correct: The steaks now boasted noticeably richer flavor. On to the spice rub.

Our plan was to treat the steak with the salt-and-glutamate-packed paste first, wait an hour, and then apply a second, more conventional dry rub right before grilling. We tried a variety of rubs, but we found that those made mostly with dried herbs lost their flavor, while those based on spices fared better. It turns out that the flavors in herbs like rosemary, sage, and thyme

GRILLED STEAK WITH NEW MEXICAN CHILE RUB

A STAY-PUT SPICE RUB TURNS CHEAPER STEAK INTO "CHOICE"

1. Cut shallow slits into steak to help salt paste and spice rub adhere to meat and penetrate more deeply.

2. Tenderize meat and boost beefy flavor with paste of onion and garlic powders, salt, tomato paste, and fish sauce.

3. Toast, then grind dried chiles and spices for substantial crust with complex flavor.

4. Lightly mist spice rub with oil to bloom spices on grill and help rub cling to meat.

fade in the intense heat of the grill, but the compounds in spices do much better, particularly those containing capsaicin—namely, peppers, chiles, and paprika. Thus, rubs made predominantly from chile or pepper were clearly the way to go.

First we tried rubs made with preground spices, but these formed a coating that was more pasty than crunchy.

Since we had some time to spare between applying the salty glutamate rub and firing up the grill, we tried toasting some whole spices (cumin, coriander, red pepper flakes, and black peppercorns) in a skillet along with some earthy-tasting dried New Mexican chiles, and then we ground them coarsely in a coffee grinder. To round out the flavors, we also incorporated sugar, paprika, and ground cloves before pressing the rub onto the surface of the steaks.

Tasters pronounced these steaks juicy, tender, and flavorful, and they greatly preferred the robust texture of this home-ground rub. Still, there were two problems to be solved. First, despite the toasting step, the spices retained a slightly raw taste, the result of being cooked with very little fat, so the flavors couldn't "bloom." Second, tasters requested a more substantial crust. We admitted that there had been more rub when we started grilling, but half of it had been left on the cooking grate. We needed to find a way to help the spices stick to the steak.

We remembered when a coworker who was developing a recipe for pan-fried pork chops had difficulty persuading the breading to adhere to the meat. He eventually came up with the clever solution of making shallow cuts into the meat to give the breading more purchase. Doing the same with the steaks before adding the first rub seemed likely to be doubly advantageous: It would increase the surface area, which could give that first rub more opportunity to really get into the meat, plus it could help the spice rub stick to the meat.

As we liberally greased the cooking grate in preparation for grilling our newly crosshatched steaks, we wished that there were some way to put a layer of oil on the steaks themselves without disturbing their spice crust (which—we were pleased to see—was sticking quite nicely). The easy solution: A light spritz of vegetable oil spray or oil from a mister helped the steaks keep their rub intact throughout the grilling process.

These steaks were crusty and crunchy on the outside, with just enough heat and spice to complement the meat's rich flavor, and that little bit of added fat imparted by the oil spray gave the spices the fully developed "bloomed" flavor that tasters were after. The tender and juicy meat belied its $5.99-per-pound price tag. Our inner cheapskate quietly rejoiced.

Grilled Steak with New Mexican Chile Rub

SERVES 6 TO 8

Shell sirloin steak is also known as top butt, butt steak, top sirloin butt, top sirloin steak, and center-cut roast. Spraying the rubbed steaks with oil helps the spices bloom, preventing a raw flavor.

STEAK

- 2 teaspoons tomato paste
- 2 teaspoons fish sauce
- 1½ teaspoons kosher salt
- ½ teaspoon onion powder
- ½ teaspoon garlic powder
- 2 (1½- to 1¾-pound) boneless shell sirloin steaks, 1 to 1¼ inches thick, trimmed

SPICE RUB

- 2 dried New Mexican chiles, stemmed and seeded, flesh torn into ½-inch pieces
- 4 teaspoons cumin seeds
- 4 teaspoons coriander seeds
- ½ teaspoon red pepper flakes
- ½ teaspoon black peppercorns
- 1 tablespoon sugar
- 1 tablespoon paprika
- ¼ teaspoon ground cloves
   Vegetable oil spray

1. FOR THE STEAK: Combine tomato paste, fish sauce, salt, onion powder, and garlic powder in bowl. Pat steaks dry with paper towels. With sharp knife, cut ¹⁄₁₆-inch-deep slits on both sides of steaks, spaced ½ inch apart, in cross-hatch pattern. Rub salt mixture evenly on both sides of steaks. Place steaks on wire rack set in rimmed baking sheet; let stand at room temperature for at least 1 hour. After 30 minutes, prepare grill.

2. FOR THE SPICE RUB: Toast chiles, cumin seeds, coriander seeds, pepper flakes, and peppercorns in 10-inch skillet over medium-low heat, stirring frequently, until just beginning to smoke, 3 to 4 minutes. Transfer to plate to cool, about 5 minutes. Grind spices in spice grinder or in mortar with pestle until coarsely ground. Transfer spices to bowl and stir in sugar, paprika, and cloves.

3A. **FOR A CHARCOAL GRILL:** Open bottom vent completely. Light large chimney starter mounded with charcoal briquettes (7 quarts). When top coals are partially covered with ash, pour two-thirds evenly over grill, then pour remaining coals over half of grill. Set cooking grate in place, cover, and open lid vent completely. Heat grill until hot, about 5 minutes.

3B. **FOR A GAS GRILL:** Turn all burners to high, cover, and heat grill until hot, about 15 minutes. Leave primary burner on high and turn other burner(s) to medium.

4. Clean and oil cooking grate. Sprinkle half of spice rub evenly over 1 side of steaks and press to adhere until spice rub is fully moistened. Lightly spray rubbed side of steak with vegetable oil spray, about 3 seconds. Flip steaks and repeat process of sprinkling with spice rub and spraying with oil spray on second side.

5. Place steaks over hotter side of grill and cook until browned and charred on both sides and center registers 120 to 125 degrees (for medium-rare) or 130 to 135 degrees (for medium), 6 to 8 minutes. If steaks have not reached desired temperature, move to cooler side of grill and continue to cook. Transfer steaks to clean wire rack set in rimmed baking sheet, tent loosely with aluminum foil, and let rest for 10 minutes. Slice meat thin against grain and serve.

VARIATIONS

Grilled Steak with Ancho Chile–Coffee Rub
Substitute 1 dried ancho chile for New Mexican chiles, 2 teaspoons ground coffee for paprika, and 1 teaspoon cocoa powder for ground cloves.

Grilled Steak with Spicy Chipotle Chile Rub
Substitute 2 dried chipotle chiles for New Mexican chiles, 1 teaspoon dried oregano for paprika, and ½ teaspoon ground cinnamon for ground cloves.

RATING HOT SAUCE

Hot sauce isn't just for spicy dishes—we call for it in many other recipes to give dishes a little kick. We wanted to find the best all-purpose hot sauce, so we gathered eight brands in the traditional Cajun or Mexican style, plus one Sriracha, a thicker, sweeter Asian hot sauce that has grown in popularity in recent years, and sampled them on steamed white rice and in a Buffalo sauce on chicken tenders. Tasters preferred brands that had more salt (at least 100 milligrams per teaspoon), garlic, and a decent—but not overpowering—amount of vinegar. When it came to the variety of chile itself, tasters liked hot sauces made with mild, fruity-tasting cayenne and red jalapeño, both of which offer a moderate heat that allows other flavors to shine through. In the end, we had two winners that offered just the right combination of punchy heat, saltiness, sweetness, and garlic flavor. Sodium is per 1-teaspoon serving. Brands are listed in order of preference. See AmericasTestKitchen.com for updates and further information on this testing.

HIGHLY RECOMMENDED

HUY FONG Sriracha Hot Chili Sauce
PRICE: $4.29 for 17 oz (25 cents per oz)   **SODIUM:** 100 mg
INGREDIENTS: Chiles (red jalapeños), sugar, salt, garlic, distilled vinegar, potassium sorbate, sodium bisulfite, xanthan gum
COMMENTS: Despite its unconventionally thick consistency and sweeter profile, this squeeze-bottle condiment (which we threw into the mix as a ringer) impressed tasters with its "full," "rich," "bright" heat. We even enjoyed its heavier body in Buffalo sauce; several tasters remarked that it coated the chicken "perfectly."

FRANK'S REDHOT Original Cayenne Pepper Sauce
PRICE: $2.29 for 12 oz (19 cents per oz)   **SODIUM:** 190 mg
INGREDIENTS: Aged cayenne red peppers, distilled vinegar, water, salt, garlic powder
COMMENTS: "Hello, Frank!" said one taster, who recognized this familiar-tasting condiment as the base for the original Buffalo sauce recipe. In both applications, it struck a perfect balance between tanginess and "tomatoey sweetness," with heat that "wasn't too hot" and "added to the food rather than overpowering it."

RECOMMENDED

ORIGINAL LOUISIANA Hot Sauce
PRICE: $0.99 for 6 oz (17 cents per oz)   **SODIUM:** 240 mg
INGREDIENTS: Peppers (cayenne), vinegar, salt
COMMENTS: Even with just three ingredients, this sauce had a "complex," "balanced" profile and "mild punch." A few tasters even picked up on "smoky," "roasted" notes with "a pleasant fruitiness." Its sodium content was at least double or even triple the amount found in most other brands.

TAPATÍO Salsa Picante
PRICE: $1.95 for 10 oz (20 cents per oz)   **SODIUM:** 110 mg
INGREDIENTS: Water, red peppers (undisclosed), salt, spices, garlic, acetic acid, xanthan gum, sodium benzoate
COMMENTS: Several tasters noted that this Mexican condiment delivered a "smoky" sweetness that reminded them of barbecue sauce or even Worcestershire sauce. Most of us agreed that the warm spice flavor is unusual for Buffalo sauce but not necessarily unwelcome.

RECOMMENDED (cont.)

TEXAS PETE Hot Sauce
PRICE: $1.55 for 12 oz (13 cents per oz)   **SODIUM:** 100 mg
INGREDIENTS: Red peppers (3 undisclosed types), salt, xanthan gum, benzoate of soda
COMMENTS: When sampling it over rice, tasters found this bright red sauce "pleasingly hot and spicy," with a burn that "builds and lingers." A few tasters felt that the heat petered out a little once the condiment was mixed into Buffalo sauce, turning this hot sauce into a "milder," more "ketchup-y" version of Frank's.

EL YUCATECO Salsa Picante Roja de Chile Habanero
PRICE: $2.69 for 4 oz (67 cents per oz)   **SODIUM:** 90 mg
INGREDIENTS: Water, habanero peppers, tomato, salt, spices, acetic acid, xanthan gum, citric acid, sodium benzoate, FD&C red No. 40, calcium disodium EDTA
COMMENTS: This habanero-based sauce was "mouth-meltingly" hot but also "sweet," thanks to the addition of a little tomato. Those who liked it praised its "earthy, almost fruity" flavor, but others felt that it was out of place on Buffalo chicken.

RECOMMENDED WITH RESERVATIONS

CHOLULA Hot Sauce, Original
PRICE: $3.69 for 5 oz (74 cents per oz)   **SODIUM:** 85 mg
INGREDIENTS: Water, peppers (arbol and piquin), salt, vinegar, spices, xanthan gum
COMMENTS: Some tasters appreciated this Mexican sauce's "sweet" flavor and "mild smokiness," but others were unimpressed. Criticisms revolved around its low salt content, which a few tasters felt rendered the sauce "washed out."

NOT RECOMMENDED

TABASCO Pepper Sauce
PRICE: $3.49 for 5 oz (70 cents per oz)   **SODIUM:** 35 mg
INGREDIENTS: Distilled vinegar, red peppers (tabasco), salt
COMMENTS: Tasters described this top-selling hot sauce as "flavorless," "vinegary," "out of balance." Its consistency was off, too, saturating rather than saucing the chicken. (Tabasco also sells Buffalo Style Hot Sauce; we didn't test it since we were looking for an all-purpose product.)

RASPBERRY SORBET

✔ **WHY THIS RECIPE WORKS:** For our raspberry sorbet recipe, we super-chilled the base and used just the right ratio of sweeteners to water to ensure the finest-textured ice crystals possible. We also bumped up the berries' natural amount of pectin to give the sorbet stability both in the freezer and out.

SORBET HAS ALWAYS BEEN THE NEGLECTED STEPCHILD of homemade frozen desserts. This is a shame, because good sorbet can hold its own against ice cream any day. A well-made batch is almost as creamy and smooth as its dairy-based relative, but rather than finishing with mouth-coating richness, it should be delicately icy and dissolve on the tongue, leaving behind an echo of clean, concentrated fruit flavor.

But delicacy is where most recipes get hung up. The majority of homemade sorbets don't have super-fine ice crystals—they have big, jagged crystals that raze the tongue—and are so hard they're impossible to get out of the carton. We've also scooped plenty of versions that are crumbly, coarse, and dull and have watched seemingly stable sorbets melt into syrupy puddles within minutes of leaving the freezer.

Despite this long list of hazards, we were determined to figure out a way to pull off the perfect batch. For flavor, we were set on raspberry—not only is it a quintessential summer fruit but the berries also freeze well, meaning we could make this summertime flavor any time of year.

Before we got to churning, we reviewed what we knew about sorbet. Regardless of how ripe, sweet, and juicy the fruit is, freezing a puree of straight berries doesn't work. The relatively small amount of moisture in the fruit will freeze completely and its crystals will be separated only by the berries' fibers. The result—a solid, impenetrable block—wouldn't be pretty.

To get sorbet with the ideal consistency—delicately icy, velvety smooth, and easily scoopable—adding both water and sugar is crucial. The two work in tandem. Some of the water freezes, which creates ice crystals. But because sugar depresses the freezing point of water, some of it will

also remain liquid. This so-called "free" water lubricates the ice crystals, producing a smooth, scoopable texture. Our challenge, then, would be to achieve just the right balance of water and sugar in the base.

With that in mind, we mixed up our first batch of the base in a blender using 4 cups of berries, ½ cup of water, and ¾ cup of sugar—which we hoped could sweeten the mixture just enough and provide exactly the right ratio of sugar to water. Once the mixture was smooth, we strained it and poured it into the ice cream machine; churned it for 30 minutes, until it froze to a soft-serve consistency; transferred it to a container; and put it in the freezer overnight.

The next morning we summoned our colleagues for a taste. We weren't expecting perfection on the first go-round, but from their frowns we could tell we were far from our goal. It wasn't the flavor that needed help. It was the texture that was in all sorts of trouble. Though not rock hard, the sorbet was still too solid to scoop (even when thawed at room temperature for a while). Worse, it was as grainy as a granita.

At this point we understood sorbet well enough to know that adding more water to the mixture would solve the hardness problem by creating more free water, and by the time we'd doubled the liquid the sorbet was perfectly scoopable. But by solving the first problem we'd exaggerated the second, as the ice crystals were now larger and coarser than ever. Apparently, increasing the amount of free water in the base came at a cost.

Fortunately, we had an idea about how to keep the water at 1 cup while still enhancing scoopability and minimizing the size of the crystals: separating out a small amount of the base and freezing it separately, then adding it back into the rest. Our science editor had explained to us that, because the small portion would freeze much more rapidly than if we tried to freeze the whole batch, there wouldn't be enough time for large ice crystals to grow, and instead very small ice crystals would be formed. Then, when we added this frozen mix back to the rest of the base (which would have been chilled in the meantime), the tiny crystals would act as a catalyst, triggering a chain reaction that very rapidly forms equally small crystals in the bigger mix. (In technical terms, the seed crystals provide "nucleation sites" for new crystals to form.) We gave this a whirl, freezing

RASPBERRY SORBET

a small amount of the base before churning it together with the rest of the base. It was certainly a worthwhile move; everyone agreed that this latest batch was noticeably smoother. But it still hadn't achieved the velvety texture of professionally made sorbet.

One thing we hadn't yet tried was playing with the amount of sugar. At the same time that it depresses the freezing point of water so that some of the water never freezes, it also reduces the tendency of ice crystals to grow large, thus contributing to smoother texture.

The only problem was that, flavor-wise, we had the sugar right where we wanted it. When we tried increasing it to 1 cup, it smoothed out the sorbet's texture but created an achingly sweet dessert. That got us thinking of another trick we used in our ice cream recipe: swapping some of the sugar for corn syrup. Like sugar, this sweetener interrupts the flow of water molecules, preventing the formation of large crystals. But because corn syrup tastes a lot less sweet than sugar, we could use a fair bit of it without oversweetening the sorbet.

We moved forward with that idea in our next several batches, swapping in varying amounts of corn syrup for sugar. The more sugar we replaced with syrup the softer and smoother the texture became. The winning batch contained ½ cup plus 2 tablespoons of sugar and ¼ cup of corn syrup, the combination of which offered an ideal balance of sweetness, smoothness, and scoopability.

At last, the texture of the sorbet was ideal when eaten straight out of the freezer. But once it sat for even a few minutes at room temperature, it began to liquefy into a soupy mess. This is the potential downfall to depressing the freezing point of a frozen dessert: The unfrozen water is literally free to move about and quickly leaks from the mixture, leaving the ice surrounded by syrupy puddles.

Professional sorbet manufacturers get around this problem with stabilizers like guar gum and locust bean gum. These additives act like sponges, corralling the free water within a loose matrix so that it can remain unfrozen while still not flowing freely. We couldn't get our hands on either of those products, but we did have access to

EQUIPMENT CORNER

ICE CREAM GADGETS

Nothing beats a scoop of ice cream or sorbet when you need to beat the summer heat, and making your own is easy enough to do, provided you have the right equipment. Looking for the best ice cream machine, we tested six models, priced from $20 to $300. Our lineup included two styles: pricey self-refrigerating models that let you make batch after batch, or cheaper models with a removable canister that must be refrozen each time. Our favorite self-refrigerating model is the **Whynter SNÖ Professional Ice Cream Maker**, which makes incredibly creamy, dense, smooth ice cream that's firm enough to eat right away. However, at $220, it makes homemade desserts a pricey proposition. For a more affordable alternative, we also like the **Cuisinart Automatic Frozen Yogurt, Ice Cream, and Sorbet Maker**, which is our best buy and cost just $49.95. Though its canister must be prefrozen and the ice cream needs to be chilled until firm, this model produced creamy ice cream that rivaled ice cream from our top-rated machine, but at a fraction of the price. And to serve that homemade ice cream or sorbet, how about a homemade ice cream cone? We tested two ice cream cone makers, both of which look and work like a waffle iron. Once the batter has set into a browned wafer, it must be removed and rolled around a cone-shaped mold until it hardens, which takes just a few seconds. Both machines were fast, easy to use, and made crisp, professional-looking cones, but one outshone the other. The **Chef's Choice 838 Waffle Cone Express**, $49.95, was solidly built and made perfect, evenly golden-brown waffle cones every time. See AmericasTestKitchen.com for updates and further information on these testings.

WHYNTER SNÖ PROFESSIONAL ICE CREAM MAKER

CUISINART AUTOMATIC FROZEN YOGURT, ICE CREAM, AND SORBET MAKER

CHEF'S CHOICE 838 WAFFLE CONE EXPRESS

two other possibilities: gelatin and pectin, both of which we tried in subsequent batches.

When it came to curbing melting, both products got the job done, but the gelatin had a downside: It left the sorbet with an unpalatable plasticlike firmness, even when used sparingly. No deal, said our tasters. Pectin, on the other hand, was an all-around success. After testing with varying amounts of the powder, we learned that a mere teaspoon (bloomed first in the water) was enough to keep the sorbet from immediately puddling without overdoing the firmness as the gelatin had. Besides, raspberries (like most fruits) naturally contain pectin in their cell walls. We were just adding more of a good thing.

Our sorbet was finally starting to come together, save for one nagging problem: The quality of the churned base was inconsistent. Every few batches, the mixture came out of the canister not with a soft-serve consistency but with a crumbly, fluffy texture and a noticeably duller berry flavor that more closely resembled a raspberry snow cone. Since some batches were coming out perfectly smooth and brightly flavored, we suspected that the problem was the result of our churning method and not the base itself. Were we under- or overchurning the sorbet?

Admittedly, we hadn't paid much attention to the churning time before that point. In fact, we'd never given much thought to how long any frozen dessert should be churned because most ice cream and sorbet recipes we've made end with the same directive: "Churn according to manufacturer instructions." But the more we thought about it, the more we realized that this vague set of instructions made no sense. Just as mixing times will vary for different types of cake batter, so, too, should the churning times be specific for different types of frozen desserts. We also thought some visual cues would be helpful. With a timer and a thermometer at the ready, we poured several identical batches of our sorbet base into canisters and let the mixtures churn for increasing lengths of time, noting their temperatures and how their consistencies varied based on churning time. Then we proceeded as usual, transferring each batch to a container that we stuck in the freezer.

The results were surprising: The longest-churned batch was the thickest coming out of the canister but also the most granular and snowlike after freezing. We'd assumed

that, just as with ice cream, the longest possible stay in the machine would result in a smoother sorbet because the constant agitation would help prevent large ice crystals from forming after the move to the freezer, but this test proved us wrong. Instead, longer churning times seemed to give the free-water and ice crystal mixture more time to grow ever-larger ice crystals. In fact, the best batch came from a base that we stopped churning almost as soon as the mixture started to thicken up, right around 18 degrees and the 20-minute mark.

To look at this batch, you wouldn't have expected it to turn into a nicely dense, stable sorbet; at the point at which we stopped the machine, it had a loose, pourable consistency, like a milkshake, because less water was frozen. But after an overnight stint in the freezer, it set up perfectly. A little research explained the difference between the two frozen desserts: During churning, air gets incorporated in the mixture. However, unlike with ice cream, in which a certain amount of incorporated air—known as "overrun"—contributes a pleasing lightness to the custard, that air renders sorbets loose and crumbly and dulls their flavor. This is because ice cream contains fat and protein, both of which act to stabilize the air bubbles. Sorbet, on the other hand, contains no cream. The only thing it has available to surround and stabilize the air bubbles is ice crystals, and they are not very good at the job, particularly as they grow larger in the freezer overnight (or with longer churning). The added air also dilutes the concentration of flavor in every bite. The upshot: a loose and crumbly, duller-tasting dessert that easily falls apart after overnight freezing.

To guarantee good results, we came away with a visual cue, which ensured that the sorbet would turn out dense and smooth no matter what ice cream machine was used: The color of the mixture began to lighten up considerably soon after it started to thicken, a sure sign that it was beginning to take on air and was in need of a transfer to the freezer.

With our sorbet finally smooth and stable every time, the only remaining tasks were to punch up the berries' intensity—a pinch of salt did the trick—and dream up a few flavor variations. Fruity ruby port made for a natural pairing, as did bracing ginger and mint, not to mention the healthy shot of lime juice we added to make a "rickey" version. With four recipes on file, we knew this sorbet formula would get us through a summer's worth of entertaining—and that this frozen dessert would no longer play second fiddle to a quart of ice cream.

Raspberry Sorbet

MAKES 1 QUART

Super-chilling part of the sorbet base before transferring it to the ice cream machine will keep ice crystals to a minimum. If using a canister-style ice cream machine, be sure to freeze the empty canister for at least 24 hours and preferably 48 hours before churning. For self-refrigerating machines, prechill the canister by running the machine for 5 to 10 minutes before pouring in the sorbet mixture. Allow the sorbet to sit at room temperature for 5 minutes to soften before serving. Fresh or frozen berries may be used. If using frozen berries, thaw them before proceeding. Make certain that you use Sure-Jell engineered for low- or no-sugar recipes (packaged in a pink box) and not regular Sure-Jell (in a yellow box).

1 cup water

1 teaspoon Sure-Jell for Less or No Sugar Needed Recipes

⅛ teaspoon salt

1¼ pounds (4 cups) raspberries

½ cup (3½ ounces) plus 2 tablespoons sugar

¼ cup light corn syrup

1. Combine water, Sure-Jell, and salt in medium saucepan. Heat over medium-high heat, stirring occasionally, until Sure-Jell is fully dissolved, about 5 minutes. Remove saucepan from heat and allow mixture to cool slightly, about 10 minutes.

2. Process raspberries, sugar, corn syrup, and water mixture in blender or food processor until smooth, about 30 seconds. Strain mixture through fine-mesh strainer, pressing on solids to extract as much liquid as possible. Transfer 1 cup mixture to small bowl and place remaining mixture in large bowl. Cover both bowls with plastic wrap. Place large bowl in refrigerator and small bowl in freezer and cool completely, at least 4 hours or up to 24 hours. (Small bowl of base will freeze solid.)

3. Remove mixtures from refrigerator and freezer. Scrape frozen base from small bowl into large bowl of base. Stir occasionally until frozen base has fully dissolved. Transfer mixture to ice cream machine and churn until mixture has consistency of thick milkshake and color lightens, 15 to 25 minutes.

4. Transfer sorbet to airtight container, pressing firmly to remove any air pockets, and freeze until firm, at least 2 hours. Serve. (Sorbet can be frozen for up to 5 days.)

VARIATIONS

Raspberry–Lime Rickey Sorbet

Reduce water to ¾ cup. Add 2 teaspoons grated lime zest and ¼ cup lime juice to blender with raspberries.

Raspberry-Port Sorbet

Substitute ruby port for water in step 1.

Raspberry Sorbet with Ginger and Mint

Substitute ginger beer for water in step 1. Add 2-inch piece of peeled and thinly sliced ginger and ¼ cup mint leaves to blender with raspberries. Decrease amount of sugar to ½ cup.

SOLVING THE PROBLEMS OF SORBET

We had to solve four problems before we arrived at a scoopable, smooth, dense, and stable sorbet.

PROBLEM 1: TOO HARD TO SCOOP
THE TESTS: VARY WATER AND SUGAR AMOUNTS
For sorbet that's soft enough to scoop, some water should freeze but some should remain liquid and "free" to flow between the ice crystals, providing the sensation of creaminess. Added water and sugar are critical. Water ensures that there's enough of it in the mix to remain free. Sugar aids the process by getting in the way of the water freezing.

ROCK SOLID
Straight fruit puree with no added water or sugar freezes into an impenetrable mass.

GETTING SOFTER
A half cup of water plus ¾ cup of sugar creates some free water, and the sorbet starts to soften.

JUST RIGHT
One cup of water and nearly 1 cup of sugar and corn syrup produce a creamy, scoopable texture.

PROBLEM 2: ICY, GRAINY TEXTURE
THE TEST: SPEED UP FREEZE TIME
Big ice crystals turn sorbet grainy. Freezing the base as fast as possible is the antidote. First, it doesn't give the base time to form large crystals. Second, once small "seed" crystals get started, they trigger a chain reaction, continuously turning more unfrozen water into equally tiny crystals.

TRADITIONAL SLOW FREEZE
When the whole base is transferred directly to the ice cream maker, it freezes slowly, giving large, grainy ice crystals time to form.

FAST FREEZE
Freezing 1 cup of the base allows it to freeze rapidly, forming small "seed" crystals. When it is combined with the refrigerated remainder, it initiates a chain reaction, causing more small crystals to form immediately.

PROBLEM 3: CRUMBLY TEXTURE, DULL TASTE
THE TESTS: CALIBRATE CHURN TIMES
Too much churning has a negative effect on the final texture of sorbet: Because the dessert has no fat or protein to stabilize the air bubbles incorporated during churning, longer churning times produce sorbets that are loose, crumbly, and dull-tasting.

40 MINUTES
Overchurned sorbet looks promisingly thick but freezes up crumbly and dull-tasting.

30 MINUTES
As the churning time is reduced, less air is incorporated, improving the texture of the final product.

20 MINUTES
Churning just long enough for the mixture to reach the consistency of a thick milkshake produces dense, flavorful sorbet.

PROBLEM 4: RAPID MELTING
THE TESTS: TRY STABILIZERS
Sorbet is prone to rapid melting once it is scooped and served. Commercial manufacturers stave off melting by incorporating ingredients like guar gum and locust bean gum that trap some of the free water so it won't readily leak out at room temperature. Instead of those additives, we tried gelatin and pectin.

NO STABILIZER
Once out of the freezer, stabilizer-free sorbet quickly melts into a watery mess.

1 TEASPOON GELATIN
While it greatly improves stability, gelatin creates a sorbet that is strangely rubbery.

1 TEASPOON PECTIN
Pectin, which is also found naturally in berries, slows melting and produces a likable texture.

SHORT RIBS AND CHOPS
Hit the Grill

A luscious mustard glaze is brushed over our short ribs multiple times for a crusty, flavorful exterior.

WE COOK A LOT OF MEAT ON THE GRILL. AND BY MEAT, WE MEAN a lot of chicken, burgers, and steak. What gives? Let's break out of our backyard barbecue rut and develop recipes for grilled pork chops and short ribs.

Grilling pork chops isn't unheard of, but most people hesitate to cook thin, boneless chops because they can dry out so quickly. We were sure there was a way to develop a grilling method for this convenient cut, one that would deliver juicy meat and a flavorful browned crust. We'd start with brining, our go-to method for keeping lean meat juicy, but we knew that we'd also need to find another path to deliver a flavorful exterior. And the grill setup would be important too: Such a thin piece of meat needs special care on the grill.

While most of us have grilled pork chops, few have attempted short ribs. Short ribs are for braising, right? Sure, but we grill other ribs, so why not ultra-meaty short ribs? Before we pulled out our grill, we had some questions to answer. Bone-in or boneless ribs? And how would we flavor them? We wanted to distinguish these luxe ribs from the usual backyard barbecue. Finally, what would our grilling method be? Short ribs are bulkier than other ribs we grill and we didn't want to constantly be turning them over a hot fire to ensure that they cooked evenly. Fire up your grill, we're having short ribs and pork chops.

EASY GRILLED BONELESS PORK CHOPS WITH ORANGE, JÍCAMA, AND PEPITA RELISH

EASY GRILLED PORK CHOPS

✔ **WHY THIS RECIPE WORKS:** To produce juicy, well-charred boneless center-cut loin chops on the grill, we used a two-pronged approach. We brined the chops to improve their ability to hold on to juices during cooking, provide seasoning throughout, and increase their tenderness. To ensure we'd get a substantial browned crust before the interior overcooked, we looked to a unique coating of anchovy paste and honey.

GRAB A PACK OF THIN, BONELESS, CENTER-CUT PORK chops from the supermarket, fire up the grill, and you're moments away from an inexpensive, simple, and satisfying supper. Or you would have been, half a century ago when American pork was still well marbled and stayed juicy on the grill. Because today's pigs are bred for leanness rather than flavor, modern chops present a perennial challenge: How can you get a flavorful, browned crust without sapping the interior of its already meager juices?

Most recipes for grilled pork chops tend to produce either beautifully charred slices of cardboard or juicy chops that are also pale and bland. Frustrated by these half measures, we wanted to develop a recipe that paid equal attention to juiciness and browning. At the same time, we aimed to retain the speed and ease that have always made grilled pork chops such an attractive weeknight dinner in the first place.

The most obvious way to guarantee juiciness in meat is to cook it at a gentle, low temperature and be vigilant about pulling it off the heat just before it reaches the desired final temperature (to allow for the effects of carryover cooking). On a grill, low temperatures are usually achieved through indirect heat, which can be produced by stacking the coals beneath one side of the grate and cooking the food on the opposite side. Meat grilled this way is often first given a few minutes directly above the coals to brown and char before it's moved to the cooler side of the grill to finish cooking. But that technique was not an option for our thin pork chops, which needed every second they could get over the coals in order to have a fighting chance at browning before they were cooked through.

Luckily, we've done a lot of testing over the years to figure out how to keep meat juicy during cooking—even when exposed to high heat. Two of the most effective methods we've found are salting and brining. Both slightly alter muscle fibers so they remain tender and are better able to hold on to moisture. Salting is a dry process that first pulls moisture from the meat and then allows it to reabsorb, while brining actually increases the amount of moisture in the meat. We ran a quick side-by-side test, and the brined chops, with their added moisture, won hands down.

While brining provided a bit of insurance against overcooking, we were still fighting a losing battle; even when we cooked the chops over an entire chimneyful of coals stacked in a thick layer, they refused to develop nicely browned lines and rich flavor in the short time (8 to 10 minutes) it took them to reach medium, or 140 degrees. We needed help, so we turned to our science editor for some guidance. What we got was a new way of thinking about browning.

While we often talk of browning as a process of creation—one that develops flavor, color, and texture—it would be more accurate to describe it as a process of destruction. Heat breaks down large meat proteins into their amino-acid building blocks, while trace amounts of carbohydrates are split into simple sugars like fructose, glucose, and lactose (known collectively as reducing sugars). It's only after this destruction has taken place that the Maillard—or browning—reaction can begin. We always knew that cooking temperature had an impact on the speed of the reaction, but it turns out that both the amount and type of amino acids released, as well as the concentration of reducing sugars, play big roles as well. Meat browns relatively slowly because its proteins break down gradually in the presence of so much moisture (meat is about 70 percent water) and it doesn't contain very many carbohydrates to transform into reducing sugars. This information led us to two potential methods for faster browning: We could either find a way to crank up the heat and overcome pork's inherent shortcomings or coat the chop in something with a composition designed for speedy browning.

Our first move was to play with the grill setup. Up to this point, we'd been emptying a full chimney of coals

onto half of the grill and cooking our chops over this relatively hot fire. We didn't want to use any more coals for such a quick-cooking meal, but what if we could bring the chops closer to the flames? We tried raising up the coals by stacking them on top of an inverted, perforated disposable roasting pan, but the glowing-hot coals melted right through the aluminum. A real roasting pan didn't have that problem, but it severely restricted airflow, choking the fire. Next we tried partially freezing the chops so that they could spend more time over the fire without overcooking. It worked to some extent but required careful timing lest the chops freeze solid, which made them cook up stringy and dry. After a few smoky afternoons grilling in the back alley, we gave up on this direction and turned our focus to the second option.

To get the pork chops to brown faster, we'd need a coating that contained both protein and reducing sugars. We started working from a list of ingredients provided by our science editor. One of the most interesting options was dry milk powder, which is rich in both protein and lactose. We dusted a few chops with milk powder and popped them on the grill. We got rapid browning, but the taste test was disappointing. The chops didn't taste like milk—but they didn't taste especially meaty either. Next we tried coating them with flour (which contains proteins as well as lots of carbohydrates that break down into reducing sugars), but again, while the chops browned

more quickly, they didn't taste that meaty. Disheartened, we went back to our science editor.

We soon learned that our folly had been in thinking that all browning was created equal. In reality, meat muscle proteins produce far more complex flavor and aroma than other types of proteins, due to their high levels of sulfur-containing amino acids. Milk protein contains only about half as many, and wheat flour protein even fewer. That explained why we were getting the appearance of browned meat while the flavor was falling short. Frustrated by our lack of progress, we took a break from grilling and threw together a quick pasta dish for lunch. We softened some sliced garlic in olive oil and then tossed in a few minced anchovies and marveled at how quickly they turned a rich golden brown in the hot oil. Why were they browning so quickly? It turns out that not only are anchovies a particularly concentrated source of muscle proteins, but their protein has already been broken down through fermentation into many sulfur-containing amino acids. We suspected that we might have finally hit the browning jackpot. We dropped everything and excitedly brined another batch of chops, patted them dry, and applied a super-thin layer of anchovy paste to both sides. Back on the grill, these chops browned much faster than plain chops and emerged with a rich, meaty-tasting crust without a hint of fishiness, thanks to the flavor contributed by browning and the smoke from the grill. With a solution finally within reach, we regained our confidence—and even got a bit greedy. Could we get the chops to brown even better and faster?

After all, we now had plenty of amino acids but still little in the way of reducing sugars. But we had a ready source of fructose right in the pantry—honey. We mixed up the anchovy paste with some honey and a little vegetable oil (which made the mixture easier to spread) and smeared the concoction over both sides of six chops. In just 4 minutes over the fire, the underside of the chops had turned a gorgeous burnished brown dotted with spots of real char. Another 4 to 6 minutes on the second side and they were ready to eat. Juicy? Check. Well browned? Check. Meaty? Check. Just as important, these chops can be prepped for the grill in about the time it takes to ready the charcoal. Mission accomplished.

Easy Grilled Boneless Pork Chops

SERVES 4 TO 6

If your pork is enhanced, do not brine it in step 1. Very finely mashed anchovy fillets (rinsed and dried before mashing) can be used instead of anchovy paste.

- 6 (6- to 8-ounce) boneless pork chops, ¾ to 1 inch thick
- 3 tablespoons salt
- 1 tablespoon vegetable oil
- 1½ teaspoons honey
- 1 teaspoon anchovy paste
- ½ teaspoon pepper
- 1 recipe relish (optional) (recipe follows)

1. Cut 2 slits about 1 inch apart through outer layer of fat and connective tissue on each chop to prevent buckling. Dissolve salt in 1½ quarts cold water in large container. Submerge chops in brine and let stand at room temperature for 30 minutes.

2. Whisk together oil, honey, anchovy paste, and pepper to form smooth paste. Remove pork from brine and pat dry with paper towels. Using spoon, spread half of oil mixture evenly over 1 side of each chop (about ¼ teaspoon per side).

3A. FOR A CHARCOAL GRILL: Open bottom vent completely. Light chimney starter filled with charcoal briquettes (6 quarts). When top coals are partially covered with ash, pour evenly over half of grill. Set cooking grate in place, cover, and open lid vent completely. Heat grill until hot, about 5 minutes.

3B. FOR A GAS GRILL: Turn all burners to high, cover, and heat grill until hot, about 15 minutes. Leave primary burner on high and turn off other burner(s).

4. Clean and oil cooking grate. Place chops, oiled side down, over hot part of grill and cook, uncovered, until well browned on first side, 4 to 6 minutes. While chops are grilling, spread remaining oil mixture evenly over second side of chops. Flip chops and continue to cook until chops register 140 degrees, 4 to 6 minutes longer (if chops are well browned but register less than 140 degrees, move to cooler part of grill to finish cooking). Transfer chops to plate and let rest for 5 minutes. Serve with relish, if using.

Onion, Olive, And Caper Relish

MAKES ABOUT 2 CUPS

- ¼ cup olive oil
- 2 onions, cut into ¼-inch pieces
- 6 garlic cloves, sliced thin
- ½ cup pitted kalamata olives, chopped coarse
- ¼ cup capers, rinsed
- 3 tablespoons balsamic vinegar
- 2 tablespoons minced fresh parsley
- 1 teaspoon minced fresh marjoram
- 1 teaspoon sugar
- ½ teaspoon anchovy paste
- ½ teaspoon pepper
- ¼ teaspoon salt

Heat 2 tablespoons oil in 10-inch nonstick skillet over medium heat until shimmering. Add onions and cook until softened, about 5 minutes. Stir in garlic and cook until fragrant, about 30 seconds. Transfer onion mixture to medium bowl; stir in remaining 2 tablespoons oil, olives, capers, vinegar, parsley, marjoram, sugar, anchovy paste, pepper, and salt. Serve warm or at room temperature.

NOTES FROM THE TEST KITCHEN

WHERE GRILLED CHOPS GO WRONG
Boneless, center-cut pork chops are widely available, but their lack of fat makes them almost impossible to cook well.

JUICY BUT NO COLOR

LOTS OF COLOR BUT DRY

Tomato, Fennel, and Almond Relish

MAKES ABOUT 2 CUPS

¼ cup olive oil
1 fennel bulb, stalks discarded, bulb halved, cored, and cut into ¼-inch pieces
6 garlic cloves, sliced thin
2 tomatoes, cored and cut into ½-inch pieces
¼ cup green olives, pitted and chopped coarse
3 tablespoons sherry vinegar
¼ cup slivered almonds, toasted
3 tablespoons minced fresh parsley
1 teaspoon sugar
   Salt and pepper

Heat 2 tablespoons oil in 10-inch skillet over medium heat until shimmering. Add fennel and cook until slightly softened, about 5 minutes. Stir in garlic and cook until fragrant, about 30 seconds. Stir in tomatoes and continue to cook until tomatoes break down slightly, about 5 minutes. Transfer fennel mixture to medium bowl; stir in remaining 2 tablespoons oil, olives, vinegar, almonds, parsley, sugar, ¾ teaspoon salt, and ½ teaspoon pepper. Serve warm or at room temperature.

Orange, Jícama, and Pepita Relish

MAKES ABOUT 3 CUPS

1 orange
¼ cup olive oil
2 jalapeño chiles, stemmed, seeded, and sliced into thin rings
3 shallots, sliced thin
6 garlic cloves, sliced thin
2 cups jícama, peeled and cut into ¼-inch pieces
¼ cup pepitas, toasted
3 tablespoons chopped fresh cilantro
3 tablespoons lime juice (2 limes)
1 teaspoon sugar
   Salt and pepper

Cut away peel and pith from orange. Quarter orange, then slice crosswise into ¼ inch-thick pieces. Heat 2 tablespoons oil in 10-inch skillet over medium heat until shimmering. Add jalapeños and shallots and cook until slightly softened, about 5 minutes. Stir in garlic and cook until fragrant, about 30 seconds. Transfer jalapeño-shallot mixture to medium bowl; stir in orange, jícama, pepitas, cilantro, lime juice, sugar, ¾ teaspoon salt, and ½ teaspoon pepper. Serve warm or at room temperature.

SCIENCE DESK

BETTER BROWNING IN A HURRY

For grilled pork chops with deeply seared crusts and juicy centers, speedy browning was crucial—but wasn't easy to come by. Trouble is, before the Maillard reaction (the scientific principle behind browning) can kick in, heat needs to do some work. It must break down proteins into amino acids and carbohydrates into so-called reducing sugars. Plus, moisture on the meat's surface inhibits browning. Dredging the exterior of the chops in something dry and absorbent seemed like a potential fix, so we tried flour (full of carbohydrates and some protein), as well as milk powder, which is loaded with not only protein but also the reducing sugar lactose. But while both ingredients significantly sped up browning, neither was particularly meaty tasting.

   Then we discovered a breakthrough combination: honey and anchovy paste. Honey is loaded with the reducing sugar fructose, while anchovy paste has three benefits: First, it has the same concentration of meaty-tasting amino acids as pork. Second, the fermentation process dehydrates anchovies, so they contain very little browning-inhibiting water. Third, their large proteins are already broken down into the fast-reacting amino acids. Those traits added up to faster browning and big, meaty flavor.

FAILED
Flour expedited browning but didn't enhance meatiness.

FAILED AGAIN
Milk powder also hastened crust development but not savory flavor.

WHO'D'VE THUNK?
Honey plus anchovy paste produced quick, flavorful browning.

RATING PRESSURE COOKERS

Pressure cookers can be intimidating, but unlike models used by our grandmothers, pressure cookers on the market today are as safe as any other cookware, and they're surprisingly simple to use. And the best news? In most cases, pressure cookers deliver long-cooked dishes like braises and stews in just 45 minutes. Pressure cookers work by raising the boiling point of liquid. In a tightly sealed pot under high pressure, the superheated steam makes food cook much faster. And because the pot stays closed, cooking requires much less liquid than usual, so flavors concentrate. Looking for the best pressure cooker, we started our testing with 12 brands, including both stovetop and electric models, but we strongly preferred stovetop cookers, so we narrowed down our list to eight stovetop brands. After preparing risotto, chicken stock, beef stew, baked beans, and meaty tomato sauce in the pressure cookers, we found a few key attributes shared by higher-ranked cookers. We preferred cookers that were short and wide, as they were easier to reach into to stir the pot's contents and provided a greater surface area for browning meat and vegetables. Though all of the pressure cookers had disk bottoms—basically a disk of aluminum attached to the bottom of the pan and covered by stainless steel—those with the broadest, thickest bottoms performed best, as they retained and regulated heat especially well. Higher-ranked models also reached 250 degrees (or close to it), which is the temperature for generating the preferred pressure standard for "high pressure" in recipes. We also liked models with pressure indicators that were brightly colored and easy to read at a glance. Brands are listed in order of preference. See AmericasTestKitchen.com for updates and further information on this testing.

HIGHLY RECOMMENDED

FISSLER Vitaquick 8-Liter (8½-quart) Pressure Cooker
MODEL: 600 700N 08 079   PRICE: $280   WEIGHT: 8.95 lb
BOTTOM THICKNESS: 7.24 mm   COOKING SURFACE DIAMETER: 9 in
DEPTH: 6½ in   HIGHEST TEMPERATURE: 253°F
EVAPORATION LOSS: ★★★   COOKING: ★★★   EASE OF USE: ★★★
COMMENTS: Solidly constructed, with a low, wide profile that made browning and stirring easy, this cooker was straightforward to seal, with an automatic lock, and an easy-to-monitor pressure valve. It was the only cooker to reach 250°F at high pressure, allowing it to cook food to perfection in the time range given.

FAGOR DUO 8-Quart Stainless Steel Pressure Cooker
MODEL: 918060787   PRICE: $89.99   BEST BUY   WEIGHT: 6.85 lb
BOTTOM THICKNESS: 7.15 mm   COOKING SURFACE DIAMETER: 9 in
DEPTH: 6¾ in   HIGHEST TEMPERATURE: 246°F
EVAPORATION LOSS: ★★★   COOKING: ★★★   EASE OF USE: ★★★
COMMENTS: Performing much like our winner at a fraction of the price (though lighter and less smooth to latch), this cooker's low sides and broad cooking surface helped in browning and stirring; its bright yellow pressure indicator was easy to monitor; and a clearly marked dial let us set pressure or release steam easily. It fell short of the 250°F target, but still performed well.

RECOMMENDED

PRESTO 8-Quart Stainless Steel Pressure Cooker
MODEL: 01370   PRICE: $64.54   WEIGHT: 6.2 lb
BOTTOM THICKNESS: 4.76 mm   COOKING SURFACE DIAMETER: 8½ in
DEPTH: 7 in   HIGHEST TEMPERATURE: 249°F
EVAPORATION LOSS: ★★★   COOKING: ★★½   EASE OF USE: ★★
COMMENTS: The lowest-priced brand in our lineup, it felt more flimsy than the top two models, and its recessed pressure indicator was hard to monitor; also, its bulging sides encouraged scorching. However, we appreciated its low, wide profile for browning and stirring. Also, it produced tender, flavorful meats and intact, creamy beans. Note this model only cooks at high pressure; it has no low-pressure setting, which we've found useful for cooking grains uniformly.

RECOMMENDED (*cont.*)

TRAMONTINA 8-Quart Heavy-Duty Pressure Cooker
MODEL: 80130500   PRICE: $99.95   WEIGHT: 6.7 lb
BOTTOM THICKNESS: 5.19 mm
COOKING SURFACE DIAMETER: 7¾ in   DEPTH: 7¾ in
HIGHEST TEMPERATURE: 243°F
EVAPORATION LOSS: ★★   COOKING: ★★½   EASE OF USE: ★★
COMMENTS: A narrower cooking surface made us brown meat in more batches than did the top-rated cookers, and the sides are slightly taller than we prefer, but the bright red pressure indicator was simple to monitor and its controls are straightforward. However, it vented more than top-rated cookers, and didn't reach 250°F, so we wound up with slightly too-firm beans and risotto at the end of recipe cooking times.

RECOMMENDED WITH RESERVATIONS

KUHN RIKON Duromatic 8-Quart Stockpot Pressure Cooker
MODEL: KU3326   PRICE: $179.99   WEIGHT: 6.25 lb
BOTTOM THICKNESS: 7.09 mm
COOKING SURFACE DIAMETER: 8¼ in   DEPTH: 8¼ in
HIGHEST TEMPERATURE: 240°F
EVAPORATION LOSS: ★   COOKING: ★★½   EASE OF USE: ★½
COMMENTS: This cooker's performance didn't quite match its sleek looks. This pot's extra-small disk bottom forced us to keep flames very low, which delayed reaching pressure, or we'd risk scorching food around the perimeter. It is deeper and narrower than we prefer (the company sells a low, wide 8-quart model, but its price is over $400). The pressure indicator was easy to monitor—a good thing, because it often dipped, forcing us to hover to adjust the temperature, and causing it to lose steam.

GRILL-ROASTED BEEF SHORT RIBS WITH MUSTARD GLAZE

GRILLED SHORT RIBS

✔ **WHY THIS RECIPE WORKS:** Beef short ribs are a meaty cut that can require a lot of time and tending on the grill. We began our testing by coating our ribs with a simple spice rub. We jump-started the cooking process by giving the ribs a pit stop in the oven. In a foil-covered baking dish, the fat was rendered from the ribs, and the tough, chewy collagen began to transform into moisture-retaining gelatin. Then we headed out to the grill to complete the cooking while lacquering on one of our flavorful glazes.

WE USUALLY RESERVE BUYING SHORT RIBS FOR THE frosty winter months. It's a great time of year to let the moist heat and long, slow cooking of a braise do what it does best: convert this cut's abundant collagen into gelatin, which coats the protein fibers and makes the ribs meltingly tender. But while casting around at the meat counter this summer for something new and different to grill, our eyes landed on short ribs. We wondered why we shouldn't take this supremely flavorful cut (which also happens to have more meat on it than almost any other rib around) to the grill instead of the same old steak or burger. We were envisioning ribs with tender meat with a little bit of chew and a nicely browned, crusty exterior. And to distinguish them a bit from your typical slab of barbecue ribs, we'd skip the barbecue sauce in favor of a bold spice rub and a sweet-tart glaze that would balance their richness.

The first decision: bone-in or boneless ribs? Leaving aside the glaze for the moment, we purchased some of each type and then mixed up a fragrant spice rub of salt, pepper, cayenne, ground cumin, and ground fennel. For good measure, we also threw in two commonly used pork-rib rub ingredients: garlic powder and brown sugar.

To ensure that the ribs' collagen had sufficient time to melt, we built a low-temperature indirect fire, placing some unlit briquettes on the charcoal grate and covering them with hot coals to generate a fire that would burn steadily for several hours. We sprinkled both batches of ribs with our rub and arranged them on the cooler side of the grates to grill-roast, occasionally rotating and flipping them until both were tender, about 4 hours later. But when we brought in both platters of ribs for tasting, our colleagues frowned. Instead of being beautifully marbled slabs, the boneless ribs had shrunk and blackened so much that our colleagues dubbed them "meat brownies."

What had happened? Well, without a bone to insulate the meat from the heat of the grill—low as it was—the boneless samples simply shriveled up and dried out. (If we'd pulled the ribs off the grill any sooner, the collagen wouldn't have broken down enough and they'd have been tough.) Though far from perfect, the bone-in ribs at least had a fighting chance of developing a tender interior by the time a crisp crust had formed.

Now we just needed to figure out how to optimize the texture of the bone-in ribs, which, among other problems, weren't cooking evenly. Although we'd flipped them every 30 minutes or so during cooking, there were still small pockets of unrendered fat, and some ribs were definitely more tender than others. The problem was this: In order to render fat and become tender, meat needs to reach a temperature hot enough for the tough collagen to start to melt (140 to 165 degrees). But if the meat gets too hot, so much moisture burns off that it becomes dry and jerkylike. To make matters worse, even a carefully monitored grill inevitably produces hot and cold spots, so the results within a single batch of ribs can be dramatically different. This was not a problem that was going to go away, either. Maintaining a steady, perfectly consistent grill temperature is a near-impossible feat, and let's face it: Even die-hard grillers don't want to fuss for hours on end, rearranging meat, opening and closing vents, and adding hot coals. It was clear that to make this work, we were going to need a more controlled environment. We would have to bring the ribs indoors to cook partway in the oven, where even heating is effortless and temperature adjustment is as easy as turning a dial. We hoped that by finishing the ribs on the grill we'd give them the substantial, smoky crust we wanted.

We sprinkled each of three batches of spice-rubbed meat with a little red wine vinegar to help cut richness, covered them with foil (to create a steamy cooking environment so the ribs would cook more quickly and evenly), and slid the pans into 300-degree ovens until the ribs hit 140, 165, and 175 degrees, respectively (80, 105, and 120 minutes later). Then we moved the operation outside to slowly finish each batch on the grill. When the ribs were dark and crusty an hour and a half later, we called our tasters for lunch.

The results were clear: The ribs pulled from the oven at 140 degrees were rubbery—obviously still packed with collagen. At the other end of the spectrum, so much collagen had broken down in the 175-degree batch that the meat had a disagreeable, shredded pot roast–like texture. The 165-degree ribs, on the other hand, boasted tender meat that sliced neatly.

For a foolproof indicator of final doneness, we made another batch of ribs, standing grillside after they had been on the fire for an hour, evaluating the meat's texture and taking its temperature at regular intervals. The magic number turned out to be 195 degrees: Intramuscular fat had completely melted and most of the collagen had broken down, turning the meat tender—but not so much so that it disintegrated at the touch of a fork.

With the meat of the matter sorted out, we moved on to create a few glazes. The red wine vinegar that we had added to the ribs before baking tempered their fattiness somewhat, but they could still stand up to more tangy flavors. We started with a classic Dijon mustard and brown sugar mixture and then came up with a fruity blackberry and bourbon variation. Finally, hoisin and tamarind took center stage in an Asian-inspired version.

To achieve a substantial lacquered crust, we brushed the ribs every time we rotated them on the grill. This allowed each layer of glaze to dry out and give the subsequent layer a base to which it could adhere. It was a bit of work, but any doubt we had that frequent glazing was worth the trouble was erased when tasters devoured the latest batch before we could even get our hands on one rib.

With meaty, finger-licking results like these, we'd no longer need to wait for the dead of winter to make short ribs. In fact, they are now at the top of the list for our next summer cookout.

Grill-Roasted Beef Short Ribs

SERVES 4 TO 6

Make sure to choose ribs that are 4 to 6 inches in length and have at least 1 inch of meat on top of the bone.

SPICE RUB

- 2 tablespoons kosher salt
- 1 tablespoon packed brown sugar
- 2 teaspoons pepper
- 2 teaspoons ground cumin
- 2 teaspoons garlic powder
- 1¼ teaspoons paprika
- ¾ teaspoon ground fennel
- ⅛ teaspoon cayenne pepper

SHORT RIBS

- 5 pounds bone-in English-style beef short ribs, trimmed
- 2 tablespoons red wine vinegar

- 1 recipe glaze (recipes follow)

1. FOR THE SPICE RUB: Combine all ingredients in bowl. Measure out 1 teaspoon rub and set aside for glaze.

2. FOR THE SHORT RIBS: Adjust oven rack to middle position and heat oven to 300 degrees. Sprinkle ribs with spice rub, pressing into all sides of ribs. Arrange ribs, bone side down, in 13 by 9-inch baking dish, placing thicker ribs around perimeter of baking dish and thinner ribs in center. Sprinkle vinegar evenly over ribs. Cover baking dish tightly with aluminum foil. Bake until thickest ribs register 165 to 170 degrees, 1½ to 2 hours.

3A. FOR A CHARCOAL GRILL: Open bottom vent halfway. Arrange 2 quarts unlit charcoal into steeply banked pile against 1 side of grill. Light large chimney starter half filled with charcoal (3 quarts). When top coals are partially covered with ash, pour on top of unlit charcoal to cover one-third of grill with coals steeply banked against side of grill. Set cooking grate in place, cover, and open lid vent halfway. Heat grill until hot, about 5 minutes.

3B. FOR A GAS GRILL: Turn all burners to high, cover, and heat grill until hot, about 15 minutes. Leave primary burner on medium and turn off other burner(s). Adjust primary burner as needed to maintain grill temperature of 275 to 300 degrees.

4. Clean and oil cooking grate. Place short ribs, bone side down, on cooler side of grill about 2 inches from flames. Brush with ¼ cup glaze. Cover and cook until ribs register 195 degrees, 1¾ to 2¼ hours, rotating and brushing ribs with ¼ cup glaze every 30 minutes. Transfer ribs to large platter, tent loosely with foil, and let rest for 5 to 10 minutes before serving.

NOTES FROM THE TEST KITCHEN

START IN THE OVEN
This atypical start guarantees perfectly cooked ribs.

Bake the ribs until they reach 165 degrees, 1½ to 2 hours. At this temperature, the conversion from collagen into gelatin is well under way and the ribs can be transferred to the grill.

SHOPPING FOR THE PERFECT SHORT RIB FOR GRILL ROASTING
Bone-in English-style short ribs (those with long, continuous pieces of meat and a single bone) are a must, but we found that they can vary widely from package to package. Here's what to look for in order for this recipe to work.

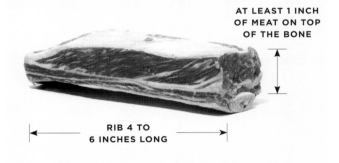

AT LEAST 1 INCH OF MEAT ON TOP OF THE BONE

RIB 4 TO 6 INCHES LONG

Mustard Glaze
MAKES ABOUT 1 CUP

½ cup Dijon mustard
½ cup red wine vinegar
¼ cup packed brown sugar
1 teaspoon reserved spice rub
⅛ teaspoon cayenne pepper

Whisk all ingredients together in bowl.

Blackberry Glaze
MAKES ABOUT 1 CUP

10 ounces (2 cups) fresh or frozen blackberries
½ cup ketchup
¼ cup bourbon
2 tablespoons packed brown sugar
1½ tablespoons soy sauce
1 teaspoon reserved spice rub
⅛ teaspoon cayenne pepper

Bring all ingredients to simmer in small saucepan over medium-high heat. Simmer, stirring frequently to break up blackberries, until reduced to 1¼ cups, about 10 minutes. Strain through fine-mesh strainer, pressing on solids to extract as much liquid as possible. Discard solids.

Hoisin-Tamarind Glaze
MAKES ABOUT 1 CUP

1 cup water
⅓ cup hoisin sauce
¼ cup tamarind paste
1 (2-inch) piece ginger, peeled and sliced into ½-inch-thick rounds
1 teaspoon reserved spice rub
⅛ teaspoon cayenne pepper

Bring all ingredients to simmer in small saucepan over medium-high heat. Simmer, stirring frequently, until reduced to 1¼ cups, about 10 minutes. Strain through fine-mesh strainer, pressing on solids to extract as much liquid as possible. Discard solids.

RATING GREAT SUMMER GADGETS

From a device that allows you to make homemade potato chips without standing over a hot pot of oil to a cooler for ice cream that allows you to enjoy this frozen treat on picnics, here are a number of gadgets that you'll want to use all summer long. See AmericasTestKitchen.com for updates to these testings.

MICROWAVE CHIP MAKER

When the weather's hot, you may not want to heat up a vat of bubbling oil to make your own potato chips. Enter the microwave chip maker, which promises to make this messy task much neater and easier. The Mastrad Topchips Microwave Chip Maker ($19.99, with slicer) turns vegetables and fruit into crisp chips in the microwave—and it does it without any oil whatsoever. This gadget consists of a perforated 11-inch silicone disk that holds 15 to 20 chips, which can be cut wafer-thin using the included slicer. After just a few minutes in the microwave (the cooking time varies depending on the food and your microwave's wattage), the slices are transformed into chips that are not only ultracrisp, they're also fat free. While we got similar results by spritzing potato slices with vegetable oil spray and microwaving them on a plate, the advantage of this model is quantity: You can stack up to three trays (a set of two additional trays is available for $19.99) to make more chips even faster. Plus, the Topchips slicer turns out chips of the perfect thickness; our mandoline-sliced chips were slightly thicker, with a bit less crunch.

WINNER: MASTRAD TOPCHIPS MICROWAVE CHIP MAKER

STRAWBERRY HULLER

If you're making strawberry pie or shortcakes for a crowd, hulling all the fruit with a paring knife can be a little tedious and take a good chunk of time. The Chef'n Stem Gem Strawberry Stem Remover, which resembles a plastic toy strawberry crossed with a syringe, promises to help. To use it, you press the green stem-shaped button to open the four spring-loaded metal prongs at the tip, insert the prongs in the top of the strawberry, and twist while releasing the button. The metal claw closes as you turn your hand, neatly slicing out the leaves, stem, and core in a cone shape that doesn't sacrifice too much fruit. It might sound confusing, but it's actually quite easy to use—we gave the gadget to three 9-year-olds who caught on in seconds. Not only is the Stem Gem easy and safe enough for kids to use (meaning you'll have extra help when you're prepping those desserts), it's also much faster than hulling strawberries with a knife. And at $7.95, it's cheap enough to be worth adding to the gadget drawer.

WINNER: CHEF'N STEM GEM STRAWBERRY STEM REMOVER

PINEAPPLE SLICER

Coring and slicing a pineapple is a messy and time-consuming task, and you can waste a lot of fruit trying to cut away the prickly skin. That's where a pineapple slicer comes in handy. We tested seven models and ultimately found our winner in the OXO Good Grips Ratcheting Pineapple Slicer. The corkscrew design makes it easy and intuitive to use. After slicing off the top of the pineapple, you use the marked measurements to get a sense of how tall the pineapple is. Then you put the corer on top and turn it like a corkscrew; because the handle is ratcheted, you don't have to keep taking your hand off and starting over with each turn, unlike other models we tested. After a few twists, simply remove the tool and you'll be left with the whole pineapple, sliced and cored. For just $19.99, this pineapple slicer is a great way to make prepping fresh pineapple much easier.

WINNER: OXO GOOD GRIPS RATCHETING PINEAPPLE SLICER

INSULATED ICE CREAM KEEPER

Ice cream is summer's perfect dessert—but a warm puddle of ice cream soup is not. The Zak! Designs Ice Cream Tubbie ($11.99) aims to prevent this problem, keeping icy treats frozen with its foam-core insulation and gel pack–lined lid. The empty container simply needs to be chilled in the freezer for 2 hours to let the gel pack freeze completely before it can be used. To test ours, we filled it with homemade vanilla ice cream and left it out on a kitchen counter. We were surprised to find our ice cream was still fully frozen 3 hours later (well past the manufacturer's promise of 90 minutes). However, there was a catch: The lid had formed such a tight seal with the base that we could twist it open only by running the container under warm water for 10 seconds. (We found that the lid is easier to open if you don't screw it on super-tight to begin with.) The Tubbie is ideal for outdoor parties and picnics and, since it fits a pint container of store-bought ice cream, long rides home from the supermarket in hot weather.

WINNER: ZAK! DESIGNS ICE CREAM TUBBIE

Ultimate Grilled
TURKEY BURGERS AND BUNS

Our potato bread dough can be used to make sesame-covered hamburger buns or pillowy dinner rolls.

TURKEY BURGERS HAVE LONG BEEN THE SECOND-CLASS CITIZENS OF the burger world. In an attempt to mask a dry burger, restaurants often camouflage their turkey burgers with a blanket of rich toppings such as caramelized onions, roasted red peppers, blue cheese, and the like. Who are they fooling? And most recipes add all sorts of binders (such as egg and bread crumbs) that make the burgers taste an awful lot like meatloaf. Why do turkey burgers suffer such indignities? The leaner composition of the meat is partially responsible. Turkey is simply drier than beef. We wanted to develop a turkey burger that was just as appealing as a beef burger. It needed to be moist, juicy, and meaty. And while a modicum of toppings is OK, we wouldn't be disguising what's under the bun.

If we were going to come up with a recipe for the ultimate turkey burger, we'd need to partner it with an outstanding bun. We've long wanted to develop a recipe for burger buns. But we wanted a two-for-one recipe for bread dough that would fit the bill as both burger buns and dinner rolls. That meant a soft, moist bread that wasn't too rich. Enter potato rolls. Potatoes have long been used to add moisture and flavor to bread dough, but some breads can turn heavy under the weight of the starch. Also, years in the test kitchen have taught us that not all potatoes are created equal. What type of potato makes the best bun? Ultimate turkey burgers and a bun to match—the challenge is on.

GRILLED TURKEY BURGERS

✔ **WHY THIS RECIPE WORKS:** To create juicy, well-textured turkey burgers, we ditched store-bought ground turkey in favor of home-ground turkey thighs, which boast more fat and flavor. To ensure that our turkey burger recipe delivered maximum juiciness, we made a paste with a portion of the ground turkey, gelatin, soy sauce, and baking soda, which trapped juice within the burgers. Finally, we added coarsely chopped raw white mushrooms to keep the meat from binding together too firmly.

WE FIGURED WE WERE LICKED BEFORE WE EVEN GOT started. The assignment was to create turkey burgers that tasted every bit as meaty, tender, and juicy as the beef kind—and the judges would be our colleagues, all of them hard-core hamburger devotees. It was a tall order for a couple of reasons: For one thing, the test kitchen brings all poultry to a much higher temperature (160 degrees) than beef (which we often cook medium-rare, or 125 degrees), which means that far more moisture will be squeezed out of the meat during cooking. What's more, turkey lacks beef's high percentage of lubricating fat. That accounts for its appeal as a healthier alternative to beef in a burger, but it also explains why these lean patties usually cook up dry, chalky, and bland.

Plenty of recipes try to compensate for those shortcomings by packing ground turkey with a slew of spices and binders that provide flavor and lock in moisture, respectively, but our tasters deemed every version that we tried a failure—and we tried many. Most burgers were still dry, and those that did offer some flavor tasted more like overdressed turkey meatloaf than burgers. We can't say we were surprised; loading up the meat with additives is a Band-Aid approach that ignores the real problem at heart: the meat itself.

The meat sounded like the right starting point to us, so we shelved our cynicism for the time being and decided to work toward a turkey burger that delivered everything we look for in a beef version—that is, tender, juicy, and

flavorful meat without the distraction of our spice cabinet or other superficial fixes. And if we could throw it over a hot grill to give the meat some smoky char, all the better.

We've been pretty clear about our stance on supermarket ground meat for burgers. It may be a timesaver, but when we want to make the meatiest, juiciest, most tender burgers we can, we grind our own—and if our test recipes were any indication, avoiding the preground stuff would be even more important when it came to turkey burgers. The vast majority of commercial ground meat is processed so fine that it turns pasty and dense, and poultry tends to be the worst offender. What's more, supermarket ground turkey is typically ultralean—an immediate setback when you're going for flavor and juiciness. Grinding our own meat would allow us to control both the cut of meat and the size of the grind.

The obvious starting point was thigh meat, as this cut boasts a decent amount of fat and flavor. We bought a large thigh (about 2 pounds), removed the skin and bone, trimmed it of excess sinew, and then followed our grinding procedure: Cut the meat into ½-inch pieces, freeze them for about 40 minutes to firm them up, and then process the meat in three batches in a food processor.

About 20 pulses gave us coarsely chopped meat that produced tender, nicely loose-textured burgers, and the flavor of these dark-meat patties was significantly richer than any turkey burger we'd had to date. But we still had plenty of work to do before we got to the juiciness and rich meatiness of a beef burger. Thanks to the requisite 160-degree doneness temperature, our all-thigh patties were still parched.

Mixing the turkey with a panade (a liquid-and-bread-crumb paste that traps moisture and prevents the meat proteins from binding together too tightly) was the most common moisture-enhancing solution we came across. But it was also universally unsuccessful. While the paste did add juiciness, it also dulled the already mild flavor of the turkey and made the patties meatloaf-like—precisely the consistency we were trying to get away from by grinding our own meat. Other recipes took a more drastic approach, "fattening up" the ground turkey with butter and bacon fat. One even mixed in turkey sausage—and, not surprisingly, the result tasted like a sausage burger. We'll admit, adding fat to the burgers did

JUICY GRILLED TURKEY BURGER

make them taste juicier (and richer), but it also felt like cheating; at that point, why not just make a beef burger?

Thinking about those two goals, however, triggered an important reminder. While developing a recent stir-fry recipe, we discovered an unlikely technique for improving tenderness and juiciness in lean pork: lightly coating it with baking soda before cooking. When applied to meat, this alkali raises the meat's pH, which tenderizes its muscle fibers and gives it a looser structure that's more capable of retaining water. The quick pretreatment had made all the difference with the pork loin; no reason it shouldn't work for turkey, too, right?

We gave it a shot, mixing up one batch of burgers with a pinch of baking soda and leaving another untreated, and then quickly seared the burgers over a hot fire. When our tasters gave us approving nods as they munched on these noticeably juicier, more tender patties, we knew we were getting somewhere. But we weren't done yet.

One of our other favorite pantry staples for improving dry meat is gelatin, which absorbs up to 10 times its weight in water. We tried hydrating varying amounts of the unflavored powder in chicken broth and adding the mixture to the turkey when grinding it. Another good move. Just 1 tablespoon of gelatin in 3 tablespoons of broth further compensated for some of the moisture lost during cooking.

Spurred on by these successes, we challenged ourselves to push the moisture factor a little further and were reminded of the recipe we'd tried with turkey sausage. It had failed for tasting too sausage-y, but it was remarkably juicy, thanks to the finely processed meat, which causes the proteins to stretch out and link up into a stronger network that traps fat and moisture. We got to thinking: If we were already grinding the turkey in the food processor, why not try making our own sausagelike mixture by grinding a portion of the meat even further? We added ½ cup of coarsely ground meat back to the processor along with salt (which activates the meat's sticky proteins), the baking soda, and softened gelatin; let it rip until the mixture turned sticky and smooth; and then, with the processor running, drizzled in 2 tablespoons of vegetable oil until incorporated.

It worked like gangbusters. When mixed into the remaining ground turkey, this emulsion trapped copious amounts of moisture and fat, resulting in the juiciest turkey burger we'd ever had. There was just one caveat, and it was predictable: Our homemade turkey sausage was binding the meat together too firmly.

In the same way that a teacher might place a balloon between two overzealous middle-school dancers, we needed to add something to the ground turkey to keep its sticky proteins from embracing too tightly. We experimented with various cooked grains and starches—even beans. But while most of them did produce more tender patties, none left us with the loose burger texture we were after, and most of them muted the turkey's flavor.

That's when we switched to mixing vegetables—both raw and cooked—into the meat and hit upon the winner: raw white mushrooms. Chopped in the food processor and then mixed into our turkey emulsion, the mushrooms actually provided three unique benefits: They interrupted some protein binding to increase tenderness; they provided extra moisture as their water-filled cells broke down during cooking; and, thanks to their high level of glutamates, they helped boost meatiness. The mushrooms also inspired us to swap in soy sauce for the salt, bumping up savoriness even more. Just 5 minutes per side over a hot fire was enough to char and cook our mouthwatering turkey burgers—now every bit as enticing as their beefy brothers.

Juicy Grilled Turkey Burgers

SERVES 6

If you are able to purchase boneless, skinless turkey thighs, substitute 1½ pounds for the bone-in thigh. To ensure the best texture, don't let the burgers stand for more than an hour before cooking. Serve the burgers with Malt Vinegar–Molasses Burger Sauce, Chile-Lime Burger Sauce, or Apricot-Mustard Burger Sauce (recipes follow).

- 1 (2-pound) bone-in turkey thigh, skinned, boned, trimmed, and cut into ½-inch pieces
- 1 tablespoon unflavored gelatin
- 3 tablespoons low-sodium chicken broth
- 6 ounces white mushrooms, trimmed
- 1 tablespoon soy sauce
  Pinch baking soda
- 2 tablespoons vegetable oil, plus extra for brushing
  Kosher salt and pepper
- 6 large hamburger buns

1. Place turkey pieces on large plate in single layer. Freeze meat until very firm and hardened around edges, 35 to 45 minutes. Meanwhile, sprinkle gelatin over chicken broth in small bowl and let sit until gelatin softens, about 5 minutes. Pulse mushrooms in food processor until coarsely chopped, about 7 pulses, stopping and redistributing mushrooms around bowl as needed to ensure even grinding. Set mushrooms aside; do not wash food processor.

2. Pulse one-third of turkey in food processor until coarsely chopped into ⅛-inch pieces, 18 to 22 pulses, stopping and redistributing turkey around bowl as needed to ensure even grinding. Transfer meat to large bowl and repeat two more times with remaining turkey.

3. Return ½ cup (about 3 ounces) ground turkey to bowl of food processor along with softened gelatin, soy sauce, and baking soda. Process until smooth, about 2 minutes, scraping down bowl as needed. With processor running, slowly drizzle in oil, about 10 seconds; leave paste in food processor. Return mushrooms to food processor with paste and pulse to combine, 3 to 5 pulses,

stopping and redistributing mixture as needed to ensure even mixing. Transfer mushroom mixture to bowl with ground turkey and use hands to evenly combine.

4. With lightly greased hands, divide meat mixture into 6 balls. Flatten into ¾-inch-thick patties about 4 inches in diameter; press shallow indentation into center of each burger to ensure even cooking. (Shaped patties can be frozen for up to 1 month. Frozen patties can be cooked straight from freezer.)

5A. FOR A CHARCOAL GRILL: Open bottom vent completely. Light large chimney starter filled with charcoal briquettes (6 quarts). When top coals are partially covered with ash, pour evenly over half of grill. Set cooking grate in place, cover, and open lid vent completely. Heat grill until hot, about 5 minutes.

5B. FOR A GAS GRILL: Turn all burners to high, cover, and heat grill until hot, about 15 minutes. Leave primary burner on high and turn off other burner(s).

6. Clean and oil cooking grate. Brush 1 side of patties with oil and season with salt and pepper. Using spatula, flip patties, brush with oil, and season second side. Place burgers over hot part of grill and cook until burgers are well browned on both sides and register 160 degrees, 4 to 7 minutes per side. (If cooking frozen burgers: After burgers are browned on both sides, transfer to cool side of grill, cover, and continue to cook until burgers register 160 degrees.)

7. Transfer burgers to plate and let rest for 5 minutes. While burgers rest, grill buns over hot side of grill. Transfer burgers to buns, add desired toppings, and serve.

Malt Vinegar–Molasses Burger Sauce

MAKES ABOUT 1 CUP

- ¾ cup mayonnaise
- 4 teaspoons malt vinegar
- ½ teaspoon molasses
- ¼ teaspoon Worcestershire sauce
- ¼ teaspoon salt
- ¼ teaspoon pepper

Whisk all ingredients together in bowl.

Chile-Lime Burger Sauce

MAKES ABOUT 1 CUP

¾ cup mayonnaise

2 teaspoons chile-garlic paste

2 teaspoons lime juice

1 scallion, sliced thin

¼ teaspoon fish sauce

⅛ teaspoon sugar

Whisk all ingredients together in bowl.

Apricot-Mustard Burger Sauce

MAKES ABOUT 1 CUP

¾ cup mayonnaise

5 teaspoons apricot preserves

1 tablespoon lemon juice

1 tablespoon Dijon mustard

1 tablespoon whole-grain mustard

¼ teaspoon salt

Whisk all ingredients together in bowl.

RATING ARTISANAL CHEDDAR

Many well-stocked supermarkets and gourmet shops now carry more than the average American cheddars that are found on burgers and in grilled cheese sandwiches. They also offer "artisanal" domestic cheddars, which claim to rival the complex, nuanced flavor of English cheeses—and charge the prices to match. We wanted to know if these gourmet cheeses were worth as much as $25 per pound and sampled 10 brands from both small and large producers. They offered a wide spectrum of flavors (from mellow and nutty to pungent) and textures (from dry and crumbly to moist and creamy). Though most brands in our lineup are produced according to traditional "cheddaring" practices that involve stacking, turning, and pressing the curds by hand, three are machine-made. But what mattered more than production method was whether the cheeses received a second dose of bacterial cultures that were different from the first strain; we found these cheeses to offer more complex flavor. Also important was the amount of time cheeses were aged. Brands that were aged for a shorter period of time performed well; cheeses aged for a longer span of time, especially if they were wrapped in plastic, fell to the bottom of the rankings. In the end, we felt that our top cheddars were worth every penny. Brands are listed in order of preference. See AmericasTestKitchen.com for updates and further information on this testing.

HIGHLY RECOMMENDED

MILTON CREAMERY Prairie Breeze
PRICE: $15.98 per lb **AGED:** 9 to 12 months
CHEDDARING: Traditional **AGING MATERIAL:** Plastic
COMMENTS: This cheese was one of the youngest in the lineup, but thanks to an extra cocktail of bacterial cultures, it wowed tasters with "deeply rich," "buttery" flavors and a "sweet" finish that reminded some of "pineapple." It boasted a "crumbly" yet "creamy" texture reminiscent of "young Parmesan."

CABOT Cellars at Jasper Hill Clothbound Cheddar
PRICE: $23.98 per lb **AGED:** 10 to 14 months
CHEDDARING: Modern **AGING MATERIAL:** Cloth
COMMENTS: Cabot's high-end line—the priciest American cheese we tasted—is also inoculated twice and won raves from tasters for its "mature sharpness" and "rich dairy flavor" that they likened to Gruyère. But the bigger draw: its "craggy" texture that broke into addictively "jagged," "crystalline" shards.

RECOMMENDED

TILLAMOOK Vintage White Extra Sharp Cheddar Cheese
PRICE: $9.50 per lb **AGED:** At least 2 years
CHEDDARING: Modern **AGING MATERIAL:** Plastic
COMMENTS: Compared with the company's other cheddars, this two-plus-year-old cheese is "vintage," but unlike some other long-aged samples, its sharpness was "appropriately bold" and "balanced." Fans of smoother cheddars will appreciate its "extremely creamy" texture—not to mention its affordable price tag.

BEECHER'S Flagship Reserve Handmade Cheese
PRICE: $25 per lb **AGED:** 12 months
CHEDDARING: Traditional **AGING MATERIAL:** Cloth
COMMENTS: Besides conventional cheddar descriptors like "nutty" and "sharp," this "firm," "grainy" clothbound cheese earned compliments for more complex flavors like "buttery walnuts" and a "gamy," "Parmesan-like" tang. No wonder: Like our two favorites, it received a second shot of nontraditional cultures.

RECOMMENDED *(cont.)*

GRAFTON VILLAGE Vermont Clothbound Cheddar
PRICE: $15.99 per lb **AGED:** At least 6 months
CHEDDARING: Traditional **AGING MATERIAL:** Cloth
COMMENTS: A classic example of clothbound cheddar, this sample was wrapped in a butter-dipped cloth and soaked up a "fruity and nutty" flavor hinting of "caramel." It broke into "firm" shards, which made it a bit tricky to slice but a pleasure to eat out of hand.

FISCALINI FARMSTEAD Bandage-Wrapped Raw Milk Cheddar
PRICE: $24 per lb **AGED:** 18 months
CHEDDARING: Traditional **AGING MATERIAL:** Cloth
COMMENTS: As artisanal cheddars go, this cheese was well liked but unremarkable. Its "complex," "fruity" aroma prompted the same pineapple analogy as our winner, but its texture was softer and creamier—even "waxy" and "squeezable," according to some.

CABOT Private Stock Classic Vermont Cheddar Cheese
PRICE: $8.49 per lb **AGED:** Up to 16 months
CHEDDARING: Modern **AGING MATERIAL:** Plastic
COMMENTS: The flavor of this "no-frills" crowd-pleaser—also our favorite supermarket cheddar—was "straight-up sharp" but "not distinctive," with a "firm and creamy" texture that reminded us of "what you'd find on the end of a toothpick at a cocktail party."

SHELBURNE FARMS 2-Year-Old Farmhouse Cheddar Cheese
PRICE: $19 per lb **AGED:** 2 years
CHEDDARING: Traditional **AGING MATERIAL:** Plastic
COMMENTS: After two years of aging in plastic, this cheddar tasted like "wet wool" and "barnyard funk"—a trait that some thought made it a "serious cheddar," while others weren't convinced. But all were agreed: The plastic's moisture-locking seal ensured a "moist, creamy," "mouth-coating" texture.

POTATO BUNS

✔ **WHY THIS RECIPE WORKS:** Mashed potatoes are hefty and substantial, but when incorporated into a bread recipe, they give the crumb a light, tender, moist texture. That's because the starches in potatoes dilute the gluten-forming proteins in flour, which weakens the structural network of the dough and makes it softer, moister, and more tender. For the lightest potato rolls, we combined ½ pound of mashed russet potatoes with high-protein bread flour. This created a potato roll dough with a stable structure, producing rolls that were not only perfectly risen but also light and airy.

THESE DAYS, BAKING BREAD ALMOST ALWAYS SEEMS to mean creating a crusty loaf with a big, irregular crumb and a sourdough tang. Maybe it's shamefully retro, but sometimes we long for a homemade bread with a soft, moist, light crumb and a delicate crust. We're not talking about the decadently buttery rolls associated with holiday dinners (though we do love those) but something a bit leaner as well as more versatile—a bread that could either be shaped into sandwich buns or formed into small dinner rolls. Our hankering, we realized, was for good old-fashioned potato rolls. This bread delivers the same soft tenderness of a classic American dinner roll but without its richness. What's more, the dough would work equally well for burger buns—something we've always wanted a great recipe for.

In the past we assumed that potato bread must boast only a little mashed potato—how else could it be so light and airy? But a roundup of recipes showed that the bread could include virtually any amount of potato, from 2 tablespoons to 2 cups. There was also no consensus on what form the potatoes should take. Some called for freshly mashed spuds (and often a bit of the cooking water), others for cold leftovers, still others for the instant kind. We even found a few recipes simply requiring the addition of dried potato starch. Almost none of the recipes specified what type of potato to use, and even peeling them wasn't a given.

To our surprise, all of the recipes we tried produced loaves that were remarkably tender and moist—even the ones made with instant potatoes and potato starch. But we did notice a few trends. First, the more potato in the mix the softer and more airy the bread—but only up to a point. Too much potato and the bread began to be weighed down by the load. Second, doughs made with warm, freshly mashed spuds seemed to rise more quickly than those that employed cold potatoes or the packaged products, and doughs that included the cooking water from the potatoes rose fastest of all.

Before we went any further, it seemed time to get at the fundamental question: How is it that mashed potato, a food that is almost synonymous with stodge, has the ability (in the right amount) to bestow such a light, soft character on bread in the first place? Our science editor enlightened us: When potatoes are boiled, their starch granules swell with water. When those swollen starches are mixed into bread dough, they physically interfere with the flour proteins' ability to link together and form gluten, thus weakening the dough's structure so that it bakes up softer and more tender. What's more, potato starch granules are four to five times larger than wheat starch granules and can thus hold much more water than the wheat starches can, making potato bread moister than straight wheat bread and contributing to our perception of the crumb as soft and light.

Armed with these facts, we were ready to figure out how much potato was optimal and what form it should take to achieve just the fluffy texture we wanted. Though the instant spuds and potato starch had actually produced decent results, we don't normally keep either product on hand. We also vetoed cold leftover mash, since that's not something we could count on having on hand either. We would start with freshly boiled peeled potatoes (tasters found that the skins contributed an earthiness that they didn't want in dough destined for sandwich rolls) and keep the amount on the lower end of the spectrum, with just ¼ cup (2 ounces) replacing 2 ounces of all-purpose flour. We also opted for russet potatoes, thinking that their floury texture would serve us best. After mashing the potatoes with butter, we kneaded them in a stand mixer with the flour, whole egg, milk (which some recipes added for a subtle dairy sweetness), salt,

POTATO DINNER ROLLS

potato's magical properties. We increased the mash by another ¼ cup, decreasing the flour by the same 2 ounces, and the rolls got even lighter and fluffier. We ended up with the same results whether we created a feathery mash using a ricer or pounded the potatoes into glueyness with a potato masher.

The more we upped the potato, the less time the dough needed to rise. We chalked that up to the dispersal of more warm potato throughout the dough, since yeast thrives in a warm environment. But when we did a little research, we learned that there was a more potato-specific reason behind the faster rise: The potassium in potatoes activates yeast, and the more of it there is the quicker and more vigorous the rise. Furthermore, when potatoes are boiled, they leach almost half of their potassium into the cooking water—helping to explain why so many recipes add the water to the dough. We found that when we switched from using 5 tablespoons of milk to the same amount of potato water, the rising times dropped still more.

Emboldened by these successes, we increased the potatoes from ½ cup to a full packed cup, reducing the flour by a corresponding 4 ounces. However, this time the dough fell flat, making coarse-crumbed rolls with a compromised rise. Could it be that a full cup of potato was just too much to cram into our bread? Before failing so dramatically, this batch had risen in record time, and we were reluctant to give that up. But maybe the problem was not with the potatoes; maybe we had chosen the wrong flour for the job.

Clearly, the protein in the more than 2 cups of all-purpose flour in our recipe wasn't providing enough muscle to support ½ pound of freeloading potato starch. But what if we switched to higher-protein bread flour? This simple swap did the trick: The increased protein provided just enough stable yet tender structure to support the potatoes, yielding rolls that were not only perfectly risen but also the lightest, airiest yet. And we could use the same dough for sandwich rolls or dinner rolls, depending on how large we made the pieces.

Now that we know how and why adding potatoes to bread improves its texture (not to mention how potatoes speed up bread preparation), we're ready to start a potato bread renaissance.

sugar, and yeast and then left the dough to rise for an hour before shaping it into sandwich rolls. After another rise—45 minutes this time—we baked the batch in a 425-degree oven.

We were on the right track: These rolls had a tenderness approaching that of richer breads, even though they contained just 2 tablespoons of butter. Excited by this effect, we wondered just how far we could push the

Potato Burger Buns

MAKES 9 ROLLS

These rolls are ideal for both burgers and sandwiches. Don't salt the cooking water for the potatoes. A pound of russet potatoes should yield just over 1 very firmly packed cup (½ pound) of mash. To ensure optimum rise, your dough should be warm; if your potatoes or potato water is too hot to touch, let cool before proceeding with the recipe. This dough looks very dry when mixing begins but will soften as mixing progresses. If you prefer, you may portion the rolls by weight in step 5 (2.75 ounces of dough per roll).

 1 **pound russet potatoes, peeled and cut into 1-inch pieces**
 2 **tablespoons unsalted butter, cut into 4 pieces**
2¼ **cups (12⅓ ounces) bread flour**
 1 **tablespoon sugar**
 2 **teaspoons instant or rapid-rise yeast**
 1 **teaspoon salt**
 2 **large eggs, 1 lightly beaten with 1 teaspoon water and pinch salt**
 1 **tablespoon sesame seeds (optional)**

1. Place potatoes in medium saucepan and add water to just cover. Bring to boil over high heat; reduce heat to medium-low and simmer until potatoes are cooked through, 8 to 10 minutes.

2. Transfer 5 tablespoons cooking water to bowl to cool; drain potatoes. Return potatoes to saucepan and place over low heat. Cook, shaking pot occasionally, until any surface moisture has evaporated, about 1 minute. Remove from heat. Process potatoes through ricer or food mill or mash well with potato masher. Measure 1 very firmly packed cup potatoes and transfer to bowl. Reserve any remaining potatoes for another use. Stir in butter until melted.

3. Combine flour, sugar, yeast, and salt in bowl of stand mixer. Add warm potato mixture to flour mixture and mix with hands until combined (some large lumps are OK). Add 1 egg and reserved cooking water; mix with dough hook on low speed until dough is soft and slightly sticky, 8 to 10 minutes.

4. Shape dough into ball and place in lightly greased container. Cover tightly with plastic wrap and allow to rise at room temperature until almost doubled in volume, 30 to 40 minutes.

NOTES FROM THE TEST KITCHEN

WHY POTATO?

Here are four good reasons why we crammed a full packed cup of mashed potatoes into our rolls.

QUICKER RISE The potassium in potatoes has a positive effect on yeast, causing it to rise faster and more vigorously than it would in wheat-only breads, which also leads to lighter texture.

SUPER-SOFT CRUMB When boiled, potato starch molecules swell and interfere with the ability of flour proteins to form gluten, ensuring tender bread.

MOIST TEXTURE Potato starch granules are about five times larger than wheat starch granules and are therefore capable of absorbing at least five times more water, resulting in a moister crumb.

LONGER SHELF LIFE Potato starch molecules hinder wheat starches from staling, thereby keeping the bread's crumb soft for days. For more information, see "Staving Off Staling in Bread," on page 230.

SUPER SPUD
The humble potato almost goof-proofs bread baking.

POTATO ROLL HIGHS (AND LOWS)

The more mashed potato we added to our dough the better the results—until we hit 1 full cup, at which point the rolls started to collapse under the weight of the spuds. But switching from all-purpose flour to higher-protein bread flour gave the dough the strength it needed to support the mash, so the rolls baked up tall, light, and fluffy.

LOW RISE
Avoid all-purpose flour.

HIGH RISE
Use high-protein bread flour.

5. Turn out dough onto counter, dusting with flour only if dough is too sticky to handle comfortably. Pat gently into 8-inch square of even thickness. Using bench scraper or chef's knife, cut dough into 9 pieces (3 rows by 3 rows). Separate pieces and cover loosely with plastic.

6. Working with 1 piece of dough at a time and keeping remaining pieces covered, form dough pieces into smooth, taut rounds. (To round, set piece of dough on unfloured work surface. Loosely cup hand around dough and, without applying pressure to dough, move hand in small circular motions. Tackiness of dough against work surface and circular motion should work dough into smooth, even ball, but if dough sticks to hands, lightly dust fingers with flour.) Cover rounds with plastic and allow to rest for 15 minutes.

7. Line 2 rimmed baking sheets with parchment paper. On lightly floured surface, firmly press each dough round into 3½-inch disk of even thickness, expelling large pockets of air. Arrange on prepared baking sheets. Cover loosely with plastic and let rise at room temperature until almost doubled in size, 30 to 40 minutes. While rolls rise, adjust oven racks to middle and upper-middle positions and heat oven to 425 degrees.

8. Brush rolls gently with egg wash and sprinkle with sesame seeds, if using. Bake rolls until deep golden brown, 15 to 18 minutes, rotating and switching baking sheets halfway through baking. Transfer baking sheets to wire racks and let cool for 5 minutes. Transfer rolls from baking sheets to wire racks. Serve warm or at room temperature.

VARIATION
Potato Dinner Rolls
MAKES 12 ROLLS

Line rimmed baking sheet with parchment paper. In step 5, divide dough square into 12 pieces (3 rows by 4 rows). Shape pieces into smooth, taut rounds as directed in step 6. Transfer rounds to prepared baking sheet and let rise at room temperature until almost doubled in size, 30 to 40 minutes. Bake on upper-middle rack until rolls are deep golden brown, 12 to 14 minutes, rotating baking sheet halfway through baking.

SCIENCE DESK

STAVING OFF STALING IN BREAD
While developing our recipe for Potato Burger Buns, we noticed that not only were the rolls incredibly soft and moist right out of the oven but, unlike other breads, they were as soft and fresh a day later. Could the potatoes be playing a role?

EXPERIMENT
We baked one batch of our potato rolls according to the recipe; in a second batch we replaced the mashed potatoes with the same weight of all-purpose flour (8 ounces), adding extra water to compensate for the moisture contributed by the mash. We stored both batches of rolls at room temperature for two days.

RESULTS
After one day, the potato rolls were almost as moist as when they came out of the oven, while the all-wheat rolls were noticeably firm and dry. After two days, the wheat rolls were inedible, but the potato rolls remained soft and remarkably fresh-tasting.

EXPLANATION
As baked bread cools, its starches begin to crystallize, trapping water inside the hardened crystal structures. This process of "retrogradation" (more commonly known as staling) explains why bread becomes firm and appears to dry out as it sits on the counter. When bread contains potato, however, this reaction is tempered. The starch molecules in potatoes contain negatively charged phosphates that deter them from recombining, and diluting flour with potato makes it harder for the wheat starches to crystallize as well. The net effect? Potato breads stay soft much longer.

RATING OIL MISTERS

Handy for lightly coating meat and vegetables for the grill or for spraying cookware and bakeware, refillable oil misters offer long-term savings over single-use nonstick sprays, plus they let you choose the oil. We recently tested five brands, pitting them against our favorite commercial spray, PAM Professional High Heat. We used the misters to spray canola oil on skillets and muffin tins to see how long they could sustain a continuous spray, and we spritzed them on brown paper to study the splatter patterns. The misters came in two types: standard and pump. The lone standard sprayer, which works with a simple downward push on the nozzle, was a bust, spitting out blobs of oil. The pump misters, in which you pump the cap (and an attached plunger) several times to build pressure before spraying, covered pans much better, although some sprayed unevenly. In the end, we found one model that consistently delivered a fine spray and thin, uniform layers. Brands are listed in order of preference. See AmericasTestKitchen.com for updates to this testing.

RECOMMENDED

ORKA Flavor and Oil Mister with Filter

MODEL: A27300   PRICE: $11.99   DISHWASHER-SAFE: Yes
TIME TO COVER 12-INCH SKILLET: 2 seconds
CONTINUOUS SPRAY, ONCE PUMPED: 9 seconds
PERFORMANCE: ★★★   EASE OF USE: ★★★
CLEANUP: ★★★
COMMENTS: It was easy to clean, fill, and monitor the oil level in this clear plastic model. Comfortable to use, it was the most consistent sprayer, sustaining a light, delicate spray far longer than other misters.

CUISIPRO Stainless Steel Spray Pump

MODEL: 837530   PRICE: $18.89   DISHWASHER-SAFE: No
TIME TO COVER 12-INCH SKILLET: 2 seconds
CONTINUOUS SPRAY, ONCE PUMPED: 9 seconds
PERFORMANCE: ★★★   EASE OF USE: ★★½   CLEANUP: ★★
COMMENTS: Our previous favorite, this mister performed well and had the strongest spray, but it was a little more finicky and slightly less consistent than our top-ranked model, and is not dishwasher-safe.

RECOMMENDED WITH RESERVATIONS

TRUDEAU Cassia Oil Spray Pump

MODEL: 0711500   PRICE: $14.99   DISHWASHER-SAFE: Bottle is, tube and nozzle are not.
TIME TO COVER 12-INCH SKILLET: 2 seconds
CONTINUOUS SPRAY, ONCE PUMPED: 8 seconds
PERFORMANCE: ★★½   EASE OF USE: ★★½   CLEANUP: ★★
COMMENTS: This tall stainless steel mister performed reasonably well in our tests but wavered between a fine, even mist and a blotchy spray pattern.

ZAK! DESIGNS Multi-Purpose Mister

MODEL: 1313-F470   PRICE: $14.95   DISHWASHER-SAFE: Yes
TIME TO COVER 12-INCH SKILLET: 6 seconds
CONTINUOUS SPRAY, ONCE PUMPED: 6 seconds
PERFORMANCE: ★★   EASE OF USE: ★★   CLEANUP: ★★★
COMMENTS: A pump-style mister that resembled a mini can of spray paint, it coated skillets and muffin tins adequately, and is dishwasher-safe, but its output was weak and spotty at times.

NOT RECOMMENDED

KUCHENPROFI Oil Sprayer

MODEL: 1005052811   PRICE: $10.30   DISHWASHER-SAFE: No
TIME TO COVER 12-INCH SKILLET: 34 seconds
CONTINUOUS SPRAY: None
PERFORMANCE: ★   EASE OF USE: ★   CLEANUP: ★
COMMENTS: The only non-pump spray we tested, the Kuchenprofi was slow and clunky and spat out messy blobs of oil. It couldn't sustain a continuous spray—it took 17 squirts to cover a 12-inch skillet—and it's not dishwasher-safe.

Spicing Up THE GRILL

Test Kitchen Director Erin McMurrer checks on the progress of jerk chicken before the cast heads out to the set.

THERE COMES A POINT DURING THE GRILLING SEASON WHEN WE want to add some spice to the fire. Enter *tacos al pastor* (shepherd-style tacos) and jerk chicken.

Tacos al pastor are not your average taco. This Mexican taqueria classic starts with chile-marinated pork that's spit-roasted until the meat turns crispy at the edges and fork-tender within. A whole pineapple, placed on the cone-shaped spit, cooks along with the pork so that its juices run down and baste the meat as it roasts. The result is a taco filling that's at once spicy, sweet, and downright succulent. Packed into a warm corn tortilla, the pork is balanced with a garnish of minced raw onion, fresh cilantro, and a squeeze of lime juice. Are you in taco heaven yet? How could we replicate these spicy pork tacos without a spit? Which cut of pork would we use and what would our marinating method be? We had a host of questions to answer.

Like tacos al pastor, jerk chicken is packed with spicy flavor. Or that's the way this Jamaican classic should be. Traditionally, the meat is marinated in a fiery mix of Scotch bonnet chiles, allspice berries, and herbs and then grill-smoked over pimento wood. But two thorny issues faced us: The thick, pasty marinade sticks to the cooking grate and pimento wood isn't that easy to find in the United States. In order to produce jerk chicken with spicy smoke flavor straight down to the bone, we'd better get busy.

SPICY PORK TACOS (AL PASTOR)

TACOS AL PASTOR

✔ **WHY THIS RECIPE WORKS:** In Mexico, super-thin slices of pork butt and pork fat are marinated in chiles and tomato, stacked and roasted on a spit, and shaved, hot and crispy, into a corn tortilla. To mimic this popular taco filling, which is often garnished with sweet pineapple, without any special equipment, we had to get creative. We braised ½-inch-thick slabs of pork butt in a mix of guajillo chiles, tomatoes, and spices until tender, before basting them with sauce on the grill until crisped and charred. Chopped into bite-size strips and topped with grilled pineapple, our simple homemade spicy pork filling lives up to the original.

TACOS AL PASTOR, OR "SHEPHERD-STYLE" TACOS, ARE a Mexican taqueria classic made from thin slices of chile-marinated pork that's been tightly packed onto a vertical spit with layers of pork fat and then roasted. The cone-shaped stack is often topped with a whole pineapple, whose tangy, sweet juices trickle down, encouraging the meat to caramelize as it turns. When the exterior is browned and crisp, thin shavings of the roasted pork and pineapple are carved off directly onto a warm tortilla and then topped with garnishes that contrast with the rich meat: minced raw onion, cilantro, and a squeeze of fresh lime.

It's an adaptation of the lamb *shawarma* (themselves inspired by Turkish *doner kebab*) introduced to Mexico by Arab immigrants in the late 19th century, and it's one of our favorite kinds of taco fillings. We've often given thought to a homemade version to satisfy our frequent al pastor cravings but have always been deterred by the fact that our home kitchens lack what you'd think would be an essential piece of equipment: a vertical spit. But no longer. We had decided to see what it would take to make this super-flavorful meat at home.

We pored over the test kitchen's library of Mexican cookbooks and came away with a half-dozen recipes. All but one called for pork shoulder, which made sense; it's what the taquerias use because it's a flavorful, well-marbled cut.

Most of the marinade formulas we found looked relatively similar, too: Some assortment of whole dried guajillo, pasilla, and/or chipotle chiles (all readily available at most supermarkets) are toasted in a skillet and then combined with tomatoes or tomatillos, cumin, garlic, citrus juices, herbs and spices, and water. The mixture is simmered until the chiles are soft and is then pureed, strained, and married with the thin-cut strips of meat. But what sounded like recipes for flavor-packed results turned out to be bland disappointments across the board. It wasn't that the marinades themselves weren't bold—the one we liked best (with fruity guajillos, tomatoes, lots of garlic, bay leaves, cumin, and cloves) was full-bodied and concentrated—but that no marinade travels more than a few millimeters beyond the surface of the meat.

That meant it was crucial that the pork be sliced as thin as possible to allow the heady chile mixture to permeate every bite—a point, we soon realized, that would be one of the biggest challenges of pulling off tacos al pastor at home. Many taquerias have the benefit of a meat slicer to shave the roast paper-thin before coating it with the marinade. We'd have to make do with a sharp chef's knife. But since raw pork is squishy and hard to control with a knife, the thinnest uniform slices we could manage still measured a good half-inch—too thick for the marinade to come through in each bite. Partially freezing the roast did make the meat firm enough to slice but also tacked an extra hour onto the process, and we didn't want to wait that long. Stymied, we decided to turn our attention to the cooking method in hopes of finding an alternative solution.

With the exception of one that opted for a skillet, all of the recipes we tried employed the broiler or a grill. The logic here seemed sound enough: Mimic the deep browning and crispy edges of authentic al pastor by exposing the marinated meat to the hottest possible heat source. According to tasters, there was no contest between the two methods; the grilled pork strips (for now, we were using our ½-inch slabs) boasted better charring and crispier edges. The downside was that neither method produced the tender, juicy results you get at a taqueria, and the problem again boiled down to a matter of equipment. When spit-roasted, the pork turns out extra-succulent because it's continually basted by the layers of melting fat. But how could we get this result without a rotisserie?

It was time to seek professional help, and we turned to our favorite local source for tacos al pastor, Taqueria el Amigo in Waltham, Massachusetts. When we stepped into owner Jorge Calderón's kitchen, we made a surprising discovery: He doesn't own a vertical spit either. Instead, he makes tacos al pastor the way his grandmother did at her roadside stand in Mexico. First, he braises finely cubed pork butt in a tomato-based chile sauce until it's supremely tender and deeply infused with flavor, and then he scoops portions of the meat onto a griddle, where it sizzles to a browned patina.

His unusual approach sounded promising: Braising the pork in the chile sauce would simultaneously tenderize it and infuse it with flavor, putting to bed the problems associated with slicing the roast by hand. We hurried back to the test kitchen to try replicating his results. After whipping up a batch of our chile-tomato sauce, we nestled the ½-inch slabs of pork (for now, we were hoping to avoid painstakingly cubing the meat) into the liquid; let it all simmer for a good 2 hours, by which time the meat was fall-apart tender; and then moved the pork slabs into a hot skillet to crisp.

It seemed our battle was half won. The braised meat was incredibly tender, juicy, and infused with the complex chile sauce, which confirmed that there was no need to cube the pork butt. But tasters missed the charred crispness of the grilled versions. Easy fix, we figured; we'd simply brown the braised strips on the grill rather than in a skillet. Indeed, searing the meat for about 5 minutes per side over a single-level fire seemed to work well until we went to flip the pieces, which fell apart and slipped through the cooking grate in shreds. Tender meat was one thing, but it had to be grillable, too, so we dialed back the braising time by 30 minutes. The result: meat that was plenty tender but still held its shape. (It was also a snap to grill some pineapple rounds right next to the pork; we coarsely chopped and transferred them to a bowl for garnishing each taco.)

To replicate the appearance and texture of meat shaved from a spit, we sliced the crisped slabs crosswise into short ⅛-inch-thick strips. Now the meat was getting really good—full-flavored, crisp at the edges, and fork-tender—but we wished it were as succulent as the spit-roasted versions we'd had. That's when it dawned on us that a crucial part of the classic setup was missing: the melted fat that drips down, basting the meat as it cooks. We weren't about to start grilling pieces of pork fat, but we did have a potful of braising liquid that was loaded with rendered drippings. We brushed the unctuous liquid over both sides of each pork slab before grilling and then, just before serving, tossed a little more of it, spiked with a bit of lime juice for brightness, with the grilled slices.

Now our tacos al pastor, imbued with all of the complexity and rich flavor of the spit-roasted originals, brought the taste of a taqueria into our own kitchen.

Spicy Pork Tacos (al Pastor)

SERVES 6 TO 8

Boneless pork butt is often labeled Boston butt in the supermarket. If you can't find guajillo chiles, New Mexican chiles may be substituted, although the dish may be spicier. To warm tortillas, place them on a plate, cover with a damp clean dish towel, and microwave for 60 to 90 seconds. Keep tortillas covered and serve immediately.

10	large dried guajillo chiles, wiped clean
1½	cups water
1¼	pounds plum tomatoes, cored and quartered
8	garlic cloves, peeled
4	bay leaves
	Salt and pepper
¾	teaspoon sugar
½	teaspoon ground cumin
⅛	teaspoon ground cloves
1	(3-pound) boneless pork butt roast
1	lime, cut into 8 wedges
½	pineapple, peeled, cored, and cut into ½-inch-thick rings
	Vegetable oil
18	(6-inch) corn tortillas, warmed
1	small onion, chopped fine
½	cup coarsely chopped fresh cilantro

1. Toast guajillos in large Dutch oven over medium-high heat until softened and fragrant, 2 to 4 minutes. Transfer to large plate and, when cool enough to handle, remove stems.

2. Return toasted guajillos to now-empty Dutch oven, add water, tomatoes, garlic, bay leaves, 2 teaspoons salt, ½ teaspoon pepper, sugar, cumin, and cloves and bring to simmer over medium-high heat. Cover, reduce heat, and simmer, stirring occasionally, until guajillos are softened and tomatoes mash easily, about 20 minutes.

3. While sauce simmers, trim excess fat from exterior of pork, leaving ¼-inch-thick fat cap. Slice pork against grain into ½-inch-thick slabs.

4. Transfer guajillo-tomato mixture to blender and process until smooth, about 1 minute. Strain puree through fine-mesh strainer, pressing on solids to extract as much

RATING MORTARS AND PESTLES

A mortar and pestle is great for grinding whole spices, making pesto, and more. In general, we prefer mortars that hold at least 3 cups, have a rough interior to help grip and grind ingredients, and come with a long, heavy pestle that keeps knuckles from scraping the mortar's edge. We tested three models that fit the bill, two made of granite and one made of volcanic rock. To test whether these tools could not only pulverize ingredients but also keep them contained, we tried crushing toasted rice, whole peppercorns, and dry tapioca to the consistency of cornmeal in each vessel. The wide, low bowl of one of the granite models had us chasing ingredients around the kitchen. While a moderately rough surface is good, the cavities of the craggy volcanic rock mortar were so large that they trapped food. Our favorite mortar and pestle has a rough (but not too rough) interior that quickly pulverized peppercorns. Heavy and stable, this mortar has tall, narrow walls that didn't let ingredients escape and a comfortable, heavy pestle. Brands are listed in order of preference. See AmericasTestKitchen.com for updates to this testing.

HIGHLY RECOMMENDED

FRIELING "Goliath" Mortar and Pestle Set
MODEL: C420128   PRICE: $49.95
MORTAR DIAMETER: 5¼ in
PESTLE LENGTH: 7½ in
COMMENTS: The extra-tall sides of this heavy, stable granite mortar kept food from escaping and its rough interior quickly reduced hard peppercorns to dust. The large, heavy pestle was comfortable to hold and made grinding a breeze.

RECOMMENDED WITH RESERVATIONS

IMUSA MEXI-2008 Lava Rock Molcajete with Gift Box
MODEL: MEXI-2008   PRICE: $26.10
MORTAR DIAMETER: 6½ in   PESTLE LENGTH: 3½ in
COMMENTS: The incredibly rough (with craters as large as 2 mm wide) inside surface of this traditional three-legged Mexican tool required a lot of TLC before it was even ready to use. It was noticeably smoother after it was seasoned though still rougher than the other mortars. We did find that this model's performance got better with use, ultimately gripping and crushing peppercorns in fewer strokes than the other two models required.

VASCONIA 4-Cup Molcajete, Granite
MODEL: 5031764   PRICE: $29.99
MORTAR DIAMETER: 6¼ in   PESTLE LENGTH: 4¾ in
COMMENTS: The squat, figure-eight-shaped pestle of this model was comfortable to hold, though it required a few more strokes than the other two models. It got the job done, but the low walls of the bowl allowed some dry ingredients to shoot out during grinding.

liquid as possible. Return puree to pot, submerge pork slices in liquid, and bring to simmer over medium heat. Partially cover, reduce heat, and gently simmer until pork is tender but still holds together, 1½ to 1¾ hours, flipping and rearranging pork halfway through cooking. (Pork can be left in sauce, cooled to room temperature, and refrigerated for up to 2 days.)

5. Transfer pork to large plate, season both sides with salt, and cover tightly with aluminum foil. Whisk sauce to recombine. Transfer ½ cup sauce to bowl for grilling; pour off all but ½ cup remaining sauce from pot and reserve for another use. Squeeze 2 lime wedges into sauce in pot and add spent wedges; season with salt to taste.

6A. FOR A CHARCOAL GRILL: Open bottom vent halfway. Light large chimney starter filled with charcoal briquettes (6 quarts). When top coals are partially covered with ash, pour evenly over grill. Set cooking grate in place, cover, and open lid vent halfway. Heat grill until hot, about 5 minutes.

6B. FOR A GAS GRILL: Turn all burners to high, cover, and heat grill until hot, about 15 minutes. Turn all burners to medium.

7. Clean and oil cooking grate. Brush 1 side of pork with ¼ cup reserved sauce. Place pork on 1 side of grill, sauce side down, and cook until well browned and crisp, 5 to 7 minutes. Brush pork with remaining ¼ cup reserved sauce, flip, and continue to cook until second side is well browned and crisp, 5 to 7 minutes longer. Transfer to carving board. Meanwhile, brush both sides of pineapple rings with vegetable oil and season with salt to taste. Place on other half of grill and cook until pineapple is softened and caramelized, 10 to 14 minutes; transfer pineapple to carving board.

8. Coarsely chop grilled pineapple and transfer to serving bowl. Using tongs or carving fork to steady hot pork, slice each piece crosswise into ⅛-inch pieces. Bring remaining ½ cup sauce in pot to simmer, add sliced pork, remove pot from heat, and toss to coat pork well. Season with salt to taste.

9. Spoon small amount of pork into each warm tortilla and serve, passing chopped pineapple, remaining 6 lime wedges, onion, and cilantro separately.

JERK CHICKEN

✔ **WHY THIS RECIPE WORKS:** Traditional Jamaican jerk recipes rely on island ingredients for both marinade and cooking technique. Fortunately, we were able to achieve the characteristic spicy-sweet-fresh-smoky balance with the right combination of stateside staples. Keeping the marinade pastelike and cooking the meat first over indirect heat prevented the jerk flavors from dripping or peeling off during grilling. Enhancing our hickory chip packet with a few spice-cabinet ingredients allowed our jerk chicken recipe to mimic the unique smoke of authentic pimento wood.

WE NEVER WOULD HAVE GUESSED THAT THE READING list for our Jamaican jerk chicken recipe would include articles in *Chemosphere* and *Journal of Sensory Studies*. After all, the roots of this approach to marinating and cooking meat date back more than 300 years, when Taino Indians inhabited the island's forests along with escaped African slaves brought over by the British when they colonized the country. There the refugees used salt, pepper, and the fragrant berries of the pimento (aka allspice) trees to flavor and preserve strips of wild boar, and they employed the tree's leaves and branches to slowly smoke the meat.

The primitive technique has come a long way since then, but the flavors still reflect the Jamaican original. Rather than boar meat smoked in fire pits, most modern-day jerk recipes call for marinating the meat—chicken, pork, and goat are all common—with an intensely flavorful liquid paste of allspice berries, fiery Scotch bonnet chiles, thyme, and a dozen or so other herbs and spices and then smoking it over pimento wood. When this is done well, the meat emerges aromatic, woodsy, spicy, and sweet (the marinade often includes a little sugar), with a clean, lingering burn from the fresh chiles—an appealing flavor profile that inspired us to come up with a recipe of our own. Chicken was our meat of choice, and for the sake of even cooking, we'd stick with individual parts rather than a whole bird.

JERK CHICKEN

Little did we know that jerk recipes are rife with pitfalls. Dense, thick spice pastes were tricky to spread evenly over the meat and tended to stick to the hot cooking grates and burn. Thinner, more liquid concoctions ran right off the chicken pieces and into the fire—but not before they saturated the skin and prevented it from rendering and browning. Drier, rublike mixtures tasted dull and dusty. Beyond that, none of the marinades hit on the ideal aromatic-sweet-spicy balance we were hoping for, and since pimento wood isn't easy to come by here in the Northeast, we were stuck with a widely available option: hickory. Needless to say, we had a lot of work ahead of us.

Nailing down the flavor and consistency of the marinade seemed like the obvious first step, so we lined up a slew of potential ingredients, set up a basic indirect fire to cook the chicken (we'd revisit the grilling method later), and got busy. Allspice, thyme, and chiles (we'd use habaneros in place of hard-to-find Scotch bonnets) were definites, as were scallions for their grassy freshness, plenty of garlic, and salt (which we've discovered is the most important element of any marinade). From there,

we went about adding—and subtracting—herbs, spices, and condiments until we'd come up with a formula that got us close to the complex balance we were after: the aforementioned core elements, plus coriander seeds and peppercorns (coarsely ground in a spice grinder with the allspice berries) and a mixture of dried thyme, basil, and rosemary for woodsy depth; ground nutmeg and ginger, plus a touch of brown sugar for warmth and sweetness, respectively; a good amount of grated lime zest and yellow mustard for brightness; and soy sauce for a savory boost.

At this point, the marinade's flavor was relatively full-bodied, but the consistency was a little too thick. So we scoured our pantry for liquid helpers and spotted vegetable oil. Sure enough, a few spoonfuls of that loosened things up just enough for the marinade to thoroughly coat and cling to the chicken pieces. Even better, between the salt and the soy sauce, the chicken tasted well seasoned after just 30 minutes of marinating. (Later on we tested the outer limits of marinating times—up to 24 hours—and happily discovered that the longer the chicken sat, the more flavorful the meat became, thanks to the water-soluble flavor compounds in the marinade ingredients penetrating even further. It's just a matter of how much time you have.)

Back to the grilling method. Cooking the chicken over the cool side of an indirect fire (where all the coals are banked to one side of the grill) was a close imitation of the traditional low-fire method, and it ensured that the chicken stayed juicy. But while gentle heat made for succulent meat, it didn't do much for the skin, which was pale and rubbery. We modified our coal setup and made use of the hotter half of the grill as well, spreading the briquettes evenly over one side, which gave us the space we needed to sear the marinated chicken pieces in one batch before finishing them on the cooler half of the grill.

Unfortunately, there was a major (albeit predictable) snag in our plans to brown and render the skin: the marinade, most of which had soldered to the metal grates by the time the skin dehydrated enough to get any color. We thought that simply switching the order of operations—from searing first to searing last—might solve the problem by allowing the marinade to dry out and set on the skin before we put it face-to-face with the hot grates, but at that point the fire had died down considerably and didn't offer enough heat for searing. Our frustration was building, but our colleagues reminded us that we had one more trick to try: a barbecue technique that we had devised for prolonging a grill's heat output. We placed a batch of unlit coals in the kettle, followed by a batch that we'd ignited as usual in a chimney starter, the idea being that the lit briquettes would slowly ignite the unlit batch. We gave it a whirl and were relieved to find that did it: The delayed fire setup accommodated both the meat and the skin.

We liked to think we were making progress, but the truth was that we'd been putting off the most challenging part of our jerk recipe—the elusive pimento wood smoke flavor—until the very end. There was no way we were shelling out for mail-order wood every time we wanted some Jamaican barbecue, but one purchase for the sake of comparing the real deal with hickory wood seemed reasonable. So we ordered some pimento chips and prepared a double batch of our recipe, one cooked over hickory and the other over the costly pimento.

The difference was clear: While the hickory wood infused the meat with an assertive smokiness, the pimento wood lent the chicken a fresher, sweeter, and more herbal smoke flavor that tasters preferred. How could we make hickory taste like pimento?

That's where the science journals came in. To get a better understanding of smoke flavor, we decided to sift through some articles about wood and the types of flavor compounds they release when they smolder. The research made sense: Depending on the type of wood, some of these compounds (known as phenols and terpenes) can be robust and meaty (like hickory) or cleaner and more delicate (like pimento). That much we'd inferred from our taste test. What was enlightening, however, was an article that we came across in *Flavour & Fragrance Journal* detailing the flavor compounds of edible spices and herbs. It had never occurred to us that we could "smoke" herbs and spices, but the idea sounded promising. Allspice berries were an obvious source of pimento wood flavor compounds, so we added a couple of tablespoons to the packet with our hickory chips, whipped up another batch

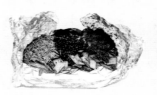 
of the jerk marinade, and got grilling. This test was a real breakthrough: We hadn't quite nailed the complexity of the pimento wood flavor just yet, but the warm fragrance of the allspice berries had made a noticeable difference. This got us wondering what else our spice cabinet might have to offer. Two bottles jumped out at us: dried rosemary and dried thyme, which both happen to contain many of the flavor compounds in the leaves of the pimento tree. Two tablespoons of each helped even out the smoke flavor, save for one familiar problem: Smoked dry, the herbs and spices were smoldering too quickly, resulting in the same carbonized off-flavors you get when wood burns too hot. We tried soaking and draining the spice mixture, but that simply washed out their flavor. So we opted for the halfway point: moistening the spices with just enough water (2 tablespoons) to dampen the smolder and still preserve their delicate flavor.

We were in Massachusetts when we took a bite of that final batch of jerk chicken, but thanks to the marinade's complexity and the delicate warmth of our faux pimento wood packet, we could just as easily have been standing in Jamaica's Boston Bay.

Jerk Chicken

SERVES 4

For a milder dish, use one seeded chile. If you prefer your food very hot, use up to all three chiles including their seeds and ribs. Scotch bonnet chiles can be used in place of the habaneros. Wear gloves when working with the chiles.

JERK MARINADE

- 1½ tablespoons whole coriander seeds
- 1 tablespoon whole allspice berries
- 1 tablespoon whole peppercorns
- 1-3 habanero chiles, stemmed, quartered, and seeds and ribs reserved, if using
- 8 scallions, chopped
- 6 garlic cloves, peeled
- 3 tablespoons vegetable oil
- 2 tablespoons soy sauce
- 2 tablespoons finely grated lime zest (3 limes), plus lime wedges for serving
- 2 tablespoons yellow mustard
- 1 tablespoon dried thyme
- 1 tablespoon ground ginger
- 1 tablespoon packed brown sugar
- 2¼ teaspoons salt
- 2 teaspoons dried basil
- ½ teaspoon dried rosemary
- ½ teaspoon ground nutmeg

CHICKEN

- 3 pounds bone-in chicken pieces (split breasts cut in half, drumsticks, and/or thighs)
- 2 tablespoons whole allspice berries
- 2 tablespoons dried thyme
- 2 tablespoons dried rosemary
- 2 tablespoons water
- 1 cup wood chips, soaked in water for 15 minutes and drained

1. FOR THE JERK MARINADE: Grind coriander seeds, allspice berries, and peppercorns in spice grinder or mortar and pestle until coarsely ground. Transfer spices to blender jar. Add habanero(s), scallions, garlic, oil, soy sauce, lime zest, mustard, thyme, ginger, brown sugar, salt, basil, rosemary, and nutmeg and process until smooth paste forms, 1 to 3 minutes, scraping down sides of blender jar as needed. Transfer marinade to gallon-size zipper-lock bag.

2. FOR THE CHICKEN: Place chicken pieces in bag with marinade and toss to coat; press out as much air as possible and seal bag. Let stand at room temperature for 30 minutes while preparing grill, flipping bag after 15 minutes. (Marinated chicken can be refrigerated for up to 24 hours.)

3. Combine allspice berries, thyme, rosemary, and water in bowl and set aside to moisten for 15 minutes. Using large piece of heavy-duty aluminum foil, wrap soaked chips and moistened allspice mixture in foil packet and cut several vent holes in top.

4A. FOR A CHARCOAL GRILL: Open bottom vent halfway. Arrange 1 quart unlit charcoal briquettes in single layer over half of grill. Light large chimney starter one-third filled with charcoal briquettes (2 quarts). When top coals are partially covered with ash, pour evenly over unlit briquettes, keeping coals arranged over half of grill. Place wood chip packet on coals. Set cooking grate in place, cover, and open lid vent halfway. Heat grill until hot and wood chips are smoking, about 5 minutes.

4B. FOR A GAS GRILL: Place wood chip packet over primary burner. Turn all burners to high, cover, and heat grill until hot and wood chips begin to smoke, 15 to 25 minutes. Turn primary burner to medium and turn off other burner(s).

5. Clean and oil cooking grate. Place chicken, with marinade clinging and skin side up, as far away from fire as possible, with thighs closest to fire and breasts furthest away. Cover (positioning lid vent over chicken if using charcoal) and cook for 30 minutes.

6. Move chicken, skin side down, to hotter side of grill; cook until browned and skin renders, 3 to 6 minutes. Using tongs, flip chicken pieces and cook until browned on second side and breasts register 160 degrees and thighs/drumsticks register 175 degrees, 5 to 12 minutes longer.

7. Transfer chicken to serving platter, tent loosely with foil, and let rest for 5 to 10 minutes. Serve warm or at room temperature with lime wedges.

RATING GREAT GRILLING GADGETS

If you're an avid griller, there's an endless number of tools and gadgets out there that promise to make your grilling experience even better. The problem is that not all of them deliver what they promise—or even close to it. Here are a few pieces of equipment that we've found do deliver and are worth having on hand next time you plan to grill. See AmericasTestKitchen.com for updates to these testings.

COOKING GRATE SET

The Weber Gourmet BBQ System allows you to replace the cooking grate on your Weber 22½-Inch One-Touch or Performer Grill with a stainless steel grate that has a removable inner 12-inch circle ($32.99) within which you can insert one of three cast-iron accessories: a crosshatched sear grate, a griddle, or a wok. We tried all three inserts and found we liked the sear grate ($32.99 or $64.99 with the stainless steel grate) the best. It created beautiful, professional-looking crosshatch grill marks on large steaks or chops. The griddle ($32.99 or $64.99 with the stainless steel grate) allowed delicate scallops and salmon to develop a great crust, although we were disappointed that the solid pan bottom didn't allow much smoke flavor to penetrate. The wok ($54.99) was our least favorite of the three; it seared meat nicely for a beef and vegetable stir-fry, but it was heavy and slow to heat. (Note: The sear grate and griddle are sold in sets with the grate for $64.99. The wok is only sold separately.)

WINNER: WEBER GOURMET BBQ SYSTEM

OUTDOOR GRILL PAN

The bars of a cooking grate are designed to be spread out, with space between them so the food above gets direct exposure to the intense heat and smoke below. Unfortunately, those gaps in the grate make it easy for small or delicate items such as seafood or vegetables to slip right through. Enter the grill pan, which acts to keep smaller foods corralled and prevent sticking but has perforations so there's enough exposure to the flames that they develop the hallmark look and flavor of grilled food. We tested nine different models, using them to grill shrimp, chopped vegetables, cod fillets, and quartered potatoes, and evaluating the pans' performance, design, user friendliness, and perforation pattern, density, and size. Our favorite was the Weber Style Professional-Grade Grill Pan ($19.99), which is made of sturdy stainless steel that retains enough heat for excellent browning and provides a generous cooking surface. Its surface is covered with narrow slits that let in grill flavor and discourage steaming.

WINNER: WEBER STYLE PROFESSIONAL-GRADE GRILL PAN

GRILL GLOVES

If you grill frequently, grill gloves, which offer serious protection for your arms and hands, are a must-have. We put five grill gloves or mitts (ranging from $25.95 to $39.90 per pair) to the test, plus our favorite oven mitt, the Kool-Tek 15-Inch Oven Mitt from Katchall ($44.95 each). We intended to pour hot coals from a chimney starter and arrange them with tongs, as well as grill zucchini and lift searing grates to add briquettes. But this was easier said than done: Thick, stiff, and oversize, most models barely let us grip our tongs. We also held gloved hands over a burner at 600 degrees. One model began to smoke after just 14 seconds; the best kept us cool for more than 90 seconds. The Kool-Tek oven mitt, offered admirable heat protection, but it's pricey, and for maximum dexterity we prefer gloves. Our winner, the Steven Raichlen Ultimate Suede Grilling Gloves ($29.99 per pair), boasts extra-long, wide cuffs that protected our forearms and supple leather that gave us great control when using tongs and grabbing hot cooking grates.

WINNER: STEVEN RAICHLEN ULTIMATE SUEDE GRILLING GLOVES

HEARTH GRILL

What if you want to grill but the weather's not cooperating? Cooking over a fire is possible indoors with the Tuscan Hearth Grill. This cast-iron set has a solid frame that fits into your fireplace. Just slide the cooking grate into one of three slots, depending on how far above the flames you want to grill. The large version ($199), with a generously proportioned grate (23½ by 30 inches), gave us enough real estate to grill and turn six strip steaks. Wood handles made the grate safe for barehanded adjustment, which proved useful when we moved the food closer to the coals as the flames subsided. Two minor objections: Adding logs to the fire was difficult once the grate was in place, so we had to make sure the fire was just right before we began cooking. Also, the set does not include a drip pan, so we used a disposable aluminum pan to keep the bottom of the fireplace grease free.

WINNER: TUSCAN HEARTH GRILL

Breakfast STANDBYS

Breakfast is almost ready as Julia plates some crusty home fries.

THERE ARE SOME BREAKFAST DISHES THAT WILL NEVER GO OUT OF fashion: a hot bowl of oatmeal to sustain you through a long morning, and the perfect partner to your favorite style of eggs: home fries.

Oatmeal made with old-fashioned, quick, or even instant oats are far more popular than steel-cut oats in this country. But the reason has nothing to do with flavor or texture—in our humble opinion, steel-cut oats are far preferable than their processed counterparts. The reason so few of us make steel-cut oats comes down to time. Who has 30 to 40 minutes on a weekday morning to be babysitting breakfast? We wanted to develop a recipe for the ultimate bowl of steel-cut oatmeal with just 10 minutes of active time: a recipe that yields a creamy porridge with deep flavor and a subtle chew.

While oatmeal is often enjoyed at home, home fries are almost exclusively a diner treat. With a large griddle or an industrial six-plus burner stove, making home fries for four or six is eminently doable. Try to make home fries in your own kitchen and you'll be monopolizing all your burners to cook the spuds evenly. You could cook home fries in batches while you keep the first couple of skillets' worth warm in the oven, but limp, warmed-over potatoes was not our goal. We wanted potatoes with crisp edges and moist, tender interiors—enough for six hungry diners. What's your order? Oatmeal or home fries? Coming up, we'll show you how to make terrific versions of both.

TEN-MINUTE STEEL-CUT OATMEAL

FASTER STEEL-CUT OATMEAL

✔ **WHY THIS RECIPE WORKS:** Most oatmeal fans agree that the steel-cut version of the grain offers the best flavor and texture, but many balk at the 40-minute cooking time. In this recipe, we decrease the cooking time to only 10 minutes by stirring steel-cut oats into boiling water the night before. This enables the grains to hydrate and soften overnight. In the morning, more water (or fruit juice or milk) is added and the mixture is simmered for 4 to 6 minutes, until thick and creamy. A brief resting period off the heat ensures that the porridge achieves the perfect consistency.

NEMO ME IMPUNE LACESSIT WAS THE MOTTO OF THE kings of ancient Scotland. It means "No one attacks me with impunity" or, more plainly, "Don't mess with me." Although the kings are long gone, that fiercely proud and sometimes downright pugnacious spirit lives on. It takes a brave (or perhaps foolish) person to criticize any aspect of Scottish identity, but as it happens we have a serious problem with one of the country's most iconic dishes: oatmeal.

We would eat traditional Scottish oat porridge every day if we could. It's delicious and sustaining, and preparing it couldn't be simpler: Steel-cut oats, which are dried oat kernels cut crosswise into coarse bits, are gently simmered in lightly salted water until the hard oats swell and soften and release some of their starch molecules into the surrounding liquid. Those freed starches bond with the liquid, thickening it until the oatmeal forms a substantial yet fluid mass of plump, tender grains. So, what's the problem? That transformation from gravelly oats to creamy, thick porridge takes 30 minutes minimum; closer to 40 minutes is preferable. There's just no way we can squeeze that into a busy weekday morning.

To reduce the prebreakfast rush, some cooks allow steel-cut oats to just barely bubble in a slow cooker overnight, but we've never had luck with that approach. After 8 hours the oats are mushy and blown out and lack the subtle chew of traditionally prepared oatmeal. If we were going to work our favorite kind of oatmeal into a regular breakfast rotation, we'd have to find a quicker way to cook it. Our goal: perfect porridge that required fewer than 10 minutes of active engagement.

Oat cookery has changed very little over the centuries, which explains why we had so few leads on alternative timesaving methods. In fact, the only Scot-sanctioned shortcut we knew was one that one of us had learned while working as a breakfast cook at a small hotel in Scotland: soaking the steel-cut oats in tap water overnight to initiate the hydration of the grain. Thinking that we'd give this approach some further scrutiny, we prepared two batches of oatmeal using a fairly standard ratio of 1 cup oats to 4 cups water. We soaked one measure of the grains overnight in room-temperature water and cooked the other straight from the package and then compared their respective cook times. As it turned out, presoaking saved some time, but not enough. Almost 25 minutes passed before the soaked oats morphed into the loose yet viscous porridge we were after—only about 15 minutes faster than the unsoaked batch. We weren't quite convinced that some sort of presoak treatment wouldn't help, but for now we went back to the drawing board.

As a matter of fact, we had a trick in mind. We'd had the same timesaving goal when developing a recipe for polenta, and we'd discovered an unlikely addition that sped things up considerably: baking soda. Introducing just a pinch of the alkali to the pot raised the pH of the cooking liquid, causing the corn's cell walls to break down more quickly, thereby allowing water to enter and gelatinize its starch molecules in half the time. We thought that the baking soda might have a similarly expediting effect with our steel-cut oats, so we dropped a pinch into the pot and waited. And waited. Twenty minutes later, we had the creamy porridge we were after, but a mere 5-minute savings wasn't going to do it. We decided to ditch the baking soda idea.

We hadn't abandoned the notion of jump-starting the hydration process with a presoak, but we obviously needed a more aggressive method than simply resting the oats in a bowl of room-temperature water. That's when our thoughts turned from presoaking to parcooking. Surely boiling water would hasten the softening of the oats faster than room-temperature water, right? To find

starch molecules to burst, which turned the oats to mush and caused the surrounding liquid to become pasty.

Still, things were looking up. A 10-minute cook time was a major step in the right direction. In our next test, we decided to split the difference between the Scottish room-temperature soak and the mushy boiled-water method. Instead of bringing the oats to a boil with the water, we boiled the water by itself, poured in the oats, covered the pot, and then left them to hydrate overnight. The next morning we got the pot going again. With this slightly more gentle method, 10 minutes later the oatmeal was perfectly creamy and not at all blown out or sticky.

We had just one other problem to solve—this one a classic oatmeal quandary. Though the finished oatmeal looked appropriately creamy in the pot, the mixture continued to thicken after we poured it into the bowl as the starches continued to absorb the water. By the time we dug in, the result was so thick and pasty that we could stand our spoons in it.

That's when we seized on one last adjustment: We would cut the heat before the oatmeal had achieved its ideal thickness and then let it sit for a few minutes, until it thickened up just enough. We gave it a whirl, simmering the oatmeal for a mere 5 minutes and then moving the pot off the heat to rest. Five minutes later we assembled tasters and all dug into bowls of perfect porridge: creamy and viscous and not the least bit pasty. Goal achieved.

Our tasters' only critical comment: Though a bowl of unadulterated oatmeal might be traditional in Scotland, on this side of the Atlantic we like ours loaded up with toppings. Of course we could easily serve our cereal with the usual fixings (brown sugar, maple syrup, dried fruit, etc.), but we wondered if we could change the flavor of the porridge more fundamentally by swapping out some of the water for more flavorful liquids and by adding some punchier ingredients.

Letting milk or juice sit out overnight might be pushing food-safety limits (water was fine), so we looked over our recipe and came up with an alternative approach that worked brilliantly: rehydrating the oats in just 3 cups

out, we brought the oats and the water to a boil together, cut the heat, covered the pot, and left it to sit overnight. When we uncovered the pot the next morning, we knew we were getting somewhere. Thanks to this head start, the coarse, gravelly oats we'd started with had swelled and fully softened. We were encouraged and flipped on the burner to medium to see how long it would take before the cereal turned creamy and thickened. About 10 minutes of simmering later, the porridge was heated through and viscous—but was also mushy and pasty like the slow-cooker oats. Simmering the oats for less time wasn't the answer: It left the liquid in the pot thin and watery. As surprising as it seemed, we could only conclude that parcooking by bringing the oats up to a boil with the water was too aggressive, causing too many of boiling water and withholding the last cup of liquid until the following morning, when it could be replaced with milk, juice, or something else right before simmering. This way, we could adjust the ingredients to make enough varieties of oatmeal to please even the most jaded palate. We came up with apple-cinnamon oats made with cider, a tropical take made with bananas and coconut milk, a carrot cake spin made with carrot juice, a cardamom-scented cranberry-orange variation made with orange juice, and a peanut-honey-banana version made with milk and creamy peanut butter.

As much as the Scots are known for being proud and stubborn, they are also known for their inventiveness and imagination. It is, after all, Scots who we have to thank for penicillin, Sherlock Holmes, and television. We're confident that our 10-minute steel-cut oatmeal will appeal to the innovative side of the national character.

Ten-Minute Steel-Cut Oatmeal

SERVES 4

The oatmeal will continue to thicken as it cools. If you prefer a looser consistency, thin the oatmeal with boiling water. Customize your oatmeal with toppings such as brown sugar, toasted nuts, maple syrup, or dried fruit.

- 4 **cups water**
- 1 **cup steel-cut oats**
- ¼ **teaspoon salt**

1. Bring 3 cups water to boil in large saucepan over high heat. Remove pan from heat; stir in oats and salt. Cover pan and let stand overnight.

2. Stir remaining 1 cup water into oats and bring to boil over medium-high heat. Reduce heat to medium and cook, stirring occasionally, until oats are softened but still retain some chew and mixture thickens and resembles warm pudding, 4 to 6 minutes. Remove pan from heat and let stand for 5 minutes. Stir and serve, passing desired toppings separately.

VARIATIONS

Apple-Cinnamon Steel-Cut Oatmeal

Increase salt to ½ teaspoon. Substitute ½ cup apple cider and ½ cup whole milk for water in step 2. Stir ½ cup peeled, grated sweet apple, 2 tablespoons packed dark brown sugar, and ½ teaspoon ground cinnamon into oatmeal with cider and milk. Sprinkle each serving with 2 tablespoons coarsely chopped toasted walnuts.

Carrot-Spice Steel-Cut Oatmeal

Increase salt to ¾ teaspoon. Substitute ½ cup carrot juice and ½ cup whole milk for water in step 2. Stir ½ cup finely grated carrot, ¼ cup packed dark brown sugar, ⅓ cup dried currants, and ½ teaspoon ground cinnamon into oatmeal with carrot juice and milk. Sprinkle each serving with 2 tablespoons coarsely chopped toasted pecans.

Cranberry-Orange Steel-Cut Oatmeal

Increase salt to ½ teaspoon. Substitute ½ cup orange juice and ½ cup whole milk for water in step 2. Stir ½ cup dried cranberries, 3 tablespoons packed dark brown sugar, and ⅛ teaspoon ground cardamom into oatmeal with orange juice and milk. Sprinkle each serving with 2 tablespoons toasted sliced almonds.

Banana-Coconut Steel-Cut Oatmeal

Increase salt to ½ teaspoon. Substitute 1 cup canned coconut milk for water in step 2. Stir ½ cup toasted shredded coconut, 2 diced bananas, and ½ teaspoon vanilla extract into oatmeal before serving.

Peanut, Honey, and Banana Steel-Cut Oatmeal

Increase salt to ½ teaspoon. Substitute ½ cup whole milk for ½ cup water in step 2. Stir 3 tablespoons honey into oatmeal with milk and water. Add ¼ cup peanut butter and 1 tablespoon unsalted butter to oatmeal after removing from heat in step 2. Stir 2 diced bananas into oatmeal before serving. Sprinkle each serving with 2 tablespoons coarsely chopped toasted peanuts.

HOME FRIES

✓ WHY THIS RECIPE WORKS: Making home fries the traditional way takes about an hour of standing over a hot skillet, after which you get only three servings at most. We wanted a quicker, more hands-off method for making a larger amount. To speed things up, we developed a hybrid cooking technique: First, we parboiled diced russet potatoes, and then we coated them in oil and cooked them in a very hot oven. We discovered that boiling the potatoes with baking soda quickly breaks down their exterior while leaving their insides nearly raw, ensuring home fries with a crisp, brown crust and a moist, fluffy interior. We added diced onions in the last 20 minutes of oven time and finished the home fries with chives to reinforce the onion flavor.

DESPITE THE COZY IMAGE CONJURED BY THE NAME, few people actually make home fries at home. That's probably because producing the perfect article—a mound of golden-brown potato chunks with crisp exteriors and moist, fluffy insides dotted with savory onions and herbs—calls for more time, elbow grease, and stovetop space than most cooks care to devote to the project. First of all, when you start with raw potatoes, achieving that ideal crisp, well-browned exterior requires frequently turning them in the pan for the better part of an hour. Then there's the matter of the yield: Even a roomy 12-inch skillet barely holds enough potatoes to serve two people. But since the prospect of juggling multiple sizzling skillets is enough to give even the most confident cook pause, making home fries for a larger gathering is out of the question. No wonder most of us eat our home fries at diners or buffet tables, where large-scale production and lengthy holding times often result in potatoes that are limp and greasy.

We wanted to find a way out of this sorry situation. Our goal: nicely crisped home fries with tender interiors that would serve six hungry people—and wouldn't chain the cook to the stove for an hour.

Since time was a priority, we decided to rule out any recipes that began with raw spuds and look for those that called for some form of parcooking. Even though it would dirty more dishes, parcooking would dramatically cut down on frying time. Our science editor also pointed out that using a moist heat method like boiling would actually aid in our goal of a crisp exterior. This is because when the starch granules in potatoes absorb water, they swell and release the water-soluble starch amylose. Once the amylose on the surface of the potato dries out, it hardens, creating a crisp shell. Parboiling it would be.

We weren't sure which type of potato would work best, so we tested the three main kinds: waxy, low-starch red-skinned spuds; all-purpose, medium-starch Yukon Golds; and floury, high-starch russets. We peeled and diced the potatoes into rough ¾-inch chunks, covered them with cold salted water, and boiled them until just cooked through. After draining the diced potatoes, we let them cool and dry slightly while we heated three cast-iron skillets. While we were frying the potatoes in the skillets with some vegetable oil for about four minutes per side, frantically flipping, we added another goal to our list: only one cooking vessel at a time.

Tasters almost universally rejected the texture of the red-skinned potatoes as too waxy for home fries. Though some praised the creaminess of the Yukon Golds, the majority preferred the earthy flavor of russets. We also knew that the higher starch content of russets would make for a crustier exterior. But as it did with the other potatoes, precooking caused the russets to become more porous, so they absorbed almost all of the oil in the pan before they'd been turned even once. The upshot was that only the first side of each cube came out golden brown while the other sides stuck to the pan, leaving their browned crusts behind. The simple fix was to boil the potatoes just until their outsides were softened but their insides were still firm. This meant that only the outermost, fully cooked layer of potato absorbed oil, leaving more oil in the pan to prevent sticking and promote even browning.

With browning under control, it was time to turn to the next pressing issue: batch size. Since we'd vowed not to repeat the stressful experience of multiple skillets, we tried successive batches in a single skillet, holding each completed batch in a warm oven until all of the

HOME FRIES

potatoes were fried. Not only was this approach too time-consuming, but the potatoes waiting in the oven grew soft outside and dry in the middle as moisture migrated from their cores to their surfaces.

We couldn't ignore the fact that the oven was ideal for large batches, so we decided to try high-temperature roasting. We were heartened to find plenty of Internet recipes purporting to make "oven home fries" without any parboiling at all. While many of these recipes produced evenly browned potatoes, they sadly did not deliver the crucial crisp texture of the real deal, plus they required nearly an hour of roasting time.

Undaunted, we decided to see if parcooking the potatoes, which at least encouraged a crisp exterior, would help. (It would also cut down on roasting time.) As before, we parboiled our potatoes for 5 minutes until they were nearly (but not completely) cooked through. We tossed them with butter (for flavor) and then transferred them to an oiled, rimmed baking sheet that we had preheated in a 500-degree oven to mimic the surface of a hot skillet. After 40 minutes of roasting (and occasional turning), the exteriors were perfectly brown and crisp—but the insides were dry and overcooked. Cutting the roasting time to 25 minutes left the insides moist and creamy but the outsides pale and soft.

Given that a baking sheet had the potential to yield three times as many servings as a skillet, we had to find a way to make the oven work. What we needed to do was somehow alter the boiling step to exaggerate the difference in doneness between the exterior and the interior of the potatoes before we roasted them. We wanted a thin outer layer of blown-out, starchy potato that would brown thoroughly in the oven but a raw middle that would stay moist during the time that it took to brown the outside. In short, we needed a method for making really bad boiled potatoes. We remembered a test kitchen potato salad recipe in which we'd discovered that adding a bit of vinegar to the boiling water keeps potatoes firm during cooking. The acid slows the breakdown of the pectin that holds the potato cells together, resulting in boiled potatoes that stay firm and intact. If a bit of acid in the water produced the best boiled potatoes, would adding its opposite—an alkaline substance—produce the worst?

We put 3½ pounds of peeled, chunked potatoes in a saucepan and covered them with 10 cups of cold water plus 2 teaspoons of alkaline baking soda, which we hoped would speed up the breakdown of pectin on the outside of the potato and turn it mushy. But after 5 minutes of boiling, the potatoes were blown out through and through. Undeterred, we cut back on the baking soda. After experimenting, we found that just ½ teaspoon produced the desired effect: floury outsides and uncooked insides. But could we take things even further? Since starting potatoes in cold water helps ensure even cooking and our goal was uneven cooking, why not chuck the spuds into boiling water? This not only made the outsides even pastier and left the insides totally raw but also reduced the parcooking to 1 minute. Perfect.

We had one more trick to try. We were already tossing the drained parcooked chunks with butter before placing them on the baking sheet, but we tossed them with kosher salt as well. In the past we've found that the coarse salt roughs up the surface of the potatoes so that moisture evaporates faster, leading to better browning. This worked beautifully to create nicely browned home fries with just the crisp, fried texture that we'd been seeking—and we'd only had to turn the potatoes twice in the oven.

Our recipe still lacked onions, so we searched for a way to incorporate them without compromising the now-perfect texture of the potatoes. Mixing chopped onions with the spuds before they went into the oven left the onions burnt on the outside and raw in the middle; mixing them in halfway through roasting had a similar effect. In the end, we found that placing oiled and salted onions in the center of the baking sheet 15 minutes into roasting the potatoes (at which point we also turned the potatoes) allowed them to soften a bit. After another 15 minutes, we mixed the onions and potatoes together and cooked them about 5 minutes longer. A pinch of cayenne tossed with the salted potatoes gave them kick, and a sprinkling of chives at the end enhanced the onion flavor.

We could now make great home fries for a group without working ourselves into a tizzy. And we didn't even need to haul out the skillet.

HOW MUSHY BOILED POTATOES LEAD TO CRISP HOME FRIES

USE RUSSETS
We like the earthy flavor that russets bring to home fries, plus their high starch content helps create a substantial golden-brown crust.

PARBOIL
Adding potatoes to boiling (not cold) water cooks them more on the outside than on the inside—just the uneven effect we want.

ADD BAKING SODA
Baking soda accentuates the uneven cooking by quickly breaking down the exteriors, leaving the insides nearly raw.

TOSS WITH SALT
Salt roughs up the drained potatoes, so their moisture evaporates more readily, leading to better crisping in the oven.

ROAST
Pretreated potatoes achieve a "fried" texture after oven roasting. This technique yields three times as many servings as frying in a skillet.

Home Fries

SERVES 6 TO 8

Don't skip the baking soda in this recipe. It's critical for home fries with just the right crisp texture.

- 3½ pounds russet potatoes, peeled and cut into ¾-inch dice
- ½ teaspoon baking soda
- 3 tablespoons unsalted butter, cut into 12 pieces
  Kosher salt and pepper
  Pinch cayenne pepper
- 3 tablespoons vegetable oil
- 2 onions, cut into ½-inch dice
- 3 tablespoons minced chives

1. Adjust oven rack to lowest position, place rimmed baking sheet on rack, and heat oven to 500 degrees.

2. Bring 10 cups water to boil in Dutch oven over high heat. Add potatoes and baking soda. Return to boil and cook for 1 minute. Drain potatoes. Return potatoes to Dutch oven and place over low heat. Cook, shaking pot occasionally, until any surface moisture has evaporated, about 2 minutes. Remove from heat. Add butter, 1½ teaspoons salt, and cayenne; mix with rubber spatula until potatoes are coated with thick, starchy paste, about 30 seconds.

3. Remove baking sheet from oven and drizzle with 2 tablespoons oil. Transfer potatoes to baking sheet and spread into even layer. Roast for 15 minutes. While potatoes roast, combine onions, remaining 1 tablespoon oil, and ½ teaspoon salt in bowl.

4. Remove baking sheet from oven. Using thin, sharp metal spatula, scrape and turn potatoes. Clear about 8 by 5-inch space in center of baking sheet and add onion mixture. Roast for 15 minutes.

5. Scrape and turn again, mixing onions into potatoes. Continue to roast until potatoes are well browned and onions are softened and beginning to brown, 5 to 10 minutes. Stir in chives and season with salt and pepper to taste. Serve immediately.

SCIENCE DESK

POTATO CHAIN REACTION

While developing a potato salad recipe not too long ago, we discovered that adding vinegar to the cooking water creates an acidic environment that slows the breakdown of the pectin that holds potato cells together, resulting in a firm, intact texture. So when our home fries required a thin outer layer of mush that would brown thoroughly in the oven, we took the opposite approach: We created an alkaline environment by adding a little bit of baking soda to the water. After just 1 minute in the pot, the exteriors of the potatoes became so soft that they were mushy—but the interiors remained raw. This lead to potatoes that more readily crisped on the outside when roasted but didn't dry out on the inside.

How could just ½ teaspoon of baking soda added to 10 cups of water be so powerful? It's because alkaline baking soda triggers a chain reaction that literally unzips the backbone of the pectin molecules and causes them to fall apart. This requires only enough alkali to raise the pH of the water high enough to start the reaction, after which it becomes self-sustaining.

BOILED WITH VINEGAR (pH 8.1)

BOILED WITH BAKING SODA (pH 3)

RATING MOKA POTS

Often referred to as poor-man's espresso machines, Italian moka pots are small, inexpensive (under $100) coffee makers that use steam pressure to force hot water from a bottom chamber up through coffee grounds. That pressure isn't high enough for true espresso extraction, but the coffee they make is stronger and more complex than anything brewed in a drip machine. We recently tested eight moka pots: three traditional 3-cup stovetop designs and five electric models with capacities twice as large. The electric mokas were universally disappointing, as they failed to deliver enough power and produced flat, characterless coffee. Conversely, two out of three of the stovetop devices, including our favorite, brewed rich, full-bodied coffee—once we mastered subtle techniques like gently tamping the grinds and immediately removing the pot from the heat. Though those two brewed a comparable cup of coffee, one was half the price of the other—making it our top-rated moka pot. Brands are listed in order of preference. See AmericasTestKitchen.com for updates and further information on this testing.

RECOMMENDED

BIALETTI Moka Express, 3 cups
MODEL: 06799   PRICE: $24.95
PERFORMANCE: ★★★   EASE OF USE: ★★
COMMENTS: This easy-to-use classic design quickly brewed rich, dense coffee. Even better, it was the least expensive model we tested.

RECOMMENDED WITH RESERVATIONS

ALESSI Moka Stovetop Espresso Maker, 3 cups
MODEL: AAM33/3   PRICE: $47
PERFORMANCE: ★★★   EASE OF USE: ★★
COMMENTS: This stovetop model looked like—and performed on par with—our favorite moka. The only significant difference? The cost, which was nearly twice as much. Hence, our reservations about recommending it.

NOT RECOMMENDED

BODUM Chambord Espresso Maker, 3 cups
MODEL: 10616   PRICE: $29.95
PERFORMANCE: ★★   EASE OF USE: ★★
COMMENTS: The only stainless steel moka we tested (the others were aluminum), this was the slowest to heat up. As a result, the top chamber became superheated before the coffee percolated, evaporating and burning the first drips of coffee as they emerged.

BIALETTI Easy Cafe 6-Cup Espresso Maker
MODEL: OH-7009   PRICE: $99.95
PERFORMANCE: ★   EASE OF USE: ★★★
COMMENTS: Despite its plug-in convenience, this pricey electric version of our favorite moka failed to generate enough steam power and, consequently, produced disappointingly flat, watery, characterless coffee.

NOT RECOMMENDED *(cont.)*

DELONGHI EMK6 Alicia Electric Moka Espresso Coffee Maker, 6 cups
MODEL: EMK6   PRICE: $49.95
PERFORMANCE: ★   EASE OF USE: ★★★
COMMENTS: We had high hopes for this electric model; one of our editors purchased a twin version in Italy, and it makes fine coffee. Unfortunately, our results were just the opposite, as the coffee this American version produced was flat, dull, and flavorless. (The manufacturer offered no explanation for the differences.)

BENECASA Bravo Espresso, 6 cups
MODEL: BC-90264   PRICE: $28
PERFORMANCE: ★   EASE OF USE: ★★★
COMMENTS: A DeLonghi look-alike, this electric moka was easy to use and featured a clear top chamber so you could watch the coffee brew and know exactly when it was done. Unfortunately, this extra feature didn't make it a better pot. The brew time was long, and the resulting coffee was flat and bitter.

LA PAVONI Caffe Mattina Electric Cordless Espresso Maker, 6 to 8 cups
MODEL: ESP-20   PRICE: $80
PERFORMANCE: ★   EASE OF USE: ★★
COMMENTS: Even though this expensive electric pot came with a number of perks—good looks, a perfectly round pour spout punched into the side of the pot, and an extra-large capacity (up to 8 espresso cups)—they didn't translate to good coffee. Like the rest of the electric mokas, it produced a flat, dull-tasting brew.

Sunday BRUNCH

Chris gets ready to roll up the sweet cinnamon filling in a classic breakfast treat, Cinnamon Swirl Bread.

EGGS AND TOAST ARE A CLASSIC BREAKFAST PAIRING. BUT BAKED EGGS and toasted cinnamon bread? That's something special. Now we're talking brunch.

The best thing about cinnamon bread shouldn't be its aroma as it bakes or toasts, but that's too often the case. We've met heavy, leaden loaves weighed down by globs of leaky "swirl" and others that barely register cinnamon. This breakfast classic should have a feathery, light crumb that's just substantial enough to support a sweet swirl of cinnamon and plump raisins. In addition to developing the right bread dough, we'd need to tackle the shaping of the bread so that the swirls would be even and compact—we didn't want any gaps or leaks. We had our work cut out for us.

Scrambled, fried, or poached: That's typically how we think of eggs. But eggs baked in individual ramekins, often with cream, are undeniably elegant and perfect for entertaining—there's no standing over a skillet like a short-order cook. The trick is getting just the right consistency—a runny, creamy yolk and a tender white. We uncovered multiple methods in our research, including one that calls for baking the whites until just set and then adding the yolks! We imagine the timing on that would drive us back to bed. We wanted a recipe for baked eggs that was both foolproof and fuss-free. Let's unlock the secrets behind baked eggs to partner with truly great cinnamon bread.

CINNAMON SWIRL BREAD

✔ **WHY THIS RECIPE WORKS:** This American classic frequently disappoints due to either precious little cinnamon flavor or, just as bad, a gloppy, oozing filling reminiscent of sticky buns. The bread itself is often an afterthought of pedestrian white bread, or else it's a cakey, dense affair. We took our inspiration from an airy, cottony Japanese white bread called *shokupan* and created a filling with a balanced mixture of cinnamon, confectioners' sugar, and vanilla. To ensure that our filling stayed put and could be tasted with every bite, we traded the traditional swirl shape for a simple yet elegant Russian braid.

CINNAMON SWIRL BREAD ALWAYS SOUNDS APPEALING in theory, but we've often been disappointed in it. Our ideal has a fluffy, delicate crumb, plump raisins, and a thick swirl of gooey cinnamon sugar. But most versions are either austere white sandwich loaves rolled up with a bare sprinkle of cinnamon or overly sweet breads ruined by gobs of filling oozing from the cracks.

When one of us finally stumbled upon the solution, it was in the unlikeliest of places: a bakery kiosk in Tokyo's Narita airport. Beneath the lightly crisp exterior, the crumb was so springy, moist, and feathery it could be pulled into cotton candy–like strands. We vowed to replicate this style of wispy, milky-sweet Japanese white sandwich bread, called *shokupan,* at home.

We decided to focus first on the bread, but when English recipes for shokupan proved hard to come by, we sought out an expert: Takeo Sakan, head baker at Boston's acclaimed Japonaise Bakery and Café. To help us better understand how shokupan is made, we compared it with American sandwich bread. The two styles share a number of the same ingredients: flour, yeast, salt, water, milk, sugar, and butter. Shokupan, however, boasts considerably more fat (roughly twice as much butter, plus an egg) and more sugar, which accounts for its particularly tender crumb. Shokupan also contains more gluten—the network of proteins that builds structure and allows bread to rise high and retain its springy crumb. To develop that gluten, Sakan uses a combination of thorough kneading and specialty high-gluten flour, which contains even more protein than the bread flour used in most American sandwich breads. It's that marriage of particularly strong gluten and tenderizers like fat and sugar that produces shokupan's airy yet sturdy crumb.

We returned to the test kitchen to mix up a batch, with one change: Since the high-gluten flour Sakan uses requires mail ordering, we'd have to stick with bread flour and worry about making up for the lack of gluten later. We mixed the flour with yeast, sugar, and nonfat dry milk powder; added water plus an egg and 8 tablespoons of softened butter for richness; and kneaded the mixture until it formed a cohesive mass. After letting the dough rest for about 20 minutes, we kneaded it for a longer stretch—about 10 minutes—until it was smoother and more workable. We mixed in a generous handful of golden raisins and let the dough proof in a turned-off oven. Because warm, humid air stimulates yeast activity and speeds rising time, we placed a pan of boiling water on the oven floor. Forty-five minutes later, we patted the dough into a rectangle, sprinkled a simple cinnamon-sugar filling over the surface, rolled it into a spiral, fitted it into a loaf pan, and let it proof for another 45 minutes, until the dough had doubled in size. We brushed the dough with an egg wash for shine and baked it until the crust was dark brown.

The crumb of the bread was far from ideal. Among other problems, it didn't have the hallmark lift and airy texture. The reason, no doubt, had a lot to do with the lower-protein bread flour. We had one solution in mind to strengthen the dough: Work in more air. Not only does oxygen provide lift to baked goods, but it also drives gluten development. To add oxygen, we tried introducing two sets of "folds" into the process. By deflating the dough and folding it back onto itself several times, we incorporated more air into it, encouraging the bread to expand and rise more. We also increased the kneading time to about 15 minutes, rendering it even more elastic

CINNAMON SWIRL BREAD

and better able to trap gas for a taller rise. This bread baked up noticeably higher, but still not as tall as the famed shokupan loaves.

We scanned our ingredient list for other ways to boost the bread's height. When we got to the butter, we paused. We knew that incorporating it into the dough at the outset was coating the flour proteins with fat, preventing them from bonding and inhibiting gluten formation. A better method, we reasoned, would be to knead the dough almost completely to develop gluten and then work in some softened butter during the final minutes of kneading. But the soft butter pieces smeared into the dough rather than incorporating evenly. Our quick fix: Tossing the pieces with a tablespoon of flour before letting them soften helped the dough grip the butter. The resulting loaf was gorgeously lofty. Our next challenge: a gooey cinnamon-sugar swirl.

We thought perfecting a thick cinnamon swirl would be easy. Halfway through baking our first loaf, the bread sprang a leak and spewed molten cinnamon sugar from its crevices. When we sliced it open, we found a mangled mix of dense bread, gaps, and puddles of cinnamon filling.

Our science editor explained: All of these issues boil down to the fact that the sugary filling and the bread don't easily bind. During proofing, the gas produced by the yeast leaks from the dough into the spiral and, because it has no place to go, the gas pushes apart the layers of dough. During baking, steam also fills the gaps. All that pressure compresses the dough, allowing the cinnamon-sugar filling to flow to the bottom of the bread and leak through its seam. What we needed was a way to encourage binding between the swirl and the dough. We added a slew of different ingredients to the filling to see if any would help it adhere: flour, eggs, pectin, corn syrup, pureed raisins, cooked caramel, crushed cinnamon cereal, and ground-up nuts. But the loaves still baked up with comically large gaps.

That's when we realized that adding extra ingredients to the swirl might not be as effective as examining the ingredients that were already in it: ½ cup of granulated sugar and 1 tablespoon of ground cinnamon per loaf. We baked more loaves, this time trading the granulated stuff for confectioners' sugar as well as tripling the cinnamon. The loaves showed significant improvement. The powdery confectioners' sugar absorbed water from the dough, dissolving and forming a sticky paste, which was thickened by the cornstarch in the confectioners' sugar and the carbohydrates in the cinnamon. The thickened paste didn't pool at the bottom of the bread and was sticky enough to help hold the layers together as the bread expanded during proofing.

This was by far the best loaf we had made to date, but unfortunately, we still got the occasional spewing leak or gaping hole. Having already fiddled with the filling ingredients, we got to thinking about the swirl itself. A spiral was attractive but impractical, and it made us wonder if there wasn't a better way to shape the dough. We tested a multitude of different shaping techniques that created crevices in the dough that would allow the problematic gas to escape, including those for monkey bread and braids. The easiest was an attractive weave called a Russian braid, which cut down on gapping and

NOTES FROM THE TEST KITCHEN

ANATOMY OF A FAILED LOAF
Cinnamon swirl bread's inherent predicament: The dough and the filling don't mix. But the problems don't stop there.

BREAD GAPS
Because the dough and filling don't readily bind, air and steam get trapped in the spiral, compressing the bread and creating significant gaps.

FILLING RUNS
The typical filling made with granulated sugar has no sticking power and puddles at the bottom of the bread.

LOAF SPRINGS A LEAK
Thanks to the gaps and the weight of the filling, the seam of the loaf is compromised, so the filling spills out.

leaking considerably. To make it, we sprinkled the filling over the dough, rolled it into a cylinder, and then halved it lengthwise to reveal the striations of dough and filling. We then stretched these two halves slightly and twisted them together to form a tight loaf. This way, any gas that would have been trapped between the layers was able to escape, and the bread baked up tightly seamed and beautifully marbled. One last tweak: To prevent any risk of burning the raisins or the bread's sugary surface, we pushed the exposed pieces of fruit into the braid and tented the loaves with aluminum foil halfway through baking.

Finally we'd come up with the bread we'd envisioned: a burnished crust encasing airy, slightly sweet bread streaked with thick lines of gooey cinnamon filling.

Cinnamon Swirl Bread

MAKES 2 LOAVES

To achieve the proper dough consistency, make sure to weigh your ingredients. The dough will appear very wet and sticky until the final few minutes of kneading; do not be tempted to add supplemental flour.

DOUGH

- 8 tablespoons unsalted butter
- 3¾ cups (20⅔ ounces) bread flour
- ¾ cup (2¾ ounces) nonfat dry milk powder
- ⅓ cup (2⅓ ounces) granulated sugar
- 1 tablespoon instant or rapid-rise yeast
- 1½ cups (12 ounces) water, heated to 110 degrees
- 1 large egg, lightly beaten
- 1½ teaspoons salt
- 1½ cups (7½ ounces) golden raisins

FILLING

- 1 cup (4 ounces) confectioners' sugar
- 3 tablespoons ground cinnamon
- 1 teaspoon vanilla extract
- ½ teaspoon salt

- 1 large egg, lightly beaten with pinch salt

1. FOR THE DOUGH: Cut butter into 32 pieces and toss with 1 tablespoon flour; set aside to soften while mixing dough. Whisk remaining flour, milk powder, sugar, and

to knead until butter is fully incorporated and dough is smooth and elastic and clears sides of bowl, 3 to 5 minutes longer. Add raisins and mix until incorporated, 30 to 60 seconds. Transfer dough to prepared bowl and, using bowl scraper or rubber spatula, fold dough over itself by gently lifting and folding edge of dough toward middle. Turn bowl 90 degrees; fold again. Turn bowl and fold dough 6 more times (total of 8 folds). Cover tightly with plastic and transfer to middle rack of oven. Pour 3 cups boiling water into loaf pan in oven, close oven door, and allow dough to rise for 45 minutes.

3. Remove bowl from oven and gently press down on center of dough to deflate. Repeat folding (making total of 8 folds), re-cover, and return to oven until doubled in volume, about 45 minutes.

4. FOR THE FILLING: Whisk all ingredients together in bowl until well combined; set aside.

5. Grease two 8½ by 4½-inch loaf pans. Transfer dough to lightly floured counter and divide into 2 pieces. Working with 1 piece of dough, pat into rough 11 by 6-inch rectangle. With short side facing you, fold long sides in like a business letter to form 11 by 3-inch rectangle. Roll dough away from you into ball. Dust ball with flour and flatten with rolling pin into 18 by 7-inch rectangle with even ¼-inch thickness. Using spray bottle, spray dough lightly with water. Sprinkle half of filling mixture evenly over dough, leaving ¼-inch border on sides and ¾-inch border on top and bottom; spray filling lightly with water. (Filling should be speckled with water over entire surface.) With short side facing you, roll dough away from you into firm cylinder. Turn loaf seam side up and pinch closed; pinch ends closed. Dust loaf lightly on all sides with flour and let rest for 10 minutes. Repeat with second ball of dough and remaining filling.

6. Working with 1 loaf at a time, use bench scraper to cut loaf in half lengthwise; turn halves so cut sides are facing up. Gently stretch each half into 14-inch length. Line up pieces of dough and pinch 2 ends of strips together.

yeast together in bowl of stand mixer fitted with dough hook. Add water and egg and mix on medium-low speed until cohesive mass forms, about 2 minutes, scraping down bowl as needed. Cover mixing bowl with plastic wrap and let stand for 20 minutes.

2. Adjust oven rack to middle position and place loaf or cake pan on bottom of oven. Grease large bowl. Remove plastic from mixer bowl, add salt, and mix on medium-low speed until dough is smooth and elastic and clears sides of bowl, 7 to 15 minutes. With mixer running, add butter a few pieces at a time, and continue

To braid, take piece on left and lay over piece on right. Repeat, keeping cut side up, until pieces of dough are tightly twisted. Pinch ends together. Transfer loaf, cut side up, to prepared loaf pan; push any exposed raisins into seams of braid. Repeat with second loaf. Cover loaves loosely with plastic, return to oven, and allow to rise for 45 minutes. Remove loaves and water pan from oven; heat oven to 350 degrees. Allow loaves to rise at room temperature until almost doubled in size, about 45 minutes (tops of loaves should rise about 1 inch over lip of pans).

7. Brush loaves with egg mixture. Bake until crust is well browned, about 25 minutes. Reduce oven temperature to 325 degrees, tent loaves with aluminum foil, and continue to bake until internal temperature registers 200 degrees, 15 to 25 minutes longer.

8. Transfer pans to wire rack and let cool for 5 minutes. Remove loaves from pans, return to rack, and cool to room temperature before slicing, about 2 hours.

NOTES FROM THE TEST KITCHEN

WEAVING CINNAMON SWIRL BREAD, RUSSIAN-STYLE
The benefit of a Russian braid—other than good looks—is that it solves the gapping that plagues swirl breads. The twisted shape tightly seals the pieces of dough together while providing plenty of escape routes for the excess air that would otherwise compress the dough and create tunnels in the loaf.

1. Using bench scraper or sharp chef's knife, cut filled dough in half lengthwise. Turn halves so cut sides are facing up.

2. With cut sides up, stretch each half into 14-inch length.

3. Pinch 2 ends of strips together. To braid, take left strip of dough and lay it over right strip of dough. Repeat braiding, keeping cut sides face up, until pieces are tightly twisted. Pinch ends together.

MAKING A STICKY FILLING THAT STICKS
The cinnamon-sugar swirl isn't just for flavor; it needs to function as an adhesive between the pieces of dough. Here's how we altered the typical formula.

POWDERED SUGAR
Confectioners' sugar contains cornstarch that thickens the filling.

LOTS OF CINNAMON
Cinnamon contains starches that thicken the filling and help it form a sticky paste.

SPRITZ OF WATER
Lightly misting the dough before and after adding the filling creates extra adhesiveness.

A BETTER BASE FOR CINNAMON SWIRL BREAD
The usual base for cinnamon swirl bread is American sandwich bread, but we looked to a different source: *shokupan,* Japan's version of the same loaf. Shokupan relies on lots of fat, high-protein flour, and thorough kneading to create a crumb that's feathery light yet still strong enough to support a gooey cinnamon filling.

JAPANESE SHOKUPAN

BAKED EGGS

✓ **WHY THIS RECIPE WORKS:** Baked eggs can be hard to get right. We wanted a creamy, slightly runny yolk and a tender white—in the same ramekin. The answer turned out to be insulation—that is, adding a spinach cream sauce to provide a barrier between the egg and the very hot sides of the ramekin. We also found that pulling the eggs from the oven before they were done and allowing carryover cooking to finish the job, delivered first-rate baked eggs.

SCRAMBLED, HARD BOILED, OR OVER EASY ARE FINE for everyday breakfast, but when we're hosting brunch, we want an egg dish with a little more substance and style. On those occasions, we're tempted to turn to baked eggs. The preparation might be a bit old-school, but when done well, it's undeniably elegant: individual ramekins (often lined with a dairy-enriched base or enhanced with savory add-ins), each filled with a gently set white surrounding a rich, runny yolk. It's a great dish for entertaining since there's no last-minute cooking at the stove.

But the reality is that most recipes fail in one of two predictable ways. We've enjoyed perfectly runny, creamy yolks and tender whites, but rarely both in the same ramekin. It turns out that there's concrete egg science behind the problem: Yolks begin to thicken and set at temperatures between 145 and 158 degrees, but, maddeningly, the whites don't set until they hit 155 to 180 degrees. That means that in order to achieve the set-white, runny-yolk ideal, the cook must work some magic, manipulating the cooking process so that the white firms up before the yolk, not the other way around. It was a tall order, so we stockpiled eggs, rounded up all the ramekins in the test kitchen, and got crackin'.

Most of the methods we came across fell into one of two categories: low and slow or high and fast. The gentlest cooked the eggs (often set in a water bath to temper the heat transfer) for 40 minutes in a 200-degree oven. The speediest called for fewer than 10 minutes of baking with the oven cranked to its maximum temperature. We even came across a more direct (and rather drastic) solution to the white-yolk differential in legendary French chef Auguste Escoffier's *Larousse Gastronomique*, in which he suggested separating the eggs, baking the whites alone until they began to set, and then adding the yolks to the ramekins. We decided not to go there, though; separating eggs and returning the yolks to the whites midway through cooking was hardly the fuss-free approach we were looking for.

Instead, we played it safe and decided to start by experimenting with gentle-heat methods. In addition to trying a water bath, we even tested nestling the ramekins in salt (a weaker heat conductor and therefore a better insulator than water). All of these approaches proved highly effective at preventing overcooked extremes—tough, rubbery whites and pasty, chalky yolks—but the yolk still invariably thickened before the white was fully set.

Maybe, we thought, increasing the heat would help establish the large temperature difference we needed between the edge of the ramekin (where the whites were) and the center (the yolks). For that we turned to the broiler. But our first attempt was a disaster. Just a few minutes under the blazing heat was too much: At the surface, the whites were blistered and the yolks dry; digging a spoon underneath revealed a loose, watery mess. We knocked the temperature down to 500 degrees and tried filling each ramekin with a tablespoon of heavy cream (the liquid would help conduct heat) and then preheating it for a couple of minutes in hopes of giving the whites a head start on cooking. When the cream-filled ramekins were hot, we slid an egg into each one and then returned them to the oven to finish. The results? Mixed. After 3 to 6 minutes of baking, the whites occasionally emerged set around partially runny yolks. Other times, though, the whites in direct contact with the scorching ramekins browned and turned rubbery. What's more, doneness varied wildly within the same batch due to hot and cold spots in the oven. Quick fixes like rotating the ramekins and changing the position of the oven racks didn't significantly improve matters. The only way to bake them all to the ideal doneness was to open the oven repeatedly for quick checks with an instant-read thermometer and then pull the ramekins out of the oven at different times to account for the uneven baking. Escoffier's separated-egg method was beginning to sound like a walk in the park.

BAKED EGGS FLORENTINE

We took a step back and reviewed our results thus far. Maybe we just needed a more substantial buffer than the skimpy layer of cream between the ramekin and the egg. With that in mind, we decided to experiment with a solid, fixing on one of our omelet favorites: spinach. We simply defrosted frozen spinach, wrung it dry, briefly sautéed it, and mixed in some heavy cream to make a more cohesive cushion for the eggs.

The result wasn't disastrous, but it wasn't perfect either, mostly because the creamed spinach was still loose enough that the egg white could swim under and around it, coming into direct contact with the bottom and sides of the hot ramekin, where it seized up and browned. Plus the simple spinach–heavy cream mixture tasted a bit too rich and dull. Our next order of business: Thicken up the spinach barrier so that the egg could no longer leak through and, while we were at it, work some supporting flavors into the mix.

We decided on a roux to tighten things up, so we melted some butter, added a minced shallot for depth, and then whisked in some flour. Instead of heavy cream, we poured in half-and-half, along with grated Parmesan cheese. We stirred the thawed and squeezed spinach into the cheesy sauce, with pinches of ground nutmeg, dry mustard, salt, and pepper. The creamy, well-seasoned mixture tasted good enough to eat on its own, so we spooned about ¼ cup into each ramekin (so there was enough to push halfway up the sides), loaded them into a large baking dish for easy transport, and popped the vessel into the hot oven to preheat for a few minutes before adding an egg to each cup.

When we pulled the baking dish out of the oven 10 minutes after adding the eggs, we knew we were on the right track. The surfaces of the eggs looked a bit scathed from the blast of heat (nothing a spritz of vegetable oil before baking couldn't fix), but the hot creamed spinach barrier had effectively cradled the whites so that they were tender throughout and the yolks were still jiggly. But as we waited a few minutes for the piping hot eggs to cool down enough to taste, we noticed the yolks firming up. And by the time we could comfortably eat a spoonful, carryover cooking had ruined our breakfast, leaving us with rubbery whites and chalky yolks.

HOW NOT TO BAKE EGGS
The inherent challenge to achieving a perfectly cooked baked egg is that the yolk needs to stay liquid (with a temperature hovering around 145), while the whites need to solidify (with a temperature of 170 degrees). Here are some of the wrong turns we took before getting both components to cook just right.

WATERBATH
THEORY: Water slows the heat transfer, giving the whites time to solidify without overcooking the yolks.
OUTCOME: Perfect whites but pasty yolks.

SALT BED
THEORY: Salt is an even better insulator than water, providing more protection to the yolks.
OUTCOME: Perfect whites; slightly less pasty yolks.

BLAZING HOT RAMEKINS
THEORY: The walls of preheated ramekins should give the whites a head start without harming the yolks.
OUTCOME: Perfect yolks— and blistered whites.

Because of residual heat, we would have to remove the eggs from the oven shy of their ideal final temperature (155 degrees) and allow them to finish cooking on the counter. After baking several more batches, we found that the eggs had to be pulled out when they looked quite underdone. This was at about the 7-minute mark, when the whites registered only 135 degrees, were just barely opaque, and trembled like Jell-O. But what a difference a 10-minute rest made. When we nicked the rested eggs with our fork, the whites were fully set (having climbed to the target 155 degrees), and the yolks gushed out their rich, golden sauce. Since taking the individual temperature of six eggs was a hassle, we were happy to find during subsequent tests that we could abandon the thermometer—the jiggly appearance of the whites was a consistent indicator of when to remove the eggs from the oven.

Knowing we had solved the great baked egg conundrum tasted almost as good as that first bite of tender egg coated in Parmesan-laced creamed spinach. The only thing missing was some toast—and perhaps a mimosa.

Baked Eggs Florentine
SERVES 6

In order for the eggs to cook properly, it is imperative to add them to the hot, filling–lined ramekins quickly. Prepare by cracking eggs into separate bowls or teacups while the filled ramekins are heating. Use 6-ounce ramekins with 3¼-inch diameters, measured from the inner lip. We developed this recipe using a glass baking dish; if using a metal baking pan, reduce the oven temperature to 425 degrees. This recipe can be doubled and baked in two 13 by 9-inch dishes. If doubling, increase the baking times in steps 3 and 4 by 1 minute.

- 2 tablespoons unsalted butter
- 1 large shallot, minced
- 1 tablespoon all-purpose flour
- ¾ cup half-and-half
- 10 ounces frozen spinach, thawed and squeezed dry
- 2 ounces Parmesan cheese, grated (1 cup)
  Salt and pepper
- ⅛ teaspoon dry mustard
- ⅛ teaspoon ground nutmeg
  Pinch cayenne pepper
- 6 large eggs
  Vegetable oil spray

1. Adjust oven rack to middle position and heat oven to 500 degrees.

2. Melt butter in medium saucepan over medium heat. Add shallot and cook, stirring occasionally, until softened, about 3 minutes. Stir in flour and cook, stirring constantly, for 1 minute. Gradually whisk in half-and-half; bring mixture to boil, whisking constantly. Simmer, whisking frequently, until thickened, 2 to 3 minutes. Remove pan from heat and stir in spinach, Parmesan, ¾ teaspoon salt, ½ teaspoon pepper, mustard, nutmeg, and cayenne.

3. Lightly spray six 6-ounce ramekins with oil spray. Evenly divide spinach filling among ramekins. Using back of spoon, push filling 1 inch up sides of ramekins to create ⅛-inch thick layer. Shape remaining filling in bottom of ramekin into 1½-inch diameter mound, making shallow indentation in center of mound large enough to hold egg yolk. Place filled ramekins into 13 by 9-inch glass baking dish. Bake until filling just starts to brown, about 7 minutes, rotating dish halfway through baking.

4. While filling is heating, crack eggs (taking care not to break yolks) into individual cups or bowls. Remove baking dish with ramekins from oven and place on wire rack. Gently pour eggs from cups into hot ramekins, centering egg yolk in filling. Spray surface of each egg with oil spray and sprinkle each with pinch of salt. Return baking dish to oven and bake until whites are just opaque but still tremble, 6 to 8 minutes, rotating dish halfway through baking.

5. Remove dish from oven and, using tongs, transfer ramekins to wire rack. Let stand until whites are firm and set (yolks should still be runny), about 10 minutes. Serve immediately.

TO MAKE AHEAD: Follow recipe through step 3, skipping step of baking lined ramekins. Refrigerate for up to 3 days. To serve, heat lined ramekins, directly from refrigerator, for additional 3 to 4 minutes (10 to 11 minutes total) before proceeding with recipe.

VARIATION
Baked Eggs Lorraine
Wash 1 pound leeks and slice white and light green parts thin. Cook 2 slices bacon cut into ½-inch pieces in medium saucepan over medium heat until crisp, about 10 minutes. Transfer bacon to paper towel–lined plate. Add leeks and cook until softened, about 10 minutes. Transfer leeks to plate with bacon. Proceed with recipe, omitting shallot and reducing butter to 1 tablespoon. Substitute bacon and leek mixture for spinach and ½ cup shredded Gruyère cheese for Parmesan.

Spicy FALL SWEETS

Sheets of fragrant gingersnaps cool on racks in preparation for filming.

CRISP, COOL DAYS IN AUTUMN ARE MADE FOR NIBBLING SWEETS laden with warm spices alongside a steaming cup of tea. But it can be tricky to bring assertive spices like cinnamon and cloves into balance in baked goods, and often the spices just serve to mask other problems in flavor and texture.

Take pumpkin bread: It has all the potential to be a quintessential fall treat. But while loaves of pumpkin bread are rarely terrible, they're usually lackluster at best. Our goal was to create a spectacular pumpkin bread—moist, with a light crumb and deep pumpkin flavor enhanced, not overwhelmed, by a balanced amount of spice. Some recipes rely on freshly made pumpkin puree, but isn't it called a quick bread? We'd be reaching for canned puree so this treat didn't become an all-day project. The problem is that canned pumpkin can taste, well, canned. We'd need to find a way to rid canned puree of its less-than-fresh taste.

In theory, gingersnaps are another perfect cool-weather treat. But these cookies rarely live up to their name; most recipes produce cookies with brittle edges but chewy centers, and store-bought versions have plenty of snap but barely any ginger flavor. Could we come up with a recipe for a crisp, crunchy cookie with a crackly top and assertive ginger flavor? To get a truly snappy gingersnap, we'd need to find ways to cut back on moisture—the culprit behind cookies without any snap. Summer's over, folks. Let's head into the test kitchen for some of our favorite fall treats.

PUMPKIN BREAD

PUMPKIN BREAD

✔ **WHY THIS RECIPE WORKS:** Although most recipes for pumpkin bread are pleasantly sweet and spicy, they're nothing to write home about. For a bread with rich pumpkin flavor and enough spices to enhance rather than overwhelm the flavor of our pumpkin, we used a few strategies. To rid canned pumpkin puree of its raw flavor and bring out its richness, we cooked it on top of the stove just until it began to caramelize. To replace some of the lost moisture from cooking the puree and offset some of the sweetness, we added buttermilk and softened cream cheese to the mix. A modest hand with spices and a sweet streusel sprinkled over the top of the bread gave us perfect pumpkin bread.

AFTER TESTING A HALF-DOZEN DIFFERENT RECIPES for pumpkin bread, we found ourselves thinking of it as the average Joe of quick breads: No loaf was remarkably bad—and none was remarkably good. They were all just OK.

But if we're going to make something, even a quick bread, we want it to be more than OK: We want it to be great, something to make guests exclaim rather than yawn. For that, we knew we'd need a bread that had just the right texture—neither too dense nor too cakey—and a rich pumpkin flavor that was properly tempered with sweetness and gently enhanced rather than obscured by spices.

We reasoned that the best pumpkin bread needed to begin with the best pumpkin puree, which, of course, would mean made from scratch rather than canned. Unfortunately, after spending 2 hours seeding, roasting, scraping, and pureeing (and then washing all the dishes) we'd changed our recipe from "quick bread" to "what-a-pain bread." And after all that, the loaf made with the from-scratch puree was only marginally better than the one made from canned. Forget that idea.

But we were definitely going to have to do something to improve the canned puree, since it had noticeable off-flavors, described by tasters as "metallic" and "raw." After we failed in our attempt to mask that canned flavor by using more spices we wondered if we were overthinking the problem: The puree tasted raw, so why not just cook it? We heated a can of puree in a saucepan and stirred it over medium heat until it just barely began to caramelize. We then cooled it down and quickly stirred together another batch of bread using this cooked-down puree. When we pulled the loaves from the oven and sliced them, tasters marveled at the way the bread had changed: The pumpkin flavor was full and rich, no longer raw-tasting or metallic.

Unfortunately, though, the texture of these loaves was a little dense and dry. By cooking down the pumpkin we had driven off some of the moisture, a problem that was easily solved by adding a bit of buttermilk. But caramelizing the puree had also increased its sweetness, throwing off the balance of flavors. We needed to add a bit of tanginess to the mix. It occurred to us that, since gently tangy cream cheese is often slathered onto slices of pumpkin bread, we might try directly incorporating it into the batter. Incorporating the cream cheese into the batter was easy. We cut a block of cream cheese into small chunks, tossed them into the pan with the hot puree, and stirred—the lumps became streaks that melted away with a few swirls of the spatula.

Now that we'd gone this far, we decided maybe we could put the mixing bowl away and just stir everything together in the saucepan. We cracked our eggs into the measuring cup with the buttermilk, gave them a quick whisk and then stirred them into the puree. Next came the dry ingredients, which were easy to mix in. We divided up the batter into the prepared pans and put them into the oven. After an anxious wait, we were rewarded with loaves with perfectly balanced flavor plus just the texture we were after: moist but not greasy.

The only thing left to tackle was adding some textural contrast to our bread. We liked toasted walnuts added to the batter, but we still wanted something to complement the bread's crumb and flavor. Well, we thought, why not add something to the top? Sprinkled on just before baking, a simple streusel gave the perfect amount of sweet crunch to each slice. As a bonus, the topping prevented the surface of the loaf from getting soggy when stored overnight, so our bread was just as delicious the next day. Average Joe no longer, this was a pumpkin bread to make you sit up and take notice.

Pumpkin Bread

MAKES 2 LOAVES

The test kitchen's preferred loaf pan measures 8½ by 4½ inches; if using a 9 by 5-inch loaf pan, start checking for doneness 5 minutes early.

TOPPING

5	tablespoons packed (2¼ ounces) light brown sugar
1	tablespoon all-purpose flour
1	tablespoon unsalted butter, softened
1	teaspoon ground cinnamon
⅛	teaspoon salt

BREAD

2	cups (10 ounces) all-purpose flour
1½	teaspoons baking powder
½	teaspoon baking soda
1	(15-ounce) can unsweetened pumpkin puree
1	teaspoon salt
1½	teaspoons ground cinnamon
¼	teaspoon ground nutmeg
⅛	teaspoon ground cloves
1	cup (7 ounces) granulated sugar
1	cup packed (7 ounces) light brown sugar
½	cup vegetable oil
4	ounces cream cheese, cut into 12 pieces
4	large eggs
¼	cup buttermilk
1	cup walnuts, toasted and chopped fine

1. FOR THE TOPPING: Using fingers, mix all ingredients together in bowl until well combined and topping resembles wet sand; set aside.

2. FOR THE BREAD: Adjust oven rack to middle position and heat oven to 350 degrees. Grease two 8½ by 4½-inch loaf pans. Whisk flour, baking powder, and baking soda together in bowl.

3. Combine pumpkin puree, salt, cinnamon, nutmeg, and cloves in large saucepan over medium heat. Cook mixture, stirring constantly, until reduced to 1½ cups, 6 to 8 minutes. Remove pot from heat; stir in granulated sugar, brown sugar, oil, and cream cheese until combined. Let mixture stand for 5 minutes. Whisk until

no visible pieces of cream cheese remain and mixture is homogeneous.

4. Whisk together eggs and buttermilk. Add egg mixture to pumpkin mixture and whisk to combine. Fold flour mixture into pumpkin mixture until combined (some small lumps of flour are OK). Fold walnuts into batter. Scrape batter into prepared pans. Sprinkle topping evenly over top of each loaf. Bake until skewer inserted in center of loaf comes out clean, 45 to 50 minutes. Let loaves cool in pans on wire rack for 20 minutes. Remove loaves from pans and let cool for at least 1½ hours. Serve warm or at room temperature.

VARIATION

Pumpkin Bread with Candied Ginger
Substitute ½ teaspoon ground ginger for cinnamon in topping. Fold ⅓ cup minced crystallized ginger into batter after flour mixture has been added in step 4.

GINGERSNAPS

✓ **WHY THIS RECIPE WORKS:** We wanted to put the "snap" back in gingersnap cookies. This meant creating a cookie that not only breaks cleanly in half and crunches satisfyingly with every bite but also has an assertive ginger flavor and heat. The key to texture was reducing the moisture in the final baked cookie. We achieved this by reducing the amount of sugar (which holds on to moisture), increasing the baking soda (which created cracks in the dough where more moisture could escape), and lowering the oven temperature (which increased the baking time.) For flavor we doubled the normal amount of dried ginger but also added fresh ginger, black pepper, and cayenne to ensure our cookie had real "snap."

SWEETENED DOUGH SPICED WITH GINGER HAS BEEN around since medieval times, but the term "gingersnap" wasn't coined until the 19th century. In our mind, this nomenclature should have settled once and for all the question of whether a ginger cookie should be crisp or chewy. We've never doubted that "snap" speaks to a cookie that breaks cleanly in half and crunches with every bite.

But most gingersnap recipes that we've tried don't live up to the name. Once you get past their brittle edges, the cookies turn soft and chewy. In fact, the only gingersnaps we've had that actually snap come from a box. But these cookies always fall short on flavor. We wanted freshly baked gingersnaps with a crackly top and a texture to rival the store-bought kind, but with all-natural ginger flavor and lingering heat.

We started with the best of all of the flawed recipes we'd tried—one that at least yielded a cookie that boasted crisp edges. Like most gingersnap recipes, it called for creaming butter and brown sugar (preferred to white sugar for its caramel-like undertone) in a stand mixer, then whipping in eggs, molasses, and vanilla and incorporating the dry ingredients (flour, baking soda, salt, and ground ginger). You then chill the dough until firm, form it into balls, and bake.

We wondered if transforming this cookie from mainly chewy to crunchy could be as straightforward as cutting down on moisture. We opted not to tinker with the molasses since the cookies wouldn't be true gingersnaps without its pleasantly bitter, smoky edge. And with just a single egg and a yolk in the recipe, the idea of adjusting the egg amount didn't seem promising either. That left us with just two potential moisture sources to work with: the brown sugar and the butter.

We turned to the sugar first. We knew that brown sugar is a double-edged sword. It contributes rich, molasses flavor—but it also creates chewiness in cookies, attracting moisture during baking. Switching to granulated sugar did produce a crispier, less chewy cookie, but the loss of flavor wasn't worth it. Our only choice was to cut back on the sweetener. We found that slashing the brown sugar almost in half—from 2 to 1¼ cups—resulted in cookies that were noticeably drier and crunchier. Reducing the sugar also allowed the ginger flavor to move to the fore.

On to the butter, which is about 16 percent water. Using less butter dehydrated the cookies a bit, but new problems emerged. Without ample fat, the leaner, stiffer dough refused to spread as it baked. More importantly, these cookies didn't taste as good. Then it occurred to us that if we browned the butter, we'd eliminate some of its water while keeping its fat (and creating a rich, nutty flavor). We were pleased to find that this lower-moisture dough yielded considerably firmer cookies, and the subtle nutty taste of the browned butter turned out to be an ideal backdrop for the ginger. Stirring in the melted butter rather than creaming seemed to help matters, too: Since we were no longer whipping air into the dough, the cookie crumb was more densely packed and firmly textured. But all was not perfect: The center of the cookie was still a little too moist and didn't have the crackly top we wanted.

Previous experiments in the test kitchen gave us an idea for creating crackles: increasing the leavening. In the next series of tests, we gradually upped the baking soda. The intentional overdose caused the cookies to rise dramatically but then collapse, leaving attractive fissures on their surfaces. After experimenting with varying amounts of baking soda, we settled on a full 2 teaspoons, which created nice deep cracks without imparting any soapy flavor. We found that the overdose had several other positive effects: better browning and crispier cookies, since the cracks in the dough were allowing more moisture to escape.

GINGERSNAPS

Though these cookies were getting close, they still didn't have quite the clean, definitive snap of the box kind, so we considered the other major variable: the oven. By reducing the temperature from 350 to 300 degrees, we nearly doubled the overall baking time, which allowed the gingersnaps to gradually (and fully) dry out without burning. We also transferred the cookies to a wire rack immediately after baking, which allowed air to circulate and steam to escape from their undersides. At last, our cookies turned out crackly crisp to the core.

There was just one glitch. When we baked two sheets at once, only the cookies on the upper rack developed a uniformly crackled top. Rotating the baking sheets halfway through baking didn't improve the situation, suggesting that the cracks were produced right at the beginning of baking, when the heat radiating down from the top of the oven caused the cookies to rise and fall rapidly. The baking sheet on the lower rack was partially shielded from the oven's heat by the sheet above, causing its cookies to expand more gradually, which resulted in smoother tops. The solution proved as simple as staggering the baking: We popped one tray onto the upper rack for 15 minutes until fissures formed, moved it to the lower rack to finish baking, then placed the second sheet of cookies on the upper rack.

With the texture and appearance of our gingersnaps right where we wanted them, all that remained was to punch up their rather mild flavor. Doubling the amount of dried ginger was an obvious starting point, as was incorporating freshly grated ginger. Warm spices seemed appropriate here, and we followed the lead of many other recipes by incorporating cinnamon and cloves. But we wanted yet another layer of heat. We perused the spice cabinet once more, landing on cayenne and black pepper. The combination lent the cookies a judicious but lingering heat. Finally, to make the spices really sing, we bloomed them in the browned butter, the hot fat helping to fully release the spices' pungent aromatic compounds.

As a finishing touch, we rolled the balls of dough in granulated sugar before baking to provide a sweet exterior foil to the spicy interiors. At last, we'd found the gingersnap that we'd been craving: snappy-textured, snappy-flavored, and a snap to make.

Gingersnaps

MAKES 80 1½-INCH COOKIES

For the best results, use fresh spices. For efficiency, form the second batch of cookies while the first batch bakes. The 2 teaspoons of baking soda are essential to getting the right texture.

2½ cups (12½ ounces) all-purpose flour
2   teaspoons baking soda
½   teaspoon salt
12 tablespoons unsalted butter
2   tablespoons ground ginger
1   teaspoon ground cinnamon
¼   teaspoon ground cloves
¼   teaspoon pepper
    Pinch cayenne
1¼ cups packed (8¾ ounces) dark brown sugar
¼   cup molasses
2   tablespoons finely grated fresh ginger
1   large egg plus 1 large yolk
½   cup (3½ ounces) granulated sugar

1. Whisk flour, baking soda, and salt together in bowl. Heat butter in 10-inch skillet over medium heat until melted. Lower heat to medium-low and continue to cook, swirling pan frequently, until foaming subsides and butter is just beginning to brown, 2 to 4 minutes. Transfer butter to large bowl and whisk in ground ginger, cinnamon, cloves, pepper, and cayenne. Let cool slightly, about 2 minutes. Add brown sugar, molasses, and fresh ginger to butter mixture and whisk to combine. Add egg and yolk and whisk to combine. Add flour mixture and stir until just combined. Cover dough tightly with plastic wrap and refrigerate until firm, about 1 hour.

2. Adjust oven racks to upper-middle and lower-middle positions and heat oven to 300 degrees. Line 2 baking sheets with parchment paper. Place granulated sugar in shallow dish. Divide dough into heaping teaspoon portions; roll dough into 1-inch balls. Working in batches of 10, roll balls in sugar to coat. Evenly space dough balls on prepared baking sheets, 20 dough balls per sheet.

3. Place 1 sheet on upper rack and bake for 15 minutes. Transfer partially baked top sheet to lower rack, rotating 180 degrees, and place second sheet of dough balls on upper rack. Continue to bake until cookies on lower tray just begin to darken around edges, 10 to 12 minutes longer. Remove lower sheet of cookies and transfer upper sheet to lower rack, rotating 180 degrees, and continue to bake until cookies begin to darken around edges, 15 to 17 minutes longer. Slide baked cookies, still on parchment, to wire rack and let cool completely before serving. Let baking sheets cool slightly and line with parchment again.

Repeat step 2 with remaining dough balls. (Cooled cookies can be stored at room temperature for up to 2 weeks.)

TO MAKE AHEAD: Dough can be refrigerated for up to 2 days or frozen for up to 1 month. Let frozen dough thaw overnight in refrigerator before proceeding with recipe. Let dough stand at room temperature for 30 minutes before shaping.

NOTES FROM THE TEST KITCHEN

PUTTING THE SNAP IN GINGERSNAPS
The hallmark of gingersnap cookie texture—big crunch—came down to one key factor: drying out the dough.

1. Butter is 16 percent water. Brown it before whisking it with sugar, eggs, and flour to eliminate moisture.

2. Brown sugar holds on to water, even after baking. Use just 1¼ cups for crispier cookies.

3. Bake cookies in low (300-degree) oven to give dough ample time to gradually—but thoroughly— dry out.

4. Stagger baking by baking each tray on top rack before moving it to cooler bottom rack to create fissures that allow moisture to escape.

RATING MOLASSES

Molasses adds a distinctive rich, caramelized flavor to many recipes, including our gingersnaps. It is made by boiling the juice of sugarcane or sugar beets and then extracting sugar crystals through a centrifuge. More stages of boiling (and extraction) may follow to produce an increasingly intense flavor. A first boil typically corresponds to mild or "Barbados" molasses; a second boil produces a style sometimes called "full"; and a third creates blackstrap, the most assertive and bitter molasses. We recently sampled five national brands, ruling out blackstrap for its overpowering flavor and including only unsulphured versions, plain and in our gingersnaps. We found that descriptive names on labels—including "mild," "original," "full," and "robust"—are not a reliable indicator of how the molasses tastes; a brand labeled "mild" rated among the strongest for flavor. But we also found that when it comes to baking, it doesn't matter what molasses you buy (as long as it's not blackstrap). Though some brands tasted bitter or burnt when sampled straight, baking mellowed out their differences. All five brands were equally acceptable in cookies, although we did identify a winner, which had a "caramelized," "spicy" taste when sampled plain. Brands are listed in order of preference. See AmericasTestKitchen.com for updates to this testing.

RECOMMENDED

BRER RABBIT All Natural Unsulphured Molasses Mild Flavor
PRICE: $4.27 for 12 oz
COMMENTS: This assertive, first-boil molasses was rated highest for strength of molasses flavor, with tasters calling it "bitter in a good way" and "acidic" yet "balanced." Its "strong and raisiny" taste was "very straightforward," and the "pleasantly bitter bite" and "deep, caramelized flavor" that were noticed when tasted plain struck a "sweet-spicy" balance when baked in cookies.

PLANTATION Barbados Unsulphured Molasses
PRICE: $7.18 for 15 oz
COMMENTS: This first-boil molasses rated sweetest in the plain tasting. Tasters picked up notes of "brown sugar," "honey," and "plum." They also dubbed this molasses "lighter," with a "politely abrupt finish" that "doesn't hit me like a punch in the face."

GRANDMA'S Molasses Unsulphured Original
PRICE: $2.89 for 12 oz
COMMENTS: This "fruity" and "cognaclike" molasses is made from unprocessed cane juice, meaning that it's packaged even before the first-boil stage, without any sugar extracted. It was "balanced," without the harshness of other brands. Tasters called it "prunelike" and "sweeter," with a "mulled apple cider" and "warm spice" flavor.

RECOMMENDED *(cont.)*

GRANDMA'S Molasses Unsulphured Robust
PRICE: $4.27 for 12 oz
COMMENTS: This first-boil molasses had a "dark and smoky" flavor that reminded our tasters of "old-fashioned candy," "Cracker Jack," and "burnt Fig Newton filling." A "hint of smokiness" was noted, with a "spicy, slightly sulfurous aftertaste."

RECOMMENDED WITH RESERVATIONS

BRER RABBIT All Natural Unsulphured Molasses Full Flavor
PRICE: $3.57 for 12 oz
COMMENTS: This molasses, which had an overpowering flavor described as "toffeelike," is a second-boil product, which may explain its acrid bitterness when sampled straight. Tasters likened it to "burnt rubber" and "coffee grounds." Its full flavor fared better in cookies, where it was deemed "deep and pleasantly sweet" as well as "complex."

Great American CLASSICS

A rotating cake stand and offset spatula aren't essential to frost Carrot Layer Cake, but it does make the job a bit easier.

IN THE PANTHEON OF ALL-AMERICAN SWEETS, TWO OF OUR LONGTIME favorites are carrot cake and peanut butter cookies. But over time, these two desserts seem to have lost their luster.

Nowadays, carrot cake is usually passed up in favor of more elegant, more elaborate confections. But carrot cake doesn't have to remain stuck in the 1970s, when it was best known as a humble but healthy dessert that used oil instead of butter. (And newsflash: It was never that healthy.) We wanted to transform this classic from simple snack cake to drop-dead gorgeous dessert. We imagined a fancy multitiered confection of sweet, delicately spiced cake layered with the trademark tangy cream cheese frosting, the whole thing covered in crunchy nuts. But beauty is more than skin deep, so we'd need to completely reengineer the recipes for both cake and frosting, so that the thin layers of cake could support the frosting and slice neatly.

Unlike traditional carrot cake, peanut butter cookies don't have a hard time getting noticed, thanks to the distinctive crosshatch pattern emblazoned on every cookie. But once sampled, they get few takers for seconds. Why? They lack real, deep, peanut flavor. We wanted a cookie that packed a peanut wallop. Our research revealed that cooking peanut butter dulls its flavor, so what's a baker to do? We thought a sandwich cookie with a fresh (read: uncooked) peanut butter filling might be the answer. That's where we'd start in our quest. Let's get baking.

CARROT LAYER CAKE

✔ **WHY THIS RECIPE WORKS:** This American classic has a lot going for it: moist cake, delicate spices, tangy cream cheese frosting. But its presentation could use some refinement. We wanted to reengineer humble carrot cake as a four-tier, nut-crusted confection that could claim its place among the most glamorous desserts. To start, we found that baking this cake in a half sheet pan meant that it baked and cooled in far less time than a conventional layer cake, and—cut into quarters—it produced four thin, level layers that did not require splitting or trimming before frosting. Adding extra baking soda raised the pH of the batter, ensuring that the coarsely shredded carrots softened during the shortened baking time. Buttermilk powder in the frosting reinforced the tangy flavor of the cream cheese without making the frosting too soft.

AS SHOWSTOPPER DESSERTS GO, CARROT CAKE IS often overlooked, and that's a shame. Carrot cake is a relatively easy option since the typical "dump and stir" method means there's no need to haul out the stand mixer. And between its moist, fragrantly spiced crumb chock-full of plump raisins and crunchy nuts and its luxurious cream cheese frosting, it brings more to the table than many desserts. But traditional carrot cake is a rather homely confection, a snack cake typically baked in a serviceable 13 by 9-inch pan and topped with frumpy-looking frosting. That's fine for an informal family dinner but not as the finale for a fancier occasion.

Building a layer cake would be the obvious way to dress it up, but stacking delicately slim slabs into a lofty tower presents plenty of obstacles. For starters, the carrots make the cake sticky and prone to breaking—and a real nightmare to slice horizontally. Additionally, a stack of moist, heavy cake comes with a risk of toppling. We've seen bakeries pull off tall, stately carrot cakes but not without compromising the frosting. To make it thick enough to keep the cake structurally sound, they load it up with powdered sugar, dulling the characteristic tang of the cream cheese. For layers that were both slender and sturdy, we'd have to lighten the crumb without sacrificing moisture and rework the frosting to support a taller profile, but we were determined to avoid a sickly sweet concoction.

Putting aside the frosting for the moment, we made a first attempt at the cake: We whisked flour, baking powder, salt, cinnamon, cloves, and nutmeg together in one bowl, and eggs, brown sugar, vanilla extract, and vegetable oil (used more often than butter) in another. We folded shredded carrots, raisins, and chopped pecans into the wet ingredients; added the dry; divided the batter between two 9-inch round cake pans; and pushed them into a 350-degree oven to bake for 45 minutes. (Because the vegetable adds moisture to the batter, carrot cakes bake longer than other types.) Once the cakes were cool, we tried to neatly trim and halve them. It was a disaster. The tacky crumbs stuck to our knife as we tried to shave off the domed top of each layer, and the blade seemed to snag every nut as we sliced the cakes horizontally. Moving the sliced layers without breaking them also proved nearly impossible.

We were starting to reconsider the layers when, on a visit to a wholesale club, we spotted a rectangular layer cake that stood four tiers high. The layers had been baked in shallow jelly roll pans, then stacked with frosting in between. The slender, uniform layers were intriguing. Could we bake our cake in a rimmed baking sheet, slice it into four equal pieces, and stack them into a tall rectangular cake?

As it turned out, this concept had a lot going for it: In a standard 18 by 13-inch rimmed baking sheet, the cake baked in a mere 16 minutes and took only 30 minutes to cool. And because the middle set almost as quickly as the edges, the cake didn't dome, rendering the trimming step unnecessary. Feeling smug, we summoned tasters—but it took only one bite of our four-tier confection for them to identify a major flaw that brought us down to earth: The carrots were crunchy. Thanks to the drastically reduced baking time, the coarse shreds hadn't had a chance to soften.

We tried cooking and pureeing the carrots before incorporating them into the batter, but their texture was completely lost. We didn't want crunch, but we did want the star of the dessert to be identifiable. Then a light bulb went on: What if we added baking soda—an alkali—to

CARROT LAYER CAKE

the batter to raise its pH and help the carrots break down? We added a teaspoon of baking soda to another batch and waited. Thanks to the baking soda's pH-boosting effect, the carrots were visible but tender, and the crumb was incredibly light yet moist, with no off-flavors. We had just two more changes to make before moving on to the frosting: Since the pecans that caught on our knife during slicing caused the cake to tear, we eliminated them for now. And because the raisins looked clunky in these slim, lighter-than-ever layers, we swapped in daintier currants.

The next step: a tangy frosting. Most recipes are basic mixtures of butter, cream cheese, and confectioners' sugar, but the ratios vary. Go heavy on the cream cheese and you get a rich, bright frosting, but one that is perilously soft and likely to trickle down the sides of the cake or—even worse—cause the layers to slip and slide. Adding sugar solves the structural issues but masks the cream cheese flavor. The standard recipe we tried fell victim to both of these faults: It was too soft and too sweet. Adding acidic lemon juice, sour cream, and yogurt punched up the tang but also introduced more liquid, necessitating more sugar for thickening—a vicious circle.

It wasn't until we started rummaging through the test kitchen pantry for ideas that we came across a potential fix: buttermilk powder. We wondered if its pleasant tang would do the trick in our frosting. We added 2 tablespoons to our frosting and were delighted to find that the mixture was not only flavorful but also markedly tangy. In fact, adding ⅓ cup of powder made the frosting so potent that we could increase the sugar by 1 cup, for a consistency that was structurally sound but still not overly sweet.

We were getting close, but our cake was not yet special-occasion ready. The cut surfaces released crumbs as we assembled the layers, so while the frosting on top of the cake looked pristine, the sides were a wreck. So we brought the nuts back into the equation. To camouflage the imperfections—and satisfy tasters who missed the crunch of the pecans in the cake—we pressed toasted pecans onto the crumb-speckled sides.

With nothing but a sheet pan and the surprise help of a few pantry ingredients, we'd managed to reengineer humble carrot cake as a four-tier, nut-crusted confection that could claim its place among the most glamorous desserts.

Carrot Layer Cake

SERVES 10 TO 12

Shred the carrots on the large holes of a box grater or in a food processor fitted with the shredding disk. Do not substitute liquid buttermilk for the buttermilk powder. To ensure the proper spreading consistency for the frosting, use cold cream cheese. If your baked cake is of an uneven thickness, adjust the orientation of the layers as they are stacked to produce a level cake. Assembling this cake on a cardboard cake round trimmed to about a 6 by 8-inch rectangle makes it easy to press the pecans onto the sides of the frosted cake.

CAKE

1¾ cups (8¾ ounces) all-purpose flour
2 teaspoons baking powder
1 teaspoon baking soda
1½ teaspoons ground cinnamon
¾ teaspoon ground nutmeg
½ teaspoon salt
¼ teaspoon ground cloves
1¼ cups packed (8¾ ounces) light brown sugar
¾ cup vegetable oil
3 large eggs
1 teaspoon vanilla extract
2⅔ cups shredded carrots (4 carrots)
⅔ cup dried currants

FROSTING

3 cups (12 ounces) confectioners' sugar
16 tablespoons unsalted butter, softened
⅓ cup buttermilk powder
2 teaspoons vanilla extract
¼ teaspoon salt
12 ounces cream cheese, chilled and cut into 12 equal
    pieces
2 cups (8 ounces) pecans, toasted and chopped coarse

1. FOR THE CAKE: Adjust oven rack to middle position and heat oven to 350 degrees. Grease 18 by 13-inch rimmed baking sheet, line with parchment paper, and grease parchment. Whisk flour, baking powder, baking soda, cinnamon, nutmeg, salt, and cloves together in large bowl.

2. Whisk sugar, oil, eggs, and vanilla together in second bowl until mixture is smooth. Stir in carrots and currants. Add flour mixture and fold with rubber spatula until mixture is just combined.

3. Transfer batter to prepared sheet and smooth surface with offset spatula. Bake until center of cake is firm to touch, 15 to 18 minutes. Cool in pan on wire rack for 5 minutes. Invert cake onto wire rack (do not remove parchment), then reinvert onto second wire rack. Cool cake completely, about 30 minutes.

4. FOR THE FROSTING: Using stand mixer fitted with paddle, beat sugar, butter, buttermilk powder, vanilla, and salt together on low speed until smooth, about 2 minutes, scraping down bowl as needed. Increase speed to medium-low; add cream cheese, 1 piece at a time; and mix until smooth, about 2 minutes.

5. Transfer cooled cake to cutting board, parchment side down. Using sharp chef's knife, cut cake and parchment in half crosswise, then lengthwise into 4 even quarters.

6. Place 6 by 8-inch cardboard rectangle on cake platter. Place 1 cake layer, parchment side up, on cardboard and carefully remove parchment. Using offset spatula, spread ⅔ cup frosting evenly over top, right to edge of cake.

Repeat with 2 more layers of cake, pressing lightly to adhere and frosting each layer with ⅔ cup frosting. Top with last cake layer and spread 1 cup frosting evenly over top. Spread remaining frosting evenly over sides of cake. (It's fine if some crumbs show through frosting on sides, but if you go back to smooth top of cake, be sure that spatula is free of crumbs.)

7. Hold cake with 1 hand and gently press chopped pecans onto sides with other hand. Chill for at least 1 hour before serving. (The frosted cake can be refrigerated for up to 24 hours before serving.)

NOTES FROM THE TEST KITCHEN

STRUCTURAL SOLUTION

For a cream cheese frosting that's stiff enough to hold several layers of cake in place, we use tangy buttermilk powder—along with confectioners' sugar—to add body.

PEANUT BUTTER SANDWICH COOKIES

✔ WHY THIS RECIPE WORKS: We wanted a cookie so packed with peanut flavor that it needed no crosshatch to identify it. In the research for our testing, we found that peanut butter flavor molecules can be trapped by flour in baked applications, so we ratcheted up the flavor's intensity by sandwiching an uncooked peanut butter filling between our cookies. Adding a full cup of confectioners' sugar to the filling made it firm enough to stay in place, and we balanced the sweetness with a relatively low-sugar cookie component. Extra liquid and extra baking soda gave our cookies the thin, flat dimensions and sturdy crunch that are vital to a sandwich cookie.

TO PEANUT BUTTER OBSESSIVES LIKE US, WE'VE ALWAYS had an issue with peanut butter cookies: The raw dough tastes better than the baked treats. This is because in the presence of heat, the starch granules in flour soak up peanut flavor molecules like a sponge, reducing their aroma and limiting their ability to interact with our taste buds. The upshot is that a traditional cross-hatched peanut butter cookie becomes flavor-challenged as soon as it hits the oven.

It occurred to us that a sandwich cookie—two peanut butter cookies enclosing a filling made primarily with uncooked (read: full-flavored) peanut butter—might be the solution. The cookies themselves would have to be quite thin and flat (so you could comfortably eat two of them sandwiched with filling) as well as crunchy, to contrast with the creamy center. We also wanted our cookies to have the simplicity of a drop cookie: no chilling of the dough, no slicing, no rolling, and no cutting.

We started with the filling. Most recipes call for blending peanut butter and confectioners' sugar (granulated sugar remains too gritty and doesn't provide much thickening power) with a creamy element, such as butter, cream cheese, or marshmallow crème. We settled on butter, which gave us the silkiest consistency and the purest peanut butter flavor. We softened 3 tablespoons of butter with ¾ cup of creamy peanut butter in the microwave

and, to keep the peanut flavor in the forefront, stirred in a modest ½ cup of confectioners' sugar. This low-sugar filling tasted great, but it was far too soft, squirting out from our placeholder cookies as soon as we pressed them together. To thicken things up, we ultimately had to double the sugar amount. We would have to balance the filling with a significantly less sweet cookie.

Setting the filling aside, we put together a dough with 3 tablespoons of butter, ½ cup of peanut butter, two eggs, 1 cup of sugar, 2 cups of flour, and ½ teaspoon each of baking soda and salt. After portioning the dough and baking it at 350 degrees for about 12 minutes, we had cookies that weren't bad for a first try, but they were too thick and soft. We wanted more spread, more crunch, and—if we could pack it in—more peanut flavor.

Our first change was to scrap one of the eggs (they make baked goods cakey), replacing it with 3 tablespoons of milk. We knew that moisture level influences how much cookie dough will spread in the oven, so we tried to increase the moisture level by cutting back on flour. Since our goal was also a super-nutty-tasting cookie, we decided to replace a full cup of flour with finely chopped peanuts, which would absorb far less moisture as well as add welcome crunch and peanut flavor. These changes helped, but the cookies still weren't spreading enough.

What would happen if we actually took out all of the flour? Flourless peanut butter cookie recipes abound on the Internet, but we found that the resulting cookies were not that much thinner. And they were also far too crumbly. We added flour back incrementally, finding that a ratio of ¾ cup of flour to ½ cup of peanut butter created relatively thin, nutty-tasting cookies that were still sturdy enough to serve as a shell for the filling. Finally, to get them thinner, we used our wet hands to squash the portioned dough into even 2-inch rounds.

We were almost there, but we had one final trick up our sleeves: tinkering with the baking soda. In other cookie recipes, we have found that adding extra soda causes the bubbles within dough to inflate so rapidly that they burst before the cookies set, flattening them. A mere ¼ teaspoon of baking soda would be sufficient to leaven the ¾ cup of flour in our recipe; when we quadrupled that amount to a full teaspoon, the cookies quickly puffed up in the oven and then deflated. *Voilà*: greater

PEANUT BUTTER SANDWICH COOKIES

spread, just as we had hoped. In addition, these cookies boasted a coarser, more open crumb, which provided extra routes through which moisture could escape. This left the cookies even drier and crunchier—a better foil for the creamy filling.

With our creamy, peanut-y filling and ultracrunchy cookies ready to go, it was time to put the two components together. But on our first few maddening attempts, the cookies shattered into pieces as we tried to spread the too-firm filling. Then we realized that it was a matter of timing: If we prepared the filling right before assembly, it could be easily scooped and squished between the cookies while it was still warm from the microwave—no painstaking spreading necessary—after which it would cool and set to an ideal firm texture.

At last, we had a cookie with a simple, understated appearance that delivered the powerful peanut wallop promised by those pretenders sporting the traditional fork marks. These cookies are unmistakably of the peanut butter variety, no crisscrosses required.

Peanut Butter Sandwich Cookies

MAKES 24 COOKIES

Do not use unsalted peanut butter for this recipe.

COOKIES

- 1¼ cups (6¼ ounces) raw peanuts, toasted and cooled
- ¾ cup (3¾ ounces) all-purpose flour
- 1 teaspoon baking soda
- ½ teaspoon salt
- 3 tablespoons unsalted butter, melted
- ½ cup creamy peanut butter
- ½ cup (3½ ounces) granulated sugar
- ½ cup packed (3½ ounces) light brown sugar
- 3 tablespoons whole milk
- 1 large egg

FILLING

- ¾ cup creamy peanut butter
- 3 tablespoons unsalted butter
- 1 cup (4 ounces) confectioners' sugar

1. FOR THE COOKIES: Adjust oven racks to upper-middle and lower-middle positions and heat oven to 350 degrees. Line 2 baking sheets with parchment paper. Pulse peanuts in food processor until finely chopped, about 8 pulses. Whisk flour, baking soda, and salt together in bowl. Whisk melted butter, peanut butter, granulated sugar, brown sugar, milk, and egg together in second bowl. Stir flour mixture into peanut butter mixture with rubber spatula until combined. Stir in peanuts until evenly distributed.

2. Using #60 scoop or tablespoon measure, place 12 mounds, evenly spaced, on each prepared baking sheet. Using damp hand, flatten mounds until 2 inches in diameter.

3. Bake until deep golden brown and firm to touch, 15 to 18 minutes, switching and rotating baking sheets halfway through baking. Let cookies cool on baking sheets for 5 minutes. Transfer cookies to wire rack and let cool completely, about 30 minutes. Repeat portioning and baking remaining dough.

4. FOR THE FILLING: Microwave peanut butter and butter together until butter is melted and warm, about 40 seconds. Using rubber spatula, stir in confectioners' sugar until combined.

5. TO ASSEMBLE: Place 24 cookies upside down on counter. Place 1 level tablespoon (or #60 scoop) warm filling in center of each cookie. Place second cookie on top of filling, right side up, pressing gently until filling spreads to edges. Allow filling to set for 1 hour before serving. Assembled cookies can be stored at room temperature for up to 3 days.

RATING SPRINGFORM PANS

Springform pans have buckle-operated, detachable sides that ease the removal of sticky or delicate cakes, such as cheesecakes and tortes, from the pan. Because some of the desserts prepared in a springform pan, like cheesecake, are baked in a water bath, the ideal pan would form a leakproof seal between the bottom and sides to prevent batter from trickling out and moisture from seeping in. In our last test of springform pans nearly a decade ago, not one pan was truly leakproof. We decided to test these pans again, and made cheesecake and summer peach cake in five different models. Once again, not one model we tested totally prevented water from entering. Even after wrapping the pans with aluminum foil before baking, we found dark, damp patches on each cheesecake's crust where moisture had snuck in. Hence, our evaluations came down to cake release, evenness of browning, and design. Nonstick coatings were essential, as the coating helped the sides release, but the lightest and darkest pans produced under- and overbrowned cakes, respectively. We also liked models with flat (not rimmed) bases that could double as a serving plate. Brands are listed in order of preference. See AmericasTestKitchen.com for updates to this testing.

RECOMMENDED

FRIELING Handle-It 9-Inch Glass Bottom Springform Pan
MODEL: 157723 **PRICE:** $49.99
BROWNING: ★★★ **RELEASE:** ★★★ **CLEANING:** ★★★
DURABILITY: ★★★ **DESIGN:** ★★★
COMMENTS: This pricey pan may not be perfect—like the other models, its seal isn't leakproof—but it boasts plenty of features that make it our favorite: evenly browned results; near flawless release; a glass bottom that helps us monitor browning; helper handles; and sturdy, dishwasher-safe parts.

NORDIC WARE 9-Inch Leak Proof Springform Pan
MODEL: 55742 **PRICE:** $15 `BEST BUY`
BROWNING: ★★★ **RELEASE:** ★★★ **CLEANING:** ★★
DURABILITY: ★★ **DESIGN:** ★★★
COMMENTS: Despite its promise of being leakproof, this pan allowed water to seep in, just like all the others. While it performed admirably, evenly browning the peach cake, its nonstick-coated base wasn't as scratch-resistant as the glass-bottomed Frieling, and it didn't release quite as easily as our winner, resulting in a cheesecake with less than perfectly smooth sides.

CUISINART Chef's Classic Nonstick Springform Pan
MODEL: 215662 **PRICE:** $13.95
BROWNING: ★★★ **RELEASE:** ★★★ **CLEANING:** ★
DURABILITY: ★★ **DESIGN:** ★½
COMMENTS: Though both peach cake and cheesecake emerged from this model almost perfectly and beautifully browned, cleanup wasn't so effortless. The narrow crevice along the bottom of the removable sides trapped crumbs, even after several rounds in the dishwasher. The upturned rim on the base made cutting slices awkward.

RECOMMENDED WITH RESERVATIONS

WILTON Avanti Everglide Nonstick Glass Bottom Springform Pan
MODEL: 218518 **PRICE:** $21.45
BROWNING: ★ **RELEASE:** ★★★ **CLEANING:** ★
DURABILITY: ★★★ **DESIGN:** ★★
COMMENTS: The other glass-bottomed model in the lineup, this pan might be considered a replica of our winner, with one crucial difference: a nonstick coating so pale that the peach cake emerged blond in spots. Release, however, was flawless, though the slim crease ringing the bottom of the removable sides stubbornly held on to crumbs.

NOT RECOMMENDED

KAISER BAKEWARE La Forme Plus Springform Pan, 9-Inch
MODEL: 654228 **PRICE:** $48
BROWNING: ★ **RELEASE:** ★ **CLEANING:** ★★★
DURABILITY: ★★ **DESIGN:** ★
COMMENTS: For the price, we expected picture-perfect results. Instead, we got a cheesecake with an unsightly seam where the buckle fastened and, thanks to the pan's exceptionally dark coating, a peach cake that overbrowned on the exterior before the middle had a chance to cook.

French Sweets,
REFINED AND RUSTIC

Test cook Lan Lam wraps up a batch of Chocolate Truffles. Our truffles can be stored in an airtight container for up to 1 week.

MOST OF THE TIME, WE'RE ON BOARD WITH ALL-AMERICAN DESSERTS like a big fudgy piece of chocolate layer cake or a wedge of apple pie à la mode, but when we're looking for a dessert that boasts a bit more refinement, we look to the French. Two desserts we've been eager to develop in the test kitchen are chocolate truffles and French apple cake.

After a rich meal, we can think of few more elegant endings than chocolate truffles. But unless you're a seasoned candy maker, preparing truffles can be downright frustrating. Too often, attempts end in chocolates that are grainy rather than lush and smooth. And home-style recipes often deliver truffles that are too soft to hold their shape. We wanted properly firm truffles that our guests could easily pluck from a dessert plate.

When chocolate doesn't feel right on the menu, consider French apple cake. This bistro-style cake is unlike anything we've seen stateside, and its simple name doesn't do it justice. The cake is made by pouring buttery batter over sliced apples. In the oven, the batter separates into two distinct layers, baking into a custardy base around the apples and turning cakey and light on the surface. Or that's the way it should be. We found that the apples in some recipes baked up dry and leathery, while others turned to mush. Goal one: Zero in on the right variety of apple for this cake. And two: Work on the cake batter, since we found it often turned sodden and heavy. On the menu tonight: desserts with a French accent.

CHOCOLATE TRUFFLES

✓ **WHY THIS RECIPE WORKS:** The problem with many homemade truffles is that they have a dry, grainy texture. There are three keys to creating creamy, silky-smooth truffles. First, start with melted chocolate. Melting the chocolate before adding the cream allowed us to stir—rather than whisk—the two together, reducing the incorporation of air that can cause grittiness. Second, add corn syrup and butter. Corn syrup smoothed over the gritty texture of the sugar, and butter introduced silkiness. Finally, cooling down the ganache gradually before chilling prevented the formation of grainy crystals.

CHOCOLATE TRUFFLES ARE INHERENTLY SIMPLE confections. These rich, dense balls of ganache often contain nothing more than good-quality bar chocolate and heavy cream. Yet they're surprisingly difficult to get right. The chocolate-to-cream ratio must be spot-on; otherwise, the truffle will be either overly dense or too soft to hold its shape. Creating a smooth, shiny coating is even more finicky—and then you've got to contend with the mess of dipping the truffle into it. Finally, there's shaping. The pros use a pastry bag, but it takes practice to produce perfectly symmetrical pieces.

Our goal was clear: Come up with an approach that would produce flawless results for anyone, regardless of their candy-making experience. Ditching the tempered chocolate coating was one way we could abridge the process; we'd go for the more rustic approach of rolling the truffles in cocoa. Beyond that, we'd have to do some experimenting.

We threw together a basic ganache: 4 ounces of warm cream poured over 12 ounces of chopped chocolate and blended in a food processor until smooth. Then we chilled the mixture, piped it into balls, firmed the pieces in the fridge, and rolled them in cocoa. What we wanted was fudgy, silky ganache. What we got, unfortunately, was dry and gritty.

We needed a way to loosen up and smooth out the texture of the ganache without pushing it into the realm of chocolate sauce, so we tried an obvious quick fix: upping the cream. This made for a ganache that was creamier, but rolling the more-fluid mixture was nearly impossible.

Paging through our research recipes for ideas, we noticed that some called for adding butter to the ganache to make it more silky. Others also incorporated a little corn syrup, which makes the ganache feel smoother by reducing the size of the chocolate's sugar crystals; when they're too large, they can be detected as grainy. Adding a little of each helped, but even then the truffles weren't as satiny-textured as we wanted.

We'd taken the ingredient list as far as it could go, so we approached the graininess problem from another angle: the mixing method. The food processor, immersion blender, and stand mixer all produced truffles that weren't as smooth as we'd hoped. Mechanical intervention was apparently not the way to go.

Our science editor quickly fingered the problem: air. Instead of smoothing out the ganache, the high-speed mixing was incorporating too much air, causing the emulsion to break. More specifically, the droplets of fat were coating the surface of the air bubbles instead of the cocoa particles; as a result, the cocoa particles absorbed water and stuck together in larger clumps that we were detecting as graininess.

That meant we needed to do everything we could to decrease the air in the ganache. We tried hand-whisking the chocolate and warm cream, but the method still required a good bit of stirring just to melt the chocolate. We were better off premelting the chocolate in the microwave until it was almost completely fluid. (While we were at it, we microwaved the cream, too.) Then we stirred the corn syrup (plus vanilla extract and salt) into the cream and poured the liquid over the mostly melted chocolate. Instead of a whisk—specifically designed to incorporate air—we grabbed a wooden spoon, gradually working in the butter before piping and chilling the ganache. The improvement was startling. The grit wasn't gone, but it was markedly reduced.

It was time to try a technique that we'd come across in our research: Instead of chilling the ganache immediately after mixing it, some chocolatiers allow it to sit at room temperature overnight, claiming that the gradual cooling makes for a creamier product. It was worth a shot.

CHOCOLATE TRUFFLES

TRUFFLE TRIALS WE OVERCAME

Truffles may be nothing more than chocolate ganache rolled in a coating, but they're full of potential pitfalls.

DULL EXTERIOR

Tempering chocolate for the coating gives it a glossy sheen—but unless you're a professional chocolatier, it's a tricky business. One wrong move and the results can easily turn matte and look smudged.

DRIPPY MESS

Chocolate-dipped truffles must be drained—and tend to drip all over the counter.

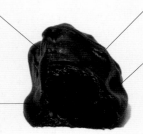

GRAINY INTERIOR

Even if the ganache looks creamy and smooth when warm, it can turn gritty and grainy as it cools.

LOPSIDED LOOKS

Piping perfectly round truffles takes a practiced, steady hand. Otherwise, the results will be lopsided.

We mixed up another batch of ganache and let it cool on the counter for 8 hours before shaping the truffles. The change was astonishing—the texture of the ganache was silky smooth, without a trace of grittiness. Our science editor explained: When melted chocolate cools and resolidifies, the crystalline structure of its cocoa butter is reorganized. Chilling the ganache in the refrigerator produced a more stable crystalline structure that melts at higher than body temperature, leading to a perception of graininess. The slower cooldown led to a different, more desirable set of crystals that literally melt in the mouth, for a sensation of ultrasmoothness. But did we really have to leave the ganache overnight? We wondered if we could get this same effect with a shorter rest at room temperature, to keep truffle making a same-day project. To our delight, we found that a 2-hour cool-down produced the same marvelously creamy texture. The only issue was that without any refrigeration, the ganache was too soft to work with. We solved this by chilling the ganache for 2 hours after cooling it on the counter—a step that didn't add back any graininess.

The only remaining glitch: shaping. We wanted to avoid a pastry bag, since perfect results take practice. But forming the truffles with a mini ice-cream scoop, a melon baller, or a measuring spoon didn't work; we ended up scraping the ganache out of the utensils with our fingers. We finally came across a promising solution from chocolatier Alice Medrich: Cool the ganache in a baking dish and then unmold the mostly solid block, cut it into squares, and roll them into rounds. This worked perfectly, the chocolate squares just soft enough to roll without cracking.

The last step before chilling, rolling the truffles in cocoa powder, was easy—provided we could keep our warm hands from smearing the chocolate. We handled the pieces as little as possible, until we realized that we could use the cocoa to our advantage. Before rolling, we lightly dusted our palms with the dry powder, which kept the melting problem in check. And once we cut the cocoa powder with a little confectioners' sugar to reduce bitterness and chalkiness, several tasters noted that they preferred this rustic, more distinct contrast to the tempered chocolate shell.

Firm, velvety smooth, and round, these truffles are plenty simple for beginners yet handsome enough to please even the most discriminating chocolatier.

Chocolate Truffles

MAKES 64 TRUFFLES

In step 5, running your knife under hot water and wiping it dry makes cutting the chocolate easier. We recommend using Callebaut Intense Dark L-60–40NV or Ghirardelli Bittersweet Chocolate Baking Bar. If giving the truffles as a gift, set them in 1½-inch candy cup liners in a gift box and keep them chilled.

GANACHE

- **2 cups (12 ounces) bittersweet chocolate, roughly chopped**
- **½ cup heavy cream**
- **2 tablespoons light corn syrup**
- **½ teaspoon vanilla extract**
- **Pinch salt**
- **1½ tablespoons unsalted butter, cut into 8 pieces and softened**

COATING

- **1 cup (3 ounces) Dutch-processed cocoa**
- **¼ cup (1 ounce) confectioners' sugar**

1. FOR THE GANACHE: Lightly coat 8-inch baking dish with vegetable oil spray. Make parchment sling by folding 2 long sheets of parchment so that they are as wide as baking pan. Lay sheets of parchment in pan perpendicular to each other, with extra hanging over edges of pan. Push parchment into corners and up sides of pan, smoothing flush to pan.

2. Microwave chocolate in medium bowl at 50 percent power, stirring occasionally, until mostly melted and few small chocolate pieces remain, 2 to 3 minutes; set aside. Microwave cream in measuring cup until warm to touch, about 30 seconds. Stir corn syrup, vanilla, and salt into cream and pour mixture over chocolate. Cover bowl with plastic wrap, set aside for 3 minutes, and then stir with wooden spoon to combine. Stir in butter, one piece at a time, until fully incorporated.

3. Using rubber spatula, transfer ganache to prepared pan and set aside at room temperature for 2 hours. Cover pan and transfer to refrigerator; chill for at least 2 hours.

(Ganache can be stored, refrigerated, for up to 2 days.)

4. FOR THE COATING: Sift cocoa and sugar through fine-mesh strainer into large bowl. Sift again into large cake pan and set aside.

5. Gripping overhanging parchment, lift ganache from pan. Cut ganache into sixty-four 1-inch squares (8 rows by 8 rows). (If ganache cracks during slicing, let sit at room temperature for 5 to 10 minutes and then proceed.) Dust hands lightly with cocoa mixture to prevent ganache from sticking and roll each square into ball. Transfer balls to cake pan with cocoa mixture and roll to evenly coat. Lightly shake truffles in hand over pan to remove excess coating. Transfer coated truffles to airtight container and repeat until all ganache squares are rolled and coated. Cover container and refrigerate for at least 2 hours or up to 1 week. Let truffles sit at room temperature for 5 to 10 minutes before serving.

VARIATION

Hazelnut-Mocha Truffles

Substitute 2 tablespoons Frangelico (hazelnut-flavored liqueur) and 1 tablespoon espresso powder for vanilla. For coating, omit confectioners' sugar and use enough cocoa to coat hands while shaping truffles. Roll shaped truffles in 1½ cups finely chopped toasted hazelnuts.

FRENCH APPLE CAKE

✔ **WHY THIS RECIPE WORKS:** For our own version of this classic French dessert, we wanted the best of both worlds: a dessert with a custardy, apple-rich base beneath a light, cakelike topping. To ensure that the apple slices softened fully, we microwaved them briefly to break the enzyme responsible for firming up pectin. And to create two differently textured layers from one batter, we divided the batter and added egg yolks to one part to make the custardy base and added flour to the rest to form the cake layer above it.

FRENCH APPLE CAKE IS A SIMPLE NAME FOR AN extraordinary dessert. The cake boasts a custardy base that surrounds the apples. It is rich, creamy, and dense but not in the least bit heavy. The butter-soft apple slices, simultaneously tart and sweet, are perfectly intact despite their tender texture. And above the rich custard sits a double layer of real cake—light and airy on the inside, with a beautifully crisp golden-brown top. Together, the contrasting layers make for a stunner of a cake.

Or that's the way it should be—not having enjoyed this cake ourselves, we were going on descriptions from friends in Paris. Instead of hopping a plane across the Atlantic, we'd have to hit the library in our quest to develop our own French apple cake.

The apple cake recipes we unearthed in our research yielded some useful clues. They all followed a simple approach: Stir eggs, milk, vanilla, and melted butter or oil together; whisk in flour, sugar, salt, and leavening until smooth; add cut-up apples; pour the batter into a springform pan; and bake until the fruit has softened and the cake has set. But the results varied widely: Some produced a crumb that was dry, airy, and cakelike, while others were moist and puddinglike. The consistency of the apples varied as well: Some held on to their shape tenaciously, even to a leathery fault, while others practically dissolved into the cake, leaving it a sodden mess. None of the cakes were particularly attractive when sliced; either they were so soft that the slices sagged or the apples dragged beneath the knife, leaving a ragged edge.

But most important, not one of these cakes displayed the stratified layers of that Parisian cake. To get that, we assumed that we'd have to create two separate batters. But for the time being, it made the most sense to focus on one layer at a time.

We started with the bottom layer—which meant we actually ended up starting with the apples. When we went back and remade the most promising of the cakes we had tested, a problem became immediately apparent. This particular cake got much of its flavor from using a variety of apples, and they cooked quite differently. Some were so soft as to be mushy, while others were dry and leathery. In addition, the different varieties released moisture into the surrounding cake to varying degrees, creating sodden patches here and there. So our first order of business would be to get the apples to cook more consistently.

The simplest way to do that, of course, would be to limit ourselves to just one type of apple. Since we wanted the apples to hold their shape entirely, we opted for Granny Smiths; among the firmer apples, their tartness stood out most clearly against the sweet, dense background of the cake. To add back some of the complexity lost by using just one kind of apple, we tossed the apples with a tablespoon

FRENCH APPLE CAKE

of Calvados, a French apple brandy, along with a teaspoon of lemon juice, and we substituted neutral-flavored vegetable oil for the butter used in the original batter, since the butter flavor tended to obscure that of the apples.

As for texture, the Granny Smiths held their shape nicely after baking, but they were susceptible to leatheriness, which made the cake difficult to slice cleanly. We tried macerating the slices in sugar to soften them, but that only made them drier and therefore tougher when baked. In the end, precooking them in the microwave for a few minutes—just to the point that they were pliable—was all the head start they needed. In the finished cake, the apples were tender and easily sliced but still retained their structure.

We could now focus on the texture of the custardy cake layer itself. Even with apples that released less water, the cake remained somewhat soupy at the center. We assumed that the batter itself contained too much liquid, so we tried reducing the amount of milk or increasing the amount of flour it contained, but both adjustments only served to make the cake pasty and grainy. Adding another egg did firm it up a bit, but it also left it a bit tough because of the extra white. We then tried adding just another egg yolk. This was a step in the right direction, as it gave the cake more cohesiveness while also enhancing its custardlike qualities. Adding a third yolk improved things even further.

But our cake was still wet at the center. After some thought, we wondered whether the problem was not too much moisture in the batter but rather that it wasn't cooking long and low enough. This cake wasn't merely custardlike; it was a real custard, especially with two extra egg yolks in the mix. We'd been cooking it at 375 degrees, but maybe it could stand to be cooked more gently, allowing the eggs to set up before so much moisture was wrung from the apples. So for our next test, we lowered the temperature to 325 degrees and dropped the cake one rack lower in the oven, so that it would cook from the bottom up and brown more slowly on top. After nearly an hour, a toothpick inserted into the center of the cake came out clean, and after it cooled, the cake had the perfect texture: The apples were tender and moist, fully embedded in a custardy matrix that was silky and smooth from center to edge.

At this point we had a perfect custardy base layer and could focus on creating a cakelike topping for it. We weren't that happy about having to make two separate batters, but we saw no other option if we wanted distinct layers. Rather than start from scratch completely, though, we returned to our tasting notes from those first trial recipes to find one with a batter that had a more cake-like consistency.

But when we looked more closely at the batter recipes, we noticed something interesting: Minor variations aside, they really only differed in the ratio among a few key ingredients. The drier, more cakelike ones contained more flour and fewer eggs, while the more custardy ones had a far higher ratio of eggs to flour. Was it possible that we didn't need two separate batters after all? Maybe we just needed to get one batter to behave differently depending on where it was in the cake.

To test this theory, we began by simply doubling the overall amount of batter and dividing it into two portions. We added the apples to one half, poured this mixture into the pan and then poured the remaining batter over it, and baked the cake as before. The results were promising: Though the batter was identical in both layers, the top half—since it lacked moisture-contributing apples—was already much more open and cakelike. It wasn't perfect yet, though. It was a bit too moist and dense, and it didn't form much of a crisp crust on its top surface.

But what if we just increased the flour and lost the extra egg yolks in the top batter? The simplest way to do that, we figured, would be to make the batter in two stages: First, combine all of the ingredients except for the extra egg yolks. Then divide the batter in two and add the yolks to one half and a few tablespoons of flour to the other half.

SCIENCE DESK

ENSURING TENDER APPLES
Why do apples that go straight into the cake batter bake up too firm, while those same raw apples come out soft and tender if microwaved a bit before heading into the oven? Common sense might suggest that precooking simply hastens the fruit's breakdown. But there's more to the answer than that. As so often happens in cooking, an enzyme is involved, in this case a temperature-sensitive enzyme called pectin methylesterase (PME). As the batter's temperature climbs and lingers between 120 and 160 degrees, the PME sets the pectin in the fruit, so the slices will remain relatively firm no matter how long they are cooked. The catch, though, is that the PME is deactivated at temperatures above 160 degrees. Enter the microwave. A three-minute zap quickly brings the apples to 180 degrees—high enough to permanently kill any activity of the PME—so the precooked fruit emerges fully soft in the finished cake.

We even double-checked the science with a side test: heating vacuum-sealed batches of both raw and microwaved apples in a *sous vide* machine to the final temperature of the cake (208 degrees) for the same amount of time it bakes (1¼ hours). The microwaved apples were predictably tender, while the slices that we didn't microwave remained firm. Furthermore, these slices never fully softened, even after we continued to cook them for another 40 minutes.

This time around, the cake was near perfection: creamy and custardy below and airy above. True, it wasn't quite crisp enough on top, but fortunately sprinkling it with granulated sugar just before it went into the oven solved that, giving our cake its own crisp top layer. Now this remarkable cake can be made at home—no pricey trip to Paris involved.

French Apple Cake

SERVES 8 TO 10

The microwaved apples should be pliable but not completely soft when cooked. To test for doneness, take one apple slice and try to bend it. If it snaps in half, it's too firm; microwave it for an additional 30 seconds and test again. If Calvados is unavailable, 1 tablespoon of apple brandy or white rum can be substituted.

- 1½ pounds Granny Smith apples, peeled, cored, cut into 8 wedges, and sliced ⅛ inch thick crosswise
- 1 tablespoon Calvados
- 1 teaspoon lemon juice
- 1 cup (5 ounces) plus 2 tablespoons all-purpose flour
- 1 cup (7 ounces) plus 1 tablespoon granulated sugar
- 2 teaspoons baking powder
- ½ teaspoon salt
- 1 large egg plus 2 large yolks
- 1 cup vegetable oil
- 1 cup whole milk
- 1 teaspoon vanilla extract
   Confectioners' sugar

1. Adjust oven rack to lower-middle position and heat oven to 325 degrees. Spray 9-inch springform pan with vegetable oil spray. Place prepared pan on rimmed baking sheet lined with aluminum foil. Place apple slices in microwave-safe pie plate, cover, and microwave until apples are pliable and slightly translucent, about 3 minutes. Toss apple slices with Calvados and lemon juice and let cool for 15 minutes.

2. Whisk 1 cup flour, 1 cup granulated sugar, baking powder, and salt together in bowl. Whisk egg, oil, milk, and vanilla together in second bowl until smooth. Add dry ingredients to wet ingredients and whisk until just combined. Transfer 1 cup batter to separate bowl and set aside.

3. Add egg yolks to remaining batter and whisk to combine. Using spatula, gently fold in cooled apples. Transfer batter to prepared pan; using offset spatula, spread batter evenly to pan edges, gently pressing on apples to create even, compact layer, and smooth surface.

4. Whisk remaining 2 tablespoons flour into reserved batter. Pour over batter in pan and spread batter evenly to pan edges and smooth surface. Sprinkle remaining 1 tablespoon granulated sugar evenly over cake.

5. Bake until center of cake is set, toothpick or skewer inserted in center comes out clean, and top is golden brown, about 1¼ hours. Transfer pan to wire rack; let cool for 5 minutes. Run paring knife around sides of pan and let cool completely, 2 to 3 hours. Dust lightly with confectioners' sugar, cut into wedges, and serve.

RATING COCOA POWDER

In the test kitchen, we reach for cocoa powder all the time for the deep flavor it gives cookies, cakes, puddings—even chili. To find the best cocoa, we sampled 10 brands in chocolate butter cookies, chocolate cake, and hot cocoa. Our taste tests made it clear that the brand used can make or break a dessert; lesser cocoas produced wan cakes and hot cocoa that tasted dusty, whereas better cocoas delivered deep chocolate flavor and luxurious butter cookies. What accounted for the differences? We suspected Dutching and/or fat levels might contribute to our preferences, but both natural and Dutch-processed cocoas performed well, and both our first- and last-placed brands contained the same level of fat. In the end, our preferred brands shared two qualities. During processing, rather than roasting the beans whole and then discarding the shells, top-rated brands shell the cacao beans first and then roast only the nibs, which allows for greater control over the cooking process. Also, these cocoas are ground to a finer particle size, which maximizes flavor release. Brands are listed in order of preference. See AmericasTestKitchen.com for updates and further information on this testing.

RECOMMENDED

HERSHEY'S COCOA Natural Unsweetened
PRICE: $3.49 for 8 oz (44 cents per oz)
ROASTING STYLE: Nib
COMMENTS: Our winner is proof that you needn't look beyond the supermarket baking aisle to find great cocoa. Because Hershey's shells the nibs before roasting them and then grinds them very fine, its cocoa boasts "assertive," "pronounced" chocolate flavor underlined by hints of "coconut," "coffee," "orange," and "cinnamon."

DROSTE Cocoa
PRICE: $10.50 for 8.8 oz ($1.19 per oz)
ROASTING STYLE: Nib
COMMENTS: This Dutch import impressed tasters with "rich," "round," "bold," flavor and "lots of depth." Some even described it as "fudgelike." If it weren't harder to track down and didn't cost nearly three times as much as our winner, it would be an appealing alternative to Hershey's Natural.

HERSHEY'S COCOA Special Dark
PRICE: $3.49 for 8 oz (44 cents per oz)
ROASTING STYLE: Nib
COMMENTS: The sibling to our winner, Hershey's Dutched-natural blend tinted cakes and cookies a deep "purple-black" color so striking, one taster dubbed the samples "chocolate with a vengeance." Unfortunately, its "milk chocolate" flavor didn't match its intense hue, though some tasters appreciated its "fruity," "herbal" notes.

VALRHONA Cocoa Powder
PRICE: $11.99 for 8.82 oz ($1.36 per oz)
ROASTING STYLE: Proprietary
COMMENTS: This "grown-up" powder was "dynamite" in cookies, where copious amounts of butter rounded its "bitter," "smoky" notes into "deep, pronounced, rich" chocolate flavor. But its smokiness overwhelmed in the leaner cake, where one taster complained that the cake "tasted like it was cooked over wood chips."

RECOMMENDED WITH RESERVATIONS

GHIRARDELLI Natural Unsweetened Cocoa
PRICE: $5.59 for 10 oz (56 cents per oz)
ROASTING STYLE: Nib
COMMENTS: Tasters offered lukewarm praise for this sample, saying it had a "respectable chocolate flavor" that was "balanced," "soft," and "milk chocolaty" but also "grassy," and "vegetal." Or as one taster summed up its ho-hum flavor: "smooth but undistinguished."

SCHARFFEN BERGER Unsweetened Natural Cocoa Powder
PRICE: $8.79 for 6 oz ($1.47 per oz)
ROASTING STYLE: Whole bean
COMMENTS: Tasters who appreciated a lighter-bodied cocoa praised this brand's "subtle and nuanced," taste that was "more milk chocolate than bittersweet." But for most of us, it simply "lacked rich flavor." Its sky-high price also knocked it down a notch.

NESTLÉ TOLL HOUSE Cocoa
PRICE: $2.69 for 8 oz (34 cents per oz)
ROASTING STYLE: Whole bean
COMMENTS: This "kid-friendly" powder was as basic as they come, provoking the majority of tasters to put it in the "simple" and "nostalgic" category owing to its "mild, "one-dimensional" chocolate flavor.

EQUAL EXCHANGE Baking Cocoa
PRICE: $7.84 for 8 oz (98 cents per oz)
ROASTING STYLE: Whole bean
COMMENTS: Chocolate flavor was "almost an after-thought" in this last-place powder that "lacked intensity." A few tasters picked up on "slightly boozy," "malty," and "caramel" notes, but most found it unpleasantly "bitter," "sour," "acidic," and "burnt."

CONVERSIONS & EQUIVALENCIES

SOME SAY COOKING IS A SCIENCE AND AN ART. WE would say that geography has a hand in it, too. Flour milled in the United Kingdom and elsewhere will feel and taste different from flour milled in the United States. So, while we cannot promise that the loaf of bread you bake in Canada or England will taste the same as a loaf baked in the States, we can offer guidelines for converting weights and measures. We also recommend that you rely on your instincts when making our recipes. Refer to the visual cues provided. If the bread dough hasn't "come together in a ball," as described, you may need to add more flour—even if the recipe doesn't tell you so. You be the judge.

The recipes in this book were developed using standard U.S. measures following U.S. government guidelines. The charts below offer equivalents for U.S., metric, and imperial (U.K.) measures. All conversions are approximate and have been rounded up or down to the nearest whole number. For example:

1 teaspoon = 4.929 milliliters, rounded up to 5 milliliters
1 ounce = 28.349 grams, rounded down to 28 grams

VOLUME CONVERSIONS

U.S.	METRIC
1 teaspoon	5 milliliters
2 teaspoons	10 milliliters
1 tablespoon	15 milliliters
2 tablespoons	30 milliliters
¼ cup	59 milliliters
⅓ cup	79 milliliters
½ cup	118 milliliters
¾ cup	177 milliliters
1 cup	237 milliliters
1¼ cups	296 milliliters
1½ cups	355 milliliters
2 cups	473 milliliters
2½ cups	591 milliliters
3 cups	710 milliliters
4 cups (1 quart)	0.946 liter
1.06 quarts	1 liter
4 quarts (1 gallon)	3.8 liters

WEIGHT CONVERSIONS

OUNCES	GRAMS
½	14
¾	21
1	28
1½	43
2	57
2½	71
3	85
3½	99
4	113
4½	128
5	142
6	170
7	198
8	227
9	255
10	283
12	340
16 (1 pound)	454

CONVERSIONS FOR INGREDIENTS COMMONLY USED IN BAKING

Baking is an exacting science. Because measuring by weight is far more accurate than measuring by volume, and thus more likely to achieve reliable results, in our recipes we provide ounce measures in addition to cup measures for many ingredients. Refer to the chart below to convert these measures into grams.

INGREDIENT	OUNCES	GRAMS
Flour		
1 cup all-purpose flour*	5	142
1 cup cake flour	4	113
1 cup whole-wheat flour	5½	156
Sugar		
1 cup granulated (white) sugar	7	198
1 cup packed brown sugar (light or dark)	7	198
1 cup confectioners' sugar	4	113
Cocoa Powder		
1 cup cocoa powder	3	85
Butter†		
4 tablespoons (½ stick, or ¼ cup)	2	57
8 tablespoons (1 stick, or ½ cup)	4	113
16 tablespoons (2 sticks, or 1 cup)	8	227

* U.S. all-purpose flour, the most frequently used flour in this book, does not contain leaveners, as some European flours do. These leavened flours are called self-rising or self-raising. If you are using self-rising flour, take this into consideration before adding leavening to a recipe.
† In the United States, butter is sold both salted and unsalted. We generally recommend unsalted butter. If you are using salted butter, take this into consideration before adding salt to a recipe.

OVEN TEMPERATURES

FAHRENHEIT	CELSIUS	GAS MARK (imperial)
225	105	¼
250	120	½
275	135	1
300	150	2
325	165	3
350	180	4
375	190	5
400	200	6
425	220	7
450	230	8
475	245	9

CONVERTING TEMPERATURES FROM AN INSTANT-READ THERMOMETER

We include doneness temperatures in many of our recipes, such as those for poultry, meat, and bread. We recommend an instant-read thermometer for the job. Refer to the table above to convert Fahrenheit degrees to Celsius. Or, for temperatures not represented in the chart, use this simple formula:

Subtract 32 degrees from the Fahrenheit reading, then divide the result by 1.8 to find the Celsius reading.

EXAMPLE:

"Roast until chicken thigh registers 175 degrees."
To convert:

175° F – 32 = 143°
143° ÷ 1.8 = 79.44°C, rounded down to 79°C

INDEX